LONGMAN ADVANCED GNVQ

TEST AND ASSESSMENT GUIDE

LEISURE AND TOURISM

Ray Youell MSc MTS

ADVANCED
GNVQ

**Longman Advanced GNVQ
Test and Assessment Guides**

Series Editors:
Geoff Black and Stuart Wall

Titles Available:
Business
Health and Social Care
Leisure and Tourism

Due for publication in 1995:
Construction and the Built Environment
Hospitality and Catering
Science

Longman Group Ltd,
Longman House, Burnt Mill, Harlow,
Essex CM20 2JE, England
and Associated Companies throughout the world.

© Longman Group Ltd 1994

First Published 1994

ISBN 0 582 23778 5

British Library Cataloguing-in-Publication Data

A catalogue record for this book is
available from the British Library

Set by 19QQ
Produced by Longman Singapore Publishers (Pte) Ltd.
Printed in Singapore.

Contents

Acknowledgements

I am grateful to the many leisure and tourism organisations who were kind enough to provide materials and data for this book. Each is acknowledged individually in the text. Thanks also to Stuart Wall and Geoff Black for their help and encouragement throughout. Finally a big thank you to Sue, Megan and Owen for suffering again!

Ray Youell

Using this Book

The first eight units provide you with the vital information and knowledge needed in each mandatory unit, both for passing the compulsory external tests (in seven of the mandatory units) and for completing the various projects and assignments set on those units. You will find many self-check questions at the end of each element in the unit, with answers at the end of the unit. You will also find a unit test at the end of each unit of the type you will face in the external test itself, with answers and examiner comments.

After these eight mandatory units there is a major chapter on the 'Portfolio', helping you develop the skills and insights needed to gain a merit or distinction in your Advanced GNVQ. You are shown the types of evidence you can present in the portfolio. Actual examples of student assignments are also provided together with examiner comments. There is also material in this chapter on what is meant by the core skills in your GNVQ and how these can be demonstrated in your portfolio of evidence.

Introduction: Advanced GNVQ in Leisure and Tourism

In order to gain your Advanced GNVQ in Leisure and Tourism, you have to demonstrate to your tutors and teachers that you have been successful in meeting the standards for the various units on the course; in other words you will be *assessed*, in a number of different ways, to show that you have reached the required standard for each unit. The bulk of the assessment you will be asked to do will be in the form of **assignments and projects**, set and marked by the staff who teach your GNVQ. You will also need to pass the **external tests** that are set by leisure and tourism experts outside your school or college. In the case of Advanced Leisure and Tourism, there are currently seven external tests that you will need to pass. An important part of the assessment process for GNVQs is the collection of *evidence* to show that you have successfully completed the different parts of the units. This material is gathered together in a **portfolio of evidence**, which is used by your tutors, and other specialists outside your school or college, to confirm that you have covered all the necessary parts of the units and to agree your overall grade for the GNVQ.

Before we can look in greater detail at the different types of assessment in GNVQs, it is important that you understand clearly how the different parts of a GNVQ fit together. You will also need to get used to a lot of new words and phrases, so it's important that you get to grips with these from the outset.

The structure of the Advanced GNVQ in Leisure and Tourism

All GNVQs are based on **units**. Advanced GNVQs are made up of 15 units in total, shared out as follows:

- *Eight Mandatory Units* – these cover the fundamental skills, knowledge and understanding related to the leisure and tourism industry. Mandatory means that everybody studying for the Advanced GNVQ in Leisure and Tourism must complete these units.

- *Four Optional Units* – these complement the mandatory units and give students the chance to look in more depth at a particular topic. The exact options you will be studying will depend on which awarding body your school or college deals with (BTEC, City & Guilds or RSA), the skills and expertise of your tutors and your own particular interests.

- *Three Core Skill Units* – these help you to develop skills that are vital for anybody wishing to work in leisure and tourism or go on to study the subject at a higher level. You will be assessed in *communication, application of number* and *information technology*.

Don't worry if you discover that you are studying more than 15 units on your GNVQ. This is likely to be because your school or college is giving you the chance to develop a broader range of skills or study certain subjects in even greater depth, by offering you **additional units**. Additional units may be necessary for studying certain courses in higher education, at degree or HND level.

Having a number of different units that go to make up the GNVQ award allows greater flexibility in studying. Although most people studying for an Advanced GNVQ will be on a full-time course of study at school or college, some students will want to study on a part-time basis, passing one unit at a time. The way GNVQs are designed allows students to build up credit for individual units over an extended period of time.

What does a unit consist of?

At the beginning of this section, we talked about the need to meet the required **standard** in order to be successful in your GNVQ. The standards for the Advanced GNVQ in Leisure and Tourism have been developed by specialists in education and the industry as a way of defining what has to be done by students to achieve the award. The standards are set out as **units**; for Advanced GNVQs there are the eight mandatory, four optional and three core skill units we mentioned above. Figure A gives a breakdown of a unit (sometimes called a **unit specification**), showing the different parts of a unit and how they link together.

To help you understand even better how a GNVQ unit is structured, an Element from the Advanced GNVQ in Leisure and Tourism is shown in full in Figure B.

Looking at Figures A and B together shows us that each unit on the Advanced GNVQ in Leisure and Tourism has a number of different components, namely:

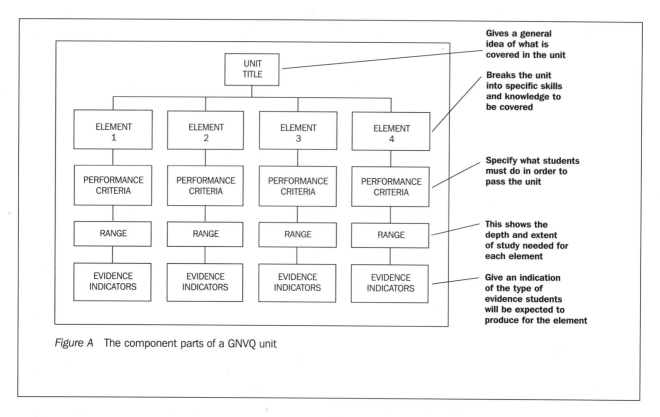

Figure A The component parts of a GNVQ unit

- Elements
- Performance criteria
- Range
- Evidence indicators

We will now look at each of these in a little more detail.

Elements

Each unit in the Advanced GNVQ in Leisure and Tourism is broken down into a number of different **Elements**, depending on the depth of material included in the unit. The first mandatory unit, for example, 'investigating the leisure and tourism industry', is attempting to set the very broad leisure and tourism industry in context and therefore needs a lot of detailed knowledge and understanding. This is why it is made up of four elements, whereas other mandatory units, for example 'maintaining health, safety and security' and 'providing management information services', have a much narrower focus which can adequately be covered by just three elements. Elements are not only found in mandatory units, however; optional and core skills units have elements as well.

In order to be successful in your Advanced GNVQ in Leisure and Tourism, you will need to produce evidence to show that you have covered *all* the elements in all the units you are studying.

Performance criteria

Each GNVQ element has a number of **performance criteria** related to it. There are five criteria in the example given in Figure B, but the number will vary between different elements. The performance criteria help to explain what that particular element is all about, by telling you what areas you need to cover to be able to pass it. In carrying out the different types of assessment for a unit, you can think of the performance criteria as a 'checklist' of evidence that you will need to collect and include in your **portfolio** to demonstrate that you have successfully met the requirements of the element.

In the course of your assessments, you must show that you have met the requirements of *all* the performance criteria for each element of your GNVQ.

Range

You will see in Figure A that, as well as having performance criteria related to it, each element will identify a **range** associated with it. The range tries to indicate the boundaries that each student will need to work within on a particular Element. In the example given in Figure A, for example, the range states that the student must provide evidence to show that they have considered the following points:

- The scale of the leisure and tourism industry
- The different contexts of the industry
- Different sources of information and advice
- Career opportunities in leisure and tourism
- Past changes in the development of the industry

To be successful in an element, the evidence that you collect must show that you have covered *all* the range points included in the unit specification.

Evidence indicators

The **evidence indicators** included in the unit specifications give a general idea as to the *sort of evidence* that would be considered suitable for successful completion of the element. In the example shown in Figure B, for example, a report on the European and UK leisure and tourism industry, given that it covered the necessary performance criteria and range, would be a suitable type of evidence. This does not mean that every student studying Element 1.1 of the Advanced GNVQ in Leisure and Tourism will be researching and writing a report to submit as evidence that they have completed all the requirements. Different schools and colleges will tackle the problem in different ways; some may ask students to make a presentation or carry out a survey, both of which are quite acceptable alternative types of evidence. There are discussions going on at the moment between the different awarding bodies

Advanced GNVQ in Leisure and Tourism

Unit 1: Investigating the leisure and tourism industry

Element 1.1: Describe the scale and contexts of the leisure and tourism industry

- **Performance criteria**
  1. Selected authoritative sources are used to describe the scale and contexts of the industry.

  2. Past changes in scale are identified and explained.

  3. Current trends in scale are identified and likely developments described.

  4. Relationships between trends in different parts of the industry are accurately described.

  5. The main areas of employment growth and decline and of career opportunities are identified.

- **Range**
  Scale: local, UK, EU; numbers employed; profitability; turnover.

  Contexts: accommodation, catering and hospitality; entertainment and education; travel and tourism; sports and recreation.

  Sources: experts; industry organizations; reference publications; trade press.

  Career opportunities: general; candidate's own.

  Past changes: historical; recent past (outline historical, report relevant detail of recent past).

- **Evidence indicators**
  An overview report of the European and UK leisure and tourism industry briefly describing the scale of different contexts, highlighting current trends and explaining differences between them. The report should include a description of significant historical developments and relevant detail of recent developments and will describe how the UK industry as a whole has evolved to its current position. Evidence should demonstrate understanding of the implications of the range dimensions in relation to the element. The unit test will confirm the candidate's coverage of range.

Figure B

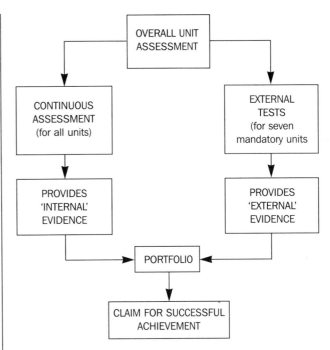

Figure C   Unit assessment in the advanced GNVQ in leisure and tourism

External tests

You will need to sit and pass external tests, set by the awarding bodies, before you can be awarded the Advanced GNVQ in Leisure and Tourism. Seven out of the eight mandatory units have external tests; Unit 5 'Planning for an event' does not have an external test, since it was thought it would be difficult to ask factual questions on the subject of events. You will therefore sit external tests in the following units:

Unit 1   Investigating the leisure and tourism industry
Unit 2   Maintaining health, safety and security
Unit 3   Providing customer service
Unit 4   Marketing in leisure and tourism
Unit 6   Providing management information services
Unit 7   Working in teams
Unit 8   Evaluating the performance of facilities

You will be told the exact dates and times of the tests by your teacher or tutor and will be given the chance to re-sit any tests that you do not pass at the first attempt. Remember, it is essential that you pass all seven external tests in the mandatory units before you can be awarded the Advanced GNVQ in Leisure and Tourism. Because it is important that you have a good grasp of the basic knowledge and understanding in each unit, the pass mark is set deliberately high at 70%. All the awarding bodies are planning to mark the tests and get the results back to you in the shortest time possible, so as to provide you with early feedback on your performance.

At present, there are no external tests for the optional or additional units, but, as with any new qualification, changes are being made all the time to GNVQs in response to feedback from students and tutors. To be absolutely sure, you should check with your teacher or tutor what the exact position is regarding tests for your particular course.

Although the seven units listed above are the only units with external tests at the moment, you may find that your particular school or college sets their own tests in some units. This is quite acceptable and will provide you with more evidence to include in your portfolio.

about the possibility of setting assessments in some units that will be the same right across the country. Even if this does happen, you will still be given assignments and projects that are specific to your school or college, in addition to any national assessments.

Types of assessment

The **assessment** in your GNVQ concentrates on two main areas:

- External tests
- Continuous assessment

The way in which the two main types of assessment link together is shown in Figure C.

Both types of assessment will produce evidence that can be filed in your **portfolio of evidence** and which will be used when deciding the overall grade that you are given for your GNVQ.

Sitting an external test is a way of showing that you have grasped the essential knowledge and understanding for a particular unit. Some people consider that having tests that are externally set and the same right across the country gives GNVQs more credibility than a qualification based entirely on continuous assessment in school or college. Passing a test will show that you understand the basic principles of a particular unit, thus providing a good grounding for working in leisure and tourism or going on to study the subject at a higher level.

What are the external tests like?
* Each test will have between 30 and 40 questions.
* Each test lasts one hour.
* You will be asked to fill in your answers on a separate answer sheet, not on the test papers themselves. Don't worry if the answer sheet has more spaces than the number of questions on your test; this is because the number of questions varies between 30 and 40 on different test papers.
* You will not be asked to answer the questions by writing sentences, but will select an answer by writing A, B, C or D on the separate answer sheet. Your answers should be written in soft (HB) pencil only, as the answer sheets are marked by machine.
* You will be allowed to use a calculator in the test, but the memory must be wiped clean before you go into the room where the tests are being taken.
* The questions on the test papers are grouped into 'focus areas' (see below).
* The tests use three different types of questions (see below).
* Tests are taken under secure conditions, on a specified day and at a specified time.

What are 'focus areas'?
You will see from the sample test papers included in Units 1–8 in the first part of this book that the questions are grouped into **focus areas**. These are simply convenient headings that have been taken from the specifications for each unit. You may find it useful when preparing for tests to structure your revision around the different focus areas in each unit. The focus areas for all seven Advanced Leisure and Tourism mandatory units that have an external test are given in Fig. D.

Types of questions
It is important that you become familiar with the three types of questions currently used in GNVQ tests. They are:

1 Multiple choice questions
2 Paired true/false questions
3 Grouped multiple choice questions

We will now look at each of these in a little more detail and study one example of each type.

Multiple choice questions

As the following example shows, these have four answer options, only one of which is correct.

Example:

The main aim of the EC Package Travel Directive is to:

A   Enable travel agents to sell more holidays

Advanced GNVQ in Leisure and Tourism

Unit		Focus areas	
1	Investigating the leisure and tourism industry	1	Trends and sources
		2	Employment and career developments
		3	Products and services
		4	Sectors and contexts
		5	Making an impact
		6	Sources of funding
2	Maintaining health, safety and security	1	Health and safety legislation
		2	Dealing with security hazards
		3	Health and safety hazards in leisure and tourism facilities
		4	Expert help and advice
		5	Proposals for health and safety measures, resource implications, viability
		6	Security hazards
3	Providing customer service	1	Customer service functions
		2	Planning a customer care programme
		3	Providing a customer care service
		4	Collecting and monitoring information
		5	Evaluating the operation of a cutomer care programme
		6	Improvements and development
4	Marketing in leisure and tourism	1	Market research and analysis
		2	Reports and presentations
		3	Provisions and opportunities
		4	Taking action
		5	Promotional activities
		6	Evaluation of a promotional campaign
6	Providing management information services	1	Information needs
		2	Recording and processing information
		3	Legal, security and contingency aspects and procedures
		4	Resources and record keeping
		5	Quality and cost-effectiveness
		6	Receivers' needs and wants
7	Working in teams	1	The purpose and structure of teams
		2	Teamwork
		3	Constraints and conflicting roles
		4	Team effectiveness
		5	Evaluating team performance
8	Evaluating the performance of facilities	1	Objectives
		2	Sources of data
		3	Aspects of performance
		4	Plans and reports
		5	Opportunities and obstacles
		6	Confidentiality and security

B   Eliminate cross-border checks for travellers in Europe
C   Give protection to the travelling public
D   Abolish duty-free allowances

A correct answer to a multiple choice question is worth one mark.

Paired true/false questions

These have two statements introduced by the phrase 'decide whether each of these statements is true (T) or false (F)'. The two statements are labelled (i) and (ii) and are always followed by the phrase 'which option best describes the two statements?'

Example:

The leisure and tourism industry provides employment for approximately 1.5 million people in the UK.

Decide whether each of these statements is true (T) or false (F).

(i) This figure of 1.5 million employees has remained static over the last 15 years.

(ii) More people are employed in accommodation, catering and hospitality than in sports and recreation.

Which option best describes the two statements?

A   (i) T   (ii) T
B   (i) T   (ii) F
C   (i) F   (ii) T
D   (i) F   (ii) F

As this example shows, there are four answer options A, B, C or D, only one of which is correct. You would choose:

- Option A if you thought both statements were true
- Option B if you thought the first was true but the second false
- Option C if you thought the first was false but the second true
- Option D if you thought both statements were false.

Take your time when deciding which option to choose; it is easy to make a wrong choice even when you know the right answer. These questions are worth one mark each.

Grouped multiple choice questions

These have four answer options A, B, C and D. These are followed by three statements which form the questions. They are numbered as three separate questions.

Example:

Questions 1–3 relate to the following information:

Four of the busiest seaports in the UK are:

A   Dover
B   Plymouth
C   Holyhead
D   Stranraer

Which is the seaport for journeys to and from:

1   Northern Ireland?
2   Brittany?
3   Southern Ireland?

You must choose from the answer options A, B, C or D, the correct answer for each of the three questions. For example, the answer to question 1 in the example is Stranraer, so you would choose option C. Each answer option may be used more than once as a correct answer. Each of the three questions is worth one mark.

Preparing for the tests

You will normally take the unit test towards the end of a period of study of one particular unit. This will make sure that the continuous assessment tasks that you have been set will help to provide information and knowledge needed to be able to answer the test questions. Each unit of this book covers the main *content* you need to know when revising for the test. You will need to spend some time, however, revising specifically for the tests. You may find it helpful to revise with another member of your group, bouncing ideas and questions off each other. Your teachers or tutors may organize revision classes or seminars, which some students find particularly useful. Use the sample tests provided at the end of the mandatory units in this book to practise your test

technique, timing yourself to make sure that you are working at the right pace. You are likely to find that there is plenty of time in which to answer all the questions on a test, so rule number one is don't rush!

Once you know the dates of your tests, it is a good idea to draw up a timetable, showing when you will be revising for particular unit tests.

On the day of the test itself, try not to get too worried so that you are able to perform to the best of your ability. Make sure you read each question very carefully before you attempt to answer it and check all answers at the end of the test. If you intend to take a calculator in with you, make sure the batteries will last. Have a spare pencil and rubber with you as well. You shouldn't think of the test as a major hurdle that you have to clear; tests are just one part of the whole assessment process for your GNVQ. Good luck!

Continuous Assessment: The Portfolio

A separate chapter at the end of this book deals with the skills and evidence you need to present for 'the portfolio', with practical examples of student work and examiner comments.

The bulk of the assessments that you carry out on your GNVQ will fall into this category. Continuous assessment can take many forms, including written assignments, projects, demonstrations, presentations and case studies. You will be given a mixture of assessments that will cover all of the elements of the GNVQ units you are studying. This is important, because you must show that you have met the required standard in *every* unit you are taking before you can be awarded the GNVQ.

An important feature of GNVQ courses is that you will be expected to take responsibility for your own learning and your own assessment. This doesn't mean that you will be setting and marking your own assignments! What it does mean is that your tutors will expect you to come up with good ideas and ways of tackling tasks. They will encourage you to look for information from many different sources, helping you to develop the vital skills that you will need in later life. You probably won't be sitting in classrooms for much of the time that you are studying for your GNVQ. You will often be 'learning by doing' with your tutors providing information, support and advice when needed.

What counts as 'evidence'?

You will quickly learn that collecting and presenting evidence is a crucial part of your GNVQ course; in fact, if you are studying for your GNVQ on a full-time course, by the end of the two years you will have heard the term 'evidence' enough times to last you a lifetime! Most of the evidence that you collect will revolve around the assignments that your tutors give you from time to time, for the different units and elements of the GNVQ; e.g. reports, letters, projects and case studies. Evidence can come from a number of different sources, however, and can be concerned with many different activities, including:

- Questionnaire surveys
- Reports of observations
- Photographs, audio and videotapes
- Computer-generated material
- Role playing

- Organizing an event or service
- Demonstrations and discussions
- Presentations and displays
- Tests set by your tutors
- Notes from lectures or classes
- Activities carried out on work experience
- Records of visits to leisure and tourism organizations

- References and certificates from previous work or study
- Log books and records of achievement

Again, the final chapter of this book will help you develop many of the skills required for the portfolio, giving examples of actual assessments and showing you what is required for a merit or distinction.

The Mandatory Units

UNIT 1

Investigating the Leisure and Tourism Industry

Getting Started

Leisure and tourism is hailed as the world's biggest industry. Statistics from the World Travel and Tourism Council (WTTC) show that tourism alone employed 127 million people worldwide in 1993 and had a gross output of nearly 3.5 billion US dollars. It is a very fragmented and highly complex industry, spanning many different activities, from theme parks to holidays, country walks to aerobics.

Leisure and tourism is growing rapidly at local, national and international levels. Locally, new facilities such as leisure centres, arts complexes and museums are being developed to meet the needs of local communities. At the national level, prestigious projects such as Alton Towers, the National Museum of Photography, Film and Television at Bradford and Wembley Arena are built with larger audiences in mind. Internationally, leisure and tourism shows steady growth, in response to higher standards of living, greater personal mobility and increasing personal incomes.

The UK leisure and tourism industry is dominated by private sector operators, who aim to maximize their profits and provide a reasonable return on investment. The public sector, however, plays a crucial role in the provision of leisure and tourism facilities and services, often providing the framework and infrastructure within which the commercial companies operate. The voluntary sector too is important in leisure and tourism, ranging from large organizations such as the National Trust to small groups with specific local aims.

The scale of the leisure and tourism industry means that it can offer significant economic, social and cultural benefits to urban and rural communities in Britain, particularly those experiencing higher than average levels of unemployment. In contrast, the rapid growth in leisure and tourism has led to criticism that the benefits it offers may well be cancelled out by the negative impacts which much of its activities can generate.

This unit provides a comprehensive foundation on which the study of the other units of the Advanced GNVQ in Leisure and Tourism is based. It contains valuable statistical information about the scale and structure of the industry, which the student will find a useful source of data when studying Units 2–8.

Balance of Payments Statement of the inflows and outflows of money to and from a particular country. Leisure and tourism is an invisible item on the balance of payments.

Compulsory Competitive Tendering (CCT) The process by which the management of local services such as leisure, traditionally provided by the local council, are opened up to competition from the private sector.

Impacts Economic, environmental and socio-cultural factors that can have negative and positive influences on communities and their environment.

Leisure Time Time left over when an individual has completed all necessary personal, employment and household tasks. Time at the disposal of the individual when he or she has the freedom to choose what to do.

Private Sector Commercial organizations, such as hotels, tourist attractions and coach companies, which aim to maximise their profits.

Public Sector Organizations largely funded by central or local government, such as local councils and the Department of National Heritage, which provide a service to local communities and the public at large.

Quangos Bodies that are funded by central government but enjoy a large degree of autonomy. Examples include the Sports Council and the English Tourist Board.

Tourism Concerned with people being away from their normal place of residence, on short-term, temporary visits, for purposes normally associated with tourism. May be subdivided into business tourism and leisure tourism.

Voluntary Sector Organizations and facilities managed and operated mainly by volunteers, with non-profit making objectives. They vary in size from a local club or society to the National Trust.

Element 1.1 begins by seeking to define leisure and tourism and goes on to consider the history of the industry, its structure, scale of operation and employment opportunities. It concludes with an analysis of the future of the industry. The second part of the unit, Element 1.2, looks in detail at the wide range of products on offer in UK leisure and tourism, the infrastructure which supports the industry and the frame- work of natural resources in Britain. Element 1.3 considers leisure and tourism's impact at the local level, with informa- tion on the positive and negative economic, environmental and social/cultural aspects of the industry. The unit concludes with Element 1.4 which looks at how leisure and tourism is financed in the private, public and voluntary sectors.

Essential Principles

1.1 The scale and contexts of the leisure and tourism industry

Leisure and tourism defined

Agreeing on a comprehensive definition of the terms leisure and tourism is not an easy matter. Most people associate **leisure** with either leisure time or leisure activities; they choose to use their spare time in ways which give them the most satisfaction. To many people, **tourism** is their annual holiday, perhaps a week in the Algarve, a family holiday to Legoland in Denmark or a trip to stay with their relations in Cornwall.

To those who plan, manage and work in leisure and tourism, these simple ideas mask a highly complex industry, which includes many different activities, including:

- International tourism
- Arts and entertainment
- Heritage and other attractions
- Community leisure provision
- Sport and physical recreation
- Hotels and other accommodation
- Countryside recreation
- Hospitality
- Transport
- Travel agents and tour operators
- Home-based leisure

In order to understand fully the nature of the leisure and tourism industry, we will turn first to defining leisure, followed by consideration of the definition of tourism.

What do we mean by 'leisure'?

'Leisure' means different things to different people. Some people consider it to be **time** when they are not at work, while others equate leisure with specific **activities** which they do in their free time, such as gardening, listening to the radio, playing tennis or going to the cinema. Some people say that Britain is moving towards becoming a 'leisure society' with the decline in many aspects of our industrial base and a move towards service industries, of which leisure is one of the most important. These different perceptions of the term 'leisure' highlight the difficult task faced by anybody trying to define exactly what is meant by leisure.

A dictionary definition of the term 'leisure' says that it is 'time free from employment'. This, too, does not give a complete answer to the question; it fails to take into account the many necessary duties and functions that we all have to perform in our daily lives such as eating, sleeping and carrying out domestic chores. Unemployed people do not fit very easily into such a definition either, with most agreeing that they have more leisure time than they want.

A comprehensive definition of the term leisure would necessarily include all of the following elements:

- time outside sleeping, eating and personal hygiene functions
- time outside of a formal employment situation
- time over and above that devoted to necessary household chores
- time at the disposal of the individual
- time when an individual has the freedom to choose what to do

The last two elements concerning an individual's freedom of choice are perhaps getting us closer to the true meaning of leisure. Rather than a mechanistic calculation of the time left over when all necessary tasks have been completed, leisure is much more about time when an individual can strive to reach his or her potential as a human being and become a productive member of society.

Leisure activities

Sources such as the General Household Survey (GHS) and *Social Trends* divide **leisure activities** into those that are *home-based* and those which take place *outside the home*.

Home-based leisure activities include:

- Listening to radio, records and tapes.
- Reading books.
- Gardening.
- Visiting or entertaining friends or relatives.
- Watching TV.
- DIY.
- Dressmaking, needlework and knitting.

The following are some of the activities categorized as leisure away from home:

- Visiting tourist attractions.
- Taking holidays and day trips.
- Taking part in indoor sports, games and physical activities (e.g. snooker, swimming, badminton, ice skating, darts etc.).
- Taking part in outdoor sports, games and physical activities (e.g. walking, cycling, fishing, sailing, jogging etc.).
- Going to watch football matches.
- Going to the cinema, theatre and ballet.

It is clear that leisure activities differ greatly in the degree of physical effort required from the individual; *passive* activities, such as watching television or listening to the radio, involve little in the way of exertion, whereas *active* leisure activities, e.g. gardening, sports and DIY, demand much greater effort.

What factors affect leisure activity?

There are many factors which influence an individual's ability to participate in leisure, some outside of his or her immediate control. Those working in leisure and tourism need to be aware of these factors, since they will influence both the products that are on offer and the way in which the public has access to them. Some of the more important factors are:

1 **The availability of leisure time** – this is one of the most basic factors, since without leisure time there will be no leisure activity. Statistics published in *Social Trends* show, not surprisingly, that retired people have the most leisure time; in a typical week in 1991–2, retired men enjoyed nearly 90 hours of leisure time and retired women 74 hours. Women in full-time employment also have less leisure time compared with their male counterparts, the result of spending more time on household chores and looking after children.

2 **Personal mobility** – car ownership has risen dramatically in Britain in the last 50 years (see page 7). One-third of the population of the UK, however, neither owns nor has access to a motor car. This can influence greatly the ability

to get involved in local leisure activities; the problem is particularly acute in rural districts and other areas where public transport provision is poor.

3 **Provision of facilities** – people who live in areas which offer high quality facilities at reasonable prices are more likely to seize the leisure opportunities made available to them.

4 **Income** – those on low incomes have little, if any, money to spend on leisure activities for which there are charges. Many facilities offer concessions for these people to help to alleviate the problem.

5 **Culture and demography** – factors such as age, marital status, gender, education, skills, cultural background, social class and personality will all influence leisure participation and choice.

What do we mean by 'tourism'?

The following is perhaps the most widely accepted current definition of **tourism** in use in the UK today.

> Tourism is the temporary, short-term movement of people to destinations outside the places where they normally live and work, and activities during their stay at these destinations; it includes movement for all purposes, as well as day visits or excursions
>
> (*Tourism Society* 1976)

It clearly demonstrates that people we would categorize as tourists are:

- Away from their normal place of residence (although they will be returning home).
- On a visit that is temporary and short-term (but the definition gives no indication if there is a maximum or minimum time for a visit to be classed as 'tourism').
- Engaged in activities which would normally be associated with leisure and tourism.
- Not necessarily staying away from home overnight; they may be on a day-trip or excursion.
- Not always away from home for holiday purposes; they could be on business but would still qualify as tourists.

Tourism is more than just holidays

Contrary to popular belief, tourism is concerned with much more than just holidays. Tourist activity is often divided into **leisure tourism** and **business tourism**; Fig. 1.1 indicates the main purposes under each of these two categories. As you can see, leisure tourism includes many of the types of activities which most people think of as 'tourism'. However, business tourism is an increasingly important sector since it is often of high value and earns hoteliers, caterers and transport operators significant income. Indeed, many city-based travel agents operate a separate department geared exclusively to the needs of the business client.

Some examples from each of the categories shown in Fig. 1.1 are given in Fig. 1.2 to give a clearer understanding of the true meaning of tourism.

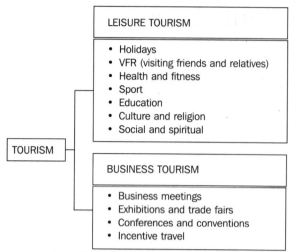

Figure 1.1 Different forms of tourism

LEISURE TOURISM	
Holidays	• A weekend break in a guesthouse in York • A two-week family holiday to the Algarve staying in a self-catering villa • A murder/mystery weekend at a hotel in Torquay
VFR	• A fortnight staying with a friend who lives in France • Staying for three months with your sister-in-law in New Zealand • A family party in your sister's house 100 miles away
Health and fitness	• A cycling tour in France • A weekend in a hotel with a fitness room and health suite • A walking holiday in Scotland
Sport	• The British team's visit to the Olympic Games in Barcelona • Visiting Old Trafford to watch a one-day international cricket match • A weekend break to watch the Monaco Grand Prix
Education	• A week at an Open University summer school in Durham • A weekend sailing course in Plymouth • A French student attending a college in Brighton to learn English
Culture and religion	• A week studying Celtic folklore in the West of Ireland • A Roman Catholic visiting the Vatican to see the Pope • A weekend studying the churches of East Anglian villages
Social and spiritual	• A weekend reflexology workshop • A one-parent family holiday to Suffolk • A week-long meditation course in the Lake District

BUSINESS TOURISM	
Business meetings	• A British sportswear manufacturer on a two-week fact-finding tour of the west coast of the USA • An advertising executive taking a train journey from her home base for a meeting with a client in Leeds • A Member of the European Parliament flying to Brussels for the day for meetings with EU officials
Exhibitions and trade fairs	• A representative of the English Tourist Board visiting the Scottish Travel Trade Fair in Glasgow • The Gardeners' World exhibition at the NEC Birmingham • Attending the World Travel Market in London
Conference and conventions	• Lawyers from EU countries attending a two-day conference on EU Directives in Copenhagen • Attending the TUC Conference in Blackpool • The ABTA domestic conference in Llandudno
Incentive travel	• A weekend golfing break at Gleneagles for achieving top monthly sales for your company • Free car hire for one week on your holiday for completing an important project on time • Two weeks in Florida for you and your family for clinching a new multi-million pound contract

Figure 1.2 Examples of leisure and business tourism categories

Tourism is more than just overseas package holidays

There is a common misconception in Britain that tourism is only concerned with taking holidays abroad; this couldn't be further from the reality of the situation. Later in this unit (see Fig. 1.8), we shall see that Britons take nearly five times as many tourist trips within the UK compared with visits abroad. Also, overseas visitors to Britain contribute nearly £8 billion per year to the UK economy according to British Tourist Authority statistics.

> ### Did You Know ?
>
> British people take nearly five times as many trips within the UK, compared with trips abroad.

The three principal strands within the tourism industry are: domestic, outbound and incoming/ inbound.

Domestic tourism:	When people take holidays, short breaks and day trips in their own country. For example, the Smith family from Birmingham enjoying a two-week holiday in a caravan in Scarborough.
Outbound tourism:	A form of international tourism which concerns people travelling away from their main country of residence. The Smith family from Birmingham deciding to give Scarborough a miss this year and taking a week's holiday at EuroDisney instead.
Incoming/inbound tourism:	That form of international tourism which deals with people entering another country from their own country of origin or another country which is not their home. For example, M et Mme Du Pont from Limoges sampling the delights of Cardiff as part of a driving tour of England and Wales

The history of leisure and tourism

Ancient Times

In ancient times there was little opportunity for true leisure pursuits and the distinction between work and leisure was often blurred. The leisure opportunities which did present themselves were usually associated with festivals and celebrations of a religious or spiritual nature. The early **Egyptian** civilization displayed a primitive social structure which rewarded the 'upper classes' with time to enjoy such activities as archery, dance, music and drama. Travel in early times tended to be confined to one of two forms, either for the purpose of trade or associated with religious activities. There is evidence, however, of some travel for purely recreational purposes with the first Olympic Games taking place in 776 BC.

The Greek Civilization

The **Greeks,** and particularly the Ancient Greek philosophers, were the first to begin to distinguish clearly between work and leisure. They commended the sensible use of free time and promoted a balance between work and play as the route to a healthy individual and a healthy society.

> ### Did You Know ?
>
> Many of the words which we associate with sport and recreation today derive from Ancient Greek, eg stadium, decathlon and gymnasium.

The Romans

Leisure activity in **Roman** times (27 BC until the fourth century AD) can be characterized as 'leisure with a purpose'; gone were the aesthetic pleasures which the Greeks so enjoyed. The great Roman engineers built public facilities for the masses of the urban populations who practised recreation for physical fitness and in readiness for war. The extensive road network developed by the Romans meant that travel was faster and more convenient. Travel within the Empire for trade and to visit friends and relatives expanded and excursions further afield were not uncommon. The healing powers of spa waters were first recognized in Roman times.

The Middle Ages

The time between the fall of the Roman Empire (AD 400) until AD 1000 was known as the **Dark Ages**. As their name implies, these were austere times with few opportunities for the mass of the population to take part in leisure activities. The rise of Christianity during this period relegated leisure activities to those associated with worship and religious festivities. During the **later Middle Ages** (up to approximately AD 1500) leisure continued to be the privilege of those in power who enjoyed hunting, jousting, music and dance. The 'holy days' designated by the church were the main source of leisure for the bulk of the population; the familiar term holiday is derived from 'holy day'. Travel for religious purposes was evident with pilgrimages to holy shrines increasing in popularity. Leisure in general towards the end of the Middle Ages was beginning to take on an unpleasant character with activities such as gambling, drinking and blood sports becoming the pastimes of the increasingly corrupt nobility.

Renaissance and Reformation

Renaissance literally means 'rebirth'; it signals that time in the history of civilization (the fifteenth century) when we changed from a medieval system to a modern Western culture. In terms of leisure, the Renaissance heralded a time when leisure was no longer available only to the privileged classes; the loosening from the religious ties of medieval times meant that such leisure activities as music, drama and dance were opened up to the masses. However, during this time the **Reformation** movement was also developing in Europe leading to the 'Protestant work ethic' which attacked the excesses and corruption of the pleasure-seeking nobility and led to a sharp decrease in the availability and respectability of leisure.

Post-Reformation leisure and tourism

During the seventeenth century, attitudes towards leisure and tourism were changing once again. From 1670 onwards, young gentlemen were sent on the **Grand Tour** of the cultural centres of Europe to widen their education prior to seeking positions at court on their return. Centres such as Paris, Venice and Florence gave such gentlemen the opportunity to sample different cultures, societies and experiences. In the early seventeenth century, the healing powers of spa waters became widely accepted among the aristocracy, leading to the development of **spa resorts** both in Britain and on the Continent. Spa towns such as Buxton, Leamington Spa, Llandrindod Wells and Bath prospered until well into the eighteenth century, recognizing the wider opportunities that tourism can create. Baden-Baden in Germany was one of the most frequented spa resorts in Europe.

The Industrial Revolution

The **Industrial Revolution** of the eighteenth and nineteenth centuries brought about profound changes to the way of life in Britain, not least in relation to leisure and tourism. There was rapid urbanization in response to greater mechanization and mass production techniques and a flow of population from the countryside to the towns. The often overcrowded housing conditions, with long working hours and low wages, gave few opportunities for leisure activities to the mass of the population. In the late nineteenth century it was not uncommon for men, women and even children to work in excess of 60 hours per week. Once again, however, there was a privileged minority (the emerging 'middle classes') who were fortunate enough to be able to indulge in all manner of leisure pursuits ranging from horse racing to prize fighting; leisure was available to those who could afford it.

As the Industrial Revolution gathered momentum, the 'working class' element of society began to demand greater freedom from work. The physical nature of their employment, coupled with dirty and often dangerous working environments, made people want to escape the urban sprawl and experience the relative calm and tranquillity of the countryside and coast. The Bank Holiday Act of 1871 created four public holidays per year which, with the increased spending power of the more prosperous working people, led to the development of a variety of leisure and tourism facilities to meet their needs.

The rise of seaside resorts

Doctors in the early eighteenth century began to realize that the healing and relaxing minerals that were present in spa waters were also to be found in the sea; Scarborough, with the twin benefits of spa and sea-water, was quick to exploit its benefits. It was not until 1752, however, with the publication of Dr Richard Russell's noted medical work *Concerning the Use of Sea-water* that **seaside resorts** such as Southend, Brighton and Blackpool began increasing in popularity.

Accommodation, catering and entertainment facilities were developed in the resorts, some of which benefited from the introduction of steamboat services in the early nineteenth century, a factor which led to the construction of many of the piers still seen at seaside resorts today.

The development of railways and steamships

The development of steam power was to have a profound impact on leisure and tourism patterns with the introduction of the **railways** from 1830 onwards and passenger **steamships** from 1840.

The first passenger train service between Manchester and Liverpool was opened in 1830. There followed a massive expansion of the network, principally to service industrial centres, but with the capacity to bring many of the seaside resorts within easy reach of the centres of population; Brighton was a notable success with some 132,000 visitors recorded on Easter Monday in 1862. The expansion of the railway network led a number of entrepreneurs to consider

how they could capitalize on this new form of travel. One of the most successful was **Thomas Cook** who was destined to have a far-reaching impact on the early development of travel. In 1841 he organized an excursion from Leicester to Loughborough for his local Temperance Association. Within 15 years, spurred on by the success of his first trip, he was running a fully commercial travel company arranging tours and excursions both at home and overseas, including the Great Exhibition in London in 1851 and 'inclusive tours' to the Paris Exhibition in 1855.

The early nineteenth century saw the introduction of a new generation of steamships serving North America, the near Continent and the Far East. The Peninsular and Oriental Steam Navigation Company (P&O) began the first regular long-distance services to India and the Far East in 1838, followed two years later by The Cunard Steamship Company with services to North America. Following on from successes in Britain and on the Continent, Thomas Cook organized the first excursion to America in 1866.

Formal sport and recreation in the Industrial Revolution

The Victorian era saw the public taking part in organized **sport and recreation** in ever increasing numbers; mass participation in leisure was becoming a reality. Sports such as football, rugby, cricket, tennis and hockey became regulated with modern rules being drawn up by governing bodies; the Football Association was founded in 1863. More informal recreational pursuits such as cycling, roller skating and swimming also increased in popularity; the Cyclists' Touring Club was founded in 1878. Leisure was at last available to all but the most deprived in society.

Did You Know ?

In 1903 the first major hotel company – Trust Houses – opened a chain of hotels throughout Britain.

Leisure and tourism in the twentieth century

Leisure

The First World War (1914–18) brought a temporary halt to the more active forms of *leisure* with much time being spent on home-based activities such as needlework, knitting, board games and reading. The inter-war years (1918–39) saw a return to many of the leisure pursuits which had become popular in Victorian times. 'Taking fresh air and exercise' was regarded as a very healthy activity in the countryside around towns and cities and at seaside resorts. New forms of communication, such as posters, guide books and radio, stimulated the public to travel further afield in search of different leisure experiences.

The economic boom of the 1950s, after the ending of the Second World War (1939–45), created more employment and meant that people had greater disposable income with which to purchase the many new consumer and leisure products which were coming onto the market. New labour-saving devices, many originating from the USA, meant that more time was available for leisure pursuits both inside and away from the home.

Fashion, music and youth culture were to have important influences on the pattern of leisure during the 1960s, 1970s and 1980s. The television became a powerful source of home entertainment at the expense of, for example, cinema attendances. 'Fads' such as ten-pin bowling and skateboarding were to come and go. Sport at the highest level was becoming dominated by money with the amateur/professional divide becoming blurred. The decade of the 1980s is sometimes referred to as 'the Thatcher years' after the Prime Minister of that time. During these years, the gap between the rich and poor widened; the terms 'yuppie' (young urban professional) and 'dinky' (double income/no kids) were coined; such people spent extravagantly on leisure and consumer products generally. High-risk activities such as hang-gliding, power boat racing and ballooning became commonplace for these privileged individuals.

Tourism

The twentieth century has seen the unparalleled growth of *tourism* in the Western world. Four factors can be singled out as major twentieth century developments in the industry:

- Increasing personal mobility
- The development of holiday camps
- The development of jet aircraft
- The introduction of package holidays

Increasing personal mobility

The increase in car ownership after the Second World War began to have serious effects on other public forms of travel, particularly rail and coach journeys. In 1970 there were approximately 11 million private cars on the roads of Britain compared with 2.3 million in 1950 and around 20 million in 1993. The dramatic rise in the use of the private car for tourism purposes has led to new types of accommodation being developed, e.g. motels, and growth in activities such as caravanning and day visits to tourist attractions.

The development of holiday camps

The first purpose-built holiday camp (what the industry now refers to as holiday centre) was opened by Billy Butlin in 1936 at Skegness. Holiday camps worked on the simple principle that if the children were happy on holiday then the parents would be happy as well. The camps provided entertainment and activities for parents and children at a low, all-inclusive rate with the added bonus of a child-minding service to allow the parents to enjoy themselves. Butlins and Warners became market leaders in this type of holiday which still survives to this day, albeit in a different form.

The development of jet aircraft

The technological advances in aircraft design which resulted from developments during the Second World War, led to air travel becoming a reality for the masses of the population from the 1950s onwards. The Boeing 707 jet was introduced in 1958 and led to a surge in scheduled and charter flights, the latter being combined with accommodation, transfers and courier services to form the 'package holiday' which is so familiar to us all today.

The introduction of package holidays

The 1960s saw the beginning of the rapid development of package holidays on offer to British holidaymakers. Destinations such as the coastal areas of Southern Spain, the Balearic Islands and Greece were favourite locations for British and other European travellers. The convenience of an all-inclusive arrangement, coupled with the increased speed which the new aircraft brought, caught the imagination of the British travelling public. The age of mass tourism had truly arrived.

Did You Know **?**

Just three tour operators (Thomsons, Airtours and First Choice Holidays), sell over 50% of all package holidays in the UK.

Today's leisure and tourism industry

This section will look at the following aspects of leisure and tourism:

- The scale of the industry
- The structure of the industry
- Employment in leisure and tourism

The scale of the industry

Leisure in Britain is a multi-billion pound industry. According to figures compiled by Leisure Consultants, consumer spending on leisure in 1993 was valued at £102.9 billion and was forecast to rise to more than £130 billion by 1998 (see Figure 1.3).

	1988	1989	1990	1991	1992	1993	1994	1995	1996	1997	1998
TIME – Hours of leisure											
Full-time worker											
Annual hours	2513	2509	2519	2542	2546	2552	2567	2579	2594	2621	2648
% change	*–0.3*	*–0.1*	*0.4*	*0.9*	*0.2*	*0.2*	*0.6*	*0.5*	*0.6*	*1.0*	*1.0*
All people 16+											
Total hours (billion)	125.5	124.9	125.5	128.2	130.0	131.1	131.9	132.4	133.1	134.3	135.5
% change	*–0.8*	*–0.5*	*0.5*	*2.1*	*1.4*	*0.8*	*0.6*	*0.4*	*0.5*	*0.9*	*1.0*
All ages											
Total hours (billion)	151.0	150.4	151.3	154.3	156.4	158.0	159.2	160.0	160.8	162.0	163.4
% change	*–0.8*	*–0.4*	*0.6*	*2.0*	*1.4*	*1.0*	*0.8*	*0.5*	*0.5*	*0.8*	*0.9*
MONEY – Consumer spending on leisure											
Value (£ billion)	76.33	83.78	89.94	94.52	99.82	102.90	107.54	113.55	120.16	126.23	130.84
Leisure as % of all consumer spending	25.0	25.0	24.7	24.9	25.1	24.5	24.2	24.2	24.2	24.1	23.7
% change on year ago											
in value	*9.2*	*9.8*	*7.4*	*5.1*	*5.6*	*3.1*	*4.5*	*5.6*	*5.8*	*5.1*	*3.6*
in price	*4.8*	*6.9*	*7.5*	*8.0*	*5.6*	*3.5*	*2.5*	*3.3*	*3.2*	*3.1*	*3.0*
in volume	*4.3*	*3.3*	*–0.4*	*–3.1*	*0.2*	*0.1*	*1.3*	*2.4*	*2.8*	*1.9*	*0.3*

Figures include spending by foreign tourists where relevant. Alcoholic drink includes off-licence sales in UK.
Leisure time is time left after essential activities (sleeping etc.) and paid work.

Source: Leisure Consultants (1994)

Figure 1.3   Leisure time and money 1988–98

	1988	1989	1990	1991	1992	1993	1994	1995	1996	1997	1998
Reading	*5.1*	*5.0*	*5.2*	*5.1*	*5.2*	*5.3*	*5.3*	*5.3*	*5.2*	*5.2*	*5.2*
Home entertainment	9.8	9.6	9.2	9.0	9.1	9.4	9.5	9.4	9.2	8.9	8.8
House and garden	8.1.	7.8	7.5	7.5	7.5	7.7	7.8	7.8	7.8	7.9	8.0
Hobbies and pastimes	5.4	5.7	5.6	5.7	5.8	5.8	5.8	5.8	5.7	5.6	5.6
IN THE HOME	28.4	28.1	27.6	27.3	27.6	28.2	28.4	28.3	27.9	27.7	27.6
Eating out	19.4	19.7	19.6	19.2	18.5	18.2	18.0	17.9	17.9	17.8	17.8
Alcoholic drink	24.6	23.6	24.1	25.0	24.7	24.3	24.0	23.7	23.4	23.2	23.0
Eating and drinking	*44.0*	*43.3*	*43.7*	*44.2*	*43.1*	*42.5*	*42.1*	*41.6*	*41.3*	*41.0*	*40.8*
Local entertainment	2.5	2.5	2.6	2.7	2.7	2.6	2.6	2.6	2.6	2.6	2.7
Gambling	3.4	3.4	3.4	3.3	3.2	3.2	3.1	3.2	3.1	3.0	3.0
Sport	4.2	4.5	4.8	4.6	4.1	4.1	4.2	4.3	4.4	4.5	4.6
Neighbourhood leisure	*10.2*	*10.4*	*10.8*	*10.6*	*9.9*	*9.9*	*9.9*	*10.1*	*10.2*	*10.2*	*10.2*
Sightseeing	0.5	0.5	0.6	0.6	0.6	0.7	0.7	0.7	0.7	0.7	0.7
UK holiday accommodation	5.2	5.8	6.8	6.5	6.3	6.1	6.1	6.1	6.2	6.3	6.3
Holidays overseas	11.7	11.9	10.5	10.8	12.4	12.6	12.9	13.2	13.7	14.1	14.3
Holidays and tourism	*17.4*	*18.2*	*17.9*	*17.9*	*19.4*	*19.3*	*19.6*	*20.0*	*20.6*	*21.1*	*21.4*
AWAY FROM HOME	71.6	71.9	72.4	72.7	72.4	71.8	71.6	71.7	72.1	72.3	72.4
ALL LEISURE	100.0	100.0	100.0	100.0	100.0	100.0	100.0	100.0	100.0	100.0	100.0

Figures include spending by foreign tourists where relevant. Alcoholic drink includes off-licence sales in UK.
Leisure time is time left after essential activities (sleeping etc.) and paid work.

Source: Leisure Consultants (1994)

Figure 1.4   Leisure spending 1988–98 (each market as percentage of leisure total)

The breakdown of leisure spending in the UK is shown in Figure 1.4, showing the largest element of leisure spending to be eating out and drinking, followed by home-based leisure, holidays and tourism, and neighbourhood leisure.

How much do we spend on leisure?

Government statistics show that average weekly expenditure by British people on leisure items in 1981, 1986 and 1991 was as follows:

Year	Total Weekly Expenditure	Percentage of Total Household Expenditure
1981	£16.82	13.4
1986	£28.76	16.1
1991	£41.14	15.9

Source: Social Trends 23

Over the same 10-year period, 1981–91, expenditure on some leisure activities and products more than doubled, including purchases of home computers, DIY, holidays, trips to the theatre and admissions at sports events (other than football matches).

Internationally, spending on leisure is an important element of total household spending in many industrialized nations. Data from the Statistical Office of the European Communities shows that, at the top end of the scale, Irish people spend 10.5% and the Japanese 10.2% of their total expenditure on leisure, while the people of Luxembourg and Greece spend the lowest proportion on leisure, with 4% and 5.6% respectively.

The scale of the tourism industry

Tourism is commonly referred to today as 'the world's biggest industry'. According to the World Travel and Tourism Council (WTTC), in 1990 the industry:

- Employed 118 million people worldwide
- Generated an annual turnover equivalent to 5.9% of world gross national product
- Contributed over 5.6% to total tax payments worldwide
- Accounted for over 6.7% of the world's capital investment

Figure 1.5 shows that world travel and tourism gross output (total revenue) grew steadily between 1987 and 1993 and is now worth nearly $3500 billion.

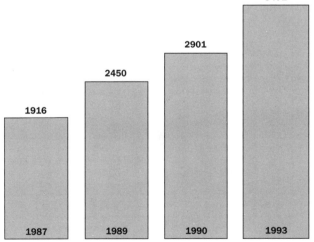

Source: World Travel and Tourism Council   **(US$ billion)**

Figure 1.5 Travel and tourism gross output

The growth in total world tourist arrivals 1970–89 is shown in Figure 1.6. Apart from the early 1980s when the world was experiencing a recession, Figure 1.6 shows a steady growth pattern over two decades culminating in more than 400 million tourist arrivals in 1989.

Year	Arrivals	Rate of growth (%)
1970	159.7	11.6
1971	172.2	7.9
1972	181.9	5.6
1973	190.6	4.8
1974	197.1	3.4
1975	214.4	8.8
1976	220.7	3.0
1977	239.1	8.3
1978	257.4	7.6
1979	274.0	6.5
1980	284.8	4.0
1981	288.8	1.4
1982	287.0	-0.7
1983	284.4	-0.8
1984	311.2	9.4
1985	325.9	4.7
1986	333.9	2.5
1987	358.9	7.5
1988	390.0	8.7
1989	405.3	3.9

Figure 1.6 World international tourist arrivals 1970–89 (millions) *Source:* World Tourism Organization (1990)

Tourism in Europe

Europe is by far the world's most popular tourist region as shown in Fig. 1.7. Europe welcomed nearly two-thirds of all worldwide travellers in 1988 and is sure to dominate the international travel scene well into the next century. It can boast:

- Eight of the top ten world tourist destinations (in terms of receipts).
- Sixteen of the top twenty destinations visited.

Region	Arrivals	Percentage Share
Africa	12.0	3
Americas	72.5	19
East Asia and the Pacific	42.0	11
Europe	251.5	64
Middle East	9.0	2
South Asia	3.0	1
World Total	390.0	100

Figure 1.7 International Tourist Arrivals by Region 1988 (millions) *Source:* World Tourism Organization (1989)

However, Europe is coming under increasing pressure from other world destinations such as America, the Far East, the Caribbean and Australasia who are marketing themselves aggressively worldwide and increasing the products they offer to tourists. During the 1980s, Europe's share of world tourist arrivals actually fell by 6%, so the European tourism industry must work hard to regain its market share.

Did You Know ?

Europe attracts more international visitors per year than all the other continents put together.

Tourism in the UK

During 1992, UK adults and children accompanying them took more than 118 million trips of one night or more away from home (see Fig. 1.8). These trips lasted for a total of nearly 653 million nights and resulted in a total expenditure of £25,070 million. Contrary to popular belief, trips and nights taken within the UK far outweighed those taken abroad; it is only when the figures for total **spending** are examined that figures for travel overseas exceed those within the UK.

tendering (see page 14), the distinction between the two is becoming increasingly blurred. Unlike private sector provision where profit maximization is generally the main objective, the public sector is concerned with providing a service to the local community and the wider public. This does not mean that public sector providers are not concerned with giving value-for-money within the facilities they provide. Increasing competition from rival facilities has forced public sector managers to adopt many private sector practices in order to survive and expand their operations.

UK RESIDENTS' TOURISM IN 1992						
	Trips		**Nights**		**Spending**	
	million	% of all destinations	million	% of all destinations	million	% of all destinations
All destinations	**118.9**	**100**	**653.3**	**100**	**25,070**	**100**
UK	95.6	80	399.7	61	10,665	43
England	77.2	65	306.4	47	8,080	32
Scotland	8.9	7	42.3	6	1,220	5
Wales	8.3	7	40.1	6	930	4
N. Ireland	1.1	1	5.3	1	135	1
Non-UK (rest of the World)	**23.7**	**20**	**253.6**	**39**	**14,410**	**57**

Figure 1.8   UK residents' tourism in 1992   *(Source: Insights)*

Notes: **A tourist trip** is a stay of one or more nights away from home for holidays, visits to friends or relatives, business, conference or any other purpose except such things as boarding education or semi-permanent employment.

Tourist nights are those spent away from home using any type of accomodation, or in transit, on a tourist ship.

Tourist spending is expenditure while away from home and on advance payments for such things as fares and accommodation. Spending by the tourist on other people, e.g. children, is included. Spending on behalf of the tourist by other people, e.g. their spouse, is excluded.

Overseas tourism to the UK

In spite of the problems generally in the global tourist industry resulting from the world economic recession, Britain earned a record £7.89 billion from the 18.53 million trips by overseas visitors to all parts of Britain in 1992 (British Tourist Authority Annual Report 1993). Figure 1.9 charts the steady progression in the number of overseas visitors to Britain since 1981.

The structure of the leisure and tourism industry

In broad terms, the leisure and tourism industry in Britain is made up of three types of providers:

- The public sector
- The private sector
- The voluntary sector

Each sector has its own distinct aims and objectives and different ways of managing its affairs.

Public sector leisure and tourism

Public sector leisure and tourism facilities in Britain exist side by side with those in the private sector. Indeed, with the trends towards **privatization** (the transfer from public to private sector ownership and control) and **compulsory competitive**

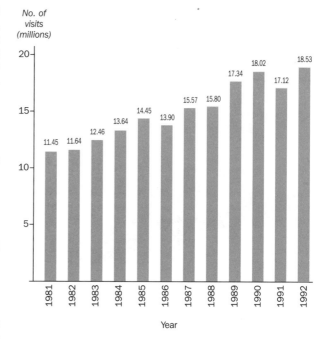

No. of visits (millions)

Source: BTA Annual Reports 1991–2 and 1993

Figure 1.9   Overseas visits to Britain 1981–92

Facilities provided by the public sector include:

- Libraries and museums
- Arts centres and galleries
- Visitor attractions
- Special events
- Sports and leisure centres
- Tourist information centres
- Parks, sports grounds and play areas
- Swimming pools
- Community centres

Public sector provision can be at either one of two levels:

- Central government
- Local government

Central government involvement in leisure and tourism

The **Department of National Heritage** (DNH) was created after the general election of April 1992 as a totally new Ministry which would try to co-ordinate the many different activities which make up leisure and tourism within Britain. The Department, which is headed by a Cabinet Minister, the Secretary of State for National Heritage, has responsibility for:

- Tourism
- Sport
- National heritage
- Broadcasting
- The arts
- The film industry
- The Millennium Fund (dedicated to projects to celebrate the start of the twenty-first century)

Before the DNH was formed these activities were the responsibility of many different government departments resulting in overlap and unnecessary duplication of effort. Staff have been transferred from these departments into the DNH which has five directorates:

- Heritage and Tourism Group
- Broadcasting, Films and Sport Group
- Arts and Lottery Group
- Libraries, Galleries and Museums Group
- Resources and Services Group

Figure 1.10 shows the structure of the Department of National Heritage. The DNH sponsors a number of public bodies, including the Arts Council of Great Britain, the British Tourist Authority, the English Tourist Board, English Heritage and the Sports Council. These are sometimes referred to as **quangos** (quasi-autonomous non-governmental organizations) which, although linked to a government department, are left, to a greater or lesser extent, to manage their own affairs, free from political bias.

Did You Know ?

The Department of National Heritage allocated nearly £1 billion of public money in 1992.

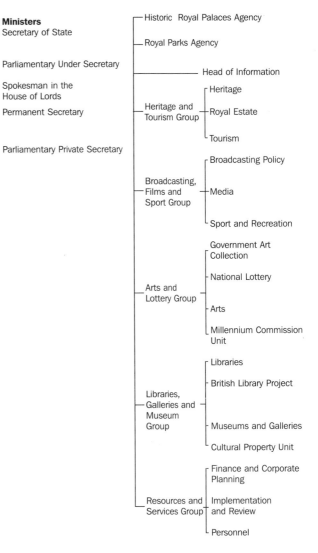

Source: DNH Annual Report 1993 (Reproduced with permission of the Controller of Her Majesty's Stationery Office)

Figure 1.10   Organizational structure of the Department of National Heritage.

Factfile 1: The Sports Council

The **Sports Council** is an independent body, established in 1972 by Royal Charter, and funded largely through funds from the Department of National Heritage. It has a remit covering British sport as a whole although there are separate Councils for Scotland, Wales and Northern Ireland. It consists of members appointed by the Secretary of State and around 550 permanent employees.

The Sports Council has four main aims:

- To increase participation in sport and physical recreation
- To increase the quality and quantity of sports facilities
- To raise standards of performance
- To provide information for and about sport

Increasing Participation

The Council has an extensive programme to increase participation by:

- Providing regional participation grants to help a range of local organizations to encourage local people into sport.

- Running campaigns to persuade people to become involved in sport.
- Funding development staff to help **governing bodies** to increase participation in their particular sport.
- Organizing programmes such as 'Action Sport' to promote sport through a wide range of formal and informal agencies.

Facilities

The Council works to improve facilities by:

- Encouraging the development of new or improved sports facilities through advice and financial assistance.
- Preparing standard design solutions for sports buildings and systems.
- Developing innovative facilities and systems such as artificial playing surfaces.
- Identifying examples of good practice in facilities and management.
- Funding research into local and national sports facility requirements.

Raising Standards of Performance

Action by the Sports Council in the area of standards of performance includes:

- Running five **centres of excellence** at:
  Crystal Palace (National Sports Centre)
  Bisham Abbey (National Sports Centre)
  Lilleshall (National Sports Centre)
  Holme Pierrepont (National Water Sports Centre)
  Plas y Brenin (National Centre for Mountain Activities)
- Offering support to governing bodies of sport.
- Financing the **National Coaching Foundation** (NCF) to help meet the demand for trained coaches.
- Encouraging sponsorship of sport by the private sector.
- Running the campaign against drug abuse in sport.

The Council is the country's main central *source of information* and data about sport. It provides a national information centre and a network of nine regional centres based at its regional offices. The Sports Council researches and publishes a wide range of data on sport, briefs journalists, politicians and other interested parties and runs sport's largest annual conference 'Recreation Management'.

Source: Sports Council

which includes the Crafts Council, British Film Institute, the Scottish and Welsh Arts Councils and the ten Regional Arts Boards (see Fig. 1.11).

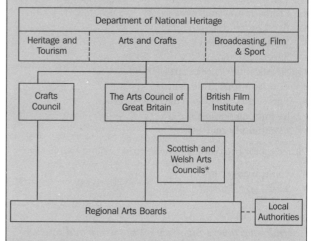

* Autonomous bodies from April 1994   *Source: Arts Council*

Figure 1.11   The arts funding structure in Great Britain

Since April 1994, the Scottish and Welsh Arts Councils have become autonomous and directly accountable to their respective Secretary of State. A separate Arts Council will be set up with a new charter to continue the work of the current Council in England.

Funding

The Arts Council received £225.63 million for 1993–94 from the Department of National Heritage. It allocated £44 million to the Regional Arts Boards and £23 million and £13 million to the Scottish and Welsh Arts Councils respectively.
Four per cent of the Council's grant is spent on administration of the Arts Council itself.

Priorities

The Arts Council has identified the following priorities for its work:

- Quality in the arts generally
- Access for all to the arts
- Growth of the arts economy
- Quality of service

Source: Arts Council

Factfile 2: The Arts Council of Great Britain

The **Arts Council** is the national body established to foster the arts throughout Britain. It was formed in 1946 to continue in peacetime the work begun by the Council for the Encouragement of Music and the Arts during the Second World War.

The Council operates under a Royal Charter which defines its objectives as:

1 To develop and improve the knowledge, understanding and practice of the arts.
2 To increase the accessibility of the arts to the public throughout Britain.
3 To advise and co-operate with departments of government, local authorities and other bodies.

Structure

The Arts Council is the central part of a funding structure

Public sector tourism

Public sector involvement in UK tourism can be traced back to before Victorian times when many 'resorts', both inland and on the coast, benefited from investment in tourist facilities by their local councils. **Central government** recognition of the economic significance of tourism was not forthcoming until as late as 1969, with the passing of the **Development of Tourism Act**. This first piece of tourism legislation, now 25 years old, still applies today, although the nature and scale of the industry has changed dramatically. The principal outcomes of the Act were:

1 The establishment of the British Tourist Authority (BTA), English Tourist Board (ETB), Wales Tourist Board (WTB) and Scottish Tourist Board (STB).
2 The introduction of 'Section 4' grants for tourist developments.

3   The establishment of a hotel development grants scheme.
4   Legislation to introduce a compulsory registration scheme for accommodation.

The Northern Ireland Tourist Board was not included in the Act since it had already been set up in 1948.

The structure of public sector tourism

Figure 1.12 shows the relationships between the various public sector organizations with an interest in tourism in the UK.

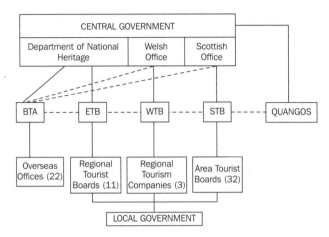

Figure 1.12   The structure of public sector tourism in the UK

While the DNH can be regarded as the 'lead' government department when it comes to tourism matters, other departments, including the Department of the Environment and the Ministry of Agriculture, all undertake activities which can impinge on tourism. **Quangos** (quasi-autonomous non-governmental organizations) include bodies such as Highlands and Islands Enterprise and the Welsh Development Agency, who have interests in tourism in their respective regions.

Factfile 3: British Tourist Authority

The 1969 Development of Tourism Act established the **British Tourist Authority** (BTA) along with the Wales, English and Scottish Tourist Boards; the Northern Ireland Tourist Board was set up in 1948. Unlike the national tourist boards who try to encourage visitors to their own particular country, the BTA is responsible for promoting **the whole of Britain** to overseas visitors. BTA's objectives are:

- To maximize the benefit to the economy of tourism to Britain from abroad while working worldwide in partnership with the private and public sector organizations involved in the industry and the English Tourist Board, Scottish Tourist Board and Wales Tourist Board.
- To identify the requirements of visitors to Britain, whatever their origin, and to stimulate the improvement of the quality of the product and the use of technology to meet them.
- To spread the economic benefit of tourism to Britain more widely and particularly to areas with tourism potential and higher than average levels of unemployment.
- To encourage tourism to Britain in off-peak periods.
- To ensure that the Authority makes the most cost-effective use of resources in pursuing its objectives.

In order to meet these objectives, BTA works in close co-operation with the national and regional tourist boards, local authorities, the media and trade interests as shown in Fig. 1.13.

Figure 1.13   BTA's co-ordinating role

As well as running the British Travel Centre in London, BTA operates a network of 22 offices worldwide which act as information points for potential visitors to Britain and pass on information about the market from that particular country to the BTA's headquarters in London. This 'market intelligence' helps shape the various travel and tourism products that Britain has to offer to overseas visitors. In 1991–92 BTA received a £29.2 million grant from the government and generated a further £13.6 million from other commercial activities. The grant-in-aid figure for 1993–94 was £32 million.

Source: BTA

Local government involvement in leisure and tourism

Local government in England and Wales consists broadly of three tiers. Working from the most local, these are:

- Parish or community councils
- District or borough councils
- County councils

Each level has elected representatives (known as councillors) who implement central government decisions at local level. Local government officers, the equivalent of civil servants in central government, carry out the decisions of the councillors which, if the democratic system is functioning correctly, should reflect the views and wishes of the majority of the local people.

Local authorities exist to provide services to the local population; whether a service is provided by the county or district, for example, is not always clear-cut. In general, county councils are concerned with broader issues such as education, social services, highways and strategic planning while the district councils confine themselves to more local needs such as refuse collection, environmental health, leisure and housing.

Did You Know ?

The British Association of Tourism Officers (BATO) has been established to represent the interests of local authorities throughout Britain.

Local Authority provision of leisure and tourism facilities

There is no **statutory** (legal) duty on local authorities to provide the range of leisure and tourism facilities which we see in most areas of the country today. They only have a legal duty to provide recreational opportunities through schools and libraries but most go far beyond this and use their wide **discretionary** powers to provide the best possible leisure and tourism facilities within their local area. This discretionary provision does have its drawbacks, however, since in times of financial cutbacks it is often leisure and tourism which has its budget cut first.

Local authorities use their resources to provide a wide range of leisure and tourism facilities, which in a typical district might include:

- Parks and gardens
- Playing fields
- Playgrounds
- Libraries
- Tourist information
- Art galleries and museums
- Theatres
- Sports/leisure centres and swimming pools
- Outdoor activity centres

Some of these facilities may be dual use or joint use when, for example, a college and the local community share the use of a sports centre in order to make better use of the facility.

The importance of local government leisure and tourism provision

Local authorities play an extremely important role in the provision of facilities and amenities for leisure and tourism. In purely financial terms, local authorities were estimated to have spent nearly £1.5 billion on such provision in the financial year 1992–3 (DNH figures). This compares with approximately £1 billion spent at national level by the DNH itself.

Local councils in England and Wales are also significant employers within the leisure and tourism sector. Employment in libraries, museums, art galleries, sports and other recreational services amounted to 380,000 in 1993, according to Department of Employment figures, out of a national leisure and tourism employment figure of around 1.4 million.

Compulsory competitive tendering (CCT)

This is the process by which many local services, traditionally provided exclusively by local authorities, are opened up to competition from the private sector. It is not privatization in the strict sense of the word, since the local authority retains ownership of the facilities involved. Within the leisure and recreation sector, all local authorities in England and Wales were required to have put the management of their sports and leisure facilities out to **tender** by the end of 1993. 'Management' in this case includes:

- Taking bookings
- Providing catering services
- Marketing and promoting the facility
- Collecting and accounting for fees and charges
- Making the facility secure
- Cleaning and maintaining the facility
- Hiring out equipment
- Providing instruction
- Supervising activities

Current employees of the local authorities may submit a bid for the management of a facility and, if their tender is successful, they are known as the DSO (Direct Service Organization).

Sport and leisure facilities which fall within the scope of CCT include sports and leisure centres, golf courses, cycle tracks, athletic grounds and bowling greens.

The principle underlying CCT is that increased competition will provide an improved service and better value for money for the local population. Opponents of the legislation argue that CCT may lead to certain services and facilities being withdrawn since they are unprofitable even though they are fulfilling an important local need, such as providing services for the disabled.

Leisure and tourism in the private sector

The **private sector** is built around business units, both large and small, owned by individuals or groups of people whose principal aim is to maximize their profits. Revenue from the sales of their services or goods will hopefully be greater than the costs of operating the business so as to leave a surplus which can be either taken as profit or re-invested in the business in order to build a solid foundation for future success for owners, directors, employees and any shareholders who may have bought a stake in the business.

The range of leisure and tourism facilities provided by the private sector is huge and includes:

- Travel agencies and tour operators
- Theatres
- Cinemas
- Restaurants, cafés, pubs and bars
- Discotheques and nightclubs
- Hotels and other forms of accommodation
- Airlines
- Transport operations
- Tourist attractions
- Health and fitness clubs and studios
- Mixed retail and leisure complexes

Private sector leisure and tourism has a lively and dynamic image since the survival of many of its companies and individuals is dependent on adapting to new trends and fashions in society. For the same reason, customer service and customer care are vital components of any professional concern in the leisure and tourism field. One of the biggest private sector leisure and tourism organizations in the UK is Rank.

Factfile 4: The Rank Organisation PLC

The Rank Organisation was founded and created by J. Arthur Rank more than 50 years ago. Rank became the dominant influence in the British film industry by the end of the Second World War and has subsequently developed and expanded into other leisure and entertainment businesses. Today it is one of the world's leading leisure and tourism organizations and one of the 100 largest companies in the UK. It currently employs some 40,000 people in four operating divisions:

- Film and television
- Holidays and hotels
- Recreation
- Leisure

Film and television operations include the famous Odeon Cinemas which have been part of the Rank Organisation for over 50 years. Odeon operates over 300 screens at more than 70 locations in the UK and has an important presence in London's West End where the Odeon in Leicester Square often stages Royal Film Premieres. All Odeon cinemas are equipped with computerized box offices and offer advance booking facilities. Rank owns Pinewood Studios near London, the premier and best-known film studio in Europe, offering facilities to producers of feature films, TV commercials, training films and corporate videos. Other film and television work includes film distribution, video duplication and film processing services. In all, the film and television division employs approximately 7000 staff.

Butlin's is the jewel in the crown of Rank's **holidays and hotels** division. Butlin's is a brand leader in the UK holiday market and sells in the region of 1.6 million holidays per year. It operates five Holiday Worlds and five Holiday Hotels at UK coastal resorts. The Holiday Worlds provide facilities for the family market, with a range of sports and leisure facilities, while the Holiday Hotels are aimed at older customers. Butlin's is the leading contractor of star entertainers in the UK. Rank also owns HavenWarner, offering self-catering and half-board holidays in 60 UK locations and, through its Haven France and Spain brand, self-drive and caravan holidays at some 40 parks in Europe. HavenWarner sells over 1 million holidays each year. Shearings is part of the Rank Organisation and is the leading coach holiday operator in Europe with a fleet of some 350 coaches travelling to 300 UK and 250 continental European destinations.

Through its **recreation** division, Rank operates businesses which are regulated by the Gaming Board of Great Britain. These include around 150 amusement centres spread throughout the UK and 28 casinos trading under the Grosvenor Clubs banner. Rank is the leading bingo and social club operator in the UK with some 160 outlets known by the 'Top Rank' and 'Mecca' brand names, attracting about 700,000 customers each week.

Rank's **leisure** division operates around 50 nightclubs and theme bars, the best-known being Ritzy, Fifth Avenue and Central Park. The division also develops and manages multi-leisure centres which typically include a mix of multi-screen cinema, bingo, ten-pin bowling, nightclub, amusement centre, bars and restaurants. Resorts USA owns and operates 14 'Outdoor World' campground resorts on the Eastern seaboard of the USA and sells second homes in Pennsylvania. Rank Leisure USA owns and operates 10 Hard Rock Cafés in Europe and America. There are also 12 franchised Hard Rock Cafés in other parts of the world.

Rank is also an equal partner in Universal Studios Florida, a film and TV studio complex and motion picture theme park which opened in Orlando in June 1990.

(Information courtesy of the Rank Organisation PLC)

Structure in the private sector

As with many other sectors of the economy, businesses in leisure and tourism can be categorized into one of the following five classifications:

1 Sole trader
2 Partnership
3 Private limited company
4 Public limited company (PLC)
5 Co-operative

Sole trader

As the name implies, a business run by a **sole trader** is owned and controlled by that one person. Within leisure and tourism, such people often provide ancillary or support services for larger organizations, e.g. as couriers, guides, chauffeurs, caterers, fitness counsellors and instructors. Much maintenance work on property and equipment is also often entrusted to sole traders. It is not uncommon in the leisure and tourism business to find that an individual who used to work for a large organization decides to leave and start a business as a sole trader free from the bureaucracy which sometimes frustrates talented employees.

This highlights one of the main *advantages* of being a sole trader, namely the ability to have personal control of the business and to be able to make decisions quickly. There are, however, *disadvantages* which include the fact that the owner is personally liable for all the debts of the business and, often overlooked, the long hours which the sole trader will have to work in order to be successful.

Partnership

There must be between two and 20 people in business together for a **partnership** to be legal. Not all of the partners are necessarily involved in the day-to-day running of the business. Indeed some may choose only to put up capital in the hope of a return on their investment and show no interest in the management of the business at all; such individuals are referred to as 'sleeping partners'. An important point about partnerships is that the decision of any one partner is binding on all the other partners; this may cause problems if one partner proves to be unreliable or untrustworthy. In leisure and tourism, partnerships are often found in the hotel and catering field, with many pubs, cafés, restaurants, small hotels, guesthouses and inns being run as partnerships.

Advantages of partnerships are that extra capital is injected into the business when compared with the sole trader and that the responsibilities are shared by the partners. One disadvantage has already been highlighted, namely that the decision of one partner is binding on the others; with the increased numbers involved in the partnership, decision making may be slower than is the case with the sole trader.

> ### Did You Know ?
>
> Sole traders and partners risk losing their personal possessions should the business fail.

Private limited company

Any organization within leisure and tourism which has the abbreviation 'Ltd' after its name is a private limited company. 'Limited' means that the company enjoys the benefit of **'limited liability'**, meaning that the investors in the business are only liable for the company's debts up to the amount they have actually invested; this is in stark contrast to both sole traders and partnerships who do not have limited liability. Those who invest in the business are known as **shareholders** although the shares of **private limited companies** are not offered for sale on the Stock Exchange as is the case with PLCs (*public limited companies*). Many leisure and tourism businesses are private limited companies, with examples as diverse as tourist attractions, leisure centres and country house hotels.

Public limited company (PLC)

Public limited companies (PLCs) are large organizations often with hundreds and even thousands of people on their payroll. Some of the best known leisure and tourism companies in the UK are PLCs, e.g. Grand Metropolitan PLC, Ladbroke Group PLC, Airtours PLC, Forte PLC, Rank Organisation PLC and British Airways PLC, to name but a few. Investors in PLCs have the benefit of limited liability in the same way as those investing in private limited companies. The difference between the two lies in the word 'public' which indicates that the shares of a PLC are listed on the Stock Exchange and are therefore available to the public at large. Public limited companies often have a **parent** company acting as the head of a group with a number of **subsidiary** companies working beneath it, e.g. Forte Travelodge and Little Chef are subsidiaries of Forte PLC, the parent company.

As well as the advantage of limited liability, private limited companies and PLCs also have greater opportunities for expansion compared with sole traders and partnerships. There may also be significant tax advantages of operating as a limited company. Disadvantages of private and public limited companies are that there is less confidentiality since they are both required to publish their accounts annually and they may be unable to react quickly to new market opportunities unless management and workforce are very flexible.

Figure 1.14 shows the turnover of some of the largest limited companies involved in leisure and tourism in 1989.

Company Name	Turnover (£000s)
Grand Metropolitan PLC	9 298 000
Ladbroke Group PLC	3 659 500
Whitbread PLC	2 488 300
Granada Group PLC	1 636 400
Rank Organisation PLC	1 093 000
Mecca Leisure Group PLC	588 438
Stakis PLC	143 223
Chrysalis Group PLC	95 590
Wembley PLC	76 275

Figure 1.14 Turnover of selected leisure and tourism companies 1989. *Source:* Jordan's (1992)

Co-operatives

The number of **co-operatives** within leisure and tourism is quite small, but they are to be found in community activities such as art galleries, music workshops, street theatre entertainment and countryside groups. Co-operatives work on very democratic principles with one vote per shareholder rather than one vote per share. They work within simple guidelines with elected managers organizing the venture on behalf of the workers.

Voluntary sector leisure and tourism

A third important source of provision in leisure and tourism, the **voluntary sector**, exists to supplement private and public facilities and services.

The voluntary sector includes charities and trusts involved in:

- Community activities
- Play schemes
- Clubs and societies
- Conservation/environment
- Heritage
- Minority groups
- Youth organizations
- Cultural/entertainment organizations
- Arts, drama and music projects

Voluntary organizations vary enormously in their *size* and *aims*. At one end of the scale, there are large organizations such as the National Trust and the Royal Society for the Protection of Birds, each having its own objectives in terms of environmental conservation. In contrast, a small group of like-minded people may decide to form a rambling club in their local village purely for the purpose of improving their level of fitness and enjoyment of the countryside.

Voluntary organizations at both national and local level often receive advice and financial help from both public and private sector sources, sometimes in the form of grants or sponsorship (see Element 1.4 on page 30).

> ### Did You Know ?
>
> The National Trust welcomes some 11 million visitors to its properties every year.

Voluntary sector organization

The grouping of individuals to achieve a common purpose may be either formal or informal. The more formal an organization, the more structured it is likely to become. Taking the earlier example of the group of people deciding to form a rambling club, it is likely that they will form a **committee** to manage the affairs of the club. As a minimum, the committee will normally include:

- A **chairperson**
- A **secretary**
- A **treasurer**

There may also be a **social secretary** or **membership secretary** and **co-opted members** (people who are appointed because of their particular skills or experience). The committee is elected by the members of the club and all who volunteer to serve on the committee are accountable to all club members for its smooth running.

Larger organizations within the voluntary sector are not able to meet all their needs through the recruitment of volunteers alone. Salaried staff are employed, sometimes alongside volunteers, to manage the affairs of the organization and to help it to meet its objectives. Certain individuals may be invited to become honorary members in recognition of loyal work or exceptional financial contributions to a particular organization. Ordinary members are members of the general public who wish to further the cause of an organization by paying a membership subscription. A particular society or trust may invite a celebrated individual to become its patron to add prestige to the organization; the Queen, for example, is the patron of the Youth Hostel Association.

> ### Factfile 5: The National Trust
>
> **Introduction**
>
> The **National Trust**, or to give it its full title The National Trust for Places of Historic Interest or Natural Beauty, was founded in 1895 as an independent charity in response to the spread of industrialization, which was affecting both town and countryside at the end of the last century. Although its name might suggest that it is run by the government, the Trust is jealously independent of the State. It depends on the generosity of those who give it properties and the money to maintain them, on more than 2 million subscribing members and on its friends and supporters everywhere. Today, the National Trust protects more than 600,000 acres of land in England, Wales and Northern Ireland as well as over 200 houses and parks.
>
> **Structure**
>
> The day-to-day administration of the Trust is carried out by its executive staff at head office in London and in 16 regional offices covering England, Wales and Northern Ireland. The

governing body is a council of 52 members, half of whom are elected by the members and half appointed by relevant bodies.

Activities

The Trust plays host to an immense number of people. Each year, some 11 million people visit its 400 buildings and gardens open at a charge, and on a fine summer weekend untold millions freely enjoy the coastline, hills and woodlands which the Trust preserves for us all. The Trust must ensure the right balance between the often conflicting interests of preservation and presentation to the public. Too great a pressure of visitors could destroy the atmosphere they seek. The Trust is at present running several special appeals including **Enterprise Neptune**, launched by the Duke of Edinburgh in 1965, which aims to preserve unspoilt coastline and set itself an initial target of raising £2 million. By the end of 1992, the appeal had raised £17.5 million and over 530 miles of coastline were under the permanent protection of the National Trust.

Source: National Trust

Employment in leisure and tourism

We saw earlier how tourism alone is estimated to employ 118 million people worldwide and, closer to home, how leisure and tourism creates a significant number of jobs in the private, public and voluntary sectors. Leisure and tourism's ability to create jobs is one of its main *economic benefits* and often the principal reason why a country, region or local area considers tourism as an option for economic development.

How many people work in leisure and tourism?

Figures from the Employment Department give the breakdown shown in Fig. 1.15 of employment in the different sectors of the leisure and tourism industry in Britain for June 1992.

As the figure shows, the bulk of jobs are to be found in the private sector. The total employment figure for the same month was approximately 1.5 million. In addition to this, the Labour Force Survey estimates that there are around 183,000 **self-employed** in the leisure and tourism sector.

Category	%
Restaurants, cafes etc.	20.5
Public houses and bars	22.3
Nightclubs and licensed clubs	9.4
Hotels and other tourist accommodation	20.6
Libraries, museums, art galleries, sports and other recreational services	27.2
	100.0

Source: Employment Gazette

Figure 1.15 Leisure and tourism employment in Britain, June 1992.

Trends in leisure and tourism employment

Much of the growth in jobs in leisure and tourism is very recent. In the case of tourism, it is only with the introduction of package tours and the advent of 'mass tourism' within the past 30 years or so that we have seen the industry develop as a signifi-

cant provider of jobs. Sectors of leisure and tourism employment which have grown rapidly over this time period include:

- Airlines
- Travel agency and tour operations
- Restaurants and cafés
- Licensed entertainment venues

One or two areas, notably employment in hotels and public sector leisure and tourism, have remained fairly static over this time period, while the number of jobs in cinemas has actually fallen. The recent upsurge in popularity of home-based leisure activities (watching TV and video, playing video games, etc.) is creating new jobs, but sometimes at the expense of others. For example, jobs in video rental go up while those in cinemas go down.

Along with other sectors of industry, leisure and tourism is likely to see more *part-time* and *short-term* employment particularly in times of economic recession. The nature of tourism means that many jobs are seasonal, only employing people for part of the year. Many agencies, however, are working hard to encourage more use of facilities and attractions *off-peak* so as to increase further the economic benefits of tourism.

Work skills in leisure and tourism

People who work in leisure and tourism, or who are considering a career, need to think very carefully whether they have the right *skills* and *attitude* to be able to work in an industry which, although it offers exciting opportunities, is not always quite as glamorous as it appears. Those employees who are successful in their leisure and tourism careers tend to be:

- Good at working under pressure.
- Willing to be flexible in the hours they work.
- Genuinely interested in working with people.
- Able to learn new skills quickly.
- Good at finding things out.
- Aware of the need for excellence in customer care.

Staff working in leisure and tourism benefit from having a rewarding job which presents new challenges every day, which offers a high degree of job satisfaction, which may offer opportunities to travel which offers excellent prospects, often at a young age, for those with talent and determination.

Figure 1.16 lists examples of the wide-ranging career opportunities that exist in the leisure and tourism industry.

CAREERS IN LEISURE AND RECREATION

- Hotel management
- Conference planning
- Leisure Centre management
- Sportsman/woman
- Arts administration
- Pub or restaurant management
- Countryside management

- Contract catering
- Event management
- Teaching/lecturing
- Outdoor pursuits
- Sports coaching
- Casino/betting shop management
- Sports administration

CAREERS IN TOURISM AND TRAVEL

- Airlines and airports
- Tour operators
- Tourist attractions
- Coach operators
- Tourist Information Centres
- Ferry and cruise companies

- Travel agencies
- Local authority tourism departments
- Hotels and other accommodation
- Car hire companies
- Guiding
- Training

Figure 1.16 Career opportunities in the leisure and tourism industry

The future of leisure and tourism

Leisure and tourism has developed very rapidly to become one of the world's biggest industries. But what does the future hold? Will this dramatic growth be sustained or will the bubble burst? Figure 1.17 shows the factors which will determine whether and in which direction the leisure and tourism industry will develop in the future.

- SOCIAL FACTORS
- POLITICAL and ECONOMIC FACTORS
- ENVIRONMENTAL and CULTURAL FACTORS
- TECHNICAL FACTORS

Figure 1.17   Factors affecting future developments in leisure and tourism

Social factors

Changes in society and demographic trends (those concerned with the characteristics of the population) will have important impacts on the future development of the industry up to and beyond the year 2000. The fact that people are living longer, that there is a fall in the number of young people, that there is an increase in one-parent households, that there are more couples choosing not to have children or to delay having children until later in life, all point to the fact that the *demand* for leisure and tourism products and services will change dramatically as we move into the next millennium.

Political and economic factors

At an international level, the late 1980s has seen historic world developments with countries emerging from State control and embracing the Western 'market economy'. Events such as the demolition of the Berlin Wall will have profound effects on leisure and tourism developments; tourists from Western countries are now more able to visit the former Eastern bloc countries, while those from the former East will be curious to sample Western hospitality by travelling further afield. The completion of the Single European Market in 1993, with the easing of border controls, has the potential to increase travel within EU member countries. Closer to home, recession will continue to hold down expansion in certain sectors of leisure and tourism.

Cultural and environmental factors

Britain has seen the emergence of a greater environmental awareness over the last 20 years and a society which has begun to value its health and level of fitness. These factors are likely to remain important influences on leisure and tourism developments in the future with so-called 'green issues' high on the agenda. Tourists will increasingly demand holidays and other travel products which conform to the principles of sustainable development. Lifestyle concerns such as environmental protection and education will have a profound influence on leisure patterns and demand.

Did You Know ?

Green Flag International is a group of leisure and tourism organizations which promotes sustainable development.

Technological factors

The leisure and tourism industry has always made extensive use of new technology equipment and systems. Central reservation systems (CRS), the use of computers in leisure centres and sophisticated databases for marketing purposes are now commonplace in many organizations. Increasing competition within the industry will force organizations to use new technology to the full. New developments in transportation make extensive use of new technology; the Channel Tunnel is a good example of this as are the advances in aircraft design, opening up new 'long haul' destinations such as Goa, the Gambia and Sri Lanka.

Taking these social, political, economic, environmental and cultural factors into account, it is likely that the following leisure and tourism activities will increase in popularity in the short-term:

- New forms of home electronic entertainment and education
- Creative and productive leisure
- 'Green', healthy and active leisure
- Purposeful travel
- Social and community leisure

Of declining interest up to the year 2000 are likely to be:

- Established 'mass' leisure (e.g. cheap package holidays, network TV)
- Socially discouraged activities (e.g. heavy drinking)
- Activities with health or environmental hazards (e.g. some DIY goods)
- Young adult leisure (e.g. going to pubs, discos and pop concerts)

Self Check ✔ Element 1

1. Thinking of your own situation, calculate the proportion of your leisure activities that are home-based and how much activity is 'leisure away from home'.

2. Explain how a person's age, marital status and gender will influence the way they spend their leisure time.

3. Explain why the Industrial Revolution had such a far-reaching impact on the UK leisure and tourism industry.

4. Explain why overseas visitors are so important to the UK leisure and tourism industry.

5. Explain why the distinction between public and private sector leisure and tourism provision is not always clear-cut.

6. Explain why local authorities provide leisure and tourism facilities and services, even though they are not legally obliged to do so.

7. What could the owner of a country house hotel do in order to offer year-round employment to his staff.

8. Consider how tour operators might respond to the growing concern for the environment shown by their customers.

_____

_____

9. Examine the ways in which technology will influence the development of home-based leisure activities.

_____

_____

_____

1.2 Investigating UK leisure and tourism products

We tend to associate the term 'product' with goods that we buy and use in our everyday lives, such as food, clothing, cars, cookers and newspapers. In leisure and tourism, a product is anything which is developed and offered for sale or use by people in their leisure time. The difference with leisure and tourism products, however, is that most are _intangible_, i.e. we can't see or touch them; examples are holidays, short breaks, aerobics sessions, swimming lessons and West End shows. Tangible leisure and tourism products include sports goods, restaurant meals and travel goods.

This element looks at the full range of leisure and tourism products available in the UK, but concentrates first on the **natural resources** to be found in the different parts of Britain, which influence many of the products on offer.

Natural resources

Climate

The **weather** plays a crucial role in determining how we use our leisure time. British people will often travel thousands of miles to escape our **cool temperate climate** in the hope of milder weather. There are marked differences in climate even across Britain, with the south generally experiencing warmer summers and less severe winters than the north of the country. This is due in part to the warming influence of the _Gulf Stream_, an air current which originates in the warm atmosphere of the Gulf of Mexico and gives places such as the West Country, Wales and western Scotland mild conditions. Weather will play a part in influencing the location of many sports and leisure activities in Britain; swimmers and surfers will usually prefer the warmer waters of Cornwall to the cooler climate of, say, North Yorkshire. Britain's wet climate necessitates indoor activities and the use of _all-weather surfaces_ for sports events. The west and south of Britain do best of all when it comes to _sunshine_ hours, but the west has the areas with the greatest rainfall, a consequence of the highest _altitudes_ and the prevailing westerly wind which the British Isles experiences.

Did You Know ?

As a result of the Gulf Stream, many regions including Devon and Cornwall, west Wales and the west of Scotland enjoy the benefits of a mild climate.

Topography

The varied **landscapes** found in Britain today are the result of man's activities over thousands of years, the climate and the underlying geological formations. The dramatic scenery of North Wales, the Pennines and the Scottish Highlands, for example, attracts visitors in their millions. Some choose simply to sit and marvel at these works of nature while others follow active leisure pursuits such as rock climbing, walking, fell running or camping. The 'patchwork' of fields in the traditional British landscape, when coupled with the delights of clusters of small towns and villages, are a magnet for home and overseas visitors alike. As a result of the last Ice Age, the countryside abounds with natural lakes, some of which are extensively used for leisure activities such as windsurfing, sailing, water-skiing and power boating.

UK leisure and tourism products

Element 1 showed us that leisure and tourism products and facilities are provided by organizations which are in the private, public or voluntary sectors of the industry. The private sector dominates the supply of leisure and tourism products, with hoteliers, tour operators, travel agents, transport operators and leisure companies, to name but a few, providing a wide range of services and products to meet the needs of every sector of the market. Products such as short breaks, holidays, flights, health clubs, hotels and catering outlets are most commonly found in the private sector. The public sector, in the form of central and local government, offers a broad range of leisure and tourism products, including leisure centres, tourist information centres and sports facilities. The voluntary sector of the industry plays an important role in conservation, providing access to historic monuments and countryside areas.

We will now look in more detail at these, and other, leisure and tourism products, highlighting the key features of each.

Holidays

Holidays are a very important part of many people's lives. A lot of British people save up for a whole year, or go without other luxuries, in order to be sure of having a good time on their annual holiday. The development of package holidays has meant that overseas holidays are now within the reach of all but the lowest income earners. Most holidays abroad are booked with _tour operators_, who negotiate with hoteliers and airlines to put together packages, which would normally include:

- Accommodation (full-board, half-board, bed and breakfast, or room only)
- Flight or ferry crossing
- Transfer arrangements at the holiday destination
- The services of a courier or representative

The tour operators invite _travel agents_ to sell the holidays on their behalf to the general public. For this service, the operator pays the agent a _commission_ (an agreed percentage of the total holiday price, normally in the region of 10%, although this fluctuates according to the level of sales).

By a process known as **vertical integration** (where companies at different levels of the distribution chain are linked), the major tour operators have gained control of the biggest travel agency chains. For example, the number one tour operator in terms of volume of sales, Thomsons, owns the Lunn

Poly travel agency. Similarly, Going Places is owned by tour operator number two, Airtours. The third biggest tour operator, First Choice Holidays, has an 'alliance' with Thomas Cook agencies. Some operators also have their own airlines, e.g. Thomson owns Britannia. **Horizontal integration** is when companies at the same level in the distribution chain merge, e.g. the recent takeover of Dan Air by British Airways.

Did You Know ?

Lunn Poly, Portland Holidays, Britannia Airways and Thomson Holidays, are all owned by the same company.

Short breaks

Short breaks have been a resounding success story since the early 1980s, with many companies capitalizing on the decline of the traditional British two-week holiday. Many innovative accommodation operators and destinations have responded to the need to fill their bedspaces at weekends and slack periods of the year by offering short holidays, often based on a theme or activity. According to independent research quoted by Cresta, one of the main short-break operators, the total outbound short-break market is also developing, with a growth rate of 67% since 1987, with city breaks alone accounting for 600,000 travellers per year. The top operator is the Bridge Group (including Paris Travel Service) with 136,000 clients in 1991, substantially ahead of Thomson Citybreaks at 80,000. Travelscene and Cresta each carry over 60,000, the next biggest being BA Holidays and Time Off each carrying well over 20,000.

The popularity of short breaks lies in the changing leisure habits of much of the population, linked to changes in working practices, making the traditional 14-day break unpopular with a large section of the travelling public, many of whom have sufficient disposable income to be able to enjoy more than one holiday each year.

Sports facilities

Most **sports facilities** in Britain are provided by local authorities, sometimes with financial assistance from the Sports Council or other funding agencies. Although sport is very popular in Britain, the level of participation remains low. According to Sports Council figures, 56.5% of adults participate in sport of some kind, only 66.7% of all men and 47.6% of all women. One-third of the population play an indoor sport at least once a month and 40% participate outdoors. Local councils, as well as the Sports Council itself, are doing a great deal to raise the overall level of participation by offering as wide a selection of products as their resources allow. A local authority is likely to offer:

- Sports coaching
- Events for young people
- Sports facilities
- Health and fitness programmes
- Events for 'minority' groups, e.g. disabled, ethnic minorities

Some sports facilities will be provided by the private sector wherever they can ensure a reasonable return on their investment. Most of the large spectator sports facilities, such as football grounds, are provided by private sector companies, e.g. Tottenham Hotspur PLC.

Entertainment venues

Facilities such as casinos, nightclubs, discos and bingo halls are major money-spinners for the private sector, with such names as the Rank Organisation and Granada being major players. Most of these **venues** combine entertainment with bar and catering services, ranging from fast-food to themed restaurants.

Did You Know ?

The Rank Organisation operates a wide range of leisure facilities including Odeon Cinemas and Hard Rock Cafés.

Accommodation services

Visitors to Britain and UK residents can choose to stay in a wide range of establishments, all of which can be classified as 'accommodation'. There are city-centre hotels, motels, farm guesthouses, country house hotels and self-catering cottages, to name but a few. For those looking for something a little different, the Landmark Trust specializes in self-catering accommodation in unusual settings, including a lighthouse and a disused railway station!

The accommodation sector in Britain is essentially a private sector concern although the voluntary and public sectors are represented to a small degree, e.g. the Youth Hostels Association and outdoor activity centres operated by local authorities. UK accommodation can be classified in a number of ways:

- Either serviced or self-catering
- Commercial or non-commercial
- Urban or rural
- Static or mobile

Perhaps the most usual classification is to categorize a type of accommodation as either **serviced** or **self-catering**. As its name implies, the term 'serviced accommodation' is used when a service is provided along with the overnight stay, for example meals and housekeeping. In this category, therefore, we find:

- Hotels
- Motels
- Guesthouses
- Bed and breakfast establishments
- Youth hostels
- Farm guesthouses

Self-catering, or self-serviced accommodation, includes:

- Cottages
- Villas and apartments
- Chalets and log cabins
- Camping and caravan sites
- Hired motorhomes
- Second homes
- Timeshare
- Educational institutions
- Camping barns
- Home 'swaps'

The distinction between serviced and self-catering accommodation is not quite as clear as these lists suggest; for example, it is quite common now for self-catering establishments, particularly if they form part of a complex, to offer visitors the option of buying food and ready-to-eat meals. Some even have on-site restaurants, cafés and snack bars.

Timeshare is the name given to the purchase of the right to stay in a particular property at a specific time in the year, rather than buying the property outright. Timeshare is usually sold in blocks of weeks, with a week in the high season costing more than the same length of time out of season. The person who buys the week or weeks has the option of letting the property out for rent or swapping properties with another timeshare owner, perhaps in another country. The week or weeks can also be offered for sale. Timeshare is most common in the USA and Mediterranean countries, but there are properties in Britain including apartments in country house hotels, in major cities and in seaside resorts, such as Torquay, as well as purpose-built timeshare villas in Wales, the Lake District, Scotland and other country areas.

Arts and entertainment

While much sport, leisure activity and tourism takes place in the *outdoor* environment, many **arts and entertainment** activities take place *indoors*, including in the home. We have seen that **home-based leisure** is set to grow substantially up to the end of the century, based to a great extent around electronic media. While such products are provided by private sector companies, the public sector does have an important role in providing arts facilities in the local community, e.g. art galleries, museums and theatres.

Visitor attractions

Attractions are a vital component of the UK tourism scene; indeed, they are often the very reason why visitors decide to venture out. BTA estimates that there were in the region of 350

Note: The Broads is not a National Park, but has equal status.

Figure 1.18 The National Parks in England and wales

million visits to tourist attractions in the UK in 1992.

Visitor attractions may be either *natural* or *man-made*.

Natural attractions

Britain has an abundance of fine landscapes, from Land's End to John o' Groats. Visitors are attracted to the beautiful coastline, the rugged mountains and the picturesque dales. Many of these areas have been given special status to protect the environment and provide facilities for their enjoyment by the public. The job of overseeing these 'protected' areas in England lies with the Countryside Commission, whose aim is to conserve and enhance the natural beauty of England's countryside and help give people better opportunities to enjoy and appreciate it. The Countryside Council for Wales does a similar job in the Principality. The main areas for which they are responsible are as follows.

- **National Parks**

  The ten **National Parks** in England and Wales (see Fig. 1.18) were established under the 1949 National Parks and Access to the Countryside Act (the Broads in Norfolk and Suffolk is not a National Park as such but has equal status). The word 'national' does not mean that the Parks are owned by the government; most of the land within National Park boundaries is privately owned and often under severe pressure from visitors and their vehicles. The Peak District National Park is a good case in point, being located between the huge conurbations of Sheffield and Manchester. The total number of visitors to the National Parks in England is more than 70 million in a typical year and, including the three Welsh Parks, all ten Parks cover approximately one-tenth of the land area of England and Wales.

- **Areas of outstanding natural beauty (AONBs)**

  Thirty-five of England's most cherished landscapes are protected as **AONBs**. They range from the wild open *moorlands* of the North Pennines to the *Green Belt* countryside of the Surrey Hills and the intimate valley of the Wye, which straddles the border with Wales (there are another four AONBs wholly within Wales itself). AONBs can be popular destinations for leisure and tourism, although, unlike National Parks, they are not designated for their recreational value. The Countryside Commission has proposed stronger measures for their management and more funding for their upkeep. In total, AONBs in England cover around 15% of the landscape.

- **Heritage Coasts**

  There are 44 **Heritage Coasts** in England and Wales. They are among the most precious assets for wildlife and landscape, as well as for leisure and tourism. Concern over the harmful impact of increasing numbers of visitors led to their designation and a plan of action which includes creating and repairing footpaths, cleaning up bathing water and removing litter.

Man-made attractions

The term 'tourist attraction' usually brings to mind a purpose-built facility, designed to provide fun and entertainment. If asked to give the name of the first major tourist attraction in Britain which comes to mind, an overseas visitor may well mention the Tower of London, while a UK resident is likely to name

Alton Towers, the well-known theme park in Staffordshire. The range of man-made attractions in Britain is vast and includes heritage attractions, theme parks, stately homes, zoos, sports facilities, amusement parks and leisure complexes. Figure 1.19 shows the top 10 UK tourist attractions for 1992 which charged for admission, while Figure 1.20 lists those which offered free entry.

1	Alton Towers, Staffordshire	2,501,379
2	Madame Tussaud's, London	2,263,994
3	Tower of London	2,235,199
4	Natural History Museum, London	1,700,000
5	St Paul's Cathedral, London	1,400,000[a]
6	Tower World, Blackpool	1,300,000
7	Science Museum, London	1,212,504
8	Chessington World of Adventures	1,170,000
9	Thorpe Park, Surrey	1,026,000
10	Royal Academy, London	1,018,114

[a]Estimated

Figure 1.19: Top ten UK attractions charging admission 1992. *Source: Insights*, July 1993

Attraction	Number of visits 1992
1 Blackpool Pleasure Beach	6,500,000[a]
2 British Museum, London	6,309,349
3 National Gallery, London	4,313,988
4 Strathclyde Country Park, Motherwell	4,220,000[a]
5 Palace Pier, Brighton	3,500,000[a]
6 Pleasure Beach, Great Yarmouth	2,250,000[a]
7 Pleasureland, Southport	2,000,000[a]
8 Tate Gallery, London[b]	1,575,637
9 Bradgate Park, Leicestershire	1,300,000[a]
10 Frontierland, Morecambe	1,300,000[a]

[a]Estimated [b]Free entry most or all of the time

Figure 1.20: Top Ten UK free attractions 1992. *Source: Insights*, July 1993

Blackpool Pleasure Beach remained the UK's most popular free attraction of 1992 and, for the first time ever, Alton Towers had the highest number of visitors of all attractions which charged for admission, overtaking Madame Tussaud's in London which held the top spot in 1991.

Did You Know ?

Blackpool Pleasure Beach was Britain's most popular tourist attraction in 1992.

- **Holiday Centres**

  The old concept of the holiday camp has been replaced by the new **holiday centre**. Butlins camps underwent a major refurbishment in the 1980s to create Butlins Holiday 'Worlds', e.g. Summer West World in Minehead. Center Parcs have introduced to Britain their well-tried and tested European formula of a complex centred on a covered leisure pool and offering up-market villas in a woodland setting for those seeking an active break or holiday. The first British Center Parcs was built in

Sherwood Forest, the second near Cambridge, with a third planned to open at Longleat in Wiltshire in July 1994.

- Theme parks

  Some of the most successful UK **theme parks** are Alton Towers in Staffordshire (nearly 2 million visitors per year), Chessington World of Adventures (1.5 million) and the American Adventure in Derbyshire (1 million visitors). The bigger British theme parks have been modelled on North American examples, principally the immensely popular Disneyworld in Florida and Disneyland in California. Theme parks often provide thrilling 'white knuckle' rides and a range of other attractions and catering facilities aimed at families and young adults who usually pay one all-inclusive entry fee which permits an unlimited number of rides.

- Leisure pools

  Many local authorities and private operators have upgraded existing swimming pools or built new complexes to house **leisure pools**. In many cities, towns and rural areas, the stark, rectangular municipal baths have been replaced with pools boasting such facilities as wave machines, jacuzzis, saunas, flumes, waterslides and splash pools. These leisure pools often have themed events, e.g. a Caribbean evening or a birthday party, in order to maximize revenue and make full use of the facility.

- Museums

  In recent years, many museums have tried to change their image from one of dark, dreary and unwelcoming places to one where visitors can find fun, excitement and entertainment. Some have been changed into **living museums**, for example Beamish Open Air Museum, Ironbridge and Wigan Pier, where actors and actresses play the roles of those who lived in the past to entertain the visitors. Others have made imaginative use of new technology to bring history to life through animated displays; two good examples are the Jorvik Viking Centre in York and the Oxford Story. To appeal directly to children, some museums have introduced a **'hands-on'** policy which allows people to touch exhibits, e.g. Eureka! in Halifax, recently named as Museum of the Year for 1993.

Factfile 6: Eureka! The Museum for Children

Introduction

Eureka! is the first museum of its kind in Britain. It is wholly designed to teach children between the ages of 5 and 12 about the world in which they live using a 'hands-on' educational approach. Visitors to the museum in Halifax are encouraged to touch, listen and even smell, as well as look; Eureka! is truly at the forefront of the new breed of 'inter-active' museum attractions. It draws on the traditions of the international community of children's museums which are to be found all over the USA and throughout the world.

Since its official opening in July 1992 by HRH The Prince of Wales, the museum has been a runaway success – so successful that it has recently been voted Museum of the Year 1993 in the ETB 'England for Excellence Awards'. Within six months of opening, Eureka! had attracted 250,000 visitors and the figure at nine months had risen to over 375,000. The museum is well on course to reach its target of 500,000 visitors per year within its first three years of operation and will welcome its millionth visitor towards the end of 1994.

Aims

The aims of Eureka! The Museum for Children are as follows:

- To promote, maintain, improve and advance public education by the creation of an informal learning centre, designed primarily for children up to the age of 12.
- To pay particular attention to children with special needs and the adults who care for them.
- To offer an educational resource for use both in the context of schools and the National Curriculum, and as a leisure facility.
- To encourage dialogue between adults, children and all sections of the community who have an interest in children's development and welfare, such as the family, the school and industry.
- To enable children to become aware of their future importance as citizens, examining the issues and problems of today.
- To help visitors, both child and adult, to discover their unexpected abilities, and to give them a desire to learn new skills.

Museum facilities

Eureka! is housed in a new 4500 square metre building designed by Building Design Partnership (BDP). The steel, stone and glass structure has been designed to be the biggest exhibit of all. Development costs totalled £9 million, a third coming from private sponsors and the remaining two-thirds from the Clore and Duffield Foundations. Eureka!, a registered charity, was conceived and built without any local or central government funding.

The focus of the museum is the exhibition which has three main parts, entitled:

- **Me and My Body** – where children are encouraged to explore how the body and senses work.
- **Living and Working Together** – which investigates how the individual fits into an extended family and into society.
- **Inventing and Creating** – which provides opportunities for children to use their imagination, shared skills and knowledge to solve the problems of today and to open up new perspectives for tomorrow.

The market

The prime target market for Eureka! are the 8.5 million people who live within a 90-minute travelling distance of Halifax, of whom 2.7 million are in family groups with children under the age of fourteen. The museum is situated at the centre of a densely populated area, with major conurbations including:

- Greater Manchester   population 2,500,000
- West Yorkshire   population 2,053,000
- Merseyside   population 1,468,000
- South Yorkshire   population 1,298,000

School groups account for 25% of all visitors and tend to be from within a 50-mile catchment area. Weekends outside the main holiday periods tend to attract family groups from a 50 to 60-mile radius. Most visitors during peak holiday times tend to be on holiday in the region.

The future

There is talk of Eureka! Mk 2, which may be housed in the Great Northern Railway shed adjacent to the existing building and would be aimed at the 12 to 14-year age group. Continuing the phenomenal achievements of the present museum will be no easy task.

(Information courtesy of Eureka! The Museum for Children)

Leisure and tourism infrastructure

The term **infrastructure** is used to denote all the services that an area needs in order to develop its full potential for leisure and tourism and provide the level of facilities that both local people and visitors demand. Infrastructure includes transport networks, such as roads, railways, airports and seaports, and the supply of services such as water, power and communications.

The infrastructure of a region can be thought of as the skeleton around which the **superstructure** components (hotels, attractions, etc.) are built. In most cases, the public sector will take on the responsibility for developing the infrastructure and the private sector the superstructure, although partnerships between the private and public sectors are increasingly common in leisure and tourism.

Transportation

A good **transport network** is vital for a country, region or local area to develop its full economic potential for leisure and tourism. We have seen in Element 1 that the number of cars on our roads is set to increase dramatically up to and beyond the year 2000 with the government pledging even more money to expand the motorway network and bypass towns and villages. Figure 1.21 shows Britain's network of principal **motorways** and main **ports** of entry and exit.

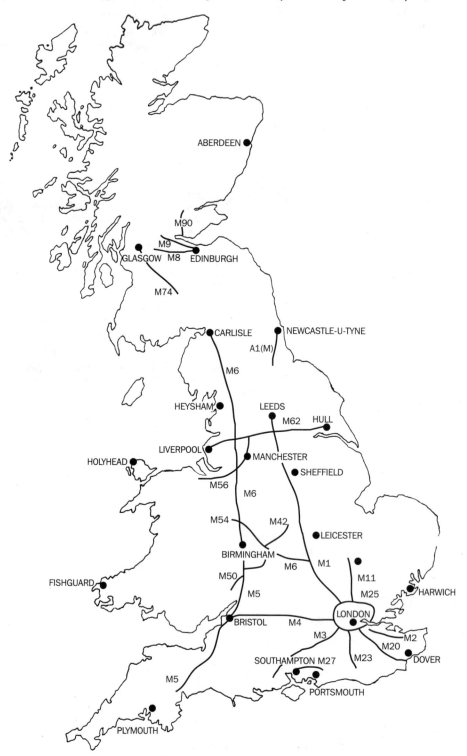

Figure 1.21   Britain's principal motorways and ports

The **private car** is the dominant means of travel for leisure and tourism in Britain, whether by UK residents or overseas visitors. The car accounted for 78% of holiday tourism trips in 1990, and if hire cars, bus and coach travel are included in the statistics the figure rises to 87% (see Fig. 1.22).

Increasing car ownership and access to private transport has meant that the use of cars for tourist trips has grown dramatically since 1951, at the expense of rail and coach/bus travel, both of which have experienced dramatic losses in market share.

Figure 1.22 shows that the number of people using **rail services** for tourism has fallen significantly over the last 40 years.

Britain's **airports** are important 'gateways' for overseas visitors, with Heathrow and Gatwick between them handling over 70% of all UK air passenger traffic.

Year	Car %	Train %	Coach/bus %
1951	28	48	28
1961	49	28	23
1971	63	10	17
1981	72	12	12
1985	70	10	14
1990	78	8	9

Figure 1.22: Modes of transport used for holiday travel in the UK 1951–90. *Source: Insights*, January 1993

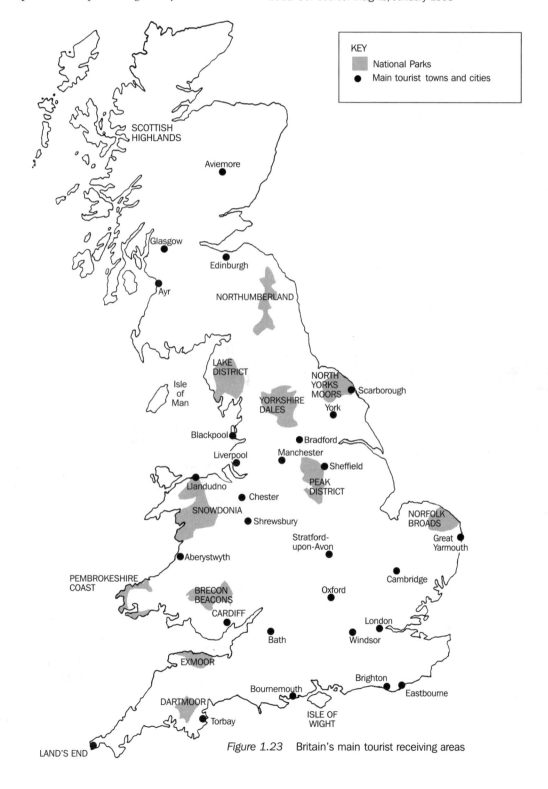

KEY

▨ National Parks

● Main tourist towns and cities

Figure 1.23   Britain's main tourist receiving areas

Main tourist receiving areas

The section on the historical development of tourism in Element 1, showed that seaside resorts and spa towns were some of the first areas to be developed for tourism in Britain. Today, seaside towns are still popular with the British and many spa towns are enjoying something of a revival, e.g. Llandrindod Wells and Cheltenham. What we have seen in Britain in more recent times has been the rise of **inland 'resorts'**, e.g. the historic towns of Chester and Shrewsbury, towns exploiting their industrial heritage (Bradford and Ironbridge are good examples) and towns and cities attracting visitors via imaginative events and excellent sporting facilities, e.g. Edinburgh and Sheffield respectively. Figure 1.23 shows some of Britain's most popular tourist receiving areas, including the National Parks, inland cultural cities and coastal resorts.

Self Check ✔ **Element 2**

10. Consider some of the reasons why the participation rate for women in sport is lower than that for men.

_____

_____

11. Explain why the National Parks are under particular pressure from leisure and tourism.

_____

_____

12. Examine the impact that rail privatization is likely to have on the leisure and tourism industry in the UK.

_____

_____

_____

13. Look again at Fig. 1.23. Identify the main cultural and historic cities for tourism.

_____

_____

_____

1.3 Local leisure and tourism services and products

We saw in Element 1 that, on a global scale, leisure and tourism is arguably the world's biggest industry. It employs more than 100 million people worldwide and generates approximately $3500 billion. In Britain, some 1.5 million are employed in the leisure and tourism industry, with many regions relying heavily on the industry for their economic well-being. At the **local** level, leisure and tourism sustains employment and generates revenue for communities, as well as providing them with a range of facilities and services aimed at improving their quality of life.

There are three main types of impacts that leisure and tourism can have at national, regional or local level:

• Economic
• Environmental
• Social/cultural

It is important to remember that within each of these categories, the impact that leisure and tourism can have may be either *positive* or *negative* or, as is often the case, a mixture of the two. For example, the building of a new leisure centre in a local area will undoubtedly bring economic benefits in the form of new jobs and income generation, but it will also carry with it an economic cost in terms of increased taxes for local people to finance the development.

Economic impacts

The generation of income

The leisure and tourism industry generates income and wealth for private individuals, local authorities, companies, voluntary bodies and national governments. At the national level, tourism can make a considerable contribution to a country's **balance of payments**, which is a statement of the inflows and outflows of currency to and from a particular country. Tourism and leisure are services and are known as **invisible**

Year	Earnings from inbound tourism (£m)	Spending on overseas tourism (£m)	Balance (£m)
1976	1768	1068	+700
1977	2352	1186	+1166
1978	2507	1549	+958
1979	2797	2109	+688
1980	2961	2738	+223
1981	2970	3272	−302
1982	3188	3640	−452
1983	4003	4090	−87
1984	4614	4663	−49
1985	5451	4877	+574
1986	5405	5927	−522
1987	6260	7280	−1020
1988	6184	8216	−2032
1989	6945	9357	−2412
1990	7475	9905	−2430

Figure 1.24: Britain's Travel Balance 1976–90. *Source*: BTA/ETB figures

items on the balance of payments, while **visibles** include goods such as food and manufactured items. Figure 1.24 shows Britain's travel balance between 1976 and 1990. As you can see, the balance has gone into a negative (deficit) situation in recent years reflecting the growth in overseas holidays taken by British people and a slowdown in the growth of overseas visitors to Britain.

Did You Know ?

The British Tourist Authority forecasts that the number of overseas visitors to Britain will rise to 23.9 million by 1997, spending an estimated £11 billion.

At the local level, revenue generated by leisure and tourism facilities is often vital to the economic well-being of an area and is boosted by an important concept known as the **multiplier effect**. Research has shown that the amount spent by visitors to an area is re-circulated in the local economy (by, for example, the wages of somebody working in a leisure centre being spent on goods and services in local shops) and is actually worth more to the area than its face value. For example, £200 spent by a couple on a short break in a hotel could be worth £200 × 1.4 (the hotel multiplier effect for that area), i.e. a total of £280.

The actual value of the multiplier (1.4 in the above example is merely an illustration) varies between regions and different sectors of the leisure and tourism industry. The multiplier for, say, a farm guesthouse is likely to be greater than for, say, a city centre hotel which is part of a large multinational chain. This is because the farm guesthouse is likely to buy its food and other services locally, while the goods and services for the large hotel may well be brought in from outside the area as part of a national distribution contract. This loss of income from an area is known as a **leakage** from the local economy.

The economic importance of tourism to a local area is demonstrated by looking at figures for the seaside resort of Scarborough. According to statistics produced by Scarborough Borough Council, the town generated a revenue of £245 million from leisure and tourism activities in 1992, with 11,000 people employed in the industry. The historic city of York earned £170 million for the same year, with 5900 employees in leisure and tourism.

Employment creation

The creation of new jobs is one of leisure and tourism's major benefits. Local authorities and national tourist boards see leisure and tourism as a way of **boosting employment**, especially in areas suffering from high levels of unemployment. Jobs in leisure and tourism can often be provided at a much lower cost than similar opportunities in more capital-intensive industries, such as engineering and construction.

Investment in leisure and tourism

Investment in large and small leisure and tourism projects not only provides short-term benefits for an area in terms of jobs in construction, for example, but also offers a base for the longer-term economic regeneration of regions by providing employment and revenue for many sectors not directly related to the industry, e.g. more business for petrol stations, printers, accountants, etc. Leisure and tourism is increasingly used as a 'springboard' for the regeneration of run-down areas of towns and cities; the Albert Dock in Liverpool and the Castlefield development in Manchester are excellent examples of this.

Factfile 7: Castlefield Urban Heritage Park, Manchester

Introduction

The Castlefield area of Manchester markets itself as 'Britain's first Urban Heritage Park' and has been the focus for substantial investment over the last few years by both the public and the private sector. The area has been recognized by the English Tourist Board as having significant tourism potential, currently attracting around 1 million visitors per year to its two main attractions:

- The Museum of Science and Industry
- Granada Studios Tour

Other attractions within the Castlefield area include:

- G-Mex Exhibition Centre
- Castlefield Gallery
- Roman fort
- Canals
- Castlefield Hotel
- Salford Quays

The job of controlling the regeneration of the area rests with the Castlefield Management Company Limited, a separate arm of Central Manchester Development Corporation (CMDC), which was established by the government in 1988 for a period of five years and given the remit of revitalizing the Castlefield area.

The area is characterized by a railway and canal network which has played an important role in its history. The whole area is currently undergoing rapid transformation with old warehouses being renovated, new hotels and attractions being built, and significant environmental improvements taking place.

Aims of the scheme

Castlefield Management Company has two principal aims:

1 To improve standards of management and maintenance in the area.
2 To improve visitor facilities and services.

It is hoped that the presence and work of the Management Company will result in:

- Increased cleanliness of the waterways.
- Improved litter control.
- Better maintenance of public areas and private land.
- Improved visitor services.
- Increased activities and events in the area.
- Increased numbers of visitors.
- Increased security.
- Improved co-ordination of the management of the area.

Objectives

In seeking to achieve its overall aims, the Castlefield Management Company has identified the following specific objectives:

- To set up and manage an Urban Ranger service for the Castlefield area.
- To establish measurable maintenance standards for the area, identify maintenance problems and encourage those responsible to take remedial action.
- To establish and gain commitment to measurable cleanliness standards for the area, identify problems and find solutions.
- To establish good working relationships with local owners and operators.
- To play an active role in establishing a programme of events and ways of marketing the area to draw in additional visitors and maximize their enjoyment of Castlefield.

The ranger service

The unique Castlefield Urban Rangers, complete with distinctive uniforms, radios and mountain bikes, patrol daily around the Heritage Park ensuring the canals and towpaths are kept free of debris and taking up environmental issues with tenants and businesses. They also provide a link to local authority services, inform Castlefield residents of events happening in the area through an in-house newsletter *Castlefield Today*, give guided tours around the site and enhance visitor interpretation through the provision of interpretation boards and trail leaflets.

Funding and the future

During the first three years, funding for the Castlefield Management Company came from a mix of private and public sector agencies:

- Central Manchester Development Corporation
- English Tourist Board via its Area Initiative Fund
- Local authorities of Manchester and Salford
- Local landowners and businesses

Future funding will be dependent on the Manager's ability to convince the sponsoring bodies of the effectiveness of this form of area management. CMDC's financial support will continue in an appropriate form if the project proves viable beyond the life of the Corporation.

(Information courtesy of Castlefield Management Company Limited)

Environmental impacts

Although leisure and tourism can have positive environmental benefits to a local area, e.g. the Britain in Bloom scheme, restoration of redundant buildings and improvements to derelict areas, there is much evidence to suggest that the industry could do much to improve its negative environmental impacts. In Britain, the coast, countryside, towns and cities all suffer from the pressures of increasing numbers of visitors and their transportation. Some of the worst problems include:

- **Pollution** – of water and air, not forgetting noise pollution
- **Physical erosion** – the wearing away of soil and vegetation by walkers, horse-riders, cyclists, cars and motor-cycles
- **Litter** – both an eyesore and a threat to safety
- **Congestion** and overcrowding – in popular holiday areas we all see the effects of too many people and too many cars
- **Spoiling of the landscape** which people have come to see and enjoy
- **Loss of habitats** for flora and fauna

Improved visitor and traffic management techniques, better education, use of the price mechanism and better signposting are some of the possible solutions which are being tried in our towns and countryside to reduce the harmful environmental effects of leisure and tourism.

Social/cultural impacts

Some people believe that the negative social and cultural impacts of leisure and tourism, and particularly tourism, are far more harmful in the long-term than the environmental problems we have just discussed. This is based on the belief that many of the negative environmental impacts can be easily corrected with the right management and funding. The social and cultural problems, however, can be far more deep-rooted and may take generations to improve. Some of these problems are:

- In rural areas, traditional activities such as farming may lose labour to the seemingly more attractive jobs in leisure and tourism
- Local languages may be lost through under-use
- Tourists' behaviour can distort local customs
- Religious codes may be altered to adapt to the needs of visitors, eg Sunday opening of facilities
- Traditional crafts may be lost in favour of mass-produced souvenirs
- Overcrowding, which may cause a reduction in the quality of life for the '**host community**' (those living in the area visited by the visitors)

Leisure and tourism can, however, have *positive* impacts such as the revitalization for visitors of neglected regions, the rebirth of local arts and crafts, refurbishment of local architecture and a greater understanding of cultures.

Concern about the harmful environmental and social/cultural impacts of tourism has led to a lively debate about 'green' or sustainable issues in relation to the industry. The Tourist Boards and private sector companies are developing principles and practices which all sectors of the leisure and tourism industry will need to consider in order to ensure a healthy industry for the future.

Self Check ✔ **Element 3**

14. What are the likely negative economic effects of a major new tourist attraction financed by a local authority?

_____

_____

_____

15. What measures could a leisure and tourism department in a local authority wishing to expand its activities, recommend to limit the negative social and cultural impacts of tourism?

_____

_____

_____

1.4 Sources of income for leisure and tourism facilities

All leisure and tourism organizations must have **income** in order to survive and develop. Without sources of revenue, there will not be the finances needed to meet the day-to-day operating costs of the enterprise, such as wages, interest charges and advertising costs, nor the longer-term investment needs, such as new buildings, vehicles and equipment, often referred to as capital items.

The **sources** of the necessary income vary, depending on whether the leisure and tourism organization is in the private, public or voluntary sector. We will look at each in a little more detail.

Funding in the private sector

The sources of funding for a **private sector** leisure and tourism organization often depend on the size of the business and its legal identity. A sole trader, for example, may start his or her business purely from private savings or gifts from friends and relatives. A large public limited company (PLC), however, will raise funds by selling **shares** in its business on the Stock Exchange, in return for which its shareholders will expect a return on their investment, known as a **dividend**.

The **clearing banks** (high street banks) are usually the first port of call for most new or existing leisure and tourism businesses looking for funding. The banks all offer a wide range of services to new or expanding businesses, through either their branch network or specialized subsidiaries. The banks can offer **overdrafts**, usually the cheapest type of borrowing with the lowest rate of interest, for short term needs, often important with the peaks and troughs of cash-flow experienced by some leisure and tourism operators. **Loans** are offered by the banks for periods ranging from up to three years (short-term) to over 10 years (long-term). They are usually for the purchase of capital items such as replacement equipment or new land and buildings; **commercial mortgages** are also on offer for this type of purchase. In all cases of loans and mortgages, the bank will require security from the borrower in case repayments are not met; this can take the form of deeds on property or insurance policies.

Other types of funding in the private sector include hire purchase and leasing, where equipment is not purchased outright.

Once a company is established, **income from sales** is vital for leisure and tourism companies in order to have a healthy cash-flow and to be able to trade profitably. In the case of companies which have shareholders, there will need to be sufficient profits generated to be able to pay a reasonable dividend. Some businesses within leisure and tourism, mainly those working as agents, will receive their income in the form of commission, which is an agreed percentage of the total price of a product or service which is retained by the agent for services rendered. A travel agent, for example, earns commission on the sale of package holidays; if the agent sells a holiday valued at £1000 and is given a 10% commission by the tour operator, the agent will forward £900 to the operator and retain £100. In a similar way, many tourist information centres offer a bed-booking service for which they charge a small commission.

Private sector companies can apply to a whole host of public sector organizations and quangos within leisure and tourism for either a grant or a loan to help with expansion or improvements to their facilities. These non-commercial sources of finance include:

- National Tourist Boards (except ETB)
- Arts Council
- Sports Council
- Department of the Environment
- Countryside Commission
- English Heritage
- Forestry Commission
- English Nature
- Rural Development Commission

Sponsorship is an important, if uncertain, source of income for some sectors of the leisure and tourism industry, particularly spectator sports and the arts. The extent of sponsorship varies enormously, from the local builder paying for the match ball for his local football team to Carling's multimillion pound deal to sponsor the Premier League in English soccer. The principle, however, is the same. Both the builder and the brewer expect a return on their investment in the form of wider publicity leading to increased sales; the builder is likely to see his picture in his local paper while Carling's name will be mentioned many dozens of times per week in the national media.

Funding in the public sector

The way in which funds are generated and distributed in **public sector** leisure and tourism is shown in Figure 1.25. The diagram shows how a typical local authority receives funding from a number of sources, including:

- **Central government** – through its *fiscal* (tax) policy, the government levies taxes on private individuals and companies. These may be either direct taxes, such as income tax on individuals and corporation tax on companies, or indirect taxes, such as VAT and duty on petrol and alcohol. A proportion of these funds is given to each local authority to provide services in its local area.

- **Council Tax** – this is a tax levied by the local authority on people living in its area in order to supplement national government funding for local services. Council Tax used to be known as the rates and, more recently, the Community Charge (Poll Tax).

- **European Union** (formerly EC) funds – some local authorities will bid for funds from the European Union (EU) for specific projects, which often include leisure and tourism because of its economic and social benefits. The main EU sources for leisure and tourism projects

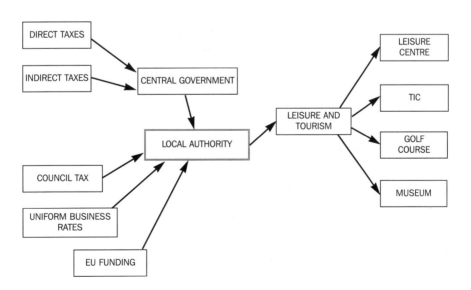

Figure 1.25   The funding of leisure and tourism in the public sector

tend to be the European Social Fund and the European Regional Development Fund, which provide finance for schemes such as infrastructure improvement and the development of new facilities.

- **Uniform Business Rate** – in the same way that local residents pay Council Tax, local businesses, such as shops and restaurants, have to pay Uniform Business Rates to the local authority for services provided.

Once it has received its funding, the local authority will decide on its own priorities and allocate **budgets** to each of its departments accordingly. The diagram shows how the leisure and tourism department will then allocate individual sums to its facilities, e.g. to a leisure centre, golf course or tourist information centre, so as to provide the best level of service to both the local community and visitors to their area.

Department of National Heritage (DNH)

The **DNH** was established in 1992 as the single Ministry which would co-ordinate government involvement in the field of leisure and tourism (see Fig. 1.10 for details of the structure of the DNH). The expenditure plans of the DNH for 1993–4 are shown in Fig. 1.26.

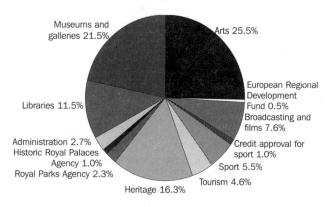

Source: DNH Annual Report 1993 (Reproduced with permission of the Controller of Her Majesty's Stationery Office.)

Figure 1.26   Expenditure plans of the DNH 1993–4

Figure 1.26 shows that sout of a total allocation for the year of £990.5 million from the Treasury, more than a quarter was allocated to the arts, over 20% to museums and galleries, and 16.3% to heritage.

Voluntary sector funding

Many **voluntary sector** leisure and tourism organizations have **charitable status** since they aim to promote a cause or help individuals rather than make a profit. There are benefits to being a charity, such as exemption from certain forms of taxation and reductions in business rates. Whether a voluntary body is very large, as is the case with the National Trust, or very small, such as a local playgroup, the funding opportunities and sources open to them are very similar, including:

- **Grants from central and local government** – a local council may make a grant to its local choral society, while the Arts Council gives grants to individuals and organizations which it considers are advancing the cause of the arts. The Countryside Commission gives grants towards training in countryside management and for environmental improvement projects.

- **Sponsorship** – the sports goods company Hi-Tec contributes to the printing costs of the YHA, while a local countryside trust may be sponsored by a local company.

- **Donations and gifts** – perhaps part of the estate of a deceased person, as is often the case with the National Trust.

- **Fund-raising events** – anything from a sponsored walk to a jumble sale can help boost funds for voluntary leisure and tourism groups.

- **Retail income** – larger voluntary organizations have set up shops and mail order subsidiaries as a way of generating income, e.g. National Trust shops and the Science Museum in London.

- **Fees** – can be levied for certain services, e.g. hiring out of equipment and entrance fees for events.

- **Subscriptions from members** – the Royal Society for the Protection of Birds, English Heritage and many local clubs receive funds from this source.

In times of economic recession, voluntary sector leisure and tourism organizations will find it harder to attract funding from both individuals and organizations. Private companies will generally have less money available for sponsorship purposes, local authorities may have to cut back on their grants, while private individuals will have less discretionary income to contribute to the operation of clubs, societies and national organizations.

Self Check ✔ Element 4

16. What were the reasons behind Carling deciding to sponsor the Premier League?

17. List the major sources of funds to support local authorities in their promotion of leisure and tourism.

18. Comment on the importance of the Department of National Heritage in the support of leisure and tourism.

Unit Test This test is one hour long. Answer all the questions.

Focus 1: TRENDS AND SOURCES

Question 1
Which government department is responsible for allocating funding to the English Tourist Board and the Sports Council?

A Department of the Environment
B Department of Employment
C Department of National Heritage
D Department for Education

Questions 2–4 relate to the following information:
Information on changing trends within leisure and tourism can be obtained from:

A The General Household Survey
B Caterer and Hotelkeeper Magazine
C The Tourism Society
D The Sports Council

Which of these potential sources of information is:

Question 2
A professional body?

Question 3
Trade press?

Question 4
A quango?

Questions 5–7 relate to the following information.
The following are four of the most dynamic contexts within the UK leisure and tourism industry:

A Travel and tourism
B Accommodation, catering and hospitality
C Sports and recreation
D Entertainment and education

Which of these contexts does each of the following fall into:

Question 5
The development of a new city centre hotel?

Question 6
The addition of a leisure complex to a country house hotel?

Question 7
A newly-refurbished casino?

Focus 2: EMPLOYMENT AND CAREER DEVELOPMENTS

Question 8
The leisure and tourism industry provides employment for approximately 1.5 million people in the UK.

Decide whether each of these statements is true (T) or false (F).

(i) This figure of 1.5 million employees has remained static over the last 15 years.

(ii) More people are employed in accomm[...] and hospitality than in sports and recreation.

Which option best describes these two statements?

A (i) T   (ii) T
B (i) T   (ii) F
C (i) F   (ii) T
D (i) F   (ii) F

Question 9
What was the main reason for the rise in the number of staff working in travel agencies in the 1960s?

A Travel agency pay rates rose substantially
B There was an expansion of self-catering holidays in the UK
C There was significant growth in the package holiday market
D Most agencies began opening on Saturdays

Question 10
There have been many changes in employment in the UK leisure and tourism industry. Which new job has been 'created' in the last 40 years?

A Tour operator
B Professional athlete
C Hotel receptionist
D Theatre usherette

Questions 11–13 relate to the following information.
The following statements can be used to describe trends in employment in leisure and tourism:

A Steady decline
B Steady growth
C Little change
D Irregular movements

Which statement best describes the trend in UK employment, over the past 20 years, in:

Question 11
Seaside guesthouses?

Question 12
Budget hotels and 'lodges'?

Focus 3: PRODUCTS AND SERVICES

Question 13
Local authority leisure centres?

Question 14
Decide whether each of these statements is True (T) or False (F).

(i) 'Travel News' lists job opportunities in travel and tourism
(ii) 'Leisure Opportunities' only lists private sector job opportunities

Which option best describes these two statements?

	(i) T	(ii) T
ﺏ	(i) T	(ii) F
C	(i) F	(ii) T
D	(i) F	(ii) F

Questions 15–17 relate to the following information:
Four of the busiest seaports in the UK are:

A   Dover
B   Plymouth
C   Holyhead
D   Stranraer

Which is the seaport for journeys to and from:

Question 15
Northern Ireland?

Question 16
Brittany?

Question 17
Southern Ireland?

Question 18
Dartmoor National Park attracts millions of visitors every year.
Decide whether each of these statements is true (T) or false (F).

(i) Dartmoor is very accessible via the UK motorway network
(ii) Dartmoor falls within the Southern Tourist Board region

Which option best describes these two statements?

A   (i) T   (ii) T
B   (i) T   (ii) F
C   (i) F(ii) T
D   (i) F(ii) F

Question 19
Decide whether each of these statements is true (T) or False (F).

(i) Tourists wishing to travel from London to Cardiff using a motorway should choose the M5
(ii) Cardiff has its own airport

Which option best describes these two statements?

A   (i) T   (ii) T
B   (i) T   (ii) F
C   (i) F(ii) T
D   (i) F(ii) F

Question 20
National and Regional Tourist Boards in Britain fulfil an important role in leisure and tourism by:

A   Providing a range of accommodation facilities
B   Providing all-weather facilities for tourists
C   Promoting their areas to tourists
D   Supplying staff for tourism operators

Questions 21–23 relate to the following information:
Four of the busiest airports in the UK are:

A   Manchester
B   London Heathrow
C   London Gatwick
D   Birmingham International

Which airport best fits the following description?

Question 21
The nearest airport for the National Exhibition Centre (NEC)

Question 22
The airport which has a direct link to London via the London Underground

Question 23
The nearest airport for travellers to Chester

Focus 4: SECTORS AND CONTEXTS

Question 24
The National Trust is a major owner of land and historic properties in England and Wales.

Decide whether each of these statements is true (T) or false (F).

(i) The National Trust is a public sector organization
(ii) The National Trust is owned by English Heritage

Which option best describes these two statements?

A   (i) T   (ii) T
B   (i) T   (ii) F
C   (i) F   (ii) T
D   (i) F   (ii) F

Question 25
Which service is most likely to be provided by the private sector?

A   A venture scouts' activity weekend
B   A creche at a leisure centre
C   Golfing lessons
D   A 'fun run' for charity

Questions 26-28 relate to the following information:
The providers of leisure and tourism products in the UK can be categorized as follows:

A   Public sector
B   Quango
C   Private sector
D   Voluntary sector

Which category best describes the following organisations?

Question 26
The Rank Organisation PLC

Question 27
The National Trust

Question 28
The Arts Council

Question 29
Which form of travel is operated mainly by the public sector?

A   Cruising
B   Car hire
C   Rail travel
D   Ferry travel

Focus 5: MAKING AN IMPACT

Question 30
A major multinational leisure corporation is intending to build a major theme park on the outskirts of a large town in the Midlands.

Decide whether each of these statements is true (T) or false (F).

(i) A positive economic impact of the proposed development will be the creation of new jobs
(ii) The loss of woodland to make way for the theme park will be a negative social impact of the proposed development.

Which option best describes these two statements?

A (i) T (ii) T
B (i) T (ii) F
C (i) F (ii) T
D (i) F (ii) F

Question 31

The manager of a local swimming pool has received a suggestion that more should be done for mothers with young children at the pool.

Which of the following measures is likely to satisfy the mothers the most?

A Better promotion of life-saving sessions
B Offering special off-peak swimming sessions
C Increasing the number of changing cubicles
D Redesigning the pool leaflets

Questions 32–34 relate to the following information:
Locally, leisure and tourism enterprises can have positive as well as negative impacts. These include:

A Environmental impacts
B Economic impacts
C Social impacts
D Cultural impacts

Choose the type of impact which is concerned with:

Question 32

The creation of income via the multiplier effect

Question 33

Damage to hedgerows and fences caused by ramblers

Question 34

More visitors to local shops leading to long queues

Focus 6 : SOURCES OF FUNDING

Question 35

Some leisure businesses operate as franchises. Which of the following is a good reason for choosing a franchise operation?

A The company offering the franchise will cover all losses

in the event of failure.
B A franchise is a cheap way of obtaining an overdraft.
C The company offering the franchise will provide promotional and managerial support.
D Franchise operators are able to pay their staff lower wages.

Questions 36–38 relate to the following information.

A local authority leisure services department can obtain revenue from a variety of sources, including:

A Council Tax
B Rate Support Grant
C Uniform Business Rates
D European Union

Which source of funding is concerned with each of the following?

Question 36
Revenue from central government

Question 37
Revenue from local businesses

Question 38
Revenue from local residents

Question 39

An independent art gallery in Shrewsbury is considering extending its premises to provide a tea shop.
Decide whether each of these statements is true (T) or false (F).

(i) The project would be eligible for English Tourist Board Section 4 funding
(ii) An overdraft would be the most likely form of funding offered by a high street bank for this type of development

Which option best describes these two statements?

A (i) T (ii) T
B (i) T (ii) F
C (i) F (ii) T
D (i) F (ii) F

Question 40

A small specialist tour operator offering walking tours in the Peak District wants to expand and purchase two extra vehicles. The owner needs advice on how best to finance this expansion.

Which of the following is the most appropriate source of this advice?

A Her local authority
B Her bank manager
C The English Tourist Board
D A local garage

Answers to self-check questions (selective – as appropriate)

2. A person's age has a direct bearing on the way in which they spend their leisure time. An older person will tend to take part in more passive activities, such as watching television, reading and knitting, while younger people enjoy active pursuits, including sport, mountain biking and visiting entertainment venues. Patterns of leisure can change dramatically when a couple decide to marry and set up a home; DIY will be important, as will social activities such as eating out and visiting friends and relatives. Research has shown that women have less leisure time

compared with men, a reflection of the increased proportion of household work and child-rearing they carry out.

3. The Industrial Revolution had far-reaching impacts throughout the whole of the British economy. Country people moved to towns and cities to work in the factories and workshops to produce goods that were exported all over the world. Housing conditions were often squalid and there was exploitation of labour, including child workers. In terms of leisure and tourism, the Industrial

Revolution provided workers with regular wages that could be used for purposes other than merely buying food and other essential items. As a reaction to the hard working conditions, people sought the peace and tranquillity of the countryside and seaside, helped by the introduction of the railways from 1840 onwards. The Industrial Revolution was to lay the foundation for the mass participation in leisure across all sections of society that we see today.

4.   Overseas visitors not only are important to the national economy, as shown in the UK balance of payments figures, but they also help local and regional economies by injecting income and thereby creating employment. The income from overseas visitors can also help to sustain the arts and cultural heritage of the UK and can help to improve the environment. Local people often benefit from facilities and services that have been developed primarily to serve the needs of the overseas visitors.

5.   The Conservative government of the 1980s accelerated the concept of privatization, when previously state-controlled organizations were sold to the private sector. A form of privatisation at the local level, CCT (compulsory competitive tendering), gave private organizations the chance to bid for the provision of services, including the management of leisure facilities. These factors have meant that public sector facilities are now operated under more commercial regimes, with a movement of managers and staff across both the private and public sectors.

6.   Local authorities are charged with providing a range of facilities and services for their local communities. They are legally obliged to provide many of these, e.g. housing, social services, refuse collection, etc. There is no statutory obligation on local councils to provide leisure and tourism facilities, although they all do. The provision of leisure and tourism facilities is part of any local authority's concern for the 'quality of life' of its local people and meeting its social objectives. Leisure facilities can lead to a healthier and happier community, with potential savings in terms of a reduced demand for social services and less crime.

7.   In order to be able to provide year-round employment for his staff, the owner of the hotel would need to increase the turnover and profitability of the business by widening the customer base, e.g. offering different products for different sectors of the market. Examples could include activity holidays outside the peak season, business meetings and conventions, and gourmet weekend breaks.

8.   A tour operator could respond to the growing environmental concern in two ways: first, by carrying out an environmental audit of the organization and its operation, with a commitment to such matters as energy efficiency, the use of unleaded fuel and recycling of waste materials; second, by offering products that are not harmful to the environment in the countries featured in its programmes.

9.   The pace of change in technology is dramatic; new equipment and systems are constantly developed with new features and gadgets. Much of the forecast growth in home-based leisure up to the year 2000 will be directly related to electronic games, satellite television and computer networking on a global scale.

10.   One of the basic reasons why women participate less than men in sport is that they have less available leisure time than men. Although UK society is sometimes considered to be moving more towards equality of opportunity for both men and women, research still shows that women devote more time than men to household duties and child-rearing. The fact that women are not well represented on the governing bodies of some sports has also been cited as a possible reason for their lower participation in sporting activities.

11.   Giving an area the title National Park immediately leads visitors to think that it is solely for their enjoyment and recreation. National Parks are, in fact, no different from many other tracts of the countryside in that they have people living and working within their boundaries every day of the year. The Parks located near to major urban areas are under particular pressure, both from holidaymakers and day-trippers. Authorities have to ensure the right balance between access for recreation, the conservation of the environment and the everyday lives of those who live and work in the National Parks.

12.   The underlying concept of the privatization of British Rail is that it will offer a more responsive and well managed service under private sector control. Customers should experience an enhanced level of service. Privatization may, however, result in the loss of services that are unprofitable, many of which will be in rural areas. People living in the countryside, as well as those visiting for their enjoyment and recreation, may well be faced with problems when it comes to travelling by rail in certain parts of Britain.

13.   These could include York, London, Bath, Stratford-upon-Avon, Shrewsbury, Oxford, Cambridge, Windsor and Chester.

14.   The main negative economic effect of a major new tourist attraction financed by a local authority, is that the local community will have to pay for the costs of its development and management via their council taxes. The local authority may have been successful in attracting European funding for part of the development costs, but a proportion will have to be borne by local people.

15.   The local authority could recommend a range of measures to limit the impact of such matters as congestion on roads, increased litter, more pollution, extra queueing in shops and public buildings and difficulties in car parking. Park-and-ride schemes, whereby cars are left outside a town or city and tourists take a bus, are very effective in reducing traffic problems. Pedestrianization of town centres can lead to a more pleasant environment for locals and tourists. Price can also be used as a way of managing traffic and visitor numbers. Tourist taxes can help to pay for measures put in place to deal with litter.

16.   Carling saw the sponsorship of the Premier League as an investment that would pay a substantial dividend, in terms of increased sales of their products. Sponsorship on this large scale has to be approached from a commercial standpoint. The extensive media coverage and mentioning of the Carling name will influence drinkers' purchasing decisions and so increase profits for the company.

17.   These include central government via the rate support grant, the Council Tax, Uniform Business Rate (UBR) and European funds.

18.   The Department of National Heritage has provided a focus for the support of tourism, sport, heritage and the arts in the UK.

Answers to Unit Test

1.	C	9.	C	17.	C	25.	C	33.	A
2.	C	10.	B	18.	B	26.	C	34.	C
3.	B	11.	A	19.	C	27.	D	35.	C
4.	D	12.	B	20.	C	28.	B	36.	B
5.	B	13.	B	21.	D	29.	C	37.	C
6.	C	14.	B	22.	B	30.	B	38.	A
7.	D	15.	D	23.	A	31.	B	39.	D
8.	C	16.	B	24.	D	32.	B	40.	B

Unit Test Comments

Q1: Answer is C – Department of National Heritage.
While the Department of the Environment, Department of Employment and Department for Education do indirectly fund some leisure and tourism organizations, the Department of National Heritage specifically provides funding for the English Tourist Board and the Sports Council.

Q2: Answer is C – the Tourism Society.
The Tourism Society is the professional body that represents people working in public and private sector tourism, as well as tourism educators.

Q3: Answer is B – Caterer and Hotelkeeper Magazine.
'Trade press' is the name given to magazines and journals aimed at people working in the industry. 'Consumer press' is printed material aimed directly at the public, e.g. BBC Holidays magazine.

Q4: Answer is D – the Sports Council.
The term 'quango' means quasi-autonomous non-governmental organization. Quangos are funded primarily from the public purse, but are given greater autonomy than many other public sector organizations. Some people think that quangos lack accountability.

Q5: Answer is B – accommodation, catering and hospitality.
Hotels are part of the very broad accommodation, catering and hospitality context in leisure and tourism. They fall within the 'serviced' sector.

Q6: Answer is C – sports and recreation.
Many hotels are adding leisure complexes to meet the needs of both leisure and business (corporate) guests.

Q7: Answer is D – entertainment and education.
Casinos, along with 'superbowls', nightclubs and discos, fall within the entertainment and education context, which is dominated by private sector operators.

Q8: Answer is C.
The number of employees in the leisure and tourism industry has grown over the last 15 years, making statement (i) false. It is true, however, that Department of Employment statistics show that more people are employed in accommodation, catering and hospitality than in sports and recreation.

Q9: Answer is C – there was significant growth in the package holiday market.
Mass market package holidays took off in the 1960s, resulting in a rise in the number of travel agencies and therefore the number of people employed in them.

Q10: Answer is B – professional athlete.
Tour operators, hotel receptionists and theatre usherettes, have been in existence for many hundreds of years. *Professional* athletes, however, are a product of more recent times.

Q11: Answer is A – steady decline.
The popularity of the traditional seaside guesthouse has fallen over the past 20 years, as a result of increased demand for foreign holidays and accommodation with a greater range of facilities.

Q12: Answer is B – steady growth.
Budget hotels and 'lodges' have developed rapidly along the UK motorway and trunk road network to meet the needs of business and leisure travellers.

Q13: Answer is B – steady growth.
Most local authorities have invested heavily in new leisure centres over the past 20 years, thus providing new employment opportunities at local level.

Q14: Answer is B.
'Travel News' does list job opportunities in travel and tourism, making statement (i) true. 'Leisure Opportunities', however, lists job opportunities in both the private and public sector, making statement (ii) false.

Q15: Answer is D – Stranraer.
Stranraer is the only port listed which has direct routes to Northern Ireland; Holyhead only operates services to and from the Irish Republic.

Q16: Answer is B – Plymouth.
Plymouth is the only port listed which has direct routes to Brittany; Dover offers services to other parts of France, but not to Brittany.

Q17: Answer is C – Holyhead.
Holyhead is the only port listed which has direct routes to Southern Ireland; Stranraer offers services to Northern Ireland.

Q18: Answer is B.
Dartmoor is close to the M5 motorway and within easy reach of major conurbations such as Bristol, Birmingham and London; statement (i) is therefore true. However, Dartmoor does not fall within the Southern Tourist Board region; it is the the West Country Tourist Board region, which has its headquarters in Exeter.

Q19: Answer is C.
Tourists wishing to travel from London to Cardiff via a motorway should take the M4, not the M5. Cardiff does have its own airport, catering for holidaymakers and business travellers.

Q20: Answer is C – Promoting their areas to tourists.
National and Regional Tourist Boards in Britain do not themselves provide accommodation or other facilities for visitors. They help other people, both private and public sector, to do this. Nor do they provide staff for tourism operators; they are usually very small employers in their own right. One of their most important roles, however, is to promote their areas to tourists, both at home and overseas.

Q21: Answer is D – Birmingham International.

Q22: Answer is B – London Heathrow.
The Piccadilly Line of the London Underground links Heathrow to central London. Gatwick does not have an Underground link, but does have British Rail's 'Gatwick Express'.

Q23 : Answer is A – Manchester.

Q24: Answer is D.
The National Trust is financed by voluntary contributions, therefore falling within the voluntary sector of leisure and tourism. English Heritage is a quango financed from central government and has no direct link with the National Trust.

Q25: Answer is C – golfing lessons.
A venture scouts' activity weekend and a 'fun run' for charity are most likely to be provided by the voluntary sector, while a creche at a leisure centre will fall within public sector provision in leisure and tourism. The private sector is most likely to offer the golfing lessons, since they will provide income and help the private organization maximize its profits.

Q26: Answer is C – private sector.
The Rank Organisation PLC is one of the foremost private sector leisure and tourism organizations in the UK.

Q27: Answer is D – voluntary sector.
The National Trust is a major voluntary sector organization with over 1 million members.

Q28: Answer is B – quango.
The Arts Council is funded principally by the Department of National Heritage.

Q29 : Answer is C – rail travel.
At present, rail travel is operated by British Rail, a public sector monopoly. In the very near future, however, parts of the network will be privatized. Cruising, car hire and ferry travel are all dominated by the private sector.

Q30: Answer is B.
The theme park will undoubtedly create new jobs, making statement (i) true. The loss of woodland, however, will not be a negative *social* impact, but rather a negative environmental impact.

Q31: Answer is B – offering special off-peak swimming sessions.
While options A, C and D will have an indirect effect on mothers with young children, the measure which is most likely to satisfy them is the off-peak swimming sessions, when charges will be lower and the pool less busy.

Q32: Answer is B – economic impacts.
The multiplier effect is the process by which money spent in an area is worth a greater amount to the economy than its face value, since it is re-spent and re-circulated in the local area.

Q33: Answer is A – environmental impacts.
Damage to hedgerows and fences is an unfortunate consequence of allowing access to the countryside.

Q34: Answer is C – social impacts.
Local people in popular holiday areas often complain that their 'quality of life' is damaged by an influx of visitors into their community.

Q35: Answer is C – the company offering the franchise will provide promotional and managerial support.
People who opt to operate a franchise are not covered for losses by the franchise company, nor is a franchise a cheap way of obtaining an overdraft. Operating a franchise does not give a company the opportunity of paying lower wages to its staff, but it does offer the chance to run a business with substantial managerial and promotional support. Budget Rent-a-car operates on a franchise basis.

Q36 : Answer is B – Rate Support Grant.
Central government provides local authorities with a sum of money, known as the Rate Support Grant, which is used to help provide local services.

Q37 : Answer is C – Uniform Business Rates.
Uniform Business Rates are paid to the local authority by local businesses.

Q38 : Answer is A – Council Tax.
Local residents pay Council Tax to their local authority for the provision of local services, including leisure and tourism facilities. Council Tax replaced the Community Charge (Poll Tax) and household rates.

Q39 : Answer is D.
Section 4 funding for tourism projects is no longer available in England, making statement (i) false. An overdraft is used for short-term borrowing and would not normally be offered by a bank for a long-term project such as building an extension. A loan or commercial mortgage would be more appropriate.

Q40 : Answer is B – her bank manager.
While the local authority and local garage may be able to offer general advice, the best bet for this type of financial advice would be the bank manager. The English Tourist Board would not normally be in a position to help.

UNIT 2

Maintaining health, safety and security

Getting Started

All leisure and tourism organizations aim to provide a safe and controlled environment for staff to work in and for visitors to enjoy. The very broad nature of the leisure and tourism industry means that each sector has its own particular health and safety requirements. Tourist attractions, for example, especially theme parks with complex 'rides', have to be aware of dangers to both staff and visitors from machinery and electrical installations. The managers and staff of hotels and other types of accommodation have a number of health and safety concerns which they must address, e.g. the storage and handling of food, and ensuring safe means of escape in case of fire. Indoor entertainment complexes are very large and often cater for the needs of hundreds, if not thousands, of people at any one time. Cinemas, theatres, sports stadia and indoor arenas must put health and safety very high on their list of priorities. Outdoor activity centres must ensure that staff are fully trained in supervising potentially dangerous activities such as rock-climbing, watersports and fell-walking. Leisure centres will offer a range of sports activities which, if not properly supervised, can expose the participants and spectators to potential risks. Centres which offer swimming and other water-based attractions need to be especially aware of health and safety requirements. Transport operators, including airlines, coach companies, ferry and cruise operators and car hire firms, have a duty to ensure that their vehicles are safely maintained and that all staff are capable of carrying passengers in a safe manner.

Leisure and tourism facilities are used by all sorts of people, some of whom will have special needs, e.g. the very young, disabled people and the elderly. Health and safety policies and practices must take the needs of these special categories of visitors into account.

Health and safety is the concern of all sectors of the leisure and tourism industry, private, public and voluntary. The following extract from a recent P&O press release demonstrates the importance that this private sector operator places on health and safety:

Codes of practice Advisory guidelines for employers to use when developing their policies on health and safety.

COSHH This stands for the Control of Substances Hazardous to Health Regulations (1988).

Data Protection Act Legislation to protect the public from problems arising out of the inaccuracy of data held on computer.

Duty of care The understanding that each citizen owes a duty to all others who may be affected by his or her activities, to act in a safe and responsible manner.

Health and Safety at Work etc. Act, 1974 The main legislation governing health and safety in the UK.

Health and Safety Executive (HSE) The government agency responsible for enforcing the legislation under the Health and Safety at Work etc. Act.

Legislation Acts of Parliament that govern the law of the land, e.g. the Health and Safety at Work Act etc 1974.

Regulations Statutory instruments controlling activities related to a particular Act of Parliament.

Risk assessment A systematic analysis of a workplace to identify actual and potential health and safety hazards.

PPE Stands for personal protective equipment.

Safety is of paramount importance as far as P & O European Ferries is concerned. All our ships comply with all current National and International safety rules and regulations. We operate under the British flag with an all-British crew and comply fully with the Department of Transport. Multi-lingual safety signs and tape announcements are standard on all of our ships. Our operational standards are well in excess of International standards.

Before ships leave a berth, the main cargo access doors at each end of the ship are closed. Once closed, the Chief Officer visually inspects them and then reports to the Captain that they are closed. He then double-checks using a closed-circuit television screen on the bridge. The Captain will then make an announcement to the passengers that the ship is ready to go to sea and draws their attention to the Muster Station notice boards. Before he makes the announcement, the Captain will have received additional check reports on the following:

i) Total passenger numbers
ii) Calculations of the vessel's trim and safety stability levels
iii) Passenger ramps and skywalks are clear

Our ships are equipped with more than enough life jackets and lifeboats. The superferries, for instance, carry 2620 adult and 240 children's life jackets, but the Passenger and Safety Certificate allows a maximum of only 2400 people to be on board, while the lifeboat rescue capability is at least 2422 people. All crew members are trained in emergency procedures. Frequent drills are held to ensure that this training is put into practice.

This unit looks in detail at the principles of health and safety in the leisure and tourism industry. It is divided into three elements, the first of which, element 2.1 considers the key legislation concerning health and safety issues. Element 2.2 focuses on current and potential health and safety hazard situations in leisure and tourism. It goes on to look at the measures which can be adopted to reduce risks. The final element, 2.3, tackles the subject of security in leisure and tourism, with consideration given to security of property, people, money and information.

Essential Principles

2.1 Health, safety and security arrangements in a facility

Health and safety legislation

Whatever the particular leisure and tourism context we are considering, it is important to remember that **health and safety** can no longer be thought of as a 'bolt-on' to other management tasks. Health and safety should underpin all the decisions and operations that managers and staff in leisure and tourism facilities undertake. Decisions on staffing, budgeting, types of activities, events management, equipment, maintenance and so on, all have health and safety implications. Many management decisions concerning health and safety are influenced and guided by the wealth of legislation on the subject that exists in the UK. There is a variety of legislation that imposes certain duties on the management and staff of leisure and tourism facilities in relation to health and safety issues. For anybody considering working in, or already involved with, the leisure and tourism industry *at whatever level*, it is important to be aware of the ever-increasing impact of health and safety legislation.

All operators of leisure and tourism facilities must show a common law **duty of care** to all those who may be affected by their activities, whether they are staff, guests, visitors, neighbours or contractors. If a person takes insufficient care in relation to another citizen and that person suffers damage as a result, the injured party may begin an action in the civil court to reclaim damages. However, this **civil law** only comes into action after damage has been suffered. Although the outcomes of civil cases have given the courts many opportunities to create precedents which guide the conduct of similar occurrences in the future, the **civil law** has always been considered an inappropriate instrument in the area of accident prevention. The advent of the *Health and Safety at Work etc. Act 1974* changed all this.

Health and Safety at Work etc. Act 1974

The Health and Safety at Work etc. Act (HSW Act) was introduced to provide the legislative framework to promote, stimulate and encourage high standards of health and safety at work. The Act is an enabling measure superimposed over existing health and safety legislation. In addition to placing duties of a general nature on employers, manufacturers, employees, the self-employed and others, the Act provides wide powers for the making of **regulations**. Part I of the Act, the part which concerns leisure and tourism organizations the most, aims to:

- Secure the health, safety and welfare of people at work.
- Control the storage and use of dangerous substances, e.g. chemicals, and prevent their unlawful use.
- Protect other people against risks to health or safety arising from the activities of people at work.
- Control the emission into the atmosphere of noxious or offensive substances from premises.

What is the scope of the HSW Act?

The Act states that all 'persons at work', whether employees, employers or self-employed, are covered by its measures, with the exception of domestic servants in private households. About 8 million people who were not covered by previous health and safety legislation, such as the self-employed and those employed in education, health services, *leisure and tourism industries* and some parts of the transport industry, are now protected.

Existing health and safety requirements will gradually be replaced by the HSW Act with the introduction of revised and updated provisions. These will take the form of regulations and approved codes of practice prepared in consultation with industry. *Regulations* relating to health and safety matters are usually made by the appropriate government minister on the advice of the Health and Safety Commission. In reality, most regulations are made by the Secretary of State for Employment. **Codes of practice** have a special legal status. Although they are not statutory requirements, they may be used in criminal proceedings on health and safety issues, as evidence that the statutory requirements have been contravened.

Did You Know ?

Codes of practice are not legally enforceable, but they may be used as evidence of contravention of health and safety requirements.

What are the duties of employers under the HSW Act?

It is the duty of every employer to safeguard, so far as is reasonably practicable, the health, safety and welfare of all those in his or her employment. This duty is extended to others who may be affected by the operation of the facility, e.g. contractors, visitors and members of the general public. In practice the employer must have specific regard for the following:

1 To ensure that the work environment is regularly monitored in respect of health and safety requirements.
2 To provide plant and equipment which is not a risk to health.
3 To provide safe storage for substances which could pose a threat to safety and ensure their safe use.
4 To provide a written statement of safety policy and bring it to the notice of employees (applies only to those employing five or more staff).
5 To ensure that work systems and practices are safe.
6 To provide adequate information and training for all staff in matters relating to health and safety.

Do employees have duties under the HSW Act?

The HSW Act is not only concerned with regulating the actions of employers. Employees also have a duty under the HSW Act:

- To take reasonable care to avoid injury to themselves or to others by their work activities.
- To co-operate with their employers and other agencies to ensure that the requirements of the Act are carried out.
- Not to interfere with or misuse anything provided to protect their health, safety and welfare under the Act.

HEALTH AND SAFETY AT WORK ACT 1974

Butlin's are very conscious of their responsiblility to protect the health and safety of employees and of the customers that visit the Hotel. In the buildings you will find the Company Policy statement.

A health and safety committee meet regularly so there is an opportunity for you to mention any problems you become aware of. The secret of safety is to BE ALERT because under the Act you too have a very important responsiblility.

COMPANY POLICY

Here are some guidelines to help you with health and safety:

1. Good housekeeping

   Keep the work area tidy – if you don't want to be treated like a cabbage, don't keep you work area like a pig sty.

2. Please wear the protective clothes provided. It's in your own interest.

3. Use equipment that's in good repair, e.g. steps/ladders.

4. Don't overload sockets so that they overheat – one plug, one socket.

5. Beware of wet slippery surfaces especially in kitchens and food halls when they've been washed.

6. Do not leave things lying around for people to fall over.

7. Have respect for chemicals – read the instructions. If in doubt ask!!!

8. Report any hazards or accidents to your Manager immediately.

Figure 2.1 Advice to employees in Butlin's Holiday Hotels (courtesy of the Rank Organisation PLC)

How is the HSW Act enforced?

The Health and Safety Commission (HSC) and the Health and Safety Executive (HSE) were both established under the HSW Act to provide the framework for publicizing the importance of health and safety and to begin prosecutions for breaches of the Act. The HSC is responsible to the Secretary of State for Employment for taking the necessary steps to secure the health, welfare and safety of people at work and also to protect the public against risks to health and safety arising out of a work situation. The HSE is the operating arm of the HSC and is responsible for enforcing the legislation under the HSW Act.

What do health and safety inspectors do?

The Health and Safety Executive appoints and controls teams of inspectors who have wide powers to enter premises, interview staff and examine records, to check that the Act is being complied with. Inspectors can also make enquiries into accidents which have occurred at places of employment. This covers accidents, not only to employees themselves, but also to visitors, and would include, for example, people using sports centres, hotels, visitor attractions and other leisure and tourism facilities.

If an inspector discovers a contravention of one of the provisions of the HSW Act or any of the earlier legislation that is still in force, he or she can take one of several courses of action:

- **Improvement notice** – if there is a contravention of any of the requirements of the HSW Act, an improvement notice can be served. This will give a time limit for compliance with the relevant contravention.

- **Prohibition notice** – if the inspector considers that there is a high risk of serious personal injury, a prohibition notice can be issued to put a stop to the activity in question until any specified action to remedy the situation has been completed. The notice can be served on either the person undertaking the activity or the person in control of it.

- **Prosecution** – over and above the issuing of either a prohibition notice, an improvement notice or both, any person found contravening the Act or any of its regulations is liable to prosecution. Contravention of some of the requirements can lead to prosecution in either the Magistrates' Court (Sheriffs' Court in Scotland) or the Crown Court in England and Wales (the Sheriffs' Court in Scotland). The maximum fine for most offences is £2,000 and imprisonment for up to two years can be imposed for certain offences.

- **Seizure** – an inspector has the power to seize, render harmless or destroy any substance or article considered to be the cause of imminent danger or serious personal injury.

Did You Know ?

In extreme circumstances, a health and safety inspector has the authority to close down a leisure and tourism facility.

Recent prosecutions concerning leisure and tourism organizations brought under the HSW Act include:

- In 1991 Alton Towers was fined £1500 with £1920 costs for inadequate operator training procedures. An incident occurred on the first day of the 1991 summer season when two cars on a rollercoaster collided leaving six people injured.
- A school was fined £2,000 in 1989 after admitting two breaches of the Act which led to the death of its groundsman when a new type of steel rugby post fell on him while it was being manoeuvred into position by staff and pupils.
- In 1985 inspectors of the Health and Safety Commission brought an action against Mendip District Council because they did not have enough lifeguards on duty when an 11-year-old girl tragically drowned in a pool.
- In 1983 Holiday Inns was prosecuted for contraventions in respect of the swimming pool at one of its hotels which had a number of alleged safety and supervision defects.

European directives on health and safety

Six new sets of health and safety at work regulations came into force on 1 January 1993. They apply to almost all kinds of work activity, including leisure and tourism, and, like the health and safety laws we already have, they place duties on employers to protect their employees and any other people, including members of the public, who may be affected by their activities.

These new UK regulations are needed to implement six **European Community** (now **European Union**) **Directives** on health and safety at work. The directives are part of the EU's programme of action on health and safety, which is an essential ingredient in the move towards a single European market. They are also part of a continuing modernization of existing UK law. Most of the duties in the regulations are not completely new but merely clarify what is already in current health and safety law. Any leisure and tourism organization which is already complying with the HSW Act and the regulations linked with it should not find the new regulations at all daunting.

A lot of old and out-of-date law has been repealed by the new regulations. More modern laws, e.g. COSHH (see page 43) and the Noise at Work Regulations, remain in place.

HSE inspectors' approach to the new regulations is initially to make employers aware of their existence and content. During this initial period, formal enforcement of the regulations will only take place if the risks to health and safety are immediate or what needs to be done is not new, i.e. it should have been put right under the existing legislation. Also, any employer who deliberately flouts the law will be liable to prosecution under the new regulations.

The scope of the new regulations

The new regulations cover the following six aspects of health and safety at work:

- Workplace conditions
- Health and safety management
- Work equipment safety
- Manual handling of loads
- Display screen equipment
- Personal protective equipment

Workplace conditions

The **Workplace (Health, Safety and Welfare) Regulations 1992** replace a total of 38 pieces of old law, making safety in the workplace a much easier topic to understand and making it clear what is expected of employers.

The regulations set general requirements in four broad areas.

1 **Safety**

- Construction and maintenance of floors
- Safe opening, closing and cleaning of windows and skylights
- Safe passage of pedestrians and vehicles
- Use of safety materials in transparent doors and partitions
- Safety devices on doors, gates and escalators

2 **Housekeeping**

- Cleanliness
- Removal of waste materials
- Maintenance of workplace, equipment and facilities

3 **Working environment**

- Room dimensions and space
- Temperature in indoor workplaces
- Ventilation
- Lighting
- Suitability of workstations and seating

4 **Facilities**

- Drinking water
- Washing, eating and changing facilities
- Clothing storage
- Rest areas, including arrangements to protect people from the discomfort of tobacco smoke
- Toilets
- Rest facilities for pregnant women and nursing mothers

All leisure and tourism organizations must ensure that any workplace within their control complies with the regulations. Existing workplaces have until 1996 to be brought up to scratch.

Health and safety management

The **Management of Health and Safety at Work Regulations 1992** set out broad general duties which apply to almost all work activities in Great Britain and offshore. The regulations make more explicit what is already required of employers under the HSW Act and are principally aimed at encouraging them to take a more systematic approach to dealing with health and safety matters. In general terms, the regulations require employers to:

1 Systematically assess the risks to the health and safety of employees and anyone else affected by the work activity, e.g. visitors, spectators and contractors. Employers with five or more employees will need to record their findings by drawing up a *risk assessment*.
2 Put into practice the measures outlined in the risk assessment. This will involve planning, organization, control, monitoring and review; i.e. the management of health and safety.
3 Set up emergency procedures.
4 Appoint competent people to help devise and apply the measures.
5 Co-operate with other employers who may share the same work site.
6 Provide employees with information about health and safety.
7 Provide temporary workers with specific health and safety information to meet their needs.
8 Provide adequate training for employees in health and safety.

Did You Know ?

Risk assessments can be carried out 'in house' or may be undertaken by specialist consultants.

Work equipment safety

The legislation governing the safety of equipment at work is contained within the **Provision and Use of Work Equipment Regulations**, which are designed to pull together and tidy up the laws governing equipment used at work. Instead of piece-meal legislation covering particular kinds of equipment in different industries, the Regulations place general duties on employers to have regard for the safety of *all* equipment in their workplace. They also list minimum requirements for work equipment to deal with selected hazards whatever the industry. 'Work equipment' is broadly defined to include everything from a hand tool, through machines of all kinds, to a complete plant such as a leisure centre or indoor arena.

The regulations include both *general duties* placed on employers and *specific requirements* which they must adhere to.

General duties require employers to:

- Ensure that equipment is adequately maintained.
- Make sure that equipment is suitable for its intended use.
- Provide equipment that conforms with EU product safety directives.
- Take into account the working conditions and hazards in the workplace when selecting equipment.
- Give adequate instruction, information and training.

The **specific requirements** of these regulations cover such items as the guarding of dangerous parts of machinery, stability of equipment, warnings and markings, for example.

Manual handling of loads

The **Manual Handling Operations Regulations** came into force on 1 January 1993 and replace patchy, old fashioned and largely ineffective laws with a modern, ergonomic approach to the problem. The incorrect handling of loads causes large numbers of injuries and can result in pain, time off work and sometimes permanent disablement. The regulations apply to any manual handling operations which may cause injury at work. Such operations should have been identified by the risk assessment carried out under the Management of Health and Safety at Work Regulations 1992. In the case of leisure and tourism, operations such as the bulk handling of brochures and other promotional material, movement of sports equipment and the handling of bulk foods are likely to be identified in a risk assessment as potential hazards.

Under the regulations, employers have to take three key steps:

1 Avoid hazardous manual handling operations where reasonably practicable.
2 Assess adequately any hazardous operations that cannot be avoided.
3 Reduce the risk of injury as far as is reasonably practicable.

The regulations are backed up by general guidance which can help to identify the more serious risks within any work situation.

Did You Know ?

Back injuries, often brought about by the incorrect handling of loads, are one of the most common causes of absence from work.

Display screen equipment

The **Health and Safety (Display Screen Equipment) Regulations** do not replace old legislation but cover a new area of work activity for the first time. The regulations have been introduced as a result of the extensive use of computers in industry today. Work with display screens is not generally high risk, but it can lead to muscular and other physical problems, eye fatigue and mental stress. Problems of this kind can be overcome by good ergonomic design of equipment, furniture, the working environment and tasks performed.

Under these regulations, employers have a duty to:

• Assess display screen equipment workstations and reduce risks which are discovered.
• Make sure that workstations satisfy minimum requirements.
• Provide information and training for display screen equipment users.
• Plan display screen equipment work so that there are breaks or changes of activity.

The regulations state that display screen equipment users are also entitled to appropriate eye and eyesight tests by an optician or doctor, and to special spectacles if they are needed and normal ones cannot be used. It is the employer's responsibility to provide tests and special spectacles if needed.

Personal protective equipment (PPE)

The **Personal Protective Equipment at Work (PPE) Regulations 1992** replace parts of over 20 old pieces of law. PPE includes most types of protective clothing, and equipment such as eye,

foot and head protection, safety harnesses, life jackets and high visibility clothing. Employers must supply PPE *free of charge* to their employees, and have a duty to:

• Maintain, clean and replace PPE.
• Make sure that the PPE issued is suitable for the risk involved.
• Give training, instruction and information to staff on the use and care of PPE.
• Provide storage for PPE when it is not being used.
• Ensure that PPE is properly used.

Implications of the new health and safety regulations for the leisure and tourism industry

All leisure and tourism organizations will be affected to some extent by one or more of the new regulations. Those employing five or more staff will be involved in recording health and safety information which is open for inspection by HSE staff. While each sector of the industry will have to respond to the regulations in its own particular way, there are some general implications which will need to be considered by all organizations.

• The **financial implications** of implementing the new regulations may be severe, particularly for those leisure and tourism organizations who have perhaps not given health and safety a high priority in the past. Even those organizations which have implemented previous health and safety law will be faced with the extra resource implications of the new regulations covering display screen equipment. Tour operators, airlines, hotels and travel agencies, all of whom make extensive use of VDUs, will have to find extra resources in order to be able to comply with these new regulations properly.

• The **staffing implications** will be apparent with both existing and new staff. Current employees will need training in certain aspects of all the new regulations. All new staff will need careful induction into the health and safety procedures of the organization and may require protective equipment and clothing or special furniture to comply with the regulations covering display screen equipment.

Other legislation affecting leisure and tourism

Food Hygiene Regulations

The sale of food plays a vital role in today's leisure and tourism industry. Eating out is an increasingly popular leisure activity, worth nearly £20 billion to the industry in 1993 (Leisure Consultants, 1994). The preparation, serving and sale of food is important in many areas of leisure and tourism as a way of generating income, either as the principal activity, in the case of a restaurant for example, or as a supplement to another activity, perhaps a leisure centre providing snacks for customers. Any leisure and tourism organization involved in any way with food which is offered for sale to customers or visitors, must now work within the Food Hygiene Regulations introduced under the *Food Safety Act 1990*. The regulations lay great emphasis on the proper storage and preparation of food, as well as cleanliness and sanitation. Local authorities enforce the **Food Hygiene Regulations** through their Environmental Health Departments. Environmental health inspectors have far-ranging powers, covering hotels and restaurants as well as clubs and other leisure and tourism facilities offering food for sale.

An inspector has the right to enter premises at any reasonable hour of the day to check whether the regulations are being adhered to. Penalties for breach of the regulations are severe, including heavy fines for the original offence and additional daily fines for each day the breach continues. In exceptional circumstances, the facility could be banned from serving food altogether until measures to rectify the situation are completed. Apart from the danger to the health of individuals from breaches of food safety, the adverse public relations which can be generated may have serious effects on the popularity of a facility.

THE FOOD HYGIENE REGULATIONS 1970
HOW THEY AFFECT YOU!

1. Any bit of you that comes into contact with food must be clean!!!

2. Dirty/soiled clothes must be changed.

3. NO SMOKING anywhere in a room where food/drink is prepared, stored or served.

4. Are you suffering from any of the following illnesses?
   Sickness, diarrhoea, skin infection or food poisoning.
   You must report this type of illness to the Department Manager.

5. Hands should always be clean. Fingernails short and NO NAIL VARNISH!!!

6. Always wash your hands in the wash basin provided and not in the sink.

7. Where appropriate, you must wear a suitable head covering while working with food.

Figure 2.2 Advice to employees at Butlin's Holiday Hotels (courtesy of the Rank Organisation PLC)

Hazardous substances, electricity and noise

If badly managed, leisure and tourism facilities can present very serious risks to the general public and staff working in them. Most facilities and premises will use **chemicals** of one sort or another for cleaning and disinfecting, all will have **electrical installations** and some may have machinery and equipment which generates significant **noise**. In all three areas, regulations with the force of law have come into operation since 1988.

What does COSHH mean?

COSHH stands for the **Control of Substances Hazardous to Health Regulations (1988)**. These regulations add to an employer's duties concerning the use of harmful substances as laid down in the HSW Act. Under the COSHH Regulations, employers must assess likely exposure to all hazardous substances and initiate control measures and monitoring procedures as appropriate. The definition of 'hazardous substance' is given in the regulations; it may be classed as 'toxic', 'very toxic', 'harmful', 'irritant' or 'corrosive'. It can be in solid, liquid, gaseous, vapour, dust or fume form. The following chemicals commonly found in leisure and tourism facilities fall within the scope of the regulations:

- Chemicals for the management of grassland in parks and open spaces
- Chemicals for the marking and management of sports fields
- Chemicals for the treatment of swimming or leisure pool water
- Cleaning and disinfecting chemicals such as bleach
- Chemicals for the control of insects and vermin

Electricity at Work Regulations 1989

The **Electricity at Work Regulations** came into force on 1 April 1990 and expand previous legislation relating to factories and building sites, to include *all* places of work, including leisure and tourism premises. They cover:

- Adverse or hazardous environments, e.g. swimming pools, outdoor arenas, beer and spirits storage areas, special events, etc.
- Insulation protection
- Strength and capability of electrical equipment
- Earthing
- Isolation of supply
- Competent staff for electrical work
- Connections
- Protection from excess current
- Work precautions

The managers and owners of all leisure and tourism facilities have to follow a clear programme of action to minimize risks from electrical plant and installations, including such items as regular equipment inspection, training for appropriate staff and troubleshooting.

Noise at Work Regulations 1989

These very technical regulations came into force on 1 January 1990. In simple terms, the regulations define three 'action levels of noise', above which certain measures, including the wearing of ear defenders, must be taken. Management must monitor levels of sound within leisure and tourism facilities and, if noise levels become too high, initiate measures to control the situation. In a leisure centre, for example, which may have hundreds of swimmers in the pool at any one time, or a disco with loud music, alternative means of communicating with the public must be available should the normal public address (PA) system become inaudible.

Fire precautions

The threat of fire is one of the most serious risk factors that any leisure and tourism organization must face. There is plenty of evidence to show that outbreaks of fire have often been the cause of fatalities. The friends and relatives of the 56 people who died at Bradford City Football Club in the tragedy of 1987 bear witness to this fact.

Fire Precautions Act 1971

One of the main requirements of the **Fire Precautions Act** is the need for certain leisure and tourism establishments to apply for a Fire Certificate from their local fire authorities. The Act requires that any premises providing entertainment, recreation or use of a club or association where there are more than 20 employees on the ground floor or more than 10 above ground floor level must apply for a Fire Certificate. If, after an inspection, the local fire authority are satisfied that all necessary conditions have been met, a Fire Certificate can be issued. The kind of conditions contained in the Certificate include:

- Limits to the number of people allowed on the premises.
- Keeping means of escape clear.
- Keeping records relating to fire safety matters.
- Providing employees with fire safety training.
- Fire drills at specified times.

Hotels and other serviced accommodation also fall within the scope of the Fire Precautions Act. As a general rule, a Fire Certificate will be needed if the accommodation sleeps more than six guests at first floor level or just one at either second floor level or below ground.

PREVENTING FIRES

- Cigarette smoking is an obvious hazard, e.g. food preparation areas, storage or near inflammable liquids or materials.
- Check waste and rubbish are not allowed to build up.
- Report electrical faults and gas leaks.
- Switch off plugs and disconnect when not in use.
- Do not overload electrical sockets.
- Report any fire appliances needing attention to security.

  REMEMBER

  IT IS A SERIOUS OFFENCE TO MISUSE FIRE EQUIPMENT
  AND MAY COST LIVES.

WHAT TO DO IN A FIRE

5 Point Guide

1. Familiarise yourself with your working area.
2. Be aware of all FIRE EXIT DOORS and how to open them. Keep FIRE EXIT DOORS clear at all times.
3. Be aware of FIRE ALARM CALL POINTS and the location of FIRE EXTINGUISHERS and FIRE BLANKETS.

WHAT IF I DISCOVER A FIRE?

4. Sound the ALARM by breaking the glass at the FIRE ALARM CALL POINT and call the emergency telephone number _____ .
5. Evacuate the building and go to the Assembly Point. Don't shout or use the word FIRE!! This will cause panic. Only re-enter the building when told to do so by a Manager.

Figure 2.3 Advice to employees in Butlin's Holiday Hotels (courtesy of the Rank Organisation PLC)

First aid

The HSW Act and its associated regulations place a duty on employers to provide adequate **first aid** for both *employees* and *non-employees*, which, in the case of leisure and tourism, would include guests, visitors, spectators, customers and contractors. From 1 January 1993, the new health and safety at work regulations require employers to carry out 'risk assessments'; clearly the provision of adequate first aid cover appropriate to the particular leisure and tourism activity is a crucial part of any such assessment.

Did You Know ?

The St. John Ambulance Brigade runs courses in first aid throughout the country.

The reporting of accidents and incidents

The law relating to accident/incident reporting is contained in the **Reporting of Injuries, Diseases and Dangerous Occurrences Regulations (RIDDOR) 1985**. Under the regulations, any employer, self-employed person or individual in control of a work situation, has a duty to inform the relevant authority of:

- Any *fatal* injuries to employees or other people in an accident connected with the business.
- Any major injuries to employees or other people in an accident connected with the business.

- Any of the dangerous occurrences listed in the regulations.

In the case of leisure and tourism organizations, the incidents should be reported to the local Environmental Health Department. The regulations stipulate that a particular form (form F2508) should be used for reporting injuries and dangerous occurrences (see Fig. 2.4).

Public order

Public order is sometimes a problem for those leisure and tourism organizations which deal with large numbers of people in the course of their activities, e.g. the organizers of events. However much an organization may feel that its activities are adding to the amenity of a particular area, there may be neighbouring individuals or businesses who think otherwise. The law protects the public by providing legal restraints against private or public nuisance, principally under the **Public Order Act 1986**. Aggrieved neighbours may decide to pursue an action in the courts against, for example, noisy speedway events, firework displays, rock concerts, etc. For the action to have any chance of success, there must be *continuity* of nuisance, i.e. it must occur more than once over a reasonable period of time. In certain circumstances, those who have a grievance against a leisure and tourism operator may obtain a faster result by complaining to their local environmental health department.

Occupiers' liability

Under the **Occupiers' Liability Act 1984**, the 'occupier' of a leisure and tourism facility, who will be either the owner or the person who operates it, owes a legal duty to all people who use it, including visitors and spectators, to make sure that the facility is reasonably safe for the purpose for which the people are entering. This would include, for example, equipment in an amusement park or in a holiday centre or the seating for spectators at an event. As well as a duty to those on the premises, the occupier also has a duty to neighbours and others living nearby. For example, if a golf ball strikes a pedestrian walking on a public footpath alongside the eighteenth fairway of a golf course, this is likely to result in a successful claim for negligence against the owner of the course if the incident could reasonably have been foreseen.

Sources of advice on health and safety matters

- **The Health and Safety Executive** – the HSE has a network of regional offices covering England, Scotland and Wales with staff who can advise on all issues relating to health and safety at work (Northern Ireland has a separate Health and Safety Agency which, although independent of the HSE, liaises closely with it on matters of mutual interest). The HSE operates a public enquiry service from its Sheffield offices, offering advice and information on a wide range of health and safety issues. The HSE produces a wide range of leaflets on health and safety and will advise on the implementation of the HSW Act and the new regulations produced as a result of the recent EU Directives on health and safety.

Health and Safety Executive
Health and Safety at Work etc Act 1974
Reporting of Injuries,Diseases and Dangerous Occurrences Regulations 1985

Spaces below
are for office
use only

Report of an injury or dangerous occurrence

- Full notes to help you complete this form are attached.
- This form is to be used to make a report to the enforcing authority under the requirements of Regulations 3 or 6.
- Completing and signing this form does not constitute an admission of liability of any kind, either by the person making the report or any other person.
- If more than one person was injured as a result of an accident, please complete a separate form for each person.

A   Subject of report *(tick appropriate box or boxes)* — *see note 2*

| Fatality ☐ 1 | Specified major injury or condition ☐ 2 | "Over three day" injury ☐ 3 | Dangerous occurrence ☐ 4 | Flammable gas incident (fatality or major injury or condition) ☐ 5 | Dangerous gas fitting ☐ 6 |

B   Person or organisation making report (ie person obliged to report under the Regulations) — *see note 3*

Name and address —

Nature of trade, business or undertaking —

If in construction industry, state the
total number of your employees —

and indicate the role of your company on site
(tick box) —

Post code —

| Main site contractor ☐ 7 | Sub contractor ☐ 8 | Other ☐ 9 |

Name and telephone no. of person to contact —

If in farming, are you reporting an injury
to a member of your family? *(tick box)*   ☐ Yes   ☐ No

C   Date, time and place of accident, dangerous occurrence or flammable gas incident — *see note 4*

Date ☐ ☐ 19 ☐   Time —
day month year

Give the name and address if different
from above —

ENV

Where on the premises or site —
and
Normal activity carried on there

Complete the following sections D, E, F & H if you have ticked boxes, 1, 2, 3 or 5 in Section A. Otherwise go straight to Sections G and H.

D   The injured person — *see note 5*

Full name and address —

Age ☐   Sex ☐
        (M or F)

Status *(tick box)* —

| Employee ☐ 10 | Self employed ☐ 11 | Trainee (YTS) ☐ 12 |
| Trainee (other) ☐ 13 | | Any other person ☐ 14 |

Trade, occupation or job title —

Nature of injury or condition and the
part of the body affected —

F2508 (rev 1/86)   *continued overleaf*

Figure 2.4   Form F2508 (Crown Copyright. Reproduced with permission of the Controller of Her Majesty's Stationery Office)

E Kind of accident - *see note 6*

Indicate what kind of accident led to the injury or condition (*tick one box*) —

Contact with moving machinery or material being machined ☐ 1	Injured whilst handling lifting or carrying ☐ 5	Trapped by something collapsing or overturning ☐ 8	Exposure to an explosion ☐ 12
Struck by moving, including flying or falling, object. ☐ 2	Slip, trip or fall on same level ☐ 6	Drowning or asphyxiation ☐ 9	Contact with electricity or an electrical discharge ☐ 13
Struck by moving vehicle ☐ 3	Fall from a height* ☐ 7	Exposure to or contact with a harmful substance ☐ 10	Injured by an animal ☐ 14
Struck against something fixed or stationary ☐ 4	*Distance through which person fell ☐ (metres)	Exposure to fire ☐ 11	Other kind of accident (give details in Section H) ☐ 15

Spaces below are for office use only.

☐

F Agent(s) involved – *see note 7*

Indicate which, if any, of the categories of agent or factor below were involved (*tick one or more of the boxes*) —

Machinery/equipment for lifting and conveying ☐ 1	Process plant, pipework or bulk storage ☐ 5	Live animal ☐ 9	Ladder or scaffolding ☐ 13
Portable power or hand tools ☐ 2	Any material, substance or product being handled, used or stored. ☐ 6	Moveable container or package of any kind ☐ 10	Construction formwork, shuttering and falsework ☐ 14
Any vehicle or associated equipment/ machinery ☐ 3	Gas, vapour, dust, fume or oxygen deficient atmosphere ☐ 7	Floor, ground, stairs or any working surface ☐ 11	Electricity supply cable, wiring, apparatus or equipment ☐ 15
Other machinery ☐ 4	Pathogen or infected material ☐ 8	Building, engineering structure or excavation/underground working ☐ 12	Entertainment or sporting facilities or equipment ☐ 16
			Any other agent ☐ 17

Describe briefly the agents or factors you have indicated —

☐

G Dangerous occurrence or dangerous gas fitting – *see notes 8 and 9*

Reference number of dangerous occurrence ☐   Reference number of dangerous gas fitting ☐

H Account of accident, dangerous occurrence or flammable gas incident - *see note 10*

Describe what happened and how. In the case of an accident state what the injured person was doing at the time —

☐

☐
☐

Signature of person making report ☐   Date ☐

Figure 2.4 Form F2508 Continued

- **Environmental Health Department** – operated by the local authority, this department is a good source of advice on such issues as noise pollution and control, food hygiene and safety, the EU Package Travel Directive and COSHH.

- **Fire Authority** – the local fire authority offers safety information and advice and is the body responsible for issuing Fire Certificates. It can advise on the purchase of fire safety equipment and training for staff in its use.

- **Building Control Department** – often part of the local authority planning department, building control staff can give advice on the building regulations, many of which contain instructions on the use of certain building materials and techniques to reduce fire risks and improve safety and security generally.

- **Health and safety consultants** – in view of the growing amount and complexity of legislation concerning health and safety, specialist consultants can be employed to advise on particular health and safety issues, e.g. in relation to the new regulations brought about by the EU directives. Consultancies vary enormously in size and style of operation, but there are certain points which an organization must bear in mind when selecting a consultant, such as competence and cost. The HSE can supply an information leaflet on the subject, entitled 'Selecting a Health and Safety Consultancy'.

- **Professional bodies** – are helpful in providing advice and publications relating to health and safety. Examples include the Sports Council, Institute of Sport and Recreation Management (ISRM), Institute of Leisure and Amenity Management (ILAM) and the Hotel, Catering and Institutional Management Association (HCIMA).

- **Universities and colleges** – often put on courses concerning health and safety issues and may offer consultancy services themselves.

- **Industrial training boards** – some industries have training boards, e.g. ABTA National Training Board and the Agricultural Training Board (ATB) who are active in assessing training needs in health and safety and organizing courses.

- **Solicitors and advice centres** – as with any legal matters, solicitors, the Citizens' Advice Bureau and local legal advice centres can give advice on the legislation relating to health and safety, as well as suggesting sources of further advice and information.

Self Check ✔ **Element 1**

1. Why is it necessary for leisure and tourism organizations to devote time and money to health and safety matters?

2. Which leisure and tourism organizations are likely to be most affected by the Display Screen Equipment Regulations?

3. Can you think of specific leisure and tourism organizations which will be affected by the PPE Regulations?

4. Noise in certain leisure and tourism facilities and at some events can reach dangerous levels. Can you think of any examples?

5. Which national organizations offer training in first aid?

2.2 Enhancing the health and safety of customers and staff

The identification of health and safety hazards

Under the new **Management of Health and Safety at Work Regulations 1992** examined in Element 1 of this unit (see page 40), employers have a duty to carry out risk assessments of their premises in order to highlight potential health and safety risks and to implement positive action to put matters right, thereby reducing the number of accidents in leisure and tourism facilities. Investigators of safety hazards and management have ample evidence to show that accidents are *caused* rather than just happen. Careful investigations of accidents show that many could have been prevented if somebody had taken the time and care to examine the risk potential of the particular building or facility. It may be something as simple as the replacement of a broken floor tile or a cracked window pane.

There were in the region of 180,000 leisure-related accidents during the six-month period May–October 1989, according to the Department of Trade and Industry's Leisure Accident Surveillance System (LASS). These figures indicate the scale of the problem and show why any work carried out to identify hazards in leisure and tourism facilities will go a long way towards keeping the number of accidents to a minimum.

This element will identify some of the main hazards which are likely to be found in all sectors of the leisure and tourism industry.

Sports and leisure centres

Sports and leisure centres are used for a wide range of activities by many different customers, including school groups, individuals, senior citizens, the disabled and sports teams. The variety of types of activity and types of customer, when coupled with heavy usage at peak times, places a particular emphasis on the need for strict health and safety measures including the identification of potential hazards. A typical local authority controlled leisure centre is likely to include the following areas:

- Wet sports areas
- Dry sports areas, e.g. squash courts, sports halls, etc.
- Changing rooms
- Toilets
- Refreshments areas
- Showers
- Spectator seating areas

We will look in detail at the likely *hazards* associated with each of the above.

Wet sports areas

- Slippery surfaces around pools
- Poor quality water, e.g. unclear or with ojectionable odour
- Untrained staff
- Inadequate depth markings
- Inadequate number of life savers
- Unsafe diving and other equipment

Dry sports areas

- Unguarded light fittings
- Poor lighting and ventilation
- Low level obstructions
- Damaged sports equipment
- Slippery floors
- Inadequate or insufficient storage for equipment

Changing rooms

- Litter on floors
- Inadequate storage for cleaning materials
- Broken tiles and mirrors
- Insecure fixtures and fittings
- Damaged doors
- Slippery floors

Toilets

- Broken tiles and mirrors
- Unhygienic condition
- Damaged doors and fittings

Refreshments areas

- Litter on floors
- Food storage areas at wrong temperature
- Slippery floors
- Damaged tables and chairs

Showers

- Damaged tiles on walls and floor
- Insecure fixtures and fittings
- Water too hot or too cold

Spectator seating areas

- Blocked emergency exits
- Damaged seats
- Insecure steps and handrails
- Poor signs
- Poor lighting

Any *special events* which take place at the leisure centre, such as a swimming gala or disco evening, will entail special health and safety measures appropriate to the occasion.

Visitor attractions

Information contained in Unit 1 shows that the term '**visitor attraction**' can be defined very broadly, and can include facilities such as theme parks, heritage attractions, museums, stately homes, sports facilities and the like. Even the smallest attraction will need to give attention to the health and safety needs of staff and visitors. Bad publicity given to poor (or non-existent) health and safety procedures leading to accidents involving members of the public can have disastrous effects on visitor numbers. The management at Disney resorts believe that accidents and Disney do not mix, and make sure that all staff are rigorously trained in emergency first aid techniques.

Potential *hazards* for visitors to attractions include:

- Fast-moving rides and monorails
- Poor lighting indoors and outside
- Blocked aisles
- Poor signposting
- Unguarded or unsupervised machinery and equipment
- Fire hazards
- Accidents involving animals
- Slippery or broken walkways
- Loose or broken wiring
- Leaks of steam, water, gas or oil
- Water hazards

Hotels and other accommodation

The very diverse nature of the **accommodation sector** in UK leisure and tourism gives it great appeal to domestic and overseas tourists. Serviced accommodation for business and leisure travellers comes in a vast range of sizes, styles and types – anything from a sixteenth-century half-timbered country house hotel in Herefordshire to a modern 30-storey city-centre hotel. Self-catering accommodation also enjoys a rich variety, including cottages, chalets, villas, camping and caravanning, so popular with families who enjoy the flexibility and value for money which this type of accommodation offers.

From a health and safety point of view, the wide range of accommodation on offer makes a standardized approach to analysing and eliminating risks quite impossible. The sixteenth-century country house hotel quoted above will have very different health and safety risks associated with it than, say, a caravan site with over 200 pitches.

Potential hazards in both serviced and self-catering accommodation include:

- Fire (particularly important in high-rise buildings)
- Faulty wiring and electrical appliances
- Faulty air conditioning

- Poorly maintained lifts and elevators
- Poor ventilation
- Glass doors, screens and windows
- Poor lighting
- Worn or damaged floor coverings
- Blocked corridors.
- Suspicious packages

The risk assessments, which are now an essential management function under the new health and safety at work regulations, should highlight such risks and hazards and prompt urgent action by employers. Self-catering accommodation, where by definition the owner or manager of the property may not be on-site, needs very careful attention when it comes to health and safety issues.

Catering and hospitality

Catering and hospitality is a very diverse sector of the leisure and tourism industry. It includes:

- Catering for large functions
- Catering in hotels
- Contract catering for airlines, ferry operators etc
- Independent restaurants and cafés
- Restaurants and eating places which are part of large multinational companies, e.g. Harvester is part of the Forte group
- Catering associated with sports events
- Catering at entertainment complexes
- Corporate hospitality events

There are potential health and safety *hazards* both for those working in this sector and their customers and clients. Particular examples of risks are:

- Unguarded machinery and kitchen equipment
- Food stored at the incorrect temperature
- Dangerous practices involving food preparation
- Contaminated water supplies
- Inadequate storage for potentially dangerous cleaning materials
- Poor lighting
- Inadequate ventilation

The Food Safety Act and its associated Food Hygiene Regulations have come about to protect both workers and the public in this area of concern for health and safety.

Travel agents and tour operators

The work of most **travel agents and tour operators** will be office-based, including dealing with clients, raising invoices, checking availability of flights and holidays, filing and such like. Many of the general health and safety risks and hazards associated with office premises will apply, including:

- Blocked corridors and aisles
- Poor lighting
- Faulty electrical equipment
- Fire
- Poor ventilation and air quality
- Fumes from certain felt pens and correction fluids

One area of work of travel agents and tour operators which has been causing concern with individuals and their trade union representatives for some time is the extensive use of visual display units (VDUs) and their harmful effects on users. Both travel agents and tour operators (together with airlines, coach operators and hotel reservation staff) use VDUs in all aspects of their work. The potential harmful effects of excessive use of VDUs has now been formally recognized with the introduction of the new Health and Safety (Display Screen Equipment) Regulations which came into effect on 1 January 1993 (see page 42).

It is important to remember that travel agents and tour operators are often acting on behalf of other sectors of the leisure and tourism industry, e.g. hotels and transport companies, over which they have no control. The travel agents and tour operators must be convinced that the health and safety procedures of all companies they deal with are as good as their own. Working across continents and in different languages can make this a very difficult task.

Did You Know ?

Under the terms of the EU Package Travel Directive, tour operators can no longer disclaim responsibility for health and safety problems which arise in the accommodation and transport that they contract.

Entertainment

Entertainment venues are often able to accommodate large numbers of people at any one time, e.g. cinemas, theatres, outdoor and indoor arenas, casinos, discos, etc. This puts a particular emphasis on the need for strict health and safety procedures to protect the public and those employed in the venues. Potential *hazards* include:

- Fire
- Overcrowding
- Blocked exits
- Excessive noise
- Harmful lighting effects
- Poor ventilation

Education

Schools, colleges and universities have long been used by people in their leisure time for evening, day and weekend courses. The recent severing of ties between schools/colleges and their local education authorities has increased the need to generate additional income from premises which are not usually fully occupied over a 12-month period. This independence has led to an increased awareness of the importance of health and safety procedures, both while the 'normal' pupils/students are on-site and while the premises are being put to 'different' uses, e.g. conferences and conventions, meetings, trade fairs, etc.

Leisure in the home

We saw in Unit 1 that **home-based leisure** was a significant and growing part of the total leisure and tourism industry. When looking at health and safety hazards in leisure and tourism, we must not forget that leisure in the home has risks associated with it. The DTI's Home Accident Surveillance Survey (HASS) compiles national figures from 13 accident and emergency departments on accidents in the home. It shows that a quarter of a million accidents a year (14% of all home accidents) happen in the garden. The top eight gardening accidents involving equipment in 1989 were:

- Lawn mower: 6300   accidents
- Garden fork: 4300   accidents
- Deck chair/sunbed: 4000   accidents
- Hedge trimmer: 3900   accidents
- Spade/shovel: 3300   accidents
- Wheelbarrow: 2000   accidents
- Flower pot: 2000   accidents
- Secateurs: 1900   accidents

With the projected increases in home-based leisure up to and beyond the year 2000, accidents in this area are likely to increase unless manufacturers and users alike are aware of potential risks and hazards.

The reduction in health and safety risks

We have looked in detail at many sectors of the leisure and tourism industry and have identified potential health and safety risks and hazards in each. Recent UK legislation on health and safety, primarily put in place to satisfy new EU directives, has focused the minds of those managing leisure and tourism facilities on the importance of health and safety at all levels of an organization.

When it comes to reducing health and safety risks and hazards in the workplace, management and staff should put in place systems and work practices which identify hazards. If a leisure and tourism organization takes a close look at its operation with a view to identifying and eliminating hazards rather than waiting for accidents to happen, then it will reap the benefits in a number of ways:

- **Improved image:** If customers see that a leisure and tourism organization is taking health and safety seriously, its image will be enhanced and, through word of mouth as much as anything, business will increase. If health and safety is poorly handled, the adverse public relations generated may have a serious effect on visitor attendances.

- **Better staff morale:** Involving members of staff in the planning and implementation of health and safety matters at an early stage will not only reduce incidents but also improve morale. Asking them to 'pick up the pieces' after an accident which they may have had nothing to do with is not effective management.

- **Reduced costs:** A carefully planned and costed health and safety strategy will help to cut out major incidents which may put a strain on the financial resources of the organization.

Measures to reduce health and safety risks and hazards

Probably the single most important factor in helping reduce health and safety risks is *management attitude*. If the senior management of a leisure and tourism organization is totally committed to providing a safe and controlled environment for its staff and visitors, it is likely that the organization as a whole will succeed in its efforts to reduce hazards. A committed senior management will inspire and involve its staff, suppliers, contractors and even its customers to achieve a safer environment.

Management can influence the improvement in health and safety procedures in a number of ways, including:

- Implementing legislation
- Budgeting for health and safety
- Scheduling essential maintenance

- Seeking advice
- Devising safe systems and work practices
- Training staff
- Carrying out safety audits
- Dealing with customers with special needs
- Managing visitors and traffic effectively

Implementing legislation

The many different laws, regulations and codes of practice relating to health and safety are all based on sound common-sense principles. Any leisure and tourism professional will consider it essential to become familiar with health and safety laws and implement them within the organization for the benefit of all. Management should aim to co-operate with the relevant health and safety regulatory bodies in their work.

Budgeting for health and safety

Leisure and tourism organizations must be sure to budget for health and safety matters in the same way as other elements of their operation need resourcing. Health and safety cannot be regarded as an optional extra; it should be seen as crucial to the success of the business and at the heart of a successful organization.

Scheduling essential maintenance

A programme of regular maintenance of equipment and machinery will help to reduce accidents. All areas must be kept clear of litter and other debris and there needs to be adequate storage for such items as potentially dangerous chemicals and other cleaning materials.

Seeking advice

Element 1 of this unit looked in detail at the many sources of help and advice available on health and safety issues (see page 00). Seeking advice from the experts will help to ensure both the identification of potential risks and hazards and their elimination.

Devising safe systems and work practices

As well as all staff being familiar with everyday health and safety matters, such as first aid procedures, it is essential that there are systems in place to deal with any emergencies which may arise, e.g. bomb scares, major equipment failure, major accidents, etc. Management is responsible for drawing up contingency plans to deal with such occurrences and informing all staff accordingly. Work practices need to be assessed in the light of a safe environment for staff and visitors.

Training staff

A management which is committed to providing a safe environment for all who enter its premises will put a high priority on staff training in the area of health and safety. New staff, as part of their wider induction programme, should be given details of the organization's health and safety policies and practices. There should be regular updating for all staff in health and safety matters and specific training for those working in particularly hazardous areas. Staff in leisure and tourism need to be alert, responsible, calm and collected when it comes to health and safety.

Carrying out safety audits

Many leisure and tourism organizations, as a matter of course, have been carrying out safety audits for years. As we have seen, the process of identifying potential risks has become more formalized of late with the introduction of the new EU-prompted health and safety regulations with their duty on employers to carry out risk assessments. Safety audits are invaluable in pinpointing potential hazards, but can only be fully useful if any highlighted risks are attended to.

Dealing with customers with special needs
All staff should be constantly aware of potential hazards and risks not only to the able-bodied but also to those with special needs, e.g. the disabled, very young and older customers.

Managing visitors and traffic effectively
Good signposting to help people and traffic circulation will contribute to a safe and controlled environment. Particular hazards should be identified with clear warning signs.

Self Check ✔ **Element 2**

6. Which health and safety hazards in hotels put disabled and elderly people at particular risk?
_____
_____
_____

7. Explain how a positive approach to health and safety issues can produce tangible benefits to a leisure and tourism organization.
_____
_____
_____

2.3 Enhancing security in leisure and tourism

Society's concern for security

There is little doubt that British people are concerned more than ever with their personal **security** and the security of their possessions. The 1980s and early 1990s has seen an upsurge in criminal activity, with theft from homes, theft of and from cars, assaults and aggressive behaviour constantly making the headlines in the media. Statistics show that few regions of Britain escape the worst excesses of crime; both inner cities and rural areas are experiencing the growth in crime. The reaction of many British people who now see their security threatened by this increased crime has been to adapt their lifestyles to improve their own particular circumstances. Some people, of course, will choose not to be deflected from their normal daily activity, but an ever-increasing number of people are deciding to make their own lives more secure. Installing burglar alarms and other security devices on houses and flats is now commonplace, as is the fitting of alarms and immobilizers to cars or choosing to buy cars which already have them fitted. People tend to avoid carrying large amounts of cash, choosing instead to use the more secure credit, debit and charge cards. Certain parts of urban areas are undoubtedly more dangerous than others, making people think carefully about their movements.

Security in leisure and tourism

The leisure and tourism industry has also felt the effects of this rise in criminal activity in a number of ways:

- Travel patterns to countries and areas experiencing political instability or terrorism have been altered. The obvious example of this has to be the complete destruction of the tourist industry in the former Yugoslavia. Northern Ireland's tourism industry has also suffered over a long period of time, and Florida is considered by many British people to be a 'dangerous' state following the recent murders of UK holidaymakers.
- The rise in importance of home-based leisure, which we looked at in Unit 1, is in part due to people looking for more entertainment in the comfort and, perhaps more importantly, the **security** of their own homes.
- Visitors to hotels, sports centres, tourist attractions, airports, events and other leisure and tourism facilities are no longer surprised to see security staff on duty; in fact, they expect to see them and would feel rather uncomfortable in certain circumstances if they were not there.

Did You Know ?

Rising crime and concern for personal security has meant that it is becoming increasingly difficult to attract people to events and facilities in certain inner city areas, e.g. to evening classes and sports activities.

What legislation is there to protect the leisure and tourism consumer?

As well as individuals altering their leisure habits and increasing their personal security, the law-makers in Britain and the European Union have been developing and passing **legislation** to help the security needs of those using leisure and tourism facilities and services. We looked in detail in Element 1 of this unit at the legislation affecting the health and safety of staff and visitors in leisure and tourism. There are one or two important laws concerning consumer rights, however, which directly influence the *security of the product* which the leisure and tourism customer is buying.

Trades Description Act 1968
The **Trades Description Act** protects customers against false descriptions by those who are selling or providing services, including leisure and tourism services. Any description of, for example, a hotel or leisure club must be truthful at the time it was written (if circumstances subsequently change, then the operator must inform the customer of the nature of the changes). This places a duty on owners and operators of leisure and tourism facilities to produce brochures and other promotional materials which are not intended to deceive the customer.

Sale of Goods Act 1979
The **Sale of Goods Act** applies particularly to one sector of the leisure and tourism industry, namely tour operators. The Act puts a duty on businesses such as tour operators to exercise care and attention when selecting all the elements of the packages they are putting together. Once they have done this, they cannot be held responsible under this Act for the day-to-day running of the services they have contracted. However, the newly introduced EU Package Travel directive puts a slightly different emphasis on this, and other, aspects of the security of the holiday product that the customer is buying.

EU Package Travel Directive
The **Package Travel, Package Holidays and Package Tours Directive** came into operation on 1 January 1993 in all 12

member states of the European Union (formerly EC). Its main aim is to give people buying package holidays more protection and access to compensation when things go wrong. The directive places a number of *duties* on the organizers of packages, namely:

*   Providing clear contract terms.
*   Providing information to customers on who is responsible for the package they have booked. That person or organization is then liable in the event of failure to deliver any elements of the package.
*   Providing proof of the organizer's security against insolvency and information on any available insurance policies.
*   Producing accurate promotional material including brochures.
*   Giving emergency telephone numbers.
*   Giving immediate notification with explanation of any increase in prices permitted within the terms of the contract.
*   Providing a variety of compensation options if agreed services are not supplied.

It is fair to say that the EU Package Travel directive has come as something of a shock to the UK tourist industry, since the directive covers domestic as well as outbound packages. This means that hotels, tourist information centres, resorts, conference organizers, coach operators and even school trip organizers have found that they may fall within the scope of the directive. There has also been much debate about what exactly constitutes a 'package', with Trading Standards Officers, the people given the job of policing the directive in the UK, appearing to have different views depending on where in the country they are located. The travel industry generally fears that the extra insurance needed by tour organizers to cover against claims under the directive is bound to put up the cost of holidays.

Did You Know ?

The EU Package Travel Directive applies to both domestic and outbound tourism.

Measures to enhance security in leisure and tourism

Any security measures in an organization will have been put in place to provide protection against all forms of loss arising from a number of different sources. The term **security** in leisure and tourism covers security of:

*   people
*   property
*   money
*   information

Security of people

When looking at the wide range of security concerns confronting the industry, the welfare of **people** must be the prime concern for the leisure and tourism professional. This will include staff, visitors (invited or uninvited) and any other people, such as contractors and students, who may be on the premises.

All employers have a legal duty under the Health and Safety at Work Act etc. 1974 to ensure the health, safety and welfare at work of their staff (see page 39). We have looked at the various

health and safety risks and hazards which may confront staff in leisure and tourism, but providing a safe working environment which is free from any violence is becoming an increasingly important concern for employers. The Health and Safety Executive working definition of violence is:

> Any incident in which an employee is abused, threatened or assaulted by a member of the public in circumstances arising out of the course of his or her employment.
>
> (HSE 1992)

Being a service industry involving a high degree of contact between staff and customers, those working in leisure and tourism can expect to encounter uncomfortable and sometimes violent incidents during the course of their work. Happily, physical attacks on staff are comparatively rare, but verbal abuse and threatening behaviour are all too common in many types of leisure and tourism facility.

Both employers and employees have an interest in reducing violence in the workplace. For employees, violence can cause pain, suffering and even disability or death. Physical attacks are obviously dangerous but serious or persistent verbal abuse or threats can also damage employees' health through anxiety and stress. For employers, violence can lead to low morale and a poor image for the organization, making it difficult to recruit and retain staff. It can also mean extra costs, with increased absenteeism, a higher turnover of staff and increased insurance premiums. The Health and Safety Executive recommends a seven-point plan to tackle violence in the workplace (see Fig. 2.5)

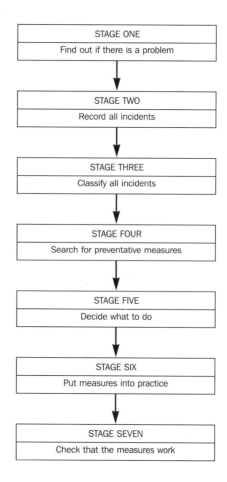

Figure 2.5 Seven-point plan to tackle violence in the workplace

Stage **one** of the plan, find out if there is a problem, may seem rather obvious, but many employers and managers are not always aware of a problem until they ask staff directly. **Stage two**, recording all incidents, will give an overall picture of the scale of the problem and any particular pattern that may exist. Classifying all incidents (**stage three**) into, for example, those which involve serious injury and those where verbal abuse or threatening behaviour occured will help management decide on the most appropriate form of action to take. **Stage four**, searching for preventative measures, will depend on the exact nature of the problem. The way jobs are carried out can help reduce the risk of violence. For example, if a leisure and tourism organization needs its staff to work late, it should either arrange for them to have a safe place to park their car or provide transport home; many nightclubs and pubs do this already, particularly for female staff. Changing from using cash to accepting cheques, credit cards or tokens can help reduce attempted thefts. **Stage five**, deciding what to do, should involve all staff and not be seen as just a management decision. Many organizations find that a mixture of measures usually works best. It is often a question of striking a balance between the fears of the staff and the needs of the public. For example, many busy tourist attractions provide entertainment for customers who are forced to queue to get in. This helps to diffuse what can sometimes turn into a threatening situation for staff on duty. Whatever measures are decided upon (**stage six**), the policy for dealing with violence should be included in the organization's safety policy statement, so that all employees are aware of it. **Stage seven**, checking that the measures work, is very important, for if the problem persists it may be necessary to go back and repeat steps two and three.

Security of property

Security of property in leisure and tourism is concerned with:

- The contents of the building.
- The fabric of the building itself, including fitments.

Security of the contents of the building

The contents of any leisure and tourism facility which are potentially at risk could include:

- The personal possessions of the staff.
- The possessions of any other people, such as contractors, who are on-site.
- Equipment, e.g. computers, sports equipment, catering equipment, furniture, museum artefacts, etc.
- Stock, e.g. wines, beers and spirits, food, sports clothing, etc.
- The personal possessions of the customers.

Most visitors will expect a facility to guard their possessions in exchange for a ticket, whether or not any payment is involved. This service is all part of making the visitor relaxed and in a better mood to enjoy his or her experience, be it a game of squash or a visit to an art gallery. Where visitors are not allowed to take possessions with them for security reasons, e.g. cameras are not allowed in certain museums and galleries, secure storage must be provided by the leisure and tourism operator.

Techniques such as the installation of alarms, fitting of security locks and the use of closed-circuit television, will help to protect equipment and possessions to a certain extent. However, over and above these technical measures, all staff must be vigilant and alert at all times to suspicious characters and circumstances. As well as ensuring a pleasant experience for all visitors, it is the job of staff and management to safeguard visitors' possessions.

Security of the fabric of buildings

Buildings used for leisure and tourism purposes can be under many different types of threat. One of the most obvious and costly is robbery, but other threats include wanton damage, often carried out by youths, and daubing with graffiti. There are some fundamental rules for securing any type of property, including:

- Fitting intruder alarms which, for large organizations, should be capable of alerting a central monitoring station which operates 24 hours a day.
- Installing security lighting particularly in high risk areas.
- Fitting security locks to doors and windows, and window bars to high risk areas such as equipment stores and bar areas.
- Introducing card access control using PIN systems to identify which parts of a building are for staff access only.
- Using closed circuit television (CCTV) or employing security personnel to monitor large areas including car parks.

Security of money

Leisure and tourism is a multi-million pound industry often revolving around **cash** transactions. It is usual to pay for many leisure and tourism products and services with cash rather than cheques or credit/debit cards; e.g.

- Paying for transport, e.g. taxi, bus and train.
- Paying for rides at an amusement park.
- Booking a court at the local leisure centre for a game of badminton.
- Gambling and betting.
- Buying drinks in a nightclub.
- Buying food and drink in pubs and cafés.
- Visiting tourist attractions.

In an industry which relies heavily on cash transactions, there is a particular need for operators to make sure that their security systems in this area are as good as possible. Where practical, leisure and tourism operators should introduce more secure means of payment such as cheques and cards to reduce the risk of *theft* and *fraud* by visitors and staff. Employees who handle cash will need careful recruitment and training in the rules and procedures of a particular organization, including:

- Locking up arrangements.
- Methods of paying in and receiving cash.
- Authorized keyholders for offices and safes.
- The use of burglar and attack alarms.

Security of information

We have seen that leisure and tourism is an increasingly competitive industry. Particularly in times of recession, when many people have only limited disposable income to spend on leisure and tourism, it is essential for organizations to safeguard their business by having secure means of storing *information*. All organizations will have a wealth of information about their performance, their customers and their employees.

The two main security hazards associated with records are *fire* and *theft*. Twenty years ago, all business records would have been held entirely on paper; nowadays, information is held in a variety of other formats including microfiche, computer disks, photographic materials and audio/video tapes. These are all vulnerable to the twin threats of fire and theft and do not inherently offer any greater security than paper. Computers, however, do give the option of storing information on 'floppy disks' which can be stored securely away from the main computer terminal, thus reducing the risk of losing information in the event of theft or fire. All computer and other sensitive information should be routinely locked in fire-proof data protection cabinets kept in controlled access rooms.

The storage of information on computers raises the issue of the **Data Protection Act 1984**. This Act was introduced to safeguard the public from problems relating to the inaccuracy of any information held about them on computer records. In leisure and tourism, the recording of customer information on computer is widespread, and includes:

- Details of travel agents' clients.
- Names and addresses of visitors to exhibitions.
- The names and addresses of hotel guests.
- Theatre booking lists.
- Membership lists for sports and social clubs.

Under the Data Protection Act customers are entitled to see any information held about them on computer and can challenge inaccuracies with the organization concerned (see Unit 6 for more information on the Data Protection Act).

Self Check ✔ **Element 3**

8. Although the EU Package Travel Directive is a welcome initiative, isn't it merely duplicating consumer legislation which already exists?

   _____
   _____
   _____

9. What measures can a leisure and tourism organization take to reduce the risk of fraud among its staff?

   _____
   _____
   _____

10. How can information stored on computers be made more secure?

   _____
   _____
   _____

Unit Test
This test is one hour long. Answer all the questions.

Focus 1: HEALTH AND SAFETY LEGISLATION

Questions 1–3 relate to the following information.
Health and safety regulations introduced as a result of EU
Directives include:
A Work equipment safety
B Display screen equipment
C Workplace conditions
D Health and safety management

Which of the regulations is concerned with:

Question 1
Poor lighting and ventilation in a tourist information centre

Question 2
An airline planning the number of staff needed for a
computerized sales office

Question 3
The owner of an outdoor activity centre carrying out a
'risk assessment' of his premises

Question 4
The main aim of the EU Package Travel Directive is to:
A Enable travel agents to sell more holidays
B Eliminate cross-border checks for travellers in Europe
C Give protection to the travelling public
D Abolish duty-free allowances

Questions 5–7 relate to the following information:
Specific legislation in place to monitor and improve health
and safety in the workplace includes legislation covering:

A Public order
B COSHH
C Food hygiene regulations
D Fire regulations and precautions

Under which category would a leisure and tourism organization be liable to prosecution if it:

Question 5
Failed to keep the area underneath a grandstand free from litter

Question 6
Failed to store toxic kitchen cleaning materials in a safe and
secure place

Question 7
Held a disco which led to complaints about noise

Focus 2: DEALING WITH SECURITY HAZARDS

Question 8
The owner of an independent travel agency is anxious to
learn more about the legislation which is in place to provide
security for his customers when they buy goods and services.

Decide whether each of these statements is true (T) or false (F).

(i) Any customers who buy the luggage that he sells in his
     agency will be covered against faulty workmanship by
     the Trades Description Act.
(ii) Misleading information contained in any brochures he
     stocks may lead to prosecution under the Sale of Goods Act.

Which option best describes these two statements?

A (i) T (ii) T
B (i) T (ii) F
C (i) F (ii) T
D (i) F (ii) F

Questions 9–11 relate to the following information.
A local authority leisure centre is becoming concerned
about security problems and decides to employ a
consultant to review its security measures.

The consultant suggests that the following measures could be
implemented:

A Internal closed circuit television
B Random searches of members of staff
C Regular patrols by security personnel
D The use of personal alarms

Which measure is the most appropriate for dealing with
each of the following situations?

Question 9
Thefts from cars parked in the centre's car park

Question 10
Graffiti on the outside walls of the centre

Question 11
Attacks on staff

Focus 3: HEALTH AND SAFETY HAZARDS IN LEISURE AND TOURISM FACILITIES

Question 12
Voluntary codes of practice are issued by the Health and Safety
Executive to help organizations operate in a safe manner.

Decide whether each of these statements is true (T) or false (F).

(i) A leisure and tourism organization is required by law
     to follow the codes of practice.
(ii) The advice contained in the codes of practice can be
     used by a leisure and tourism organization to develop
     its safety policy.

Which option best describes these two statements?

A (i) T (ii) T
B (i) T (ii) F
C (i) F (ii) T
D (i) F (ii) F

Question 13
As part of a routine fire practice, the manager of a hotel
discovers that the fire alarm cannot be heard in five
bedrooms located in an annexe.

What immediate action should she take?

A Write a letter to the guests staying in the annexe rooms
   stating that the matter will be put right as soon as
   possible.
B Close the hotel until the alarm in the annexe is repaired.
C Close the annexe rooms and move the guests into rooms
   in the main part of the hotel until the alarm is repaired.
D Put up a notice in the annexe stating that guests use
   the rooms at their own risk.

Question 14

The manager of a new leisure complex recently added to a city centre hotel is concerned about the safety of the chemicals used in the leisure pool.

Decide whether each of these statements is true (T) or false (F).

(i) An escape of chlorine gas is less dangerous than the fumes from spilt chlorine granules.
(ii) From a legal standpoint, he has no worries about the storage of the chemicals since the COSHH regulations only apply to public sector organizations.

Which option best describes these two statements?

A (i) T   (ii) T
B (i) T   (ii) F
C (i) F   (ii) T
D (i) F   (ii) F

Question 15

An assistant manager of a local authority sports centre has been asked to write a report for the manager on potential health and safety hazards in the building.

Decide whether each of these statements is true (T) or false (F).

(i) There will be fewer hazards in the dry sports areas of the centre than in the wet sports areas
(ii) All types of users of the sports centre will present the management with the same challenges in terms of health and safety

Which option best describes these two statements?

A (i) T   (ii) T
B (i) T   (ii) F
C (i) F   (ii) T
D (i) F   (ii) F

Focus 4: EXPERT HELP AND ADVICE

Questions 16–18 relate to the following information.
Advice on matters relating to health and safety in leisure and tourism is available from the following organizations:

A The police
B Health and Safety Executive (HSE)
C Local fire authority
D Local authority environmental health department

Which of these organizations is best suited to advise on the following?

Question 16

The implementation of the EU Package Travel Directive

Question 17

The temperature at which perishable foods should be stored

Question 18

The installation of window locks in a museum

Question 19

The assistant safety officer in a college has been asked by his line manager to collect some information on the organizations involved in health and safety matters in England and Wales.

Decide whether each of these statements is true (T) or false (F).

(i) The Health and Safety Executive (HSE) is responsible for establishing the general policy on health and safety.
(ii) The Health and Safety Commission (HSC) is responsible for enforcing health and safety legislation.

Which option best describes these two statements?

A (i) T   (ii) T
B (i) T   (ii) F
C (i) F   (ii) T
D (i) F   (ii) F

Focus 5: PROPOSALS FOR HEALTH AND SAFETY MEASURES, RESOURCE IMPLICATIONS, VIABILITY

Question 20

A small guesthouse has been advised by the local fire department that it must spend £10,000 on fire prevention measures before a Fire Certificate can be issued.

Decide whether each of these statements is true (T) or false (F).

(i) The guesthouse owner will be eligible for a grant from the Health and Safety Executive to cover the cost of the work.
(ii) The guesthouse owner will be eligible for a grant from the fire department to cover the cost of the work.

Which option best describes these two statements?

A (i) T   (ii) T
B (i) T   (ii) F
C (i) F   (ii) T
D (i) F   (ii) F

Questions 21–23 relate to the following information.
A bookshop in a popular tourist city wishes to double the size of its premises and include a restaurant in an extension. The owner has consulted widely on legislation concerning:

A Food safety
B Health and safety
C Planning regulations
D Trade descriptions

Which legislation applies to the following?

Question 21

A customer who trips over a trailing cable and injures her arm

Question 22

Inaccuracies in a poster advertising a Mexican evening

Question 23

The cleanliness of kitchen equipment

Question 24

The manager of an art gallery is looking for advice on health and safety issues relating to his premises. Which of the following organizations should be recommended to give this advice?

A The Arts Council
B The Health and Safety Executive
C The British Tourist Authority
D The Institute of Leisure and Amenity Management

Question 25
The operator of a commercial leisure and tourism enterprise is finding it difficult to meet the costs of urgent health and safety improvements.

Decide whether each of these statements is true (T) or false (F).

(i) Any remedial work recommended by the Health and Safety Inspector can be put right when the business is on a sound financial footing and at   a time determined by the operator.
(ii) The operator's public liability insurance will cover the cost of the necessary improvement work.

Which option best describes these two statements?

A (i) T   (ii) T
B (i) T   (ii) F
C (i) F   (ii) T
D (i) F   (ii) F

Question 26
Since 1 January 1993, leisure and tourism enterprises have had to meet new health and safety requirements. These have been established as a direct result of:

A The Development of Tourism Act
B EU Directive
C The Food Safety Act
D Act of Parliament

Question 27
The manager of a local authority leisure centre is concerned about health and safety hazards in his centre and has asked his assistant manager to carry out a safety check.

Decide whether each of these statements is true (T) or false (F).

(i) As the centre employs 12 people in total, the manager is obliged, under current legislation, to record the findings of the safety check by preparing a 'risk assessment'.
(ii) Training in health and safety is only compulsory for those staff working on reception.

Which option best describes these two statements?

A (i) T   (ii) T
B (i) T   (ii) F
C (i) F   (ii) T
D (i) F   (ii) F

Question 28
A small private zoo set in the Lincolnshire countryside is reviewing its health and safety procedures in the light of recent legislation.

Decide whether each of these statements is true (T) or false (F).

(i)The Health and Safety at Work, etc Act places duties on both the employers and employees at the zoo in respect of health and safety matters.
(ii) The theme park does not need to provide a written statement of health and safety policy as it only employs 25 people.

Which option best describes these two statements?

A (i) T   (ii) T
B (i) T   (ii) F
C (i) F   (ii) T
D (i) F   (ii) F

Question 29
A Health and Safety Inspector finds that an outdoor activity centre has serious defects in its electrical system which could result in death or serious injury to staff and visitors.

Decide whether each of these statements is true (T) or false (F).

(i) An improvement notice served on the owner by the inspector will result in immediate closure of the centre.
(ii) Prosecution of the owner is not an option that the inspector could recommend.

Which option best describes these two statements?

A (i) T   (ii) T
B (i) T   (ii) F
C (i) F   (ii) T
D (i) F   (ii) F

Focus 6: SECURITY HAZARDS

Question 30
A password is used by staff who use a leisure centre's computer system. What does this aim to prevent?

A Staff playing games on the computer
B Staff gaining access to customers' records
C Access to the system by unauthorized personnel
D Staff gaining access to databases

Question 31
An area manager of a travel agency chain is trying to raise the awareness of branch managers when it comes to security on their premises.

Decide whether each of these statements is true (T) or false (F).

(i) It is possible for the company to insure against loss of property but not loss of travellers' cheques.
(ii) Stocks of travellers' cheques should always be kept in a locked drawer.

Which option best describes these two statements?

A (i) T   (ii) T
B (i) T   (ii) F
C (i) F   (ii) T
D (i) F   (ii) F

Question 32
On cross-Channel ferries, a muster station is:

A A place where staff can obtain leaflets on safety
B A place where children are sent in the event of an emergency
C A place where a lifeboat is kept
D A place where travellers should report in the event of an emergency

Questions 33–35 relate to the following information.
A prestigious city centre art gallery and museum is having to review its security measures in the light of recent problems.

The problems include:

A Theft of small items on exhibition
B Large amounts of cash being held on reception
C Visitors straying into unauthorized areas

D Suspected thefts by staff from workrooms

Which security hazard would be helped by:

Question 33
Electronic 'tagging' of exhibits

Question 34
Random searches of employees

Question 35
Improvements to direction signs

Question 36
Security of information held on computer can present

leisure and tourism organizations with a problem.

Decide whether each of these statements is true (T) or false (F).

(i) Information can be copied without an organization ever knowing.
(ii) The use of a networked computer system will prevent access by unauthorized personnel.

Which option best describes these two statements?

A (i) T (ii) T
B (i) T (ii) F
C (i) F (ii) T
D (i) F (ii) F

Self-check Answers

1. Quite apart from the statutory (legal) necessity to provide a safe and healthy environment for both staff and visitors, it makes good business sense to give health and safety a high priority. An organization that manages its health and safety policy in a positive manner will reap the benefits of good public relations and an enhanced reputation amongst staff and the public in general.

2. Leisure and tourism organizations have been very pro-active in the way they have taken on board new technology equipment and systems. This means that the Display Screen Equipment Regulations will apply in many different contexts of the industry, including hotels, leisure centres, airlines, tour operators and travel agents.

3. The PPE Regulations are likely to apply in organizations involved with outdoor activities, grounds maintenance, water-based leisure, activity centres and motor sports.

4. Examples in leisure and tourism when noise can reach dangerous levels include rock concerts, motor sports events, discos, swimming pools and home music equipment.

5. In addition to locally based first aid courses run by local authorities in their leisure facilities, schools and colleges, the St. John Ambulance Brigade offers first aid training right across the country.

6. Elderly people are particularly susceptible to food poisoning and any risks associated with their possible impaired vision and mobility, such as blocked corridors, poor lighting and damaged floor coverings, furniture and

equipment. These hazards will also be applicable to disabled people, depending on the nature of their particular disabilities.

7. A positive approach to health and safety issues in a leisure and tourism organization can produce tangible benefits, such as an improved image, increased use, higher profits, enhanced staff morale and satisfied customers.

8. The main aim of the EU Package Travel directive is to give the travelling public greater protection when buying packaged holiday products. There is current UK legislation already in place to help travellers, for example the Sale of Goods Act and the Trades Description Act, but the Package Travel directive offers greater protection and enhanced compensation levels.

9. Fraud is an increasingly common problem for leisure and tourism organizations. An important first measure to try and reduce the risk of fraud is to have an effective recruitment policy within the organization with the aim of taking on staff with good credentials and references. While at work, staff should receive thorough training in handling cash and cards, with secure storage and access limited to named keyholders.

10. Restricting access to computers is one of the most effective ways of enhancing the security of information stored on computers. This can be achieved by using passwords and security codes to named users, or restricting the number of keyholders.

Answers to Unit Test

1.	C	7.	A	13.	C	19.	D	25.	D	31.	D
2.	B	8.	D	14.	D	20.	D	26.	B	32.	D
3.	D	9.	C	15.	D	21.	B	27.	B	33.	A
4.	C	10.	C	16.	D	22.	D	28.	B	34.	D
5.	D	11.	D	17.	D	23.	A	29.	D	35.	C
6.	B	12.	C	18.	A	24.	B	30.	C	36.	B

Unit Test Comments

Q1: Answer is C – workplace conditions.
The condition of lighting and ventilation is covered by the new EU directive on workplace conditions, which also covers such things as temperature and room dimensions and space in the work environment.

Q2: Answer is B – display screen equipment.
Under the new EU directive on display screen equipment, employers must plan work on VDUs and other computerized equipment so as to give staff breaks or changes of activity. An airline, therefore, planning the number of staff needed for a computerized sales office would need to take this into account.

Q3: Answer is D – health and safety management.
One of the requirements of the new EU directive on health and safety management is that an employer must assess the risks to the health and safety of employees and anyone else affected by their work and put into practice suitable measures to reduce risks and hazards. Organizations with five or more employees must record their findings by drawing up a 'risk assessment'.

Q4: Answer is C – give protection to the travelling public.
The EU Package Travel directive sets minimum standards that the organizers of 'package tours' have to comply with and details compensation available to travellers who are adversely affected when an organization fails to meet its obligations.

Q5: Answer is D – fire regulations and precautions.
Litter underneath a grandstand is a fire risk that organizations have to guard against and is an area which a local fire authority will investigate in the course of an inspection.

Q6: Answer is B – COSHH.
The COSHH (Control of Substances Hazardous to Health) Regulations place a duty on employers to make sure that all hazardous substances, including chemicals for cleaning, for the treatment of swimming pool water and for the control of insects and vermin, are securely and safely stored in the workplace.

Q7: Answer is A – public order.
The law protects the public against excessive and continuous noise, such as from a disco or sporting event, under the Public Order Act 1986.

Q8: Answer is D.
The Trades Description Act covers misleading information contained in brochures and other printed promotional materials, while the Sale of Goods Act is concerned with redress in the event of faulty goods or workmanship.

Q9: Answer is C – regular patrols by security personnel.
Neither internal closed circuit television, random searches of members of staff, nor the use of personal alarms would be as effective as regular patrols by security personnel.

Q10: Answer is C – regular patrols by security personnel.
The use of security personnel is most likely to reduce the incidence of graffiti on the external walls of the leisure centre.

Q11: Answer is D – the use of personal alarms.
While internal closed circuit television and regular patrols by security personnel will help to reduce the number of attacks on staff, the use of personal alarms by staff will give them the chance to summon help in the event of an attack in the workplace.

Q12: Answer is C.
Codes of practice in leisure and tourism are not enforceable in law, making statement (i) false. They can, however, be used in a court of law as evidence of contravention of health and safety requirements. They are often used by leisure and tourism organizations to develop their safety policies.

Q13: Answer is C – close the annexe rooms and move the guests into rooms in the main part of the hotel until the alarm is repaired.
In this situation it would not be necessary to close the hotel completely, since the rooms in the main part of the hotel are safe. Writing letters to the guests or putting up a notice would not be sufficient action, since the guests would still be at risk from fire.

Q14: Answer is D.
An escape of chlorine gas is just as dangerous as the fumes from spilt chlorine granules, making statement (i) false. COSHH regulations do not apply only to public sector organizations; they apply in all sectors of leisure and tourism.

Q15: Answer is D.
It is false to say that there will be fewer hazards in the dry sports areas of a leisure centre than in the wet sports areas. All parts of a centre should be treated the same from the point of view of health and safety. It is also false to say that all types of users of leisure centres present the same challenge; certain users, for example the very young, senior citizens and disabled people, will need special consideration when it comes to health and safety.

Q16: Answer is D – local authority environmental health department.
Environmental health officers have been given the task of 'policing' the EU Package Travel directive.

Q17: Answer is D – local authority environmental health department.
All matters concerning the storage, preparation and sale of food fall under the jurisdiction of the environmental health department.

Q18: Answer is A – the police.
The police have specialist crime prevention officers who advise on such matters as the installation of alarms, fitting of locks and general security of premises.

Q19: Answer is D.
The Health and Safety Commission (HSC) is responsible for the general policy on health and safety matters, while the Health and Safety Executive (HSE) actually enforces the policy, by employing inspectors and providing advice to organizations.

Q20: Answer is D.
Neither the Health and Safety Executive nor the local fire authority are in a position to offer grants to cover the cost of alterations to premises. In certain circumstances, local authorities can offer grants for improvements.

Q21: Answer is B – health and safety.
A trailing cable would be regarded as a preventable hazard under health and safety regulations.

Q22: Answer is D – trade descriptions.
The Trades Description Act would cover inaccuracies in promotional materials, including a poster advertising a Mexican evening.

Q23: Answer is A – food safety.
The cleanliness of kitchen equipment is covered by the Food Safety Act.

Q24: Answer is B – Health and Safety Executive.
Although ILAM may be able to suggest help in this case, the best source of advice is the HSE, which is specifically responsible for providing an information service to organizations on health and safety issues. Neither the British Tourist Authority nor the Arts Council would be in a position to help directly.

Q25: Answer is D.
Health and safety inspectors will determine the date by which any remedial work will need to be finished. Operators cannot wait until their financial position is healthy. Public liability insurance is to provide cover for operators against claims by individuals who sustain injuries while on their premises. It will not, therefore, cover the cost of any remedial work.

Q26: Answer is B – EU directive.
Six new sets of health and safety at work regulations came into force at the beginning of 1993, as a direct result of EU Directives on health and safety in the workplace.

Q27: Answer is B.
Any organization with five or more employees must record the findings of safety checks by preparing 'risk assessments'. Training in health and safety applies to all staff in an organization, not just those working on reception.

Q28: Answer is B.
Both employers and employees have duties under the Health and Safety at Work etc. Act The theme park will have to provide a written statement of its health and safety policy and bring it to the attention of all members of staff; this applies to all organizations employing five or more staff.

Q29: Answer is D.
In a situation as serious as this, the inspector will issue a prohibition notice which will result in closure of the centre until remedial work has been carried out. An improvement notice is for less serious situations, when the operator is given a period of time in which to put matters right. Prosecution is an option open to the inspector, regardless of whether a prohibition or improvement notice has been issued.

Q30: Answer is C – access to the system by unauthorized personnel.
Passwords are issued to staff to prevent unauthorized personnel, either from within the organization or outside, from gaining access to the computer system.

Q31: Answer is D.
It is possible for a travel agency to insure against loss of property and loss of travellers' cheques; statement (i) is therefore false. Stocks of travellers' cheques should always be kept in a locked safe, to ensure security.

Q32: Answer is D – a place where travellers should report in the event of an emergency.

Q33: Answer is A – theft of small items on exhibition.
Electronic tagging of exhibits, as well as items for sale in shops, can help reduce thefts.

Q34: Answer is D – suspected thefts by staff from workrooms.
Random searches of employees can help reduce thefts from staff areas.

Q35: Answer is C – visitors straying into unauthorized areas.
Good direction signs can help prevent visitors straying into unauthorized areas of museums, art galleries and many other types of leisure and tourism facilities.

Q36: Answer is B.
It is true that information held on computer can be copied without the owner ever knowing that there has been a breach of security. A networked computer system has the advantage that a number of different workstations can be accessed at the same time, but networking alone will not prevent access by unauthorized personnel.

UNIT 3

Providing customer service

Getting Started

Care of the customer and the awareness of his or her needs have become major issues throughout the UK leisure and tourism industry. The UK leisure and tourism industry has experienced dramatic changes over the last 10–15 years, from the boom days of the early 1980s to the recession of the late 1980s and early 1990s. The high levels of investment in new facilities and services seen in the 1980s have all but dried up. CCT (see page 00) has forced local authorities to examine the facilities they offer to their increasingly discerning visitors. The English Tourist Board has seen its government funding severely cut, putting into question the whole concept of a 'national' tourist organization.

Competition in the leisure and tourism industry is intense. Private, public and voluntary sector organizations compete for their share of the 'leisure pound' – that part of an individual's disposable income that is spent on leisure goods and services. Operators are finding it increasingly difficult to compete on price alone and are looking to improve the quality of their customers' experience in order to remain competitive.

It is fair to say that the expansion of leisure and tourism facilities seen in the 1980s was not matched by investment in the human resources of the industry – its staff. Except for some notable exceptions, the message that customer service and customer care are vital to the very survival of leisure and tourism has not been widely *practised* within the industry. It is true that many organizations have nailed their colours firmly to a 'putting customers first' strategy, but in times of financial cutbacks the resources needed for customer service training have often been sadly lacking.

Many people would argue that investing in a customer service approach is *more* important in times of recession since competition for customers and their reduced disposable income is even fiercer. A leisure and tourism organization which advocates excellence in customer service is sure to survive a recession better than one which gives the subject little attention.

It is against this background that we will look in this unit at the importance of customer service in the leisure and tourism industry. Element 3.1 begins with an analysis of the function of customer service in leisure and tourism. The detailed planning associated with implementing a customer care programme is covered in Element 3.2. The requirements of good customer service and customer expectations are featured in Element 3.3, while Element 3.4 looks at the evaluation of customer care programmes.

Customers Individuals or groups of people who buy or use a particular product, service or facility. Different customers will have different needs and requirements.

Customer orientation An approach which places the customer and his or her needs at the centre of an organization's planning and management.

Privatization The moving of previously state-controlled industries into the private sector, e.g. British Airways and the British Airports Authority (BAA).

Mission statement An organization's policy statement indicating what it is hoping to achieve and the environment in which it operates.

Non-user survey A survey that attempts to discover why people do not use a particular product, service or facility.

Evaluation A process that seeks to measure the outcomes of a course of action, such as the operation of a customer care programme.

Internal customers Colleagues in the same organization whose co-operation and support is vital to the overall success of the organization.

Essential Principles

3.1 The function of customer service in leisure and tourism facilities

Customers defined

Leisure and tourism organizations sometimes lose sight of the fact that without **customers** there would be no business. Their policies and actions do not always take account of the fact that customers are the most important people to their organization. Rather than being an interruption to the work of any leisure and tourism organization, customers are the very purpose of its existence. It is only when organizations begin to put the customer at the centre of all activity that a true customer service approach has begun.

Customers in leisure and tourism take many different forms. They may be enjoying their leisure time, or perhaps business clients. They will come from right across the age range, from different ethnic and cultural backgrounds, different social classes and varying home circumstances. Some will be extremely fit and active, while some will be less physically able, yet just as determined to make the most of their leisure time and activities. All will have different needs and will expect their needs to be met with courtesy and efficiency.

How is a customer service approach developed?

The key issues to be addressed by any organization which is committed to a positive approach to customer service include:

1 **Identifying customer needs** – knowing what your customers want is fundamental to the success of any business. In Unit 4 'Marketing in leisure and tourism' we look in detail at the various techniques which can be used to gather customer information. It is important to remember that the *gathering* of data is often relatively easy; what is often more difficult is putting into *action* the recommendations which the information suggests.

2 **Developing the right products and services** – having found out what its customers' needs are, the organization can begin to develop products which match these requirements to make sure that they are offered at the right price, in the right place, at the right time and at a profit.

3 **Measuring customer satisfaction** – customer service is a constant process to strive to be as successful as possible in satisfying customer needs. The products and services will need careful monitoring and adjusting to meet any changes which the customers are demanding.

4 **Developing internal systems** – customer service is not just about satisfying the customers 'on the other side of the counter'. Many leisure and tourism organizations, particularly large employers, will need to give attention to the needs of the *'internal customer'*, i.e. the staff working within the organization. Mechanisms to improve internal communications, including regular meetings, social events and internal newsletters, are all part of improving the overall level of customer service.

5 **Staff training** – training in customer service handling and attitude is vital for *all* staff in leisure and tourism organizations, not just those whose work brings them into daily contact with customers. Staff working 'behind the scenes', perhaps in kitchens or on maintenance duties, need to appreciate also that they have an important role to play in customer service.

Developing a customer service approach is all about creating the right **culture** within the organization. Sometimes referred to as a quality culture, TQM (total quality management) culture or customer culture, the end result should be the same, namely that customers who enjoy their experience come back again and tell their friends. Some *terms* commonly used to identify customer service approaches include:

- Quality pays
- Excellence in service
- Profit through service
- Putting customers first
- Caring for customers
- Service first

Factfile 1: Center Parcs – Customer care in action

The **Center Parcs** concept originated in Holland 25 years ago when Dutchman Piet Derksen hit on the deceptively simple idea of 'a villa in a forest', where city dwellers could escape from the stresses of everyday life and find real relaxation. The idea was so successful with the Dutch that Center Parcs expanded rapidly and now has 12 sites across Europe, with more in the pipeline.

Center Parcs opened its first UK village in Sherwood Forest in 1987, followed closely by a second at Elvedon Forest near Cambridge. A third village at Longleat in Wiltshire opened in the summer of 1994. The Center Parcs' concept is based on a high quality holiday or short break which cannot be spoiled by the weather (all UK sites have covered leisure pools with controlled temperature and atmosphere). The recipe certainly seems to work, with all villages enjoying over 95% occupancy and 365 days a year opening.

The company's customer care strategy is centred on its mission statement, which is:

> To give our guests a truly unique short break holiday experience which far exceeds their expectations.

In order to achieve its mission, the company has established a number of primary goals, which focus on:

- A visionary approach to creative management.
- Continually striving for the highest standards of product available.
- Having an approach to guest service which is second to none.
- A genuine recognition of its own employees.
- Investing in the business and the personal development of all staff.
- Stimulating repeat business.
- Optimizing profitability.
- Maintaining its position as market leader.

The company gives staff training a high priority, with all staff attending a three-day 'caring for people' course which aims to enable those attending to take personal responsibility for the delivery of excellent guest care. By the end of the course, all staff should be able to:

- Understand their contribution to the reputation and success of their department and Center Parcs as a company.
- Identify and utilize the skills necessary to create good guest relations.

- Communicate a professional, approachable image.
- Increase their personal confidence and self-esteem.
- Utilize the skills of promoting/selling the product and service.
- Identify and utilize the skills necessary to handle guest complaints effectively.

Further customer care training deals with issues such as:

- Team building
- Target setting
- Written and oral communication
- Interpersonal skills
- Problem solving
- Managing people

It is clear from the above initiatives that Center Parcs takes customer care training very seriously and is committed to the growth of a culture which stresses excellence in customer relations through individual personal development.

Why develop a customer service approach?

There may be many reasons *why* a leisure and tourism organization decides to strive for excellence in its level of customer service. In general, the factors which drive a customer-centred approach are either **internal** or **external** to the organization.

Internal factors

Organizational benefits
Implementing an improved customer service strategy can bring considerable benefits to a leisure and tourism **organization**. The principal benefits to an organization of striving for excellence in its customer service strategy are shown in Fig. 3.1.

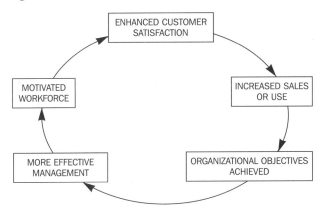

Figure 3.1 The benefits of developing a customer service approach in leisure and tourism

Figure 3.1 shows that the benefits are part of a cyclical process starting with enhanced customer satisfaction, which in turn will lead to more sales or more use of a facility. This in turn will help the organization to meet its objectives and develop a more effective management structure. Staff will gain increased satisfaction and motivation from working in a successful environment, which will again help to give customers a satisfying experience. Other tangible benefits of introducing excellence in customer service are likely to include:

- Lower staff turnover
- Fewer complaints
- Improved co-operation between departments
- Reduced absenteeism by staff
- Reduction in marketing budget (by retaining more existing customers)
- Improved security
- Less waste (of materials, time, money, etc.)
- Improved quality in other aspects of the organization's work

Most of all, the implementation of a customer-centred service approach will ensure that the organization will achieve its objectives and that all who have a stake in the business, whether they be shareholders or council-tax payers, will benefit.

External factors

The rise in consumerism
The rise in *consumerism* through the 1980s and 1990s has accelerated the emergence of customers who place quality of service, in its widest sense, above all other factors when making purchasing decisions in leisure and tourism. People are, of course, still sensitive to the price of the products they are buying. There is a growing belief among leisure and tourism organizations, however, that customers will pay a higher price for a higher quality product which is delivered with the highest levels of customer service.

Following hard on the heels of customers across the Atlantic, British consumers are becoming more vocal in their opinions of product and service quality (indeed many British people will have picked up the habit of speaking their mind in such places as the USA where customer complaints are not frowned on but used as a form of market research to be built upon). The introduction of television and radio programmes devoted to the cause of consumerism, e.g. 'That's Life' and 'You and Yours', is evidence that people are no longer willing to accept poor service and will 'vote with their feet' by taking their custom elsewhere.

Changing customer expectations
Customers in Britain today have far greater *expectations* of service quality than was the case even 10–15 years ago. In leisure and tourism today it is very much a 'buyers' market' where organizations have to compete not only on price but also on quality of service in order to win their share of customer spend. Service is no longer seen as peripheral as was the case in the recent past. There is considerable evidence to show that customers, although not always willing to complain openly about poor standards of service, will take action to show their disapproval.

Did You Know **?**

Research from the US Office of Consumer Affairs shows that one unhappy customer will tell at least nine others and that 13% of unhappy customers will tell at least 20 others.

Changes in customer expectations have been brought about by such influences as:

- Changing work patterns.
- Exposure to lifestyles from around the world via television and other mass media.
- Greater mobility.

- Changing eating patterns and food choices.
- Increased educational opportunities.
- More foreign travel with exposure to foreign customer service standards.

The result of these, and other, influences is a new breed of customer who, in leisure and tourism, is demanding improvement in both product quality and the level and standard of customer service: customers who are looking for *en suite* facilities in their hotels, who want to be able to play a game of squash at 9.30 in the evening, who want a particular newspaper with their freshly ground coffee at breakfast, who want to party until the early hours of the morning and who want to see the latest movies in plush surroundings – in a word, customers who want service excellence.

Competition

Leisure and tourism is an intensely competitive business. Organizations survive and prosper by having a *competitive edge* over the opposition and by winning customers from the competition. Because leisure and tourism is such a diverse industry, there is competition within sectors as well as between companies in the same marketplace. Competition within sectors means that the money an individual spends on leisure could be spent on any number of different leisure activities or products, e.g. a person could go to the cinema, an amusement arcade, go swimming, go to the pub or put the money towards a week's holiday in Greece. Competition between companies is commonplace with, for example, travel agents, tour operators, health and fitness clubs, theatres, etc. In such a competitive environment, excellence in customer service is vital for the survival of many organizations.

Leisure and tourism organizations are beginning to realize that they cannot compete on price alone. A number of tour operators, for example, have seen their profit margins reduced to such a level that their long-term survival is put in serious jeopardy. Many have decided to develop superior customer service strategies to help single them out from the masses. The race to attract and retain business customers in the airline industry has led to emphasis being placed on such factors as in-flight catering, standards of comfort and personal service.

Changes in the economy

The UK is experiencing a shift from a manufacturing economy to one based on service industries, such as banking, insurance, financial services, and leisure and tourism. It is estimated that about half of the country's gross national product (GNP) comes from the service sector. These fundamental changes have brought about a climate in which customers are dealing with staff in the service sector, either in person, over the telephone or in writing, on a much more regular basis than was the case in the past. This has led in turn to organizations having to respond to higher levels of customer expectation in the area of quality of service.

Did You Know ?

Economists estimate that three out of every four jobs in Britain will be in service industries by the year 2000.

Privatization, the moving of previously state-controlled industries into the private sector, was heavily promoted in the 1980s under the Conservative government. This too has led customers to demand a higher standard of customer service from the newly privatized companies such as British Telecom, British Gas and the electricity companies.

The importance of existing customers

Many leisure and tourism organizations talk about 'increasing market share' and 'targeting new customers' but sometimes overlook the importance of providing a quality service to the customers they already have. While new customers are always welcome in any organization, existing clientele provide a higher profit contribution and provide a much firmer base from which to develop further business.

Did You Know ?

It takes five times as much effort, time and money to attract a new customer than it does to keep an existing customer (*Source*: US Office of Consumer Affairs).

If an organization in leisure and tourism can develop repeat and multiple business relationships with its *existing* customers, it is more able to maximize its resources and achieve its ultimate objective. Creating excellence in customer service is obviously a crucial element in retaining loyal and valued customers.

Over and above developing a positive customer service attitude, there are many ways in which leisure and tourism organizations try to retain the customers they already have, including:

- Offering incentives to existing customers to do repeat business, e.g. frequent flyer programmes in the airline industry.
- Hosting events which are only open to existing customers.
- Giving existing clients first choice of bookings before launching them to the general public.
- Offering preferential rates for products and services to existing customers.

It is usual for customers to be categorized according to their volume of business with an organization, with those at the top receiving maximum incentives to remain loyal.

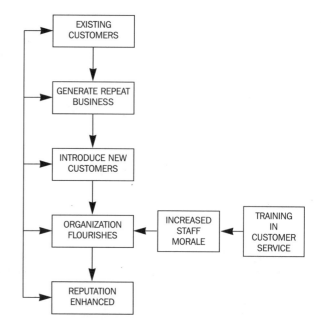

Figure 3.2 The importance of existing customers in leisure and tourism

The importance of existing customers is shown in diagrammatic form in Fig. 3.2. Figure 3.2 demonstrates the influence that existing customers can have on the success or otherwise of any leisure and tourism organization. It shows that existing customers generate repeat business and can attract new customers to help the organization to flourish. When linked to a planned programme of improving customer service, the organization's reputation is enhanced and all customers reap the benefits of an organization determined to give excellence in customer service.

Self Check ✔ **Element 1**

1. What techniques can a leisure and tourism organization use to identify its customers' needs?

    _____
    _____
    _____

2. What are the main customer needs identified by Center Parcs?

    _____
    _____
    _____

3. What might be the main *organizational benefits* from a customer-centred approach?

    _____
    _____
    _____

4. How might changing work patterns influence customer expectations?

    _____
    _____
    _____
    _____

3.2 Planning a customer care programme

The term 'customer care' is on the lips of so many professionals in the leisure and tourism industry today that we might be persuaded that it is a concept which is totally new to the industry. This is far from the truth as any study of the high standards expected by travellers in the heyday of Victorian Britain would quickly show. What is new is the almost universal acceptance that customer care is an integral part of any successful leisure and tourism organization.

Unit 4 will show us that identifying the needs of customers is an essential first stage in the whole process of marketing in the leisure and tourism industry. If identifying needs is considered as the foundation on which all marketing activity is built, then **customer care** can be thought of as one of the more important 'bricks' which go to make up the total experience being offered to the customer. Customer care is an attitude and an approach which helps to cement all the elements of the organization together.

Element 1 of this unit has shown us that adopting a positive customer service approach is essential to the survival of many leisure and tourism organizations. Customer care is a vital element of any customer service strategy since it focuses on the crucial interaction between customer and member of staff and, if planned and executed effectively, will help the organization achieve its overall objectives. There are a number of 'ground rules', however, which need to be explained before any customer care programme can be implemented.

Ground rules in customer care

There are many considerations which an organization will need to take into account before embarking on a customer care programme for its staff. Some of the more important, which we will look at in more detail, include:

*   Have clear aims and objectives.
*   Include senior management in the process.
*   Try to involve all staff.
*   Be realistic as to what can be achieved.
*   Examine your organization from the customers' point of view.
*   Be prepared to invest time and money.
*   Integrate customer care with other marketing activities.
*   Monitor the programme and evaluate results.

Have clear aims and objectives

A leisure and tourism organization which is planning a customer care programme must be clear as to *why* it is considering the scheme and *what* it is hoping to achieve from the programme. Unless management is clear on its **aims and objectives** for the programme, it will be difficult to measure whether anything has actually been achieved. The aims of the customer care programme will vary between organizations and even between different departments of the same organization. Private sector leisure and tourism companies will equate customer care with increased profitability while the public and voluntary sector providers will invest in customer care to provide enhanced levels of service to their customers.

Include senior management in the process

Every individual in the organization must be committed to carrying out a customer care programme if it is to succeed. This means starting with the **highest levels of management**, whether it be the chairman of the board, the chief executive, the head of personnel or the director of leisure services. Without their enthusiasm and support the programme will be doomed to failure. Some senior managers sometimes need convincing of the benefits of a customer care programme before they commit resources to it. This is where an individual from outside the organization can sometimes play an important role in presenting an objective view of the situation.

Did You Know ❓

Many customer care programmes fail through a lack of senior management commitment.

Try to involve all staff

Implementing a customer care programme which involves only 'front line' staff, such as receptionists and sales personnel, will do little to enhance the overall level of customer service in an organization. This piecemeal approach will not achieve the aim of promoting a customer-centred approach throughout the organization. **All staff**, whether on reception or in the plant room, will need some training in customer care and their role in helping to give the customer excellence in service. It is important also to involve staff in the planning and design of the programme, recognizing that they have valuable experience and expertise to offer. Any programme which is seen to be 'imposed from above' will create hostility and not help staff to relate to the benefits of good customer service.

Staff like to feel that they have 'ownership' of a customer care programme.

Be realistic as to what can be achieved

Management will need to be aware of not setting unrealistic targets for the customer care programme, since staff will feel that they have 'failed' if the aims are not met. Management should be in the best position to know what resources of time, money and equipment the organization can devote to the programme and any limitations or constraints that may exist. Outcomes should be framed within any limiting factors and should be planned over a reasonable timescale; it is always better to have **achievable aims** which staff will feel good about having met, rather than unrealistic outcomes which could lead to demoralized employees.

Examine your organization from the customers' point of view

Taking the time to look at your organization from the customers' perspective will pay dividends in helping to develop a customer care programme which is truly customer-focused. Managers and staff can become complacent and overlook problems which may be obvious when looked at from the customers' viewpoint. All customers have particular needs, especially:

- **Understanding** – customers value friendliness and acknowledgement.
- **Attention** – customers do not like being ignored or being given only partial attention.
- **Fairness** – they want to feel that they are being treated with fairness and honesty.
- **Control** – they like to feel in control of the situation and feel good about themselves and what they are doing.

Be prepared to invest time and money

Making the decision to plan and implement a customer care programme will have **financial implications** both in the long term and short term. Short-term costs will revolve around releasing staff from their normal duties to attend training sessions and employing a trainer to see the programme through. The trainer need not necessarily be a consultant employed on a contract basis from outside the organization; an existing employee with the right skills and attitude could be asked to do the job. However, many institutions which have used 'in-house' staff have found that their knowledge of employees and procedures within the organization sometimes acts as a barrier to fully achieving the objectives of the customer care programme.

The organization may well be faced with longer-term financial costs, since the customer care programme may highlight procedures, systems or equipment which may need to be changed in order for the staff to fully implement what they have learnt as part of the programme.

Financial help and advice for implementing customer care programmes may be available from such sources as the Department of Trade and Industry (DTI) under its 'Marketing Initiative' scheme and the Department of Employment.

Integrate customer care with other marketing activity

Customer care should not be seen by staff and management as a 'bolt-on' to other marketing and promotional work being carried out in the organization. Rather, it should be viewed as an important part of the **total marketing plan.** Staff who are striving to achieve excellence in customer care should be confident that:

- Effective market research has been carried out to determine customer needs.
- The products and services which the organization is offering reflect these customer demands.
- The products and services are effectively promoted to their intended audience.

It is only when customer care is integrated with all other marketing activity that it will achieve its full potential for the organization.

Monitor the programme and evaluate results

All the effort and expense of seeing through a customer care programme will have been wasted if measures have not been put in place to **evaluate** its effectiveness. This is why it is important to have specific objectives and outcomes against which to measure success. Techniques for receiving feedback from customers must be maintained to check whether there are measurable gains from the programme, such as the forecast increase in sales or the predicted rise in positive customer response shown via customer feedback.

Factfile 2: Wales Tourist Board – The 'Welcome Host' Programme

Welcome Host is a training programme devised by the Wales Tourist Board (WTB) with the help of the Training and Enterprise Councils (TECs) in Wales. The programme's aim is to raise the standard of service and hospitality offered to visitors to Wales. Under Welcome Host, staff from a whole range of companies and organizations who come into contact with visitors are given the opportunity to improve their customer service skills and so help the long-term future for tourism in Wales. To date, those who have attended the training seminar include staff from:

- Restaurants
- Tourist Information Centres
- Retail outlets
- Tourist attractions
- Petrol stations
- Hotels and guesthouses
- Leisure facilities
- Car hire companies

The key objectives of Welcome Host are *professionalism* and *pride.* The training concentrates on raising the level of communication when dealing with customers and visitors, and focuses on the tourism attractions of the local area. More skill and more knowledge lead to a greater level of professionalism and enjoyment at work.

The WTB considers that the benefits of the Welcome Host programme will be felt not only by those attending the training sessions but also by the *community as a whole.* For the community, Welcome Host should:

- Provide increased and improved services for residents and visitors.
- Encourage visitors to stay longer in the community.
- Stimulate repeat business.
- Encourage more spending in the local area.
- Increase visitors' local knowledge and appreciation of heritage and culture.

For *local businesses*, the Welcome Host programme is designed to:

- Provide better service standards for local consumers.
- Generate increased profits and repeat business.
- Tie into a high profile programme which is nationally recognized.
- Lead to heightened employee pride and sense of responsibility.
- Lower staff turnover and raise staff morale.

During the first 16 months of the programme, over 11,000 people attended Welcome Host training sessions, a number which far exceeded the WTB's target of 4000 for the first year of operation. Feedback from participants clearly showed that they had found that their awareness of the need for offering good customer care had been raised as a result of undertaking the training.

Source: WTB

Setting up a customer care programme

Having investigated the ground rules underlying the introduction of a customer care programme, we must now turn to the detail of the programme itself and the stages which are necessary to ensure success. Figure 3.3 shows the principal stages in carrying through a customer care programme.

Figure 3.3 Stages in implementing a customer care programme

We will look in detail at each of the stages identified in Fig. 3.3, in order to understand how it contributes to the overall success of the programme.

Organizational policy

One of the ground rules we looked at was making sure that the commitment to the customer care programme started at the top of the organization, in other words it must be embedded into its **policy**. All organizations nowadays seem to spend a great deal of time developing **mission statements**, setting out the reason for their very existence. This trend seems to be evident in all sectors of leisure and tourism, whether private, public or voluntary sector. Some mission statements are very long and detailed. For example, British Waterways' mission statement is as follows:

> Our business is the efficient management of the inland waterways system for the increasing benefit of the nation. We seek to expand business on the waterways by pursuing a commercial approach, providing a safe and high quality environment for customers, staff and local communities, and aiming for excellence in every aspect of our work. The waterways heritage and environment will be conserved, enhanced and made more viable for future generations.
> (British Waterways Leisure & Tourism Draft Strategy 1992)

In contrast, British Airways' mission statement is very brief:

> To be the best and most successful company in the airline industry.
> (BA Annual Report 1992–3)

The mission of the Wales Tourist Board is somewhat longer:

> The Board seeks to develop and market tourism in ways which will yield optimum economic and social benefit to the people of Wales.
> (WTB 1988–93 A Record of Achievement)

Mission statements are important in that they give an indication of what an organization is trying to achieve; the mission is often followed by specific objectives which will detail how it is to be achieved. Any leisure and tourism organization which is committed to excellence in its customer relations should say so in its mission statement and associated objectives. In this way, staff at all levels within the organization will be sent a clear message on the importance of positive customer relations, and customers will know what to expect.

The mission is a clear public statement which should be used as the basis for future activities by the organization. It is also essential that the mission is communicated to all staff and that they understand what the organization is trying to achieve.

Customer research

Once the leisure and tourism organization has developed a mission statement or policy which clarifies its commitment to excellence in customer care, the next stage of the customer care programme, namely **customer research**, can be put into action. It is essential to identify customer needs if we wish to provide them with a high level of customer care.

Did You Know ?

Without research, management will not have a clear and unbiased view of who their customers are and what their particular needs are.

Unit 4 looks in depth at identifying customer needs and the techniques which can be used to collect the data needed for the research process. The collection of information on customers invariably involves a survey of some sort which will collect both *factual* data (age, sex, employment status, etc.) and customer *opinions* on the facilities and services they use. Some organizations may wish to know why people do not use their services and may carry out themselves or commission a *non-user survey*. This may reveal interesting information on why people choose to use rival facilities and services and may prompt management into making changes to their own activities.

It is important to spend time and money on obtaining detailed information on customers; using inaccurate or incorrect information at this early stage of the customer care programme will put into jeopardy all that takes place from this point on.

Staff perceptions

Market research on customers will generate very useful information on their needs, habits and opinions. Just as important to any leisure and tourism organization which is striving for excellence in customer care is to know what its **own employees** think about the organization and their place within it. If staff feel undervalued and overlooked in their job, it will be difficult to inspire them in any activity aimed at improving customer relations. Depending on the size of the organization, there are different approaches which can be adopted to discover staff perceptions. A large company or public sector organization will probably carry out an *employee attitude survey*. This will often be filled in anonymously so that staff can express their feelings freely without threat of reprisal. A smaller organization may wish to interview all staff about their work attitudes or conduct a small-scale survey.

Employee attitude surveys should be filled in not just by 'front line' staff but by management as well. A survey may reveal that, although the majority of staff are very keen on the idea of improving customer care systems and practices, some senior managers may not be convinced of the merits of the idea. This may highlight the need for changes in management style which will need to be implemented if the whole drive towards a customer-centred organization is to be a success.

Customer care training for managers

All managers will need to be **trained** in their role in implementing a customer care programme and philosophy. Once the initial programme has finished, it will be the job of management to inspire the staff and ensure that the initiative is a success. Although there will undoubtedly be delegation of tasks, they will also be responsible for the monitoring of the programme and its constant refinement. Members of senior management will need updating in leadership qualities and team-building skills to ensure that the customer care programme is a success. Managers will need to be comfortable with people in their workplaces, be good listeners, trusting, open and fair. Management must keep staff fully informed of what is happening and why, which can be done through a combination of short meetings, newsletters and social events.

Customer care training for staff

We have mentioned earlier in this unit that it is a mistake to train only 'front line' staff in customer care improvement; all employees need to feel part of the drive for excellence. There are likely to be two main aims of the customer care staff training in leisure and tourism organizations:

1 To focus all staff on the new company attitude towards its customers.

2 To equip staff with the appropriate skills in dealing with customers, which will include such things as:

- Listening skills.
- Telephone technique.
- Communication skills.
- Dealing with customers with special needs.
- Dealing with difficult situations.
- Body language.

The training should deal with both *internal* and *external* customers (internal customers are people working in the same organization, who you liaise with in the course of your normal work duties). It is also important that training in customer care is seen as a continual process and not merely a 'one-off' event. Some organizations use a technique known as '*cascading*', with senior management being trained first, then middle management, who are in turn responsible for passing on the training to junior managers and staff.

Alterations to systems

All leisure and tourism organizations will have **systems** in place to handle their day-to-day processes. A commitment to improving customer relations and the establishment of a customer care programme may expose weaknesses in existing systems which will need amendment. The systems will need to be **customer-orientated** and not developed solely because they bring benefits to the organization. Looking at how customers are dealt with from their point of view will help the management to put in place systems which are far more 'user friendly' and likely to succeed.

It is at this stage in the customer care programme that management may consider pursuing external certification of their systems: *BS5750/ISO9000* or *Investors in People*. Having these certificates may give the organization a 'marketing edge' over the competition, but they require a great deal of dedication, hard work and money to put in place. The British Standard BS5750, for example, will involve the organization in extensive auditing and documentation of procedures, practices, processes and personnel related to any aspect of quality within the organization. Some leisure and tourism organizations, regardless of whether they wish to apply for full certification or not, use relevant parts of the BS5750 guidelines when developing customer care systems.

Developing customer-orientated systems for a leisure and tourism organization can only be totally successful when whoever is doing the development work has an in-depth understanding of the organization, its mission and its customers. It is only when considerable time has been spent on these three points that the actual development of the systems can take place. Once developed, the systems will need embedding in the organization and constantly updating to take account of internal changes and improvements.

Did You Know ?

Many leisure and tourism organizations are actively working towards BS5750/ISO9000 certification, as a way of improving their standards of customer care.

Monitoring and evaluation

Once the customer care programme is operational, it will need careful **monitoring** to ensure that a customer focus is being maintained. Left to its own devices, any programme will wither and die. Part of the development of systems mentioned above should be the means to measure the tangible benefits that the programme has generated, e.g. increase in profits, improvement in customer attitude, increase in usage, etc. The whole subject of the monitoring and **evaluation** of customer care programmes will be dealt with in more detail in Element 4 of this unit.

Factfile 3: Customer care at British Airways

BA is the world's largest international passenger airline with a scheduled network covering some 155 destinations in 72 different countries. It serves more leading international markets than any other European airline. According to the 1992–3 annual report, its mission is:

> To be the best and most successful company in the airline industry.

It lists seven specific goals which it is striving towards in order to fulfil its mission, including:

- To provide overall superior service and good value for money in every market segment in which we compete.
- To excel in anticipating and quickly responding to customer needs and competitor activity.

(British Airways PLC Annual Report 1992–3)

BA's customer service approach was started in earnest in the mid-1980s under the direction of Sir Colin Marshall, then Chief Executive and now President of BA. To create a clear competitive advantage, the company recognized the importance of adopting a more customer-centred approach to its activities. In 1984 a new corporate identity was introduced across all aspects of the airline, from the colour and design of staff uniforms, through changes to stationery and promotional material to the aircraft themselves. Market research was carried out with a view to establishing both customer expectations of the standard and level of service and the staff's perception of their role within the company.

The outcome of the market research was the development of a corporate training programme under the banner 'Putting the Customer First – if we don't someone else will'. The programme was launched with a series of corporate events for staff entitled 'Putting People First' aimed at fostering a spirit of teamwork and co-operation among employees. A parallel programme for managers was also introduced at the same time, with the title 'Managing People First' which encouraged a more open management style.

Subsequent advertising highlighted the excellence in customer service offered to all who chose to fly with BA.

BA obtains regular feedback from its customers via its market research department which uses a variety of data collection methods.

Quality in customer service has now become an essential part of the working practices of all BA management and staff. Individual departments have begun to introduce their own quality initiatives and individual members of staff are encouraged to put forward new ideas for improving the level of customer service. One of the major themes of BA's current work in this area is the need to *sustain* high levels of customer service and provide *consistency* throughout the company.

---

5. Why is it important for a leisure and tourism organization to integrate customer care with its other marketing activity?

6. Write down the stages involved in implementing a customer care programme.

7. How might you go about evaluating the success of a customer care programme?

3.3 Providing customer service

Good and bad customer service

Defining what is 'good' and 'bad' service is not always an easy matter. One person's idea of good service in a restaurant, for example, may be thought of by another person as only average. Whether a person is happy or unhappy with their service is essentially a *personal* experience; no two people have the same *perception* of what good or bad service means to them. The very personal nature of the customer service experience needs to be accepted by staff working in leisure and tourism organizations right from the outset. If customers are not treated as individuals, they will become disenchanted with the service they recieve and may choose to take their business elsewhere.

Although it is not always easy to define exactly what constitutes good service, we are all familiar with circumstances when the level of service we have received is either very good or very bad. In leisure and tourism, the following examples give a flavour of what a good customer service approach is all about:

- **In a hotel:** *Good* service would be when the receptionist remembers the name of a guest's child and the hotel provides a box of toys for her to play with. *Bad* service would be not attending to a broken shower in a guest's room immediately.

- **In a restaurant:** An example of *good* service would be when the management remembers that an evening booking is for a couple's first wedding anniversary and provides a complimentary bottle of champagne. *Bad* service is when a group telephones in advance to make a booking only to find when they arrive that the waiter has no record of the booking and all the tables are full.

- **In a leisure centre:** An example of *good* service would be providing free use of armbands for all the under fives in the swimming pool. *Bad* service would be the temporary receptionist telling a telephone caller that he (the receptionist) is not sure of the cost of hiring the indoor bowls hall for the day as he is new to the job and only comes in on Saturdays.

Obstacles to good customer service

Delivering good customer service, in all its forms, is a highly skilled task. It requires effort, motivation, commitment and support from both management and workforce. Introducing a customer service philosophy into an organization will inevitably involve *change*: change in attitude, change in work practices and change in the way that staff are rewarded. The majority of human beings are resistant to change and feel threatened when it happens to them in the workplace. By adopting a positive customer service approach, leisure and tourism organizations must be mindful of these anxieties on the part of their staff and may have to deal sensitively with a number of obstacles which can hinder the successful implementation of the strategy, including:

- Poor communication between staff
- Lack of staff co-operation
- Lack of commitment on the part of staff
- Lack of knowledge

Poor communication between staff

Poor communication is often the biggest single barrier to implementing a successful customer service strategy. It causes resentment among staff, frustrates managers and is often picked up by customers who are sometimes put in embarrassing situations. Managers can help to break this vicious circle by:

- Using simple language and communications methods that everybody can understand.
- Briefing all staff fully on their respective roles.
- 'Walking the job', i.e. taking the time and trouble to talk to staff about their jobs and concerns.

Did You Know **?**

An organization which looks after its staff is likely to be one that looks after its customers as well.

Lack of staff co-operation

We saw at the beginning of this unit that everybody working in a leisure and tourism organization has 'customers', whether or not they deal face to face with the general public. 'Internal customers' are people working in the same organization who you meet in the normal daily course of events and on whom you rely for services and support. Good customer service requires a team approach and a recognition that it is not just the customers 'on the other side of the counter' who need respect and consideration, but that colleagues within the organization need to be dealt with in the same supportive manner.

Lack of commitment on the part of staff

Regrettably, the 'take it or leave it' attitude is still evident in a minority of leisure and tourism organizations today; the restaurant waiter who gives the impression that he would rather be at home watching television or the sports shop assistant who is less than helpful when you try to buy some equipment. Thankfully, this negative attitude is being tackled in many organizations through positive management and staff training. In order that a customer care programme is not undermined by the indifferent attitudes of members of staff, it is the job of management to:

- Discover any underlying problems which are causing the lack of commitment.
- Put in place measures to deal with the problems, perhaps via staff training.
- Provide a supportive environment in which staff can flourish.
- Involve all staff in customer service improvement.

A commitment to the programme on the part of senior management often translates into committed individuals and staff teams.

Lack of knowledge

Some staff, particularly those new to their job, will take time to settle into their role and gain the knowledge and experience necessary to carry it out to the full. Induction training followed by detailed training on the services, products and systems of the organization should give these staff the confidence needed to sustain a high level of customer service and feel a valued member of the team. **Product knowledge** is vital within any leisure and tourism organization since it can help staff to:

- Inform customers of prices and features of the products and services on offer.
- Suggest alternatives if the client's first choice is not available.
- Give detailed information of particular services; in leisure and tourism it is often 'the little things' that either make or break the total experience for the customer.
- Raise the general level of awareness of other services and facilities that the organization can offer.

Handling difficult situations

From time to time, even the best trained and most professional members of staff will find themselves having to deal with awkward situations involving customers; two of the most common are dealing with complaints and 'difficult' customers.

Dealing with complaints

In general, British people are rather reluctant to complain. When they do, however, staff in leisure and tourism organizations must know how to handle the situation and even turn the complaint to positive advantage. Handled correctly, complaints can be thought of as another type of feedback which gives the organization a second chance to put things right and satisfy the customer.

What makes people complain?

Since all people are individuals, the reasons why they complain are many and varied. Some of the most common reasons can be broadly categorized into:

- **Being patronized** – nothing is guaranteed to turn frustration into fury quicker than a patronizing tone of voice on the part of the member of staff dealing with a customer. It is wise to assume that the customer has some knowledge of the product or service being bought and staff should be trained not to take a 'we know best' attitude.

- **Bad products or service** – to the customer, there is a strong link between quality of products and quality of service. If he or she has poor service in getting advice on buying a set of golf clubs, for example, the quality of the product itself tends to be put in doubt. Poor service, whether it be in person, on the telephone or in writing, is one of the main reasons why people complain.

- **Waiting** – people hate waiting around for attention and wasting their valuable time. The longer the wait the more likely customers are to complain. Mechanisms can be put in place to reduce conflict when a certain amount of waiting or queuing is unavoidable; entertainers are sometimes employed to keep the crowds happy outside London theatres and TV/video screens or the use of music can sometimes have a positive effect.

Specific examples of situations in leisure and tourism when customers are prone to complain include:

- Booking a window seat on a coach tour only to find that all the window seats are taken when you get on the coach.
- Not being able to get through to the information department of a tourist board as the line is constantly engaged.
- Having the time of the flight changed on your package holiday at the last minute.
- Being served a meal which has gone cold by the time it reaches the table.
- Finding that a hotel room has not been properly prepared for new guests.
- Not being able to find a parking space in a leisure centre car park.
- Being served cloudy beer in a nightclub or pub.

Did You Know ?

Research from the US Office of Consumer Affairs shows that 96% of dissatisfied customers never complain, but 90% of them will not return in the future.

How to handle complaints

Although each situation is likely to have its own particular circumstances, there are certain common approaches which are advocated for dealing effectively with complaints:

1 Listen attentively so that you get the whole story first time.
2 Thank the customer for bringing the problem to your attention.
3 Apologize in general terms for the inconvenience but do not grovel.
4 Provide support for the customer by saying that the matter will be fully investigated and matters put right immediately.
5 Sympathize with the customer and try to see the situation from their point of view.
6 Don't justify the circumstances which led up to the complaint and become defensive.
7 Ask questions if you are not clear on any points of the customer's complaint.
8 Find a solution to the problem.
9 Agree the solution with the customer.
10 Follow through to make sure that what you promised has been done.
11 In future, try to anticipate complaints *before* they happen.

'Difficult' customers

One step on from somebody who has a justifiable complaint is the customer who is intent on 'causing a scene'. Just like handling complaints, there are tried and tested ways of dealing with these awkward cases:

1 Never argue with the customer. It can often lead the member of staff into deeper trouble.
2 Never be rude to the customer, however rude they are being to you!
3 Let the customer do the talking and listen to what they have to say.
4 Try not to take any remarks personally. You may have had nothing to do with the alleged incident but are simply the nearest member of staff.
5 Try not to let them get you down or get under your skin; the fact that they wish to cause a fuss may be a sign of their own insecurity.
6 If in any doubt, seek help from another member of staff or senior management.

Factfile 4: Customer care at HavenWarner

Part of the Rank Organisation PLC, HavenWarner operates some 60 caravan and chalet parks in the UK, offering self-catering and half-board holidays under the Haven and Warner brand names. European holidays are offered through the Haven France and Spain brand using around 40 parks in Europe.

HavenWarner employs over 1000 permanent staff and up to 6000 seasonal staff at the height of the holiday months. All staff are trained in the importance of customer care through a series of training events focusing on:

1 Using the telephone effectively.
2 Why customer care is important.
3 Providing quality service.
4 How individuals can provide better customer care.
5 How to handle complaints smoothly.

All employees are given a staff guide to customer care as part of their training. The guide explains the benefits to members of staff who provide high quality customer service, including:

- Your job becomes more enjoyable.
- You acquire pride in what you are doing.
- You develop skills which make you more valuable to your employer.
- The skills you develop will be valuable wherever you go.
- You become more successful as more opportunities open up at HavenWarner.
- You become an important member of a team whose success you have helped to create.

Under the heading *'How you can provide better customer care'*, the HavenWarner staff guide mentions:

The Right Attitude

Employees with the right attitude are:

- Able to create a great first impression.
- Positive in outlook.
- Clean, neat and well groomed.
- Welcoming to customers – use their names if you can and remember a smile costs nothing.
- Proud of doing their job as well as they can.
- Ready to take the initiative.
- Friendly and sincere.
- Willing to act promptly and effectively.
- Ready to take extra trouble and make extra effort to give the customers what they need.

The Right Information

Informed employees are up to date on:

- The facilities, services and activities on the Park.
- Where the key people are located, e.g. Duty Manager, First Aiders.
- The surrounding area, e.g. places of interest, public transport, key telephone numbers.
- Health and safety procedures.
- What to do in case of an emergency.

Teamwork

No one person achieves quality service for the Park. That needs teamwork. Everybody is part of the 'team' and everybody must adopt common standards of service for the 'team' to succeed.

So be FLEXIBLE:

- Help your colleagues where necessary.
- Think about the effect your action will have on the rest of the team.
- Keep your colleagues informed.

Remember – it doesn't matter what job you do, to the customer you are the HavenWarner representative.

In the section of the staff guide concerning *handling complaints*, staff are advised:

Some 'Do's'

- Show interest.
- Show empathy.
- Listen.
- Restate the complaint.
- Agree a solution.
- Thank the customer.
- Turn the complaint into a compliment.

Some 'Don'ts'

- Don't be defensive.
- Don't 'pass the buck'.
- Don't give commands.
- Don't make unrealistic promises.

(Information courtesy of the Rank Organization PLC)

Self Check ✔ Element 3

8. What measures can leisure and tourism organizations take to counteract the most common obstacles to good customer service?

9. You run a travel company. Suggest some of the situations you might expect to bring about complaints. How might you *avoid* such complaints.

10. Suggest how you might effectively handle customer complaints.

3.4 Evaluating the operation of a customer care programme

There is always the danger when a leisure and tourism organization is implementing a customer care programme, that the staff will think their work is over when the programme is finally put in place. In reality, this is far from the case and is likely to be when the hard work really begins. If the staff and management see the customer care programme as just another campaign, it will start to falter from day one, and another campaign will need to be launched at a later date.

All those involved with the programme must realize that it is not a 'one-off' but is part of the process of creating a different *culture* within the organization, one which has customers as its focus. A customer care programme is not a 'quick fix' which will sweep away all the organization's problems overnight. Rather it is a *process* which will take time to achieve its objective of excellence in customer service. Customers' needs and expectations are constantly changing in the leisure and tourism business, so that any customer care programme must be flexible enough to meet the requirements of an increasingly discerning public.

All of these factors point to the need for constant *monitoring* and *evaluation* of the customer care programme to ensure that it is meeting the aims set by the organization. Monitoring and evaluation is the last link in the chain of customer care which begins with setting objectives and investigating customer needs, and moves through training of staff and managers to looking at alterations to existing systems. Monitoring is concerned with looking at how the customer care programme is operating in the organization, while evaluation means measuring its effectiveness. From a management perspective, evaluation is very important, because, 'If you can't measure it, you can't manage it!'

The need for monitoring and evaluation

Those leisure and tourism professionals who take quality seriously, enthuse and stimulate those working with them. To them, customer care can become a way of life, even a crusade. Following the route to excellence in customer service may change not only the way they operate at work but also their whole attitude to life in general, with a greater degree of openness and fairness. Sadly, not all staff within a leisure and tourism organization may share this same zeal or be given the opportunity to see a customer care programme through to its completion. Pressures on senior management may force them to transfer their time and commitment away from the customer care programme to some other function. At the same time, some staff may become sceptical about the benefits of the programme or there may be breakdowns in communications within the organization.

These sorts or problems highlight the need for effective monitoring and evaluation of any customer care programme. Measuring effectiveness allows an organization to do a number of things, for example:

- Develop training.
- Increase customer service awareness.
- Focus efforts.
- Evaluate the programme according to pre-determined criteria.
- Identify strengths and weaknesses.

- Reward staff accordingly.
- Monitor progress.
- Quantify achievements.

In practice, most organizations use monitoring and evaluation to achieve a mixture of the above points.

The type of questions which should be asked of any customer care programme include the following:

- What are the successes of the customer care programme?
- Are the original objectives of the programme still valid?
- How does performance to date measure against the established criteria?
- What are the major priorities for action to put things right?
- How can the organization build on these successes?
- What are the weaknesses of the programme?
- Have the customers' expectations of service quality changed?
- In which areas do improvements need to be made?

Programme evaluation in practice

There are three main elements to the evaluation of any customer care programme:

1 Setting performance standards/criteria.
2 Measuring to see if the standards are being met.
3 Implementing measures to rectify any shortcomings.

Setting performance standards

When leisure and tourism organizations strive for excellence in customer care, it soon becomes clear that it is not enough simply to encourage staff to 'give the customers a better standard of customer care'. There comes a point when the management has to define just what 'better' means. Employees need to know the standards against which their performance will be measured. Staff will need both a clear **job description** and a set of **performance standards** or performance criteria for each of the tasks they are responsible for.

Did You Know ?

Many organizations boast about their excellent customer service, but few are prepared to put in place the necessary performance standards to measure *objectively* just how good their service really is

---

Devising and implementing performance standards is a very time-consuming task and one which, if done properly, will call for an investment of financial resources from the organization. Large leisure and tourism organizations, with extensive personnel and training departments, may well carry out the task themselves. Smaller organizations are likely to appoint a consultant to devise the standards on their behalf or use criteria already available through professional bodies and other industry organizations.

Figure 3.4 shows an example of typical performance standards which could be used in a restaurant, hotel or any catering outlet. This is only a small section of a typical set of performance standards, but it shows the *detail* which is needed if the exercise is to be a success.

Staff role: Customer Service Assistant

Task: Serving a light meal or snack to a customer

Step: One – Greeting the customer

Standards: (a) Smile pleasantly while you wish the customer a pleasant good morning/afternoon/evening.
(b) Ask for the customer's order courteously.
(c) Use the customer's name if you know it to add a touch of warmth.
(d) Offer the customer a menu if he or she doesn't have one.

Step: Two – Taking the customer's order

Standards: (a) Be familiar with all items on the menu.

(b) Ask the customer for his/her order.

(c) Answer any questions the customer may have precisely and courteously.

(d) If something is requested which is not on the menu, suggest an alternative.

(e) Accept any special orders graciously.

(f) Thank the customer for his or her order and let him or her know how long the meal will take to prepare.

Figure 3.4 Typical performance standards in customer care

In addition to the detailed performance standards for specific job tasks, there will be the overall **objectives** of the customer care programme itself, which again must be specific and detailed. Examples of objectives of customer care programmes in leisure and tourism could be:

- For a leisure centre to achieve a 15% reduction in the number of complaints.
- To achieve a 10% increase in memberships sold for a golf club.
- To achieve a 10% increase in the 'excellent' category for responses to a customer satisfaction survey.
- For a hotel to achieve a 15% increase in bednights sold to business customers.

Using the objectives of the customer care programme and specific performance indicators as the yardsticks against which the effectiveness of the programme can be measured, the organization is now in a position to consider the most appropriate ways in which the measurement can take place.

Measuring to see if the standards are being met

Whereas a company in the manufacturing sector of the economy can reasonably easily set standards for the quality of its products and *measure* to see if the standards are being met, this process is much more difficult in a service sector industry such as leisure and tourism. However, although a difficult task, it is essential that any leisure and tourism organization which is committed to improving customer care develops systems and procedures to measure the effectiveness of its activities.

Some of the main techniques for measuring to see if standards are being met are:

- Surveys
- Observation
- Recording informal feedback
- Checking financial data
- Analysing customer data

Surveys

Surveys are the most common method of monitoring levels of performance in customer care. An organization will use a survey as part of a customer care programme to see if the targets it set itself are being achieved in reality. A survey provides a 'snapshot' of an organization's health at a particular point in time. If designed and carried out effectively, surveys are important to management since they measure the satisfaction levels within the organization and provide crucial information on which decisions can be made.

Surveys as part of a customer care programme can be directed at:

- **Customers** – a customer satisfaction survey at a leisure centre or a survey of visitors at a tourist attraction will provide valuable information about how the customer perceives their leisure experience; how they feel about the standard of service, the attitude of the staff, how any queries have been dealt with, etc.

- **Staff** – it is important continually to seek and act on the views of staff at the 'sharp end' of customer care. Without their continuing support, the programme will not succeed. An employee attitude survey will give them the chance to have their ideas and concerns formally noted. Management will be able to see if particular concerns are being expressed by more than one individual and act accordingly.

- **'Internal customers'** – we have seen that all staff in an organization have 'customers', whether or not they deal with the public face to face. Internal customers are colleagues in the same organization who may be in a different department but whose co-operation and support is vital if the move towards excellence in customer care is to be successful. Surveys can be a useful way of establishing whether all departments are happy with the progress of the customer care programme.

- **Management** – the managers in the organization should be surveyed routinely to see if they are clear on their role in achieving total customer satisfaction. If the management are unclear or unhappy about the culture of the organization, these fears may be transmitted to other staff and even customers.

- **Non-users** – it may be useful to find out why people are *not* using a particular facility or location but are choosing to spend their money on competitor products and services instead. Such a survey, which is normally carried out in the street or door-to-door, may highlight aspects of poor customer service which could be put right.

Observation

Observing what people do and say, whether they are customers, managers or staff, can provide useful feedback on the effectiveness of any customer care programme. It is common for an employee, who has been given clear performance standards to achieve, to be observed in the workplace by his or her *line manager*. Indeed part of the evaluation process of the programme may be a manager observing his or her staff and recording their progress over a period of time. Staff in certain leisure and tourism organizations may also be tested from time to time by management on matters such as pricing and product knowledge.

Customers may be observed in order to gain a fuller picture of their satisfaction levels. Staff may be given the task of 'mingling' with customers to listen to their views; people are often more open with their comments if they think their answers or reactions are not going to be recorded on a questionnaire. The sectors of the industry where observation of customers is a particularly useful technique include visitor attractions, restaurants and cafés, museums and art galleries.

Recording informal feedback

Any leisure and tourism organization which is striving to improve its customer care will go out of its way to seek customers' views in a variety of ways. To give the whole programme credibility in the eyes of the customer, it is vital that their views are listened to and acted upon. There are many occasions in the course of a normal day that staff in leisure and tourism will have the opportunity to receive *informal* comments from guests, clients and visitors. It is important that staff have the chance to 'pool' this feedback since it can be an invaluable management aid. It may be that staff discussion groups could be held once a week when the informal feedback could be discussed and perhaps recorded. Alternatively, customer feedback sheets could be issued to all staff for them to *record* the information as it happens, for analysis at a later date.

Checking financial data

Customer care programmes with *financial objectives* as part of their overall aims, e.g. for a hotel to achieve a 5% increase in conference business within 12 months, can be evaluated relatively easily. If the organization has a well-structured management information system, a check on sales figures should provide the necessary evidence.

> **Did You Know ?**
>
> Performance indicators (PIs) are an effective way of measuring the effectiveness of a customer care programme.

Analysing customer data

Data on customers, such as the frequency of bookings, satisfaction levels, volume of repeat business, level of customer spend, etc., are available from both surveys and internal records. *Analysing* such information, either manually or with the help of a computer-based system, will allow managers to see if performance standards and specific objectives of the customer care programme are being met.

Implementing measures to rectify any shortcomings

If the process of measuring actual performance against the performance standards and criteria shows that targets are not being met, measures to rectify the situation will need to be implemented as soon as possible to maintain the impetus of the customer care programme. The measurement exercise may highlight the need for alterations to existing *systems* and work patterns in order to improve matters, or perhaps more *training* for staff or management. Once the measures have been put in place, the process of monitoring and evaluation will continue using a mixture of the techniques described above.

Maintaining the momentum

We have seen that the planning, implementation and evaluation of a customer care programme in leisure and tourism is a very complex, time-consuming and resource-intensive process. Any faltering on the part of management or staff could lead to the whole exercise failing to meet its objectives. One of the most important tasks for management is to make sure that the momentum of the programme is maintained throughout. Some managers adopt a 'campaign' approach to this by involving staff in devising slogans, having T-shirts, posters and pens printed with the slogans, and arranging extra social and sporting activities within the organization. Such an approach is particularly useful in the early stages of the customer care programme to build staff loyalty to the scheme.

Managers and staff should not be afraid of publicizing achievements within the programme; perhaps a performance standard has not only been met but exceeded. Newsletters and noticeboards should be used to communicate such examples to all staff to help maintain the momentum.

Above all, it is essential that managers appreciate what their staff are doing to achieve excellence in customer care and reward them accordingly.

Self Check ✔ **Element 4**

11. Why is it important for a customer care programme to have clearly defined objectives?

12. Who are your 'internal customers' likely to be if you are the assistant product manager for a large mass market tour operator?

Unit Test
This test is one hour long. Answer all the questions.

Focus 1: CUSTOMER SERVICE FUNCTIONS

Questions 1–3 relate to the following information.
A large hotel on the outskirts of a Midlands industrial town has recently opened a health and fitness centre to cater for many different types of customers. These customers will have very different needs, including:

A Advice on health, exercise and diet
B Information on the availability of creche facilities
C Details of social events organized by the centre staff
D Information on advanced training programmes

Which is likely to be the main need of the following types of member?

Question 1
A single parent with two pre-school children

Question 2
The secretary of a group of local 'elite' athletes

Question 3
A new member who has recently moved to the area

Question 4
Customers visiting a theme park expect to have an enjoyable experience and are likely to come back again if the visit has been a success.

Decide whether each of these statements is true (T) or false (F).

(i) The attitude of all members of staff at the theme park will directly affect the customers' enjoyment of their visit.
(ii) The cleanliness of the site and the appearance of the buildings is unlikely to affect the customers' enjoyment of their visit

Which option best describes these two statements?

A (i) T (ii) T
B (i) T (ii) F
C (i) F (ii) T
D (i) F (ii) F

Question 5
Which of the following customer care situations would require the greatest degree of sensitivity to be shown by a waitress in a restaurant?

A Taking a person's order for food
B Helping a guest to choose from the menu
C Dealing with a complaint from a dissatisfied customer
D Presenting a customer with her bill

Questions 6
A small, independent museum has seen its visitor numbers and profits drop over the last three years and has not invested in any customer care training for its staff.

Decide whether each of these statements is true (T) or false (F).

(i) Introducing a customer care programme for employees is likely to increase staff morale.
(ii) Customer care training is unlikely to increase visitor numbers.

Which option best describes these two statements?

Focus 2: PLANNING A CUSTOMER CARE PROGRAMME

Questions 7–9 relate to the following information.
Some of the most common obstacles to planning a successful customer care programme include:

A Lack of staff commitment
B Under-resourcing
C Poor product knowledge
D Poor communication

Which obstacle is the most apparent in the following situations?

Question 7
A leisure centre receptionist who does not know the prices for the various activities in the centre's sports hall

Question 8
The management of a conference centre who, because of financial cut-backs, want their staff to attend the customer care training in their own time

Question 9
An assistant manager in a cinema who fails to pass on information about a rise in the number of complaints to the manager

Question 10
Travel agency staff on a customer care training programme have been told of their 'duty of care' to customers. Which of the following situations could lead to a successful claim on the grounds of negligence?

A An irate customer who bangs a travel clerk's desk with his fist and hurts his hand in the process
B Two customers who fight with each other over the last copy of a brochure, leading to one of them sustaining a broken wrist
C A customer who breaks her arm after tripping over a box of brochures
D An unhappy customer who tries to open the locked door of a travel agency during the lunch break and cuts his finger in the process

Question 11
The manager of a cinema where a customer recently broke her leg tripping on an unlit step in the auditorium is discussing with his assistant what would make a good defence if the customer decided to sue.

Decide whether each of these statements is true (T) or false (F).

(i) A good defence would be that a local electrician had been asked to prepare a quote for installing lighting to the steps.
(ii) A good defence would be that there was a sign in reception saying that the management accepts no responsibility for injuries, however caused.

Which option best describes these two statements?

A (i) T (ii) T
B (i) T (ii) F
C (i) F (ii) T
D (i) F (ii) F

Questions 12–14 relate to the following information.
Staff in leisure and tourism organizations are sometimes accused of:

A Showing a lack of understanding
B Being unfair towards customers
C Being inefficient
D Showing a lack of attention

Which of these characteristics is the most apparent in the following situations?

Question 12
The receptionist in a leisure centre who ignores a customer who has been waiting at reception for some time

Question 13
The operator of a ride at a theme park who charges two children of the same age a different price for the same ride

Question 14
A theatre receptionist who makes a mistake when calculating the price of a group booking

Question 15
The management of a cross-Channel ferry service is considering introducing an enhanced customer care programme for staff.

Decide whether each of these statements is true (T) or false (F).

(i) Maintenance staff should not be included in the customer care programme since they will never come into contact with travellers.
(ii) It is necessary to include senior management in the customer care programme.

Which option best describes these two statements?

A (i) T (ii) T
B (i) T (ii) F
C (i) F (ii) T
D (i) F (ii) F

Focus 3: PROVIDING A CUSTOMER CARE SERVICE

Question 16
The customer care plan for a leisure centre states that chemicals used on the premises should be stored in a safe place.

Decide whether each of these statements is true (T) or false (F).

(i) Chemicals must be securely stored to prevent accidental contact by customers.
(ii) Health and safety legislation states that dangerous chemicals must be securely stored.

Which option best describes these two statements?

A (i) T (ii) T
B (i) T (ii) F

C (i) F (ii) T
D (i) F (ii) F

Questions 17–19 relate to the following information.
Customers in leisure and tourism facilities expect that staff will be:

A Attentive
B Understanding
C Efficient
D Fair

Which of these characteristics is NOT apparent in the following situations?

Question 17
The operator of a fairground who charges two girls of the same age a different price for the same ride

Question 18
A hotel receptionist who ignores a customer who has been waiting at reception for some time

Question 19
A travel consultant who makes a mistake when calculating the price of a short break to Amsterdam

Question 20
Introducing a customer care plan is likely to have many benefits for a leisure and tourism organization.

Decide whether each of these statements is true (T) or false (F).

(i) The introduction of a customer care plan is likely to result in a higher turnover of staff.
(ii) The introduction of a customer care plan is likely to result in reduced absenteeism by staff.

Which option best describes these two statements?

A (i) T (ii) T
B (i) T (ii) F
C (i) F (ii) T
D (i) F (ii) F

Question 21
A customer in the café of a major tourist attraction complains to the duty manageress that the toilets are dirty and have no toilet paper.

What should the manageress do?

A Tell the customer that the matter will be put right when the next duty manageress takes over in two hours.
B Thank the customer and provide him with some toilet paper immediately.
C Ask a member of the cleaning staff to remedy the situation immediately.
D Tell the customer that the toilets were cleaned first thing that morning.

Focus 4: COLLECTING AND MONITORING INFORMATION

Questions 22–24 relate to the following information.
Four techniques used by leisure and tourism organizations for collecting information on their customers are:

A   Telephone survey
B   Electronic tally counter
C   Self-completed questionnaire survey
D   Focus group

Which of these is most likely to be used in the following situations?

Question 22
A major airline which is keen to have in-depth knowledge of why its business travellers choose different companies

Question 23
A tourist information centre which wants to keep track of how many people use its services

Question 24
A market research company which has been employed by the Scottish Tourist Board to discover the immediate reactions of buyers who attended the Scottish Travel Trade Fair

Question 25
Many leisure and tourism organizations now hold information on their customers on computer databases, in order to offer them the best possible standard of service.

Decide whether each of these statements is true (T) or false (F).

(i) The information held on database must be regularly updated to reduce the likelihood of errors.
(ii) Customers have a legal right to see information on them held on computer.

Which option best describes these two statements?
A   (i) T   (ii) T
B   (i) T   (ii) F
C   (i) F   (ii) T
D   (i) F   (ii) F

Question 26
The results of a visitor survey at a major tourist attraction in the Lake District reveal that customers are unhappy about the length of time they have to queue to enter the site and when waiting for refreshments. The management of the attraction decide to investigate the problem further.

Which of the following research methods would be the most cost-effective way of gaining information on the problem of queuing?

A   Postal survey
B   Face-to-face interview survey
C   Observation
D   Telephone survey

Question 27
In order to obtain reliable information on which to base its plans for expansion, a small art gallery which is open to the general public has decided to carry out face-to-face interviews throughout the summer months with a sample of its visitors.

Decide whether each of these statements is true (T) or false (F).

(i) The face-to-face interview technique is a cheap way of collecting data since no training of interviewers is involved.
(ii) Face-to-face interviews give the opportunity of gathering more in-depth information compared to self-completed questionnaires.

Which option best describes these two statements?
A   (i) T   (ii) T
B   (i) T   (ii) F
C   (i) F   (ii) T
D   (i) F   (ii) F

Focus 5 : EVALUATING THE OPERATION OF A CUSTOMER CARE PROGRAMME

Question 28
Surveys are an effective way of evaluating the effectiveness of a customer care programme in a leisure and tourism organization.

Decide whether each of these statements is true (T) or false (F).

(i) It is not helpful to interview staff to discover their thoughts and concerns on the operation of the programme.
(ii) Employing staff from outside the organization to carry out the surveys is likely to increase objectivity and reduce bias.

Which option best describes these two statements?
A   (i) T   (ii) T
B   (i) T   (ii) F
C   (i) F   (ii) T
D   (i) F   (ii) F

Question 29
Measuring the effectiveness of a customer care programme will provide an organization with much useful management information.

Which of the following information is the evaluation of a customer care programme unlikely to supply?

A   Ideas for further staff training
B   The performance of individual members of staff
C   The promotional budget of the organization
D   The focus for further development in customer care initiatives

Question 30
Individual members of staff are the key to a successful customer care programme.

Decide whether each of these statements is true (T) or false (F).

(i) Providing a member of staff with a detailed job description is essential if management expects him/her to perform effectively.
(ii) Establishing performance indicators for each member of staff will allow managers to monitor his/her progress.

Which option best describes these two statements?
A   (i) T   (ii) T
B   (i) T   (ii) F
C   (i) F   (ii) T
D   (i) F   (ii) F

Question 31
The manager of a sports centre knows that his customer care programme is effective when:

A   Staff morale is high
B   Surveys show that usage figures are rising

C   Surveys show that the number of positive customer
    comments is rising
D   There is an increase in customer enquiries

Focus 6: IMPROVEMENTS AND DEVELOPMENT

Question 32

A business travel agency has been criticized by some of its
clients for being slow to respond to requests for
information and confirmation of travel arrangements.

Decide whether each of these statements is true (T) or false
(F).

(i) The use of a fax machine would allow the agency to
    send immediate written confirmations to clients.
(ii) A dedicated telex machine would be cheaper than a fax
     machine to buy.

Which option best describes these two statements?

A   (i) T   (ii) T
B   (i) T   (ii) F

C   (i) F   (ii) T
D   (i) F   (ii) F

Questions 33–35 relate to the following information.
A consultant has reported on the operation of a customer
care programme in a major international airline. She has
concluded that extra staff training is needed in the
following areas:

A   Inter-personal skills
B   Information technology
C   Product knowledge
D   Selling skills

Which of these is concerned with the following situations?

Question 33
The use of a database for promotional purposes

Question 34
Details of the various routes that the airline operates

Question 35
A product manager being asked to form a new team for a
specific project

Self-check Answers

1. There are many techniques that a leisure and tourism organi-
    zation can use to identify its customers' needs, some formal
    and some informal. They include visitor surveys, suggestion
    boxes, observation, focus groups and staff feedback ses-
    sions. It is important to remember that informal feedback
    from customers is just as important as formal feedback via
    surveys when it comes to satisfying their requirements.

2. Centre Parcs aims to give its guests a truly unique short
    break experience which far exceeds their expectations. They
    offer high levels of customer service and quality products for
    customers seeking relaxation in a stress-free environment.

3. These will include a more motivated workforce, more
    effective management and increased sales.

4. Changing work patterns, including more part-time and con-
    tract work, will lead to changing patterns of demand for
    leisure and tourism products. Moves towards a '24-hour
    society' will mean that people will indulge in leisure pursuits
    at times which are most convenient to them.

5. Customer care should not be seen as a 'bolt-on' to other
    marketing activity, such as advertising and public rela-
    tions. A customer care programme needs to be inte-
    grated into the mainstream marketing activity in order to
    be fully effective. All marketing activities, whether an
    advertising campaign in a local paper or a sales promo-
    tion in a facility, will involve an element of customer care
    and service.

6. The main stages are 1. Organisational policy 2. Customer
    research 3. Staff perceptions 4. Customer care training
    for managers 5. Customer care training for staff
    6. Alterations to systems 7. Monitoring and evaluation.

7. Evaluation of the success of a customer care programme is
    concerned with testing that the original aims of the pro-
    gramme have been met. These might include increased
    usage, greater profits or an improvement in customer atti-
    tude.

8. Some of the most common examples of obstacles to
    good customer service include poor communication
    within the organization and a lack of commitment and
    co-operation from staff involved. Staff motivation can be
    increased by involving them from the outset in the plan-
    ning of any customer care activity. They should be fully
    briefed about their particular role and supported by man-
    agement to carry out their tasks effectively.
    Communication can be improved by holding regular
    meetings, distributing information widely and by manage-
    ment taking the time and trouble to talk to staff about
    their roles.

9. Complaints could centre around booking arrangements
    and documentation, quality of transportation and accom-
    modation or last-minute alterations to travel arrange-
    ments. Such complaints could be avoided by the
    company issuing detailed specifications to all companies
    with which it contracts travel and accommodation. Staff
    training in customer care will also reduce customer com-
    plaints.

10. A sympathetic yet firm approach is the key to handling
    complaints effectively. Staff should be trained to listen to
    complaints, agree a solution to the problem and make
    sure that what is agreed actually happens.

11. Without clearly defined objectives, a team of people
    working on a customer care programme will feel unsure
    as to what they are actually trying to achieve. This could
    affect their performance at work. Clear objectives are
    also important when it comes to evaluating the pro-
    gramme to measure what has been achieved.

12. 'Internal customers' are colleagues working in the same
    organization, on whom you rely for advice, information
    and support. In this case, they are likely to be the product
    manager, other assistant product managers, market
    research staff, people working in the flights department,
    finance personnel, brochure production staff, marketing
    people and computer systems specialists.

Answers to Unit Test

1.	B	8.	B	15.	C	22.	D	29.	C
2.	D	9.	D	16.	A	23.	B	30.	A
3.	C	10.	C	17.	D	24.	A	31.	C
4.	B	11.	D	18.	A	25.	A	32.	B
5.	C	12.	D	19.	C	26.	C	33.	B
6.	B	13.	B	20.	C	27.	C	34.	C
7.	C	14.	C	21.	C	28.	C	35.	A

Unit Test Comments

Q1: Answer is B – information on the availability of creche facilities.
A single parent is most likely to want information on the availability of creche facilities, so as to allow the parent a chance to do some activities on her or his own, knowing that the child is well cared for.

Q2: Answer is D – information on advanced training programmes.
'Elite' athletes will be particularly interested in details of advanced training programmes, which are likely to be geared to their specific needs.

Q3: Answer is C – details of social events organized by the centre staff.
People who are new to an area will want to have details of social events in order to be able to meet new people and make new friends.

Q4: Answer is B.
It is important to remember that the attitude of all members of staff at leisure and tourism facilities, not just those on 'front line' duties, is important to the customers' enjoyment. Also, that matters such as the cleanliness of the site and appearance of buildings will also affect their enjoyment.

Q5: Answer is C – dealing with a complaint from a dissatisfied customer.
Although taking a person's order for food, helping a guest to choose from the menu and presenting a customer with her bill are all important customer service functions, dealing with a complaint will call for the greatest degree of sensitivity on the part of the waitress, who will need to show respect to the customer, listen to the complaint, agree to put matters right and thank the customer for raising the matter.

Q6: Answer is B.
One of the greatest benefits of introducing a customer care programme is an increase in staff morale, since they begin to work more as a team and see tangible results from their improved customer service attitude. As a consequence, there is likely to be an increase in visitor numbers.

Q7: Answer is C – poor product knowledge.
It is essential that staff in leisure and tourism have good knowledge of the products and services they are offering to the public, so as to project a professional image and provide a high standard of customer service.

Q8: Answer is B – under-resourcing.
Asking staff to undertake customer care training in their own time is an admission by an organization that they either are not willing to commit the necessary resources to the task or do not have sufficient resources to be able to carry out the job effectively.

Q9: Answer is D – poor communication.
There must be clear lines of communication between all staff in an organization if the customer care programme is to be totally effective.

Q10: Answer is C – a customer who breaks her arm after tripping over a box of brochures.
Options A, B and D are outside the control of the travel agency staff. Option C, however, is certainly within their control and could be the grounds for a successful claim for negligence.

Q11: Answer is D.
Neither defence would be suitable in this case. Putting up signs does not compensate for negligent acts, nor does getting a quote for work to be carried out at some time in the future.

Q12: Answer is D – showing a lack of attention.
Customers who are ignored by staff may well decide to 'vote with their feet' and go elsewhere.

Q13: Answer is B – being unfair towards customers.
Staff must treat customers fairly if they do not want to create bad feeling and give their organization a poor image.

Q14: Answer is C – being inefficient.
A lack of efficiency and attention to detail can itself cause bad feeling, particularly when money is involved. Inexperienced staff should not be afraid of seeking help from other members of their team if they are having difficulty with calculations.

Q15: Answer is C.
All staff should be involved in customer care training, including maintenance staff who, although not working directly with customers, are likely to come into contact with them from time to time. Senior management should also be included in a customer care programme, so as to show their full commitment to its success.

Q16: Answer is A.
Many leisure and tourism facilities use potentially hazardous chemicals in the course of their normal activities. They must be securely stored, not only because legislation states that this has to be done (COSHH), but also because it makes normal business sense, so as to prevent accidental contact by customers.

Q17: Answer is D – fair.
A lack of fairness may lead to bad feeling and a poor image for the organization.

Q18: Answer is A – attentive.
Reception staff must be attentive at all times. If they are particularly busy, they should call for extra help, in order to retain the goodwill of their customers.

Q19: Answer is C – efficient.
Mistakes can be costly, not only in terms of lost income, but also from the point of view of a lack of confidence in the organization on the part of the customer.

Q20: Answer is C.
Many organizations that introduce customer care programmes benefit from a reduced turnover of staff and reduced absenteeism. The employees feel happier in their work and see tangible benefits in terms of satisfied customers, which in turn leads to a more motivated workforce with less absenteeism and a lower turnover of staff.

Q21: Answer is C – ask a member of the cleaning staff to remedy the situation immediately.
Telling a customer that the matter will be put right in the next shift is not good enough, nor is the fact that the toilets were cleaned first thing in the morning. Providing toilet paper for the customer is likely to turn a difficult situation into a disastrous one. Customers expect that their wishes will be seen to immediately, with as little fuss as possible.

Q22: Answer is D – focus group.
Focus groups involve in-depth analysis of customers' buying habits by highly trained researchers. They are expensive, but do yield very useful results for large leisure and tourism organizations on how their products should be developed and marketed.

Q23: Answer is B – electronic tally counter.
An electronic tally counter is a cost effective way of monitoring numbers of people or vehicles entering and leaving premises and sites, such as tourist information centres, country parks and tourist attractions.

Q24: Answer is A – telephone survey.
Although not widespread in leisure and tourism, telephone surveys are often used as a way of obtaining a fast response to an event, such as an exhibition or trade fair. They frequently operate on a business-to-business basis rather than directly with consumers.

Q25: Answer is A.
Databases of customer details must be frequently updated in order to be as cost effective as possible and to minimize the amount of misdirected information. Under the terms of the Data Protection Act, customers do have a legal right to see any information on them held on computer. They can also insist on errors being put right and may be able to claim compensation if incorrect information persists.

Q26: Answer is C – observation.
Observing the behaviour of visitors and vehicles is an effective way of finding solutions to particular problems in leisure and tourism facilities. Observation may be carried out with the help of electronic devices, such as time-lapse photography and CCTV.

Q27: Answer is C.
To be totally effective, a survey using face-to-face interviews should be carried out by trained interviewers, thereby making it a relatively expensive technique for collecting primary data. Face-to-face interviews, however, do give the opportunity of gathering more in-depth information compared with self-completed questionnaires, since the interviewers can prompt respondents and explain the meaning of questions if necessary.

Q28: Answer is C.
Staff should always be involved in evaluating the effectiveness of a customer care programme, since they may have valuable information and ideas to contribute. Organizations often employ outside agencies to carry out their research, in order to make the exercise more objective and reduce bias.

Q29: Answer is C – the promotional budget of the organization.
While the evaluation of a customer care programme is likely to suggest ideas for further staff training, highlight the performance of individual members of staff and provide ideas for further customer care initiatives, it is unlikely to supply information relating to the promotional budget of the organization.

Q30: Answer is A.
Without a clear job description, a member of staff will be unsure as to the boundaries of his or her work, which may hamper effective performance. Performance indicators (PIs) are a good way for management to monitor the progress of individual members of staff. PIs are sometimes linked to performance-related pay schemes.

Q31: Answer is C – surveys show that the number of positive comments is rising.
The fact that staff morale is high, or that usage figures are up in a facility, or that there is an increase in customer enquiries, may be the result of factors other than the introduction of a customer care programme. Rising numbers of positive customer comments, however, will be a direct result of increased standards in customer care.

Q32: Answer is B.
Fax machines are an excellent way of sending immediate written confirmations to clients. A dedicated telex machine will cost much more than a fax machine; these are now readily available in many high street stores.

Q33: Answer is B – information technology.
Databases are an important information technology aid to effective management.

Q34: Answer is C – product knowledge.
Information such as details of airline fare costs and routes is essential product knowledge for all those involved in selling and marketing.

Q35: Answer is A – inter-personal skills.
Skills such as negotiating, team building and effective communication, will be essential for a manager who is asked to form a new team.

UNIT 4

Marketing in leisure and tourism

Getting Started

Many leisure and tourism professionals consider that marketing is the single most important management function in their organization. Large sums of money may be invested in new developments such as hotels, resort complexes and leisure centres, but without effective marketing to attract customers the projects may fail.

Marketing is concerned with identifying customer needs, developing products and services to meet these needs and communicating with the customers using a range of promotional techniques. The Chartered Institute of Marketing defines marketing as:

> The management process for identifying and satisfying customer needs profitably.

There are many myths in existence concerning the concept of marketing. The most common is that marketing is the same as advertising. This is not true, although advertising is a very important part of marketing and, since it is the most conspicuous part of the process with millions of pounds spent on television and press adverts every year, it is understandable that confusion between the two exists. Advertising is just one of a number of promotional techniques used in marketing.

Another misconception is that marketing is the same as selling. Again this is not true. Selling is a vital part of marketing, particularly in leisure and tourism, but it is just that, a *part* of a much wider process.

Another myth surrounding marketing is that it only occurs in private sector leisure and tourism enterprises. It is now widely accepted that marketing is just as important in the public and voluntary sectors of the leisure and tourism industry, since, like private sector operators, they too have 'customers'.

Some leisure and tourism organizations think that they will be successful in their marketing merely by employing staff with lively personalities. A lively personality is a good starting point for training in the promotional aspects of marketing, but activities such as market research, while perhaps not so glamorous, are equally vital to successful marketing.

Element 4.1 of this unit looks at the marketing process in l eisure and tourism and the importance of identifying market needs. Element 4.2 considers the marketing mix and how it is adjusted to exploit market opportunities. Element 4.3 investigates promotional activities in leisure and tourism, while Element 4.4 looks at how promotional activities are evaluated.

Branding Giving a product or service an identifiable name so as to develop customer loyalty and increase sales.

Macro environment Factors and influences outside of an organization, over which it has little control, but which are likely to influence its operation and profitability, e.g. the state of the economy and political stability.

Marketing plan The formal identification of the marketing objectives of an organization and the means by which the objectives will be achieved.

Market segmentation The technique of subdividing the market into different groups who share similar characteristics. Allows an organization to target its marketing activity at particular market segments.

Market share An organization's share of the total market for a product or service.

Micro environment Factors that are close to an organization and over which it has some degree of control, e.g. staff and customers.

Promotion The process by which existing and potential customers are made aware of the availability of products and services.

Sampling The process by which a proportion of a total population is selected for research purposes.

SWOT analysis The strengths, weaknesses, opportunities and threats concerning an organization.

The marketing mix Also known as the 4 P's (price, product, promotion, place). Organizations will seek to balance these four variables so as to have maximum marketing impact.

Essential Principles

4.1 Identifying market needs for products and services

The marketing process in leisure and tourism

Being a service industry, the **marketing of leisure and tourism** has similarities with marketing in other sectors, particularly retail. However, leisure and tourism has certain characteristics which are specific and which, when taken together, give marketing within this sector a special character. To begin with, leisure and tourism products are *perishable* (an airline seat not sold today cannot be resold tomorrow). Also, much activity is *seasonal* which poses a particular challenge to managers in leisure and tourism. Above all, however, leisure and tourism marketing differs from so many other service sectors in that it is all about selling experiences. We shall see later in this unit that many products are *intangible*; you are not actually buying the holiday, for example, when you hand over your money to the travel company, but an *expectation* of what you hope to experience on that holiday.

The **marketing process** can be explained with the help of the simplified diagram shown in Fig. 4.1.

Figure 4.1 The marketing process in leisure and tourism

Figure 4.1 shows us that:

- Any good marketing strategy (the process by which marketing plans are put into action) should start with the customer as its focus. Organizations need to know who their customers are, where they come from, what they want from the facility, how much they are willing to pay, whether they are satisfied with the service on offer and so on, in order to be able to make the right marketing decisions.
- Once the customers' needs are known, it is much easier to develop products and services that they will want to use. By giving attention to such matters as pricing and the location/accessibility of facilities, leisure and tourism organizations will be able to give the customer what he or she wants, at the right time, in the right place and at the right price.

- There are many ways of communicating with customers, including advertising, direct mail, sponsorship, sales promotions and public relations activity.
- Marketing is not something that an organization does once and then forgets about. It is a dynamic activity which reflects the ever-changing tastes and fashions of the general public. It is essential, therefore, that all leisure and tourism organizations evaluate what they are doing at each stage of the marketing process, by asking such questions as:
  - Is our promotional work reaching its intended target?
  - Are our customers the same today as they were three years ago?
  - Does our mix of activities meet their needs today?
  - What are our competitors doing?
  - Are we offering value for money?
  - Are we providing a good level of customer service?

It is only by constantly monitoring activity that managers can be sure of success in their marketing activity.

Marketing objectives

Leisure and tourism organizations will have different *objectives* and their marketing style and practice will tend to reflect this (in addition, the size of the marketing budget will influence what is done and how it is carried out). A large multinational hotel chain, for example, may make extensive use of various 'aggressive' sales techniques (telesales, for example) in order to achieve maximum capacity in its hotels. A travel agent is likely to take a more 'low key' approach to selling by perhaps sending a quarterly newsletter to all existing clients. A leisure centre run by the local council, whose primary aim is the provision of a service to the local community, will use local newspapers, leaflet drops and local radio to get its message across. Voluntary groups may be able to secure the services of well-known personalities free of charge to help their promotional work and they may be able to get 'free' editorial coverage in the local and national press.

Market versus product orientation

We have seen the importance of putting the customer at the heart of the marketing process; this is known as **market orientation** (as opposed to **product orientation** which focuses on the products being developed rather than their intended buyers). Organizations within leisure and tourism must adopt this notion of market orientation at all levels if they are to be successful in keeping their existing customers and attracting new ones. Companies such as British Airways, Virgin and Mecca Leisure all adopt practices which put the customer first, while public sector providers, including British Rail and local authority leisures services departments, provide their staff with training in improving customer service.

Strategic versus tactical marketing

Strategic marketing is marketing activity which is planned well in advance and which has clear medium-term and long-term objectives, e.g. becoming the number one tour operator from the UK to the USA or increasing the use of a sports centre by 50% within 12 months. **Tactical marketing** is marketing activity which is unforeseen and unplanned and which is carried out in response to a particular problem or action by a competitor.

An example of tactical marketing activity would be the re-launch of brochures by a tour operator which suddenly finds that its prices have been undercut by a rival company. In an increasingly competitive marketplace, tactical marketing has to be used extensively by leisure and tourism organizations simply to hold on to their existing market share.

Identifying market needs

Characteristics of customers

In Unit 3, we saw how vital it is for any leisure and tourism organization to put the **customer** at the centre of all its activity and to develop a market- or customer-orientated culture. Organizations which fail to understand or implement this concept will not flourish in the highly competitive leisure and tourism sector of the economy.

In order to be able to put the customer as the hub of all activity, the organization will need to obtain certain basic information on the characteristics of its customers. This is likely to include:

1 How many customers are there?
2 What proportion of them are male and what proportion female?
3 What ages are they?
4 How much money do they spend at the facility?
5 How far do they travel to use the facility?
6 What is their attitude to the facility?
7 What is their income level?
8 How long do they spend at the facility?
9 Are there any improvements they would like to see?

Without these basic data, any leisure and tourism organization, be it a leisure centre, museum, art gallery, country house hotel or visitor attraction, will be basing its management decisions purely on guesswork. Decisions on pricing, design of promotional material, advertising media used and choice of menus, can only be carried out effectively with accurate knowledge of present and future customers.

Customers and markets

In the leisure and tourism industry, the term 'customer' means different things to different people. In the private sector, customers are quite obviously those individuals and groups who buy leisure goods and services: anything from a meal in a restaurant to a two-hour bingo session or a two-week holiday in the USA. In the public and voluntary sectors, the definition of a 'customer' is not quite so easy. Those who *pay* to use a local authority leisure centre are certainly customers, but so are those who use services for which there is *no charge*, such as the playground at the local park. Although there may be no direct charge for the playground, the people will have indirectly contributed to its cost by paying central and local taxes. Members of voluntary bodies, such as the Royal Society for the Protection of Birds or the Youth Hostels Association (YHA), are again 'customers' of their particular organization. They too must be treated with courtesy and respect, since without them the organization would not exist.

Leisure and tourism organizations often talk about the **market** for a particular product; this is the total number of people who currently buy or use a particular product or service (the potential market is the total number of people who *could* consume, given the right circumstances). In the private sector, the total market is usually expressed in financial terms. For example, Fig. 4.2 shows the estimated values of selected UK markets in 1988.

Item	£ million
New motor cars	17,000
Beer	9,793
Cigarettes	7,001
Casinos	1,722
Instant coffee	573
Ice cream	486
Disposable nappies	330
British people's spending on holidays	12,880
Overseas visitors' spending in the UK	7,065
Spending by British on all leisure activities	76,060

Figure 4.2 Estimated value of selected UK markets 1988. *Source*: Various including Leisure Consultants and *Social Trends*

Figure 4.2 shows that large sums of money are spent by people in Britain during their leisure time. Examples and data given in Unit 1 suggest that spending on leisure is set to go on increasing up to and beyond the year 2000.

The size of the market for a particular facility, e.g. a tourist attraction, can be calculated reasonably accurately by using population statistics readily available to the general public. Census data will indicate numbers of households and numbers of people by age groups. By calculating the population within different travel time zones, the attraction will have a good indication of its total market.

Did You Know ?

Private sector operators in leisure and tourism are constantly trying to increase, or at least maintain, their market share in an industry which is becoming increasingly competitive.

Not all customers are the same!

If we start from the point of view that everybody is unique, then the number and range of customers for any leisure and tourism product is immense. The characteristics of customers (e.g. their gender, social class and income level) will vary between different leisure and tourism facilities, while their habits, tastes and even moods will change constantly over time and in different locations. As a general rule, most British people feel better when in a sunny climate. Customers' expectations will also differ depending on, for example, their religion, education and cultural background.

An important group of customers are those with *special needs*; the elderly, young children, disabled people and ethnic minorities, will all need particular attention.

In order to simplify the marketing process and make it more effective, many attempts have been made to classify the population into different categories according to certain characteristics. Three of the best-known classification techniques are:

• Socio-economic classification
• Life cycle classification
• Lifestyle classification

We will look at each of these in a little more detail.

Socio-economic classification

For many years, this **JICNARS** (**Joint Industry Committee for**

National Readership Surveys) classification based on 'social class' was the only one available to marketeers. Individuals were placed into one of six categories according to the occupation of the head of their household (see Fig. 4.3).

Social grade	Social class	Typical occupations
A	Upper middle	Higher managerial, administrative and professional (e.g. judges, surgeons)
B	Middle	Intermediate managerial and administrative (e.g. lawyers, teachers, doctors)
C1	Lower middle	Supervisory, clerical, junior management (e.g. bank clerk, estate agent)
C2	Skilled working	Skilled manual workers (e.g. joiner, welder)
D	Working	Semi-skilled and unskilled manual workers (e.g. driver, postman, porter)
E	Those at lowest level of subsistence	Pensioners, widows, casual workers, students, the unemployed

Figure 4.3   Socio-economic classification

The underlying principle of the **socio-economic classification** is that those in each category will display similar patterns of buyer behaviour, have similar levels of disposable income and share similar values. It is assumed, also, that those at the top of the scale will have the highest level of disposable income. Clearly, there are a number of problems with this classification system:

- Many skilled manual workers (C2) may well have a higher *disposable* income than those in the C1, B or A social grades when payment for items such as private education and private health care are taken into account.
- If the Managing Director of a large PLC loses her job, she will immediately move from social grade A to social grade E.
- It is too much of a generalization to expect all those in a particular category to have similar characteristics. For example, a surgeon (social grade A) may choose to read the *Daily Mirror*, a newspaper read mostly by working class people (social grade D).
- When the whole social fabric of the nation is changing so rapidly, it is even questionable who the head of household is. Today, the heads of many households may be unemployed and in receipt of state benefits.

Life cycle classification

The shortcomings of the socio-economic classification led marketeers to investigate if there wasn't a better way of categorizing segments of the population. The **life cycle** concept puts an individual into one of nine categories which are based, not on income, but on where that person is on his or her life cycle (see Fig. 4.4).

Stage in the life cycle	Characteristics
(1) Bachelor stage	Young, single people with few ties and a reasonable level of disposable income
(2) Newly-wed/living together	Generally a higher disposable income
(3) Full nest 1	Young marrieds/living together with youngest child less than 6
(4) Full nest 2	As above but youngest child over 6. Falling disposable income
(5) Full nest 3	Older couples with dependent children, perhaps still studying. Disposable income low
(6) Empty nest 1	Older couples, childless or children all left home. Level of disposable income likely to be restored
(7) Empty nest 2	Older couples, chief breadwinner retired. Income again restricted
(8) Solitary survivor 1	Single/widowed person in work
(9) Solitary survivor 2	As above but retired. Little spare cash

Figure 4.4   The life cycle classification

Lifestyle classification

A further refinement of the process of categorization came with the introduction in Britain during the 1980s of the concept of classification according to **lifestyle**, a technique which had been previously used in North America. One of the first British companies to test the concept was Young and Rubicam, a well-known advertising agency, who developed a lifestyle classification known as the '4 Cs'. Four classes of people who were categorized according to their innermost needs into one of the following:

1   **Mainstreamers** – people who are looking for security and who live a conventional lifestyle. They usually buy well-known brands of products, such as Heinz, Daz and Fairy Liquid, rather than 'own brands'. Mainstreamers do not want to 'stick out from the crowd'. They are by far the largest of the four groups, accounting for around 40% of the British population. Their leisure habits are rather conventional, including reading, gardening, knitting and walking in the country.

2   **Aspirers** – these are people looking for status and who like to be thought of as being 'at the cutting edge' of society. They buy status symbols such as fast cars and expensive jewellery and generally like the good things in life. They are risk-takers and many aspirers run their own businesses. Leisure interests include hang-gliding, motor sports, power boating, karate and listening to hi-fi music.

3   **Succeeders** – these are people who have already achieved status and who ultimately like to be in control of their lives. They have no need for status symbols but value quality in all that they purchase. Leisure interests include gardening, entertaining, taking short breaks and playing golf.

4   **Reformers** – these are people who consider that 'quality of life' is more important than status and status symbols. They are the best educated of all four groups and tend to join groups to influence decision-making in society. They buy many natural products and 'own label' products; they are sometimes referred to as 'the Sainsbury shoppers'! Leisure is often family-orientated

and includes camping, walking, cycling, reading and playing games.

The importance of market segmentation

The three techniques which we have just investigated all attempt to subdivide the market into different groups who share similar characteristics; this process is known as **market segmentation**. One of the main benefits of segmenting the market for a particular leisure or tourism product is that it allows an organization to *target* particular individuals or groups within the segment. These people then become the focus of all the marketing effort, with the design and promotion of products and services that they will want.

Segmentation within leisure and tourism happens at a number of different levels:

- The *whole leisure and tourism industry* can be segmented into a range of different sectors, e.g. tourism, sport, arts, entertainment, community recreation, heritage, etc.
- An individual *sect*or can be segmented, e.g. tourism can be divided into accommodation, transportation and attractions.
- Individual *elements* of a sector can be further segmented, e.g. accommodation can be broken down into serviced and self-catering.
- At a fourth level of segmentation, *serviced accommodation* can be divided into hotels, guesthouses, inns, motels, etc.
- Further segmentation of hotels by the type of *guests*, e.g. business clients, groups, short break clients, conference delegates, overseas visitors, etc.

Market segmentation is therefore a tool which leisure and tourism organizations can use to satisfy the requirements of their own particular customers. Being concerned with the needs of customers, however, does mean that segmentation relies heavily on *market research* to help match the product exactly to the clients' needs.

Market research

Market research is the collection and analysis of data about customers and its use for management purposes. The term 'marketing research' has gained favour in recent years and is an all-embracing phrase to include product research, promotion research and price research. Research into *customers*, which is the subject of this particular section, is rightly called market research, and this is the terminology which will be used.

Market research data, from whatever source, is invaluable to the leisure and tourism manager in providing a sound basis for effective marketing decisions. All leisure and tourism organizations need feedback from their existing customers and many will want to know why people are *not* using their facilities but prefer what a competitor is providing. It is the job of market research to provide such data in as objective a form as possible, in other words with as little bias as possible. Not all market research activity is a costly or elaborate affair. The proprietor of a small hotel will constantly receive feedback from his guests on their opinion of his facilities and service level and will make the necessary adjustments. What he doesn't always know, of course, are the opinions of the people who say nothing; the British are notoriously reticent about complaining so that an anonymous questionnaire or comments form may produce more reliable and honest information.

> **Did You Know ?**
>
> An accurate information base is essential for effective marketing in leisure and tourism.

Sources of market research information

There are many different sources of market research data available to those managing and planning leisure and tourism facilities, some of it very *general*, such as statistics on trends in the population structure, and some *specific* to particular sectors of the industry, e.g. data on the number of visitors to tourist attractions.

Information and data *specific* to the UK **leisure** industry are available from a wide range of private and public bodies, and include:

- Data published by consultancies such as Jordan's and Leisure Consultants.
- Annual reports of various bodies including the Sports Council, CCPR, Arts Council of Great Britain, Countryside Commission, National Trust, Department of National Heritage etc.
- *Leisure Futures* published by the Henley Centre for Forecasting.
- CIPFA Leisure and Recreation Statistics.
- Annual reports of private sector leisure organizations including Forte, the Rank Organization PLC, Granada PLC etc.
- Professional bodies such as the Institute of Leisure and Amenity Management (ILAM) and the Institute of Sport and Recreation Management (ISRM, formerly IBRM).

Information and data *specific* to the UK **tourism** industry can be obtained from:

- Annual reports of the English, Scotland, Northern Ireland and Wales Tourist Boards.
- BTA Annual Report.
- The United Kingdom Tourism Survey (UKTS).
- Annual reports of commercial travel and tourism organizations including British Airways, Thomson Holidays, Airtours PLC, Thomas Cook etc.
- Trade associations such as ABTA and IATA.
- Professional bodies such as the Tourism Society and the Hotel, Catering and Institutional Management Association (HCIMA).

Material which is already available, through many different published sources, is known as **secondary data**. If the particular information is not available from existing sources, then it will be necessary to collect **primary data**.

Much of the information that an organization needs for marketing purposes may already be held within its various departments. These **internal sources** include:

- Membership lists
- Customer databases
- Gate receipts
- Sales returns
- Visitor information records

Information found outside the organization (**external sources**) is useful in giving a general picture of the state of a particular market or sector of the market. Collecting primary data about customers in leisure and tourism generally involves either direct *observation*, such as counting traffic or observing visitor flow patterns at a tourist attraction, or conducting a *survey* of one kind or another, e.g. asking hotel guests to complete a questionnaire to find out if they were happy with the facilities and service.

The collection of primary research data

If an organization wishes to collect information which is not already available, or wants to update previous information, it will need to collect **primary data**, either through observation, by carrying out a survey or through the use of focus groups.

Observation

Observation is a very useful, and often neglected, form of primary data collection in leisure and tourism. It does not always involve people actually watching what others do and recording the details systematically. Nowadays, there are sophisticated techniques available for counting and recording customer and traffic flows, such as time-lapse photography, closed circuit television (CCTV) and electronic tally counters. Particular examples of the use of observation in leisure and tourism include:

- A tourist information centre using an electronic tally counter to record the number of people using the centre.
- A large sports complex installing an electronic traffic counter to help traffic management and ease congestion.
- A large visitor attraction using CCTV to record visitor flows around the site.
- A museum using time-lapse photography to examine visitor movements.

Clearly, such equipment can be very useful for security purposes as well. When people are employed to carry out observation, rather than relying on electronic means of collection, they are often able to collect useful information on customer attitudes to a particular facility by 'mingling' with them but not revealing their identity or purpose.

Interview surveys

There are three main types of **interview survey** used to collect primary data, all of which involve the recording of responses on a **questionnaire**:

1. **Face to face interview survey:** This is usually the most effective way of gathering information on customers. As its name implies, a trained interviewer will ask questions of a respondent (the person being interviewed) and record the *responses* on a questionnaire. Although one of the best methods for getting in-depth information, since the interviewer can prompt the respondent if he or she is unclear as to the meaning of a particular question, face-to-face interviewing is very labour intensive and therefore *expensive*. The interviews can take place in a number of different locations:

   - In the street
   - At the facility (e.g. at a tourist attraction)
   - At home
   - *En route* to a facility (e.g. on board ship)
   - At work

   Leisure and tourism organizations will often employ

specialists to carry out an interview survey on their behalf so that any bias is kept to a minimum.

Did You Know ?

A visitor survey is one of the most common face-to-face interview techniques used by leisure and tourism organizations.

One of the most useful face-to-face interview surveys which is used extensively in leisure and tourism facilities is the **visitor survey**. Leisure centres, hotels, tourist attractions, catering outlets and entertainment complexes all use the information from visitor surveys to help to develop products and services that will appeal to their customers. By asking the relevant questions, a visitor survey can also indicate which media to use in promoting the facilities.

2. **Self-completed questionnaire survey:** This is a cheaper method of data collection since respondents are asked to fill in the questionnaires themselves, meaning that there is no need to employ and train interviewers. A self-completed questionnaire does have the disadvantage, however, that if the respondent is unclear about a particular question there is nobody to prompt him or her. With this type of survey, there are again different locations and methods by which the data are gathered:

   - **Postal survey** – this is a very common method in leisure and tourism involving the posting back of a completed questionnaire which may have been distributed in a number of ways:
     - (a) Given out on the return journey from a holiday, perhaps on the flight home.
     - (b) Picked up 'on site', e.g. at a sports centre, hotel or tourist attraction and posted when completed.
     - (c) Through the postal system – some tour operators mail a questionnaire to clients soon after they return home.
   - **Full 'on site' survey** – this is the cheapest self-completed survey of all since the respondents are asked not only to complete the questionnaire while they are at the facility but also to leave it behind, often in a sealed box, before they leave. Cost is minimal as there are no postal charges involved.

3. **Telephone survey:** While not widespread in leisure and tourism, telephone surveys are growing rapidly as a way of obtaining a quick response to an event or activity. In the leisure and tourism industry they are most commonly used in the commercial sector and often on a business-to-business basis. For example, the organizers of the annual British Travel Trade Fair (formerly MOOT) use the technique to contact exhibitors and trade visitors immediately after the event to gauge their reactions and comments. Hotels and other conference venues will often use telephone surveys to gain feedback on the standard of service and facilities at a particular venue.

Survey methods

There are a number of important points which relate to how

surveys are carried out using any of the *methods* just described. These include:

1 **Qualitative versus quantitative data:** An organization must be clear what it hopes to achieve by carrying out any survey. If it is only interested in *factual* (quantitative) information (how many visitors, how far have they travelled, how much have they spent, etc.), then a simple visitor survey based on a self-completed questionnaire would be sufficient. If, however, more in-depth *opinions* (qualitative) are sought, face-to-face interviews and focus groups would be more appropriate.

2 **Sampling:** In most cases it is not feasible to survey everybody who uses a particular leisure and tourism facility or buys particular products. It is therefore necessary to select a proportion of the total number known as a sample. Large samples produce more accurate results than small ones, but the increase in accuracy becomes less and less significant as the sample size is increased. Sophisticated statistical procedures are used to ensure that the sample is *representative* of the whole group and that there is *no bias* in selection.

3 **Questionnaire design:** It is important to remember that designing a questionnaire is an acquired skill, often best left to the professional. Questionnaires generally include a mix of factual and opinion questions and a number of '*profile*' questions (age, sex, marital status, occupation, etc.) to give a clearer picture of the respondent. Designing a *good* questionnaire which will achieve its intended aim can be a very time-consuming process, with constant checks to see that the questions are easily understood and in an appropriate order. Specialists in the design of questionnaires suggest the following sequence to ensure an effective finished product:

   (a) With reference to the objectives of the survey, make a list of expected 'outcomes'.
   (b) Formulate the questions which will achieve these 'outcomes'.
   (c) Produce a first draft of the questionnaire paying attention to question order, language style and overall layout.
   (d) Carry out a 'pilot' survey with a small number of respondents to check understanding and suitability of the questions.
   (e) Amend the first draft as necessary to produce a final version.
   (f) Use the final version in the survey, but be prepared to make minor adjustments if they will achieve the 'outcomes' better.

The following is a list of *guidelines* which should be followed when designing questionnaires:

- Always put 'sensitive' questions, e.g. age, occupation, marital status, etc., at the end of the questionnaire. Respondents will feel more comfortable about giving answers to such questions than if they appear at the beginning.
- Avoid ambiguous questions (questions with 'double meanings').
- Avoid using jargon.
- Make the questionnaire as short or as long as it needs to be; don't be tempted to include questions which, although interesting, will not help to achieve the 'outcomes'.

- Simple, objective, pre-coded (agree/neutral/disagree) questions will provide clearer answers than open-ended questions.
- Avoid 'leading questions', e.g. 'Don't you agree that the hotel is comfortable?' is a question which invites a positive response.
- Do not include questions which are an impossible test of the respondent's memory, e.g. 'How much did you spend on drinks per day for the first week of your holiday?'
- Use language which is appropriate to the respondent.

Focus groups

Focus groups are the bringing together of a small group of individuals under the guidance of a *facilitator*, often trained in psychology. It gives the facilitator a chance to delve into people's innermost thoughts and values with a view to exploring the influences which affect their purchasing decisions, e.g. what makes them book with tour operator A rather than tour operator B, and so on. Focus groups often produce very valuable information which cannot easily be gathered from either a face-to-face interview or a self-completed questionnaire. British Rail used the focus group technique in the early 1980s to investigate ways of improving its Inter City rail services.

Self Check ✔ **Element 1**

1. How is marketing in leisure and tourism different from marketing in other service sector industries?

2. Can you think of specific examples of tactical marketing which a theme park may have to consider when it learns that a competing attraction is to open nearby?

3. Can you think of examples of leisure and tourism organizations which regularly carry out research on their customers' needs?

4. Using the information contained in Fig. 4.4, suggest likely leisure and tourism activities for each of the nine stages in the life cycle.

5. Do you think that lifestyle classification has any weaknesses?

4.2 Identifying market opportunities

The changing market environment

Leisure and tourism organizations today operate in highly complex *environments* where the pace of change is quicker than it has ever been. This makes the role of marketing within leisure and tourism even more important, since it involves understanding this changing environment in order to identify market opportunities and mobilize the organization's resources to deliver the goods and services that the customers want.

For ease of understanding, the factors which influence the market environment are sometimes divided into those which are *internal* to an organization and those which are *external*.

Internal (micro) environment
This concerns those influences and factors which are close to an organization and over which it has some degree of control. For example:

- **Staff** – in the service sector, the role of staff is vital in determining success or failure. Given the right management style, adequate training, a supportive environment and fair pay, most staff will rise to the challenges to be found in abundance in the leisure and tourism sector.

- **Customers** – customers can be influenced, to some degree, in their purchasing habits but, at the end of the day, if they are unhappy with the product on offer or the level of service they receive, they may not come back again.

- **Suppliers** – these may be suppliers of food products for the catering side of an operation, suppliers of services such as printers, trainers or cleaners, distributors or wholesalers. They must be made aware of how their product or service fits into the overall structure of the organization and of the importance of quality and customer care.

External (macro) environment
There are certain influences outside the control of most leisure and tourism organizations but which are likely to have a direct bearing on how they survive and expand. These external factors include:

- **Economics** – the state of the economy is one of the most important influences on leisure and tourism spending. In a recession, patterns of buyer behaviour change; e.g. people eat out less but spend more on 'convenience' foods to eat at home. It is the marketeer's job to respond to these variations.

- **Competitors** – although its competitors are usually well known to an organization, having any control over their activities is difficult, if not impossible, in our democratic society. A competitor may be somebody offering exactly the same facility as yours. On the other hand, competition may come from another facility within the leisure and tourism sector, e.g. a city-centre cinema will be in competition with local restaurants to try to attract customers during their leisure time. In a wider sense, spending on leisure goods and services is in direct competition with other household expenditure, such as spending on food, clothing and energy.

- **Technology** – rapid developments in technology in leisure and tourism mean that the customer expects instant decisions on such things as bookings and availability of services and products.

- **Demographics** – these are factors concerned with the age structure and other characteristics of the population

as a whole. In general, people in Britain are living longer, fewer couples are having children and women are having children later in life. All such factors are important in the marketing of leisure and tourism products.

- **Politics** – factors such as taxation policy, regional grants and political stability will all influence the leisure and tourism sector and affect demand.

- **Environment** – recent growth in the concern for, and interest in, the environment is a powerful influence on customers' habits and spending patterns and must be taken into account by marketing personnel.

The marketing mix in leisure and tourism
The marketing mix is one of the most important concepts in marketing today, often used to identify and capitalize on market opportunities. It is commonly referred to as the 'four Ps':

- Price
- Product
- Place
- Promotion

Just as the ingredients must be in the correct quantities to make a successful cake, so the four ingredients of the marketing mix must be in the right proportions to make an organization's marketing activity successful. Different leisure and tourism providers will vary the emphasis between the four Ps to meet their particular objectives. For example:

- A tour operator who has just discovered that a major competitor has undercut its prices by 5% may restructure its **prices** in order to remain competitive.
- A visitor attraction which notices that it is receiving 50% more school parties than it had anticipated may need to look again at its **product** to see if the needs of this important sector are being met.
- A newly opened hotel will spend a lot on **promotion** to attract customers.
- **Place** must be taken into account. Market research for a major leisure company shows that there is an upsurge in electronic games played at *home*. It decides to shift resources from its chain of fast-food outlets into home-based leisure to exploit this demand.

> **Did You Know ?**
>
> The emphasis that a leisure and tourism organization places on the different elements of the marketing mix will vary over time.

The above examples show that emphasis on the elements of the marketing mix will vary over *time*, as well as between the various sectors of the industry.

We shall now look in more detail at the four components of the marketing mix.

Price
Pricing of products and services is a crucial aspect of exploiting market opportunities. Price is just as important as place, product or promotion; if the price is wrong, no amount of

advertising or other promotional work will make the customer buy the product. Getting the price right in leisure and tourism is no easy task. The fact that it is a service industry and that most of its products are intangible makes pricing difficult. It is an industry where it is customary to charge different amounts for the same product at different times of the year and even different times of the day. An all-inclusive family French camping holiday with Eurocamp, for example, will cost nearly £500 more in August than the same package in late September. Similarly, a round of golf at the local municipal course may well cost more on a Sunday morning than on a Tuesday afternoon. Pricing in leisure and tourism, therefore, is often related to **demand**.

Price is also closely allied to **value**, a concept which is notoriously difficult to define since it varies so much between individuals. Some people put a very high value on a particular leisure pursuit, while others will not be interested at all and it is clearly of little value to them. Value will also fluctuate according to particular circumstances; water-skiing on a local lake in high summer will have a greater value than the same activity taking place in the freezing temperatures of February.

Pricing is clearly a far more complex subject than simply adding up all the costs associated with providing a product or service and then adding a small margin of profit. The idea of what something is *worth* to the individual comes into play, a feature which will influence the amount he or she is willing to pay.

Before we look at some of the methods used to price leisure and tourism products, it is important to understand some of the factors which influence pricing.

- **Demand** – we have shown that the same product can command a higher price at different times according to customer demand. People will often pay high prices for *exclusivity*, e.g. a trip on the Orient Express or a flight on Concorde.

- **Costs** – it is important for the organization to be aware of the costs of providing a particular product or service when deciding on its price. This may only be the starting point of a much more complex pricing policy, however, revolving around many of the concepts discussed above.

- **Objectives of the organization** – clearly a private sector company will need to maximize revenue and will try to set prices which help to achieve this objective. Public sector and voluntary bodies may be able to offer more concessionary prices to achieve their social aims.

- **Competition** – in the highly competitive leisure and tourism industry, an organization will need to be aware of what competitors are charging and adjust its own prices accordingly.

- **State of the economy** – in times of recession, products may be reduced in price in order to gain revenue, e.g. hotel rooms are heavily discounted, particularly at weekends when the use by business clients is low, on the assumption that it is better to earn a little income for the rooms than nothing at all if they are left empty.

Pricing policies in leisure and tourism

From the many different **pricing policies** in use in leisure and tourism, the following are some of the most common:

1 **Cost plus pricing** – sometimes known as 'accountant's pricing', this is the rather simplistic approach which totals all *fixed* costs (buildings, machinery, etc.) and *variable* costs (wages, energy costs, postage, etc.) and adds a small profit margin to arrive at the price to charge. It assumes that an organization can calculate its costs accurately, something which a large leisure complex, for example, may find it difficult.

2 **Skimming** – when a high price is charged initially for a new product which is unique and which attracts people who are willing to pay the high price for status reasons. The pricing of virtual reality facilities is an example of market skimming.

3 **Competitive pricing** – sometimes referred to as 'the going rate', competitive pricing assumes that, where products or services are similar, the organization will charge the going rate, i.e. will match the price of competitors. This method often leads to very low margins and, in the long run, the collapse of some organizations, e.g. tour operators, who find their profitability is too low.

4 **Penetration pricing** – this is used by organizations wanting to break into a new market where there are existing suppliers of the same product or service. The price will be set sufficiently low to persuade customers to switch their allegiance (sometimes known as a *loss leader*). It is important that this pricing method is seen as a long-term strategy since customers will resent an early rise in price.

Product

The leisure and tourism '**product**' is very different from many other products that we buy and use. The term product is something of a misnomer since leisure and tourism is a *service* industry; it is true that a set of golf clubs, a garden spade or a football shirt are all products in the strict sense of the word, but the bulk of the leisure and tourism sector is concerned with the customers' experience and how the many elements of the sector are delivered to the customer. Below are a few examples of leisure and tourism products:

- Leisure centres
- Nature reserves
- Short breaks
- Sports facilities
- Museums
- A 30-minute session on the squash court
- Holidays
- Art galleries
- Sports equipment
- Events

As you can see, some products are *tangible*, i.e. you can touch sports equipment and see a leisure centre and its facilities. However, many leisure and tourism products cannot be seen and are therefore *intangible*. You can't, for example, see or touch a session on the squash court or a short break holiday, but you can experience it. It is this aspect of intangibility which makes leisure and tourism products so different.

It could be argued that the tangible products, such as hotels, leisure centres, tourist attractions, etc., are simply the facilities in which the intangible products are experienced; for example, the session on the squash court may well take place in a leisure centre, and the short break may well involve staying at a hotel.

Leisure and tourism products are also *non-standardized*. In other words, it is difficult to guarantee the same experience every time. A tour operator, for example, does not have control over all the elements of a package holiday. This highlights the importance of quality control in leisure and tourism.

Products in leisure and tourism also tend to be *unpredictable* and *fragile*. A customer treated badly in a leisure centre, for example, may 'vote with his feet' and go elsewhere. Training in customer care is therefore essential for a successful organization.

Branding

Many leisure and tourism products are given **brand names**, e.g. Thomson, Reebok, Slazenger, Superbowl, Happy Eater and Harvester, to name but a few. A brand name gives a product a certain *identity*, which, when coupled with promotional activities such as advertising and direct mail, helps to persuade the customer to buy that particular product. Many customers show brand loyalty, meaning that they will only buy a particular brand above all others. Branding is often linked to the concept of segmentation, with brands being developed to meet the needs of a particular segment of the market. One of the best examples of this is the wide range of products on offer from Thomson Holidays. Their brands range from 'Small and Friendly', through 'Thomson Cities' to Thomson 'A la Carte'.

Programming

Programming is an often overlooked element of marketing within the leisure and tourism sector. It is most commonly associated with leisure and sports centres, but is equally applicable to theatres, local community centres or a concert hall. In tourism, tour programmes are devised to meet particular customer needs.

Programming is all about making sure that a facility is used to its full capacity at all times and, certainly in the public and voluntary sectors, is used by as wide a cross-section of the local community as possible. It involves planning, scheduling, timetabling and implementing action and should take into account not only the needs of customers but also the availability and expertise of staff and the physical resources at the organization's disposal. Figure 4.5 shows a typical sports hall programme for a local authority leisure centre.

Place

Place, in the context of the marketing mix, is concerned not only with the location of where leisure and tourism activities are undertaken, but also with how they are made available to the customer, sometimes referred to as the channels of distribution. We shall look at each of these in turn.

Location

The right **location** can often mean the difference between success and failure for a leisure and tourism facility. A farm guesthouse, for example, which is deep in the countryside and well off the beaten track, will not benefit from 'passing trade' and, unless the proprietor is skilled in marketing, will struggle to attract guests. A travel agency, on the other hand, in a busy high street location should attract a constant stream of clients. For a leisure development company looking for a suitable site for a new theme park, the prime location is likely to be close to a major centre of population. Location is therefore closely linked to *accessibility*, at the local, regional and national level. In the public and voluntary sectors of leisure and tourism, accessibility is not just about physical access to

	5.30	6.30	7.30	8.30	9.30	10.30
MON	MILLBANK FOOTBALL CLUB	AEROBICS	AEROBICS	STEP CIRCUITS		
TUE	TEEN STEP	STEP REEBOK	STEP REEBOK	U.L.C. BADMINTON CLUB	U.L.C. BADMINTON CLUB	
WED	JUNIOR BADMINTON COURSE	TRIDENT SPORT CLUB	CYNTHIA'S CIRCUITS	WEALDEN FOOTBALL CLUB	FAIRWARP FOOTBALL CLUB	
THU	JUNIOR FOOTBALL CLUB	ALLSORTS UNITED	AEROBICS	UCKFIELD BASKETBALL CLUB	UCKFIELD BASKETBALL CLUB	
FRI		STEP REEBOK	FLYING SQUAD	FLYING SQUAD		

☐ Centre run courses or clubs   ☐ Block bookings by Centre approved clubs

☐ Available for casual use

Figure 4.5 A typical programme for a local authority leisure centre (Courtesy of Wealden District Council)

buildings, although this is important when it comes to catering for those with special needs. In these sectors, accessibility is also about providing facilities for the whole community and giving everybody equal access.

Distribution channels

When we think of the **distribution** of products, images of huge container lorries full of chilled food or fashion garments driving up and down the motorway come to mind. This has little to do with how leisure and tourism products are bought or used (except, perhaps, if the food is destined for a restaurant chain and the fashion garments are 'leisure wear'!). It is true that some tangible leisure products, such as computer games, sports goods and CDs, will pass through standard channels of distribution. The difference with many leisure and tourism products, however, is that they are consumed *at the point of production* so there is no need for distribution channels of any sort. For example, a round of golf takes place on the golf course, just as a game of tennis is played on a tennis court. In cases such as these, the important point is to make sure that the facilities are made *accessible* to the customers and that they are promoted effectively to the intended audience.

The way that holidays are sold in Britain is a good example of distribution channels in the service sector. Figure 4.6 shows the stages in the process.

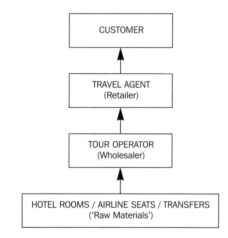

Figure 4.6 The channels of distribution in selling holidays

Figure 4.6 shows that the tour operator assembles the 'raw materials' of a typical package holiday by buying in bulk such items as hotel rooms and airline seats. Taking on the role of the wholesaler, these are then divided into smaller proportions, the package holidays themselves, which are offered for sale through travel agents (the retailers) to the customers. Although this is the usual method of selling holidays, there are certain companies who specialize in selling direct to the customer without using the services of travel agents. Some of the best known of these *direct sell* operators are Eclipse and Portland Holidays, who profess to being able to offer the public cheaper holidays because they don't have to pay commission to travel agents.

Promotion

Once the leisure and tourism product has the right features, is correctly priced and offered for sale in the right place, the fourth element of the marketing mix, **promotion**, comes into play. The next Element of this unit will look at the many ways in which leisure and tourism organizations promote their products and facilities.

4.3 Planning promotional activities

The role of promotion

Promotion is an essential part of the marketing process in leisure and tourism. An event such as the NutraSweet London Marathon which gets its promotion wrong will not only suffer embarrassment if it fails to meet its targets, but will also have to deal with the many sponsors who have invested their time and money in the expectation of tangible benefits. By the same token, a leisure centre may have the latest state-of-the-art equipment and facilities, but if it cannot promote itself effectively it is unlikely to succeed. Promotional work in leisure and tourism is concerned with *communicating* information and 'messages' to persuade people to use or buy particular products, facilities or services. The promotional activities of the YHA, for example, will be geared towards maximizing the use of YHA accommodation and activity holidays. The effectiveness of their promotional efforts will have a vital role to play in the overall success of the organization.

In the dynamic world of leisure and tourism, promotion is the most visible of the four Ps. Promotion is used:

- To **inform** customers of the benefits of one product over another.
- To make customers **aware** of the availability of leisure and tourism products.
- To **remind** customers of the existence of a product.
- To **stimulate demand** for products.
- To provide **incentives** to purchase or use products.

Promotional techniques in leisure and tourism

The leisure and tourism industry uses a number of different **promotional techniques** (sometimes referred to as '**the promotional mix**'). The most important are:

- Advertising
- Public relations
- Direct marketing
- Sales promotion
- Personal selling

Whichever technique is chosen, it is likely to follow the principle known as **AIDA**, which stands for:

- Attention
- Interest
- Desire
- Action

AIDA is just as applicable whether an organization or agency is developing an advertising campaign, writing a direct mail letter, designing an exhibition stand or selecting sales promotion materials. In the case of a newspaper advertisement for a newly opened theme park, for example, the person responsible for writing it may choose to:

- Attract **attention** to the advertisement by using colour, bold headlines, a picture of a famous personality or striking graphics.
- Maintain the readers' **interest** by keeping the wording of the advertisement as brief as possible, including language and images that the reader can easily relate to.
- Create a **desire** to visit the theme park by perhaps offering a discount voucher or other incentive as part of the advertisement.
- Trigger **action** on the part of the reader by clearly letting him or her know what to do next, e.g. by including a simple map or directions to the park, printing the address and telephone number clearly, or displaying the opening times.

Advertising

Advertising is the most obvious of all the promotional techniques in use today. We are all subjected to advertising on our television screens, on buses and trains, on commercial radio, at the side of the road and in newspapers and magazines. These are known as advertising **media**; the precise choice of media will be dictated partly by cost (a 30-second commercial on television in peak viewing time can cost as much as £30,000) and partly by the type of product. A new museum aimed at local people is unlikely to use national television advertising but will rely on advertisements in the local press.

Advertising in leisure and tourism is directed either at the customer (consumer advertising) or at those working in the industry (trade advertising). *Travel Trade Gazette* and *Leisure Management* are two examples of trade magazines which carry advertisements.

Did You Know ❓

Many small and medium-sized leisure and tourism organizations find it hard to justify the expense of advertising campaigns. They rely much more on methods such as direct marketing and public relations which can be just as effective with less investment.

Public relations

Public relations, or PR as it is often known, is used a great deal in leisure and tourism. Organizations sometimes think of it as 'free publicity', particularly when associated with a newspaper or magazine article which features its facilities. In reality, there is usually a price to be paid for such *editorial* coverage, even if it is just the cost of entertaining the journalist who wrote it!

Public relations is more than just keeping the media informed of your organization, however, although this can undoubtedly pay dividends. PR is also about making sure that all staff and functions of an organization which come into contact with the public, e.g. promotional literature, telephone technique, staff at reception, uniforms, etc. are well managed so as to gain maximum publicity and goodwill. PR is also about leisure and tourism organizations helping in the local community and getting involved in work for local and national charities. As well as providing much-needed cash, *sponsorship* can also bring PR benefits to leisure and tourism organizations. The image of a football club, for example, can be enhanced by being sponsored by a company which is regarded as successful in its own particular field.

Direct marketing

While advertising is sometimes criticized for not always hitting its intended audience (a product geared specifically to the needs of women will be of little interest to men watching a television advertisement, for example), **direct marketing** is able to *target* particular customers very successfully. **Direct mail** is the best-known method of direct marketing, a technique which is used extensively in leisure and tourism. Using a mailing list, which may have been bought, borrowed or compiled from its own records, a leisure and tourism organization can mail existing and prospective customers with a personalized letter or brochure giving details of its facilities. If planned carefully, a direct mail campaign can bring excellent results for a whole host of leisure and tourism organizations, ranging from hotels, leisure centres and travel agencies to tour operators, visitor attractions and art galleries. Direct mail is one of the fastest-growing types of promotional activity in leisure and tourism today.

Telemarketing (direct selling over the telephone) is a growing method of direct marketing in the UK. Already widespread in the USA, its use in this country in leisure and tourism is fairly new, and is limited to activities such as selling timeshare and selling services to businesses.

Sales promotion

There are many different **sales promotion** techniques used in the leisure and tourism industry. Some of the most common are:

- Competitions
- Brochures and leaflets
- Discount vouchers and coupons (often in newspapers and magazines)
- Price cuts and 'sale' offers, e.g. 10% off all brochure prices of summer holidays
- Extra product, e.g. a 'three for the price of two' offer at a restaurant
- Free gifts, e.g. free sports bag with every ten aerobics sessions booked
- Prize draws
- Displays and exhibitions
- 'Giveaways', e.g. free carrier bags, pens, balloons, hats, T-shirts, stickers etc
- Free demonstrations, e.g. of sports and fitness equipment
- Free membership of a new club in the area

The main features of all sales promotion techniques is that they are *temporary* and aim to stimulate demand in the *short term*. The fast-moving nature of leisure and tourism means that managers are constantly having to react to fluctuations in demand from customers on a daily, weekly or seasonal basis. Unlike advertising, direct marketing and public relations activities, which are essentially long-term promotional tools, sales promotion gives an organization the flexibility needed to be able to respond quickly to such changes.

Sales promotion techniques are not only targeted at members of the general public; it is common for many staff working in leisure and tourism, especially in the private sector, to be offered incentives and rewards for achieving predetermined sales targets. Travel agency counter staff, for example, may be given Marks & Spencer or Boots vouchers by tour operators in return for selling a certain number of holidays. Indeed, *incentive travel* is a growing sector of leisure and tourism. Started in the USA, incentive travel is the reward of, say, a fortnight's holiday in Florida for an employee who has achieved sales success within his or her organization.

Personal selling

Leisure and tourism relies heavily on the selling skills of those employed in order to achieve success. Selling is all about *helping people to buy* rather than selling them something they don't really want. Training in selling techniques is important for leisure and tourism staff, particularly in the commercial sector. Planning prior to a sales interview is essential as is being able to recognize buying signals, such as nodding of the head and signs of agreement from the customer. Closing the sale can be achieved by the taking of a deposit, credit card details or simply noting the customer's name and address.

Self Check ✔ **Element 3**

8. Which sales promotion techniques do tour operators use to help market their products to the trade and the public?

   _____
   _____
   _____

9. What are the main components of a direct mail package?

   _____
   _____
   _____

10. Which advertising media would be used by a large theme park which attracts over 1 million visitors per year, most living within a 50 mile catchment area?

   _____
   _____
   _____

4.4 Evaluating promotional activities

In Element 3 of this unit we looked at the many promotional techniques available to the leisure and tourism professional to stimulate demand for products and facilities. Rather than using any single promotional tool, an organization is likely to develop a 'promotional mix' which includes elements of all the techniques described. The exact proportions of each in the mix will vary over time and in response to internal and external influences.

Planning promotional campaigns and implementing them are two important stages in the process of stimulating customer demand. However, without a third crucial element, namely **evaluation of the promotional activity**, a marketing professional may say that the whole process has been a waste of time and money.

Did You Know ?

The results of any promotional work must be capable of being measured; only then can the organization say with any degree of certainty that the time and money invested in the promotion was worthwhile.

The objectives of promotional activity

Before being able to measure whether a particular promotional campaign has been successful or not, the organization must ask itself the question: 'What were we hoping to achieve from the promotion?' In other words, **promotional objectives** will need to have been developed and it is against these aims that success, or the lack of it, is measured. Such objectives should be:

1 **Specific** – it is pointless having vague objectives as this will make the task of deciding success or failure all the more difficult. For example, an objective such as 'the promotional work should increase the number of guests staying at the hotel' is not specific enough. Will just one extra guest mean that the promotion has been a success? A much better objective might be 'the promotional work should result in a 5% increase in the number of guests staying at the hotel'. Some managers shy away from setting such specific objectives since they may not feel comfortable about achieving them.

2 **Time constrained** – all objectives should be set within a particular time span so as to determine whether they have been achieved. Using the hotel example in 1, the objective may be developed into 'the promotional work should result in a 5% increase in the number of guests staying at the hotel within the next 12 months'.

3 **Realistic** – all objectives must be realistic and capable of being achieved by the organization and the staff working within it. Setting wildly unrealistic aims and targets is counter-productive and wasteful of resources. Going back to our hotel example, it would be pointless to set a target of, for example, achieving a 50% increase in the number of guests within a three-month period. When the target was not met, staff would feel demoralized and the future success of the hotel would be put in doubt.

The promotional objectives are likely to reflect the overall objectives of the organization, which, as we saw in Unit 1, are many and varied, depending on which sector of the leisure and tourism industry is being considered.

Promotional effectiveness

A leisure and tourism organization which uses just one type of promotional activity, e.g. newspaper advertising, will find it relatively easy to measure how effective it has been in attracting customers. Unfortunately, such a situation is very rare, and measuring the effectiveness of a whole range of promotional techniques is a much more complex task.

If we take the example of a newly opened health club which is reviewing its operation after its first twelve months, the management may be quite happy with the overall level of usage of the centre and will attribute much of the success to its promotional work, which could include:

- Advertising in the local press
- Mailing of leaflets to local districts
- Press releases to local newspapers and local radio
- Local radio advertising
- Promotional items such as pens, badges, carrier bags, T-shirts, etc.
- Free demonstrations of fitness facilities
- Discounts for squash club membership
- Incentive bonuses for staff to encourage sales of memberships

As you can see, the club has used the five main types of promotional activity, namely advertising, PR, direct marketing, sales promotion and personal selling.

While the management may be quite happy with the overall promotional plan, certain elements of the plan may not have been successful and money may have been wasted on these. Unless there are systems in place to monitor the effectiveness of each activity, management may be unaware of any weaknesses. If the information is readily available, funds can be taken away from the weak activity and channelled into more effective promotion.

Measuring promotional effectiveness

Measuring promotional effectiveness is harder in some activities than in others.

Advertising effectiveness is relatively easy to measure, especially press advertising which can include a coded coupon denoting which newspaper or magazine it is in. Look at coupons in newspaper advertisements and you will probably see a code such as DM17/9, which could mean that the coupon was in the *Daily Mail* dated 17 September. Television and radio advertising are a little more difficult to measure, and are often used for *image-building* purposes anyway, i.e. to create or sustain a product's image in the minds of the viewer or listener.

The effectiveness of direct marketing is reasonably easy to measure because of its very targeted nature. Mailings to households can include coded coupons or tickets which can be traced to see which particular district a customer lives in. Telephone selling can be carried out in a very structured fashion with the salesperson logging customer details.

The effectiveness of public relations activity can be very difficult to measure. Much PR activity is about image-building, making it difficult to attribute success to any particular part of a PR campaign. One area which is relatively easy to measure, however, is editorial coverage, such as articles and features in newspapers and magazines. The editorial usually stems from either a press release or a complete article sent out by the leisure and tourism organization.

Journalists are sometimes invited to sample leisure and tourism products for themselves, sometimes referred to as a familiarization (fam) trip. Such visits are common in leisure and tourism, particularly in the travel sector. The coverage, either in column inches in the case of press articles or 'air time' if the feature is on radio or television, can be easily measured and a calculation as to how much the same coverage would have cost in paid advertising can be made.

The effect of personal selling skills should be relatively easy to measure, particularly if individual staff members are given targets to achieve. Incentives can be introduced to increase sales effort and reward the high achievers, while further training can be introduced for those staff not yet meeting their targets.

Because of their very temporary and short-term nature, sales promotion activities are generally easy to measure. They often demand a firm commitment from the customer in return for which a discount, free gift or similar incentive can be gained.

Techniques for measuring effectiveness

Figure 4.7 gives some examples of **techniques** which can be used to measure the effectiveness of certain promotional activities.

Promotional activity	Measuring technique
Newspaper coupon to generate a 10% increase in the number of visitors to a tourist attraction	Tally counter Electronic counter
Local radio advertising campaign to increase the sales of caravans by 5%	Sales figures
Customer care training to improve customer attitude to a facility	Visitor survey
Promotional campaign to widen the customer base	Visitor survey
Advertising campaign to increase the number of visitors to an annual event	Tally counter Vehicle counter

Figure 4.7 Techniques for measuring promotional effectiveness

Figure 4.7 shows that not all promotional objectives are necessarily concerned with increasing profits. Certainly in the public and voluntary sectors of leisure and tourism, promotional activities may be put in place to increase the participation of a particular section of the local community. Even in the private sector, a company may wish to change its customer profile by perhaps going 'up market', which may not always involve *increased* numbers of visitors to a facility and sometimes quite the reverse.

Self Check ✔ **Element 4**

11. Why should leisure and tourism organizations always evaluate the effectiveness of their promotional work?
_____
_____

12. How would a local museum measure the effectiveness of a new advertising campaign in its local newspaper?
_____
_____
_____

Unit Test This test is one hour long. Answer all the questions.

Focus 1: MARKET RESEARCH AND ANALYSIS

Question 1
A tour operator has employed a market research company to analyse customer attitudes to new product developments. The company has decided to use 'focus groups' to achieve the aims of the research.

What is the main advantage of the 'focus group' type of market research?

A   It is a cheaper method than carrying out a questionnaire survey.
B   The information which is gathered is in-depth.
C   The information which is gathered is objective.
D   The person conducting the research does not need to be trained.

Question 2
A restaurant owner is considering opening a second outlet in a neighbouring town and is keen to carry out some market research to assess the likely demand.

Decide whether each of these statements is true (T) or false (F).

(i) On-street interviews with people living near to the site of the second restaurant would be a useful type of primary research.
(ii) Studying population figures for the neighbouring town is a form of primary research.

Which option best describes these two statements?

A   (i) T   (ii) T
B   (i) T   (ii) F
C   (i) F   (ii) T
D   (i) F   (ii) F

Question 3
Leisure and tourism organizations have access to both internal and external sources of market research information.

Which of the following is NOT an internal source?

A   Sales returns
B   Census data
C   Gate receipts
D   Membership lists

Question 4
Questionnaires are widely used in leisure and tourism organizations to collect market research data.

Decide whether each of these statements is true (T) or false (F).

(i) 'Open' questions on a questionnaire allow the respondent to give his or her opinions on a particular subject.
(ii) Questionnaires made up entirely of 'closed' questions take more time to complete than those containing 'open' questions.

Which option best describes these two statements?

A   (i) T   (ii) T
B   (i) T   (ii) F
C   (i) F   (ii) T
D   (i) F   (ii) F

Question 5
The market for a particular leisure and tourism product or service may be segmented according to a number of different factors, one of which is demographics.

Which of the following is a demographic factor?

A   The fact that a customer likes active pursuits
B   The fact that a customer is in a special interest group
C   The fact that a customer is over 55 years of age
D   The fact that a customer takes a holiday three times a year

Focus 2: REPORTS AND PRESENTATIONS

Questions 6–8 relate to the following information.
A tour operator decided to make a number of changes to its market research plan in the light of the following problems:

A   Respondents were having difficulty in understanding some of the questions on a self-completed questionnaire survey.
B   There was a lack of information available within the organization on population trends and statistics.
C   The company's database was not able to target specific customers effectively.
D   Response rates in a telephone survey were low.

Which problem is likely to be solved by:

Question 6
Using a system such as ACORN or PINPOINT?

Question 7
Running a pilot survey?

Question 8
Increasing the amount of secondary research data held in-house?

Question 9
The marketing manager of a large visitor attraction has been asked by the general manager to compile a report on the feasibility of introducing a new catering facility on the site.

Decide whether each of these statements is true (T) or false (F).

(i) Any lengthy statistics, charts and tables are best included in appendices to the report.
(ii) It would be more appropriate to use a straight-line graph rather than a pie-chart in the report to represent the amount spent on food and drink by five different categories of visitors.

Which option best describes these two statements?

A   (i) T   (ii) T
B   (i) T   (ii) F
C   (i) F   (ii) T
D   (i) F   (ii) F

Question 10
When designing questionnaires, it is important to avoid using 'leading questions', which may introduce bias.

Which of the following is an example of a 'leading question'?

A   What is your present occupation?
B   How do you think travelling by train compares with travelling by coach?
C   Do you agree that serviced accommodation is better than self-catering?
D   Are there any improvements you would like to see in the hotel?

Focus 3: PROVISIONS AND OPPORTUNITIES

Questions 11–13 relate to the following information.
An independent travel agent has noticed a trend towards late bookings for overseas package holidays among his clients.

He has identified the following specific needs of customers who book at the last minute:

A   Accurate advice on the characteristics of particular holiday destinations
B   A taxi service to travel to their departure airport
C   Special discounts on the price of late availability holidays
D   Quick access to details of late availability packages

Which customer need is likely to be met by the following services?

Question 11
Staff with good product knowledge

Question 12
A recently updated viewdata system

Question 13
Low premiums arranged with a local travel insurance company

Question 14
A city-centre art gallery is hoping to increase its number of visitors and has identified both existing and potential customers as offering marketing opportunities.

Decide whether each of these statements is true (T) or false (F).

 (i) Potential customers are only those who have visited another art gallery in the city.
(ii) It is easier to market to existing customers than to potential customers.

Which option best describes these two statements?

A   (i) T   (ii) T
B   (i) T   (ii) F
C   (i) F   (ii) T
D   (i) F   (ii) F

Question 15
A farmer in Wales has decided to open his farm to paying visitors and convert two old barns into self-catering units in order to capitalize on the increasing number of tourists to his area.

This response to a market opportunity is known as:

A   Diversification
B   Product development
C   Market segmentation
D   Market penetration

Question 16
A large hotel which is used mainly by business guests on Mondays to Thursdays, is considering ways of filling its surplus rooms at weekends by exploiting the growing demand for short leisure breaks.

Decide whether each of these statements is true (T) or false (F).

 (i) One way of responding to the opportunity would be to offer discounted room rates to tour operators so that they can put together a short break package.
(ii) The hotel would reduce its administrative workload if it handled the development, promotion and reservations associated with the short breaks itself.

Which option best describes these two statements?

A   (i) T   (ii) T
B   (i) T   (ii) F
C   (i) F   (ii) T
D   (i) F   (ii) F

Focus 4: TAKING ACTION

Question 17
A local museum in a small market town has recently run a successful promotion to increase the number of 'friends' of the museum, who pay a regular sum of money to help with development work. The manager has decided to restrict the number of employees who have access to the database of 'friends'.

Decide whether each of these statements is true (T) or false (F).

 (i) This is for reasons of confidentiality.
(ii) This is to comply with the requirements of the Data Protection Act.

Which option best describes these two statements?

A   (i) T   (ii) T
B   (i) T   (ii) F
C   (i) F   (ii) T
D   (i) F   (ii) F

Question 18
A leisure centre is looking at ways of increasing off-peak use of the facility and has identified a number of possible courses of action.

Which of the following is likely to have the most positive impact on the people living close to the centre?

A   Staging rock concerts during the winter months
B   Holding car boot sales every Sunday
C   Hiring out the centre for late night themed disco events
D   Offering early evening dance classes for adults and children

Question 19
Since the event was first held five years ago, the organizers of an annual 'fun run' have received an increasing number of complaints and bad publicity in the local press, for closing roads and diverting traffic. This year the organizers have decided to hold a public meeting beforehand to inform local people about the arrangements.

Decide whether each of these statements is true (T) or false (F).

(i) Holding a meeting is likely to increase local goodwill and help reduce criticism of the event.
(ii) Holding a meeting may produce good ideas to help reduce the negative social impacts of the event.

Which option best describes these two statements?

A   (i) T   (ii) T
B   (i) T   (ii) F
C   (i) F   (ii) T
D   (i) F   (ii) F

Questions 20–22 relate to the following information.
The owner of a new country house hotel is considering a number of ways of increasing business to his establishment, including:

A   An advertising campaign in the local press
B   Extending the hotel by adding a conservatory
C   Inviting journalists for 'fam' trips
D   Changing the logo of the hotel

Which action is likely to have the following disadvantages?

Question 20
Disruption to visitors

Question 21
Loss of current identity

Question 22
Loss of control over what is written about the hotel

Question 23
A local council is planning a series of regional events to help to raise the profile of the town for tourism.

Decide whether each of these statements is true (T) or false (F).

(i) Involving local organizations and individuals in the planning of the events will help to reduce environmental and social problems.
(ii) The local police should be consulted once all the plans are finalized.

Which option best describes these two statements?

A   (i) T   (ii) T
B   (i) T   (ii) F
C   (i) F   (ii) T
D   (i) F   (ii) F

Focus 5: PROMOTIONAL ACTIVITIES

Questions 24–26 relate to the following information.
Four of the most common promotional techniques in leisure and tourism are:

A   Public relations
B   Sales promotions
C   Direct marketing
D   Point-of-sale

Which technique is most closely associated with the following situations?

Question 24
Sending a 'mailshot' to existing customers

Question 25
Writing a press release

Question 26
Offering '3 weeks for the price of 2' when selling holidays to Spain

Question 27
An ex-teacher decides to set up her own business by running an outdoor activity centre in the Peak District.

The first objective of any promotional campaign for the centre would be to:

A   Buy new equipment
B   Evaluate the objectives
C   Create awareness of the centre
D   Reinforce brand loyalty

Question 28
A city-centre hotel invites all its current corporate clients to a complimentary winter weekend break.

The main reason for doing this is to:

A   Distribute new promotional materials
B   Reinforce customer loyalty
C   Update the hotel's database
D   Identify alternative market segments

Questions 29–31 share the answer options A–D.
An international hotel group with its headquarters in Britain, uses the following personnel when devising their UK promotional campaigns.

A   The UK Marketing Director
B   A well respected public relations agency
C   An in-house design studio
D   Marketing managers in each of the group's hotels

Who is most likely to be responsible for the following activities?

Question 29
Planning the PR strategy

Question 30
Setting up point-of-sale displays

Question 31
Producing leaflets to support the campaigns

Question 32
The marketing manager of a large travel agency chain is constantly telling his area managers that setting the budget is a crucial stage in any of their promotional campaigns.

Decide whether each of these statements is true (T) or false (F).

(i) It is important to have regard for the total budget for a campaign when setting the campaign objectives.
(ii) Once the total promotional budget has been set, it should then be divided equally between the planned promotional activities.

Which option best describes these two statements?

A   (i) T   (ii) T
B   (i) T   (ii) F
C   (i) F   (ii) T
D   (i) F   (ii) F

A   (i) T   (ii) T
B   (i) T   (ii) F
C   (i) F   (ii) T
D   (i) F   (ii) F

Focus 6: EVALUATION OF A PROMOTIONAL CAMPAIGN

Questions 33–35 share answer options A–D.
The marketing team of a major indoor arena has identified the following stages in its forthcoming winter promotional campaign.

A   Implementation
B   Planning
C   Evaluation
D   Preparation

At which stage would each of the following activities take place?

Question 33
Establishing the objectives of the campaign

Question 34
Reviewing the successes and failures of the campaign

Question 35
Taking advertising space in local newspapers

Question 36
A tourist attraction is looking for a cost-effective way of evaluating the response to a recent newspaper coupon campaign, offering one free child entry with each paying adult.

Decide whether each of these statements is true (T) or false (F).

(i) The response could be evaluated by the staff at the admission booth asking customers when they last visited the attraction.
(ii) The response could be evaluated by analysing the number of coupons handed in by visitors.

Which option best describes these two statements?

Question 37
The operator of a catering franchise at a major tourist attraction wants to increase business in his four outlets. He decides to run a short-term promotion in conjunction with a local newspaper, offering £1 off a meal on presentation of a voucher printed in the newspaper. An analysis of weekly takings shows an increase during the promotion, but lower takings after the promotion than before it.

Which of the following would be the best method of identifying why customers did not return?

A   A comparison of food versus drink sales, before and after the promotion
B   An analysis of customer comment cards completed while the promotion was taking place
C   Interviews with customers after the promotion
D   An analysis of the number of coupons presented on each day while the promotion was in place

Question 38
Investors in a new golf driving range are concerned that the venture is not proving to be as popular as they were led to believe by the developers. They have asked the company managing the range for an evaluation report.

Decide whether each of these statements is true (T) or false (F).

(i) The report will include details of usage, income and expenditure to date.
(ii) The report will include forecasts of usage, income and expenditure.

Which option best describes these two statements?

A   (i) T   (ii) T
B   (i) T   (ii) F
C   (i) F   (ii) T
D   (i) F   (ii) F

Self-check Answers

1. Unlike other service sector industries such as banking and insurance, leisure and tourism is concerned with 'selling dreams' and experiences. When we buy a holiday from a travel agent, for example, we are not buying the hotel, aircraft and other tangible components of the package, but more the expectation of the experience that all the different elements will provide. Marketing in leisure and tourism must reflect the intangible nature of the leisure and tourism product and emphasize quality and customer care.

2. Specific tactical marketing activity in this case could include an advertising campaign in the local and regional press, discounts on admission prices, free gifts, a competition, a PR campaign or an improved customer care programme.

3. The large tour operators and airlines, such as British Airways, Thomson, Airtours and Britannia, regularly research their customers' opinions and requirements. Smaller, local organizations, including leisure centres and tourist attractions, use their customers' views to shape their products and services.

4. Stage 1 Going to discos and clubs. Stage 2 Eating out. Stage 3 Self-catering holiday. Stage 4 Visits to theme parks. Stage 5 Hobbies and sports. Stage 6 City breaks. Stage 7 Gardening. Stage 8 Coach holidays. Stage 9 Watching television.

5. As with all classifications, there will be some people who do not fit easily into any of the categories of the lifestyle classification, or some who exhibit characteristics from across all four types. The classification will need constant review in order to make it applicable. Segmentation by lifestyle, however, is now regarded as one of the most effective forms of classification.

6. The fact that people are generally living to an older age means that the demand for overseas package holidays is likely to change. More older people may choose to go on extended package holidays in the winter months to escape the British weather. Older people are more likely to buy packages based on serviced rather than self-catering accommodation.

7. 'Loss leader' pricing is when an organization charges a price which is below breakeven in order to stimulate demand. It is often used when a new facility is opened in order to generate business and make the facility known to the general public.

8. Typical sales promotion techniques used by tour operators include discounts, special offers, extra product (3 weeks for the price of 2 etc.), incentives, free insurance, point-of-sale displays, 'freebies' (pens, stickers, balloons etc.) and personality endorsement.

9. Direct mail packages usually consist of four components. These are the envelope, a personalised letter, a reply device (freepost reply card for example) and another insert, such as a brochure or leaflet.

10. Such a park is likely to use advertising in local and regional newspapers, leaflet drops and local radio advertising.

11. Without a thorough evaluation of its promotional work, a leisure and tourism organization will not know whether the promotion is achieving its desired results, nor which particular promotional techniques are the most and least effective.

12. By encouraging readers to clip the coupon and exchange it for reduced price admission or a free gift, thereby giving the management an indication of the effectiveness.

Answers to Unit Test

1.	B	9.	B	17.	B	25.	A	33.	B
2.	B	10.	C	18.	D	26.	B	34.	C
3.	B	11.	A	19.	A	27.	C	35.	A
4.	B	12.	D	20.	B	28.	B	36.	C
5.	C	13.	C	21.	D	29.	A	37.	C
6.	C	14.	C	22.	C	30.	D	38.	B
7.	A	15.	A	23.	B	31.	C		
8.	B	16.	B	24.	C	32.	B		

Unit Test Comments

Q1: Answer is B – the information which is gathered is in-depth.
Focus groups are an effective, if expensive, way of obtaining in-depth information which can be used to develop new products and marketing ideas. A trained researcher questions a small team of consumers on the reasons for their purchasing habits.

Q2: Answer is B.
Primary research is concerned with collecting new information, often by conducting interviews in a number of different locations. Studying population figures is a form of secondary data collection, since the information is already available. Secondary research is also known as 'desk research'.

Q3: Answer is B – census data.
Census data (information on households in a particular area) is an external source of information, since it is collected by a government agency outside of the leisure and tourism organization. The other three options, sales returns, gate receipts and membership lists, are all held internally.

Q4: Answer is B.
'Open' questions on a questionnaire are used to discover people's opinions and views on particular subjects. An example of an 'open' question is: 'What improvements would you like to be made to the facility?' It is 'open' because there are many possible answers to the question. An example of a 'closed' question is: 'Did you use the café in the facility?' There are only two possible answers (yes or no), giving the respondent a restricted number of choices. Questionnaires made up entirely of 'closed' questions would take less time to complete than those containing 'open' questions.

Q5: Answer is C – the fact that a customer is over 55 years of age.
Demographic factors are concerned with characteristics of the population, such as age and gender. The fact that people in the UK are generally living longer, with all the implications this has for leisure and tourism organizations, is an example of a demographic variable.

Q6: Answer is C – the company's database was not able to target specific customers effectively.
ACORN and PINPOINT are computer-based database systems which can be used to target households and businesses according to a number of different factors, such as location, social class and postcode area. They often use census data and are used extensively in direct mail campaigns.

Q7: Answer is A – respondents were having difficulty in understanding some of the questions on a self-completed questionnaire survey.
Running a pilot survey (trying out a questionnaire on a small number of people before carrying out the main survey) can highlight problem questions and give the organization the chance to change them before conducting the main survey.

Q8: Answer is B – there was a lack of information available within the organization on population trends and statistics.
Information on population trends and statistics is an example of secondary data which can be held by an organization to help with its market research.

Q9: Answer is B.
So as not to break the flow of a report for the reader, it is usual to include any lengthy statistics, charts and tables as appendices towards the end of the report and to refer to them in the main body of the report.

Q10: Answer is C – do you agree that serviced accommodation is better than self-catering?
'Leading questions' are those that invite a particular answer from the respondent, rather than seeking an objective answer.

Q11: Answer is A – accurate advice on the characteristics of particular holiday destinations.
Staff in travel agencies must have good product knowledge, such as prices, details of destinations, flight times, etc., to be able to offer a professional service to their clients.

Q12: Answer is D – quick access to details of late availability packages.
Viewdata systems, such as those found in most travel agencies today, can give access to details of late availability packages and flights. They are often connected to the main computers of tour operators and airlines via a 'gateway' system.

Q13: Answer is C – special discounts on the price of late availability holidays.
A travel agent who has arranged low insurance premiums will be able to pass this saving on to the customer in the form of lower prices for holidays.

Q14: Answer is C.
Potential customers for the art gallery are not just those people who have visited other art galleries in the city. They could well be people who have never visited an art gallery before. It is easier to market to existing customers since they are more accessible, e.g. an organization may have their names on database or be able to distribute publicity material on-site.

Q15: Answer is A – diversification.
Diversification is the process by which an organization expands its operations into an area of activity that it has never tried before, in the hope of increasing its profitability.

Q16: Answer is B.
Many hotels are devising short break programmes to use their surplus rooms at weekends; most business guests stay

Monday to Thursday nights inclusive. Statement (i) is therefore true. The development, promotion and reservations associated with such a programme, however, would place an increased administrative workload on the hotel staff, should they choose to take on these duties themselves.

Q17: Answer is B.

The 'friends' of the museum may not wish it to be publicly known that they have made donations, preferring to keep such matters confidential. There is no requirement in the Data Protection Act which says that certain employees should not see information held on databases.

Q18: Answer is D – offering early evening dance classes for adults and children.

Options A, B and C are likely to have negative impacts on their local community, with increased noise, traffic and disruption to normal activities. Option D will contribute positively to the well-being of the local community.

Q19: Answer is A.

It is a very good idea to hold a meeting or series of meetings prior to the staging of an event, in order to inform local people of what is happening, thereby increasing goodwill, reducing criticism of the event and giving them the chance to put forward good ideas.

Q20: Answer is B – extending the hotel by adding a conservatory.

Any building work in a hotel or other leisure and tourism facility is bound to cause a certain amount of disruption to visitors. Management should take steps to keep disruption to a minimum and should consider closing off certain sections of buildings if major work is being carried out. Apart from anything else, health and safety issues should be considered.

Q21: Answer is D – changing the logo of the hotel.

From time to time, leisure and tourism organizations decide to change their 'corporate image'; Forte and British Airways are two organizations who have spent millions of pounds changing their image. One disadvantage of changing a logo is that there may be a temporary loss of current identity, until such time as the public grow used to the new style.

Q22: Answer is C – inviting journalists for 'fam' trips.

A 'fam' or familiarization trip is when a journalist is invited to see first hand a facility or sample a product. 'Fam' trips are very common in travel and tourism, where a journalist may go on a holiday and write an article about it on his or her return. While this can give good media coverage, the travel company will not have full control over what the journalist says or writes.

Q23: Answer is B.

Local groups and individuals are likely to have good local knowledge which can help reduce the impact of potential environmental and social problems. It is important that the local police, as well as the other emergency services, are consulted at the beginning of any plans, so that their views can be taken into account.

Q24: Answer is C – direct marketing.

Direct marketing is one of the fastest growing promotional techniques used in leisure and tourism. It includes telephone marketing, direct mail and door-to-door distribution. It is popular since it allows precise targeting of particular market sectors.

Q25: Answer is A – public relations.

Press releases are an effective way of keeping newspapers, magazines, radio and television stations up to date with what is going on in a leisure and tourism organization. Writing a good press release takes practice and skill.

Q26: Answer is B – sales promotions.

An offer such as '3 weeks for the price of 2' is a common example of a sales promotion, which also include free gifts, competitions and discount vouchers.

Q27: Answer is C – create awareness of the centre.

Any new business in leisure and tourism will want to get its name known as quickly as possible and create awareness among potential customers. It may do this by using a range of promotional techniques, including direct mail, advertising and public relations.

Q28: Answer is B – reinforce customer loyalty.

Although the hotel may well be able to distribute new promotional materials, update its database and identify alternative market segments, the main reason for offering the complimentary weekend break will be to reward its existing customers for their continued support and encourage them to use the hotel's services in the future.

Q29: Answer is A – the UK marketing director

Although he or she will rely heavily on the services of the public relations agency, the *responsibility* for the PR strategy will ultimately rest with the marketing director.

Q30: Answer is D – marketing managers in each of the group's hotels.

The marketing managers will be given the responsibility of setting up and monitoring the point-of-sale displays, since it is in the hotels that the customers will come face-to-face with the promotion.

Q31: Answer is C – an in-house design studio.

Neither the Marketing Director, nor the PR agency, nor the marketing managers will be responsible for producing promotional leaflets. This task should rightly be left to the design studio whose staff will have the necessary skills and expertise.

Q32: Answer is B.

If a promotional campaign is to be realistic, with achievable results, it is essential that the campaign objectives and techniques are decided within the overall budget limits. A television advertising campaign, for example, would be unrealistic as part of a campaign with a small budget.

Q33: Answer is B – planning.

The campaign objectives should always be established in the beginning of a campaign at the planning stage.

Q34: Answer is C – evaluation.

Evaluation takes place at the end of a campaign, when all those involved look back at its successes and failures.

Q35: Answer is A – implementation.

The time when a campaign is put into action (the implementation stage) is when advertisements are placed.

Q36: Answer is C.

Asking customers when they last visited the attraction will not give the precise detail needed to evaluate the response to the newspaper campaign. However, collecting and counting the number of coupons will give the required level of information, especially if the coupons have been coded in some way to indicate which newspaper was read or what region the visitors come from.

Q37: Answer is C – interviews with customers after the campaign.

Only option C will give the necessary depth of information needed in this case. An analysis of cards while the promotion was on or the number of coupons while the promotion was under way will not address the problem. The comparison of food versus drink sales, likewise, will not give the required information.

Q38: Answer is B.

Evaluation reports will look back at events and statistics rather than looking forward. Statement (i) is therefore true, but statement (ii) is false.

UNIT 5

Planning for an event

Getting Started

Successful events make an immense contribution to Britain's leisure and tourism industry. Large and small organizations in the private, public and voluntary sectors use events as a way of achieving their objectives. On a global scale, the world's biggest cities compete to stage major events such as the Olympic Games, the Commonwealth Games, the World Athletics Championships and the motor racing Grand Prix. At a national level, British towns and cities offer a wide range of events to attract visitors, generate revenue, raise their profile and improve amenities for local people. Locally, the money raised by a small event such as a summer fair can help voluntary groups to continue their good work in the community.

The media attention that surrounds many events today may lead the casual observer to think that events are something new. Nothing could be further from the truth: informal gatherings for religious, cultural or sporting purposes have existed since the beginning of time. The first Olympic Games was held in 776 BC and religious festivals and events were commonplace in the Middle Ages. In the mid-nineteenth century, Thomas Cook was building his reputation as a travel entrepreneur by organizing excursions to the great exhibitions in London and Paris, some of the grandest events of their day.

What has changed in recent times is the frequency, themes and locations of events. Whereas in the past, events were put on to celebrate a specific happening, today events can be created in order to meet specific objectives; their scope has gone well beyond purely recognizing the cultural importance of a particular date in the calendar. Organizers are forever dreaming up new ideas and themes for their events with the hope of catching the attention of a public which is becoming increasingly sophisticated in its leisure habits. Access to improved transport links and new technology means that events can be staged very quickly in response to changing tastes and fashions.

This unit looks at the main factors involved in planning and managing events. Element 1 considers the nature of events and the opportunities and problems that they generate. Element 2 looks in detail at the stages in event planning, while the final section, Element 3, is concerned with staffing events, including such matters as staff selection and staff training.

Contingency plans Alternative measures that will need to be planned in advance and implemented in response to particular problems.

Co-ordinator The single individual who will control the planning and management of an event.

Evaluation The process of looking back at an event, identifying good and bad points, and learning for the future.

Feasibility study An objective study that aims to determine whether the idea is practical, in an operational and financial sense.

Observers Individuals who are invited to observe an event and provide constructive comments at the evaluation stage.

Pre-feasibility The initial stage of event planning when an individual or group has an idea.

Resource implications An understanding that staging an event will demand resources, such as time, money, staff, buildings and equipment.

Steering group A selection of individuals who will oversee the planning and management of an event.

Essential Principles

5.1 The nature of events

The **types of events** that are staged by leisure and tourism organizations are as broad as the industry itself. Some of the more common events include:

- Mexican evening in a restaurant
- Beer festival
- Firework display
- Town carnival
- Swimming championships
- Athletics summer school
- Sponsored walk
- International soccer festival
- Holiday show
- Olympic Games
- Music workshop
- Festival of transport
- Air display
- Caravan rally
- Craft fair
- Opera festival
- Travel trade exhibition
- Fitness demonstration
- Garden party
- World Chess Championships

While by no means exhaustive, the list above gives an indication of the types of events which can be organized. The main *characteristics* of a public event are that:

- It is short-term.
- It is a 'one-off' or occurs infrequently.
- It provides an opportunity for the public to enjoy their leisure time.
- It allows the organizers to achieve their objectives.
- It may have a theme or celebrate a special anniversary.

Trade events, such as the World Travel Market or RecMan, give business people the opportunity to meet with suppliers and make important new contacts.

Events are to be found in all *contexts* of the leisure and tourism industry. Sport and recreation, accommodation, travel and tourism, catering and hospitality, entertainment and education, all use events as part of their strategy to win customers.

Did You Know ?

All sectors of the leisure and tourism industry (private, public and voluntary) plan and manage events.

The rationale for staging events

Events are often outside the normal activities of many leisure and tourism organizations. While this undoubtedly creates opportunities for the organizers, it can also lead to problems, particularly if the event is large scale or of national or international significance.

The reasons why people organize events are as many and varied as the types of events themselves. There are certain opportunities, however, which can be grasped regardless of the type of event. For example, events can:

- Provide facilities once the event is over, e.g. Sheffield played host to the World Student Games in 1991 and now has some of the finest sports facilities in the country, thus attracting further events and activities.
- Play an important part in the economic regeneration of an area, e.g. the Castlefield area of Manchester stages a number of events for visitors and local people every year, thereby helping the local economy.

- Introduce people to new activities, e.g. a young person going on an outdoor pursuits weekend for the first time.
- Help to change the image of a destination, e.g. the events held as part of the 'European City of Culture' celebrations helped to transform the image of Glasgow and put it firmly on the tourist map.
- Publicize a destination, e.g. the Sidmouth Folk Festival has helped put this small Devon town on the international map.
- Increase visitor numbers, e.g. as part of an overall promotional strategy.
- Improve knowledge and skills, e.g. a local quilters' guild running a weekend workshop on patchwork quilting.
- Promote a cause, e.g. a local hospital organizing a fun-run to raise funds for a new scanner.
- Increase community participation, e.g. in sport and recreation.
- Make a profit, e.g. the Los Angeles' Olympic Games.
- Provide enjoyment, fun and relaxation.

Managing events

The important thing to remember about events is that they don't 'just happen'. They have to be **planned and managed** effectively if they are to succeed. If organized well, events can be a source of great enjoyment and pride both for the organizers and those who attend. If they are badly managed, they can have a serious impact on the credibility of the organizers, any sponsors who may be involved, the location where the event is held and any other organizations or individuals who lend their names to it.

The remainder of this element focuses on three key areas of the management of events, namely:

- Problem-solving
- Resource implications of events
- Sources of advice and information

Problem-solving

Even the most well-planned event will, from time to time, encounter difficulties. The sort of **problems** which can occur when organizing events include:

- Having insufficient time to plan the event properly.
- Not having the right staff to plan and manage the event.
- Not setting clear objectives for the event.
- Having inadequate funding to see it through.
- Lack of a team effort on the part of those organizing the event.
- Poor communication between staff and outside organizations.
- Lack of consideration for those affected by the event, e.g. neighbours.
- Overspending the budget.
- Lack of, or poor, promotional activity.
- Little regard for health and safety matters.

Many problems occur because of the unique nature of many events. It is not something that management and staff in a leisure and tourism organization are used to dealing with on an everyday basis. There is no established routine for the event which will automatically make it a success. Whether the event is organized by a commercial concern, a local council or a voluntary sector organization, it will test the planning and management skills of all involved. There is nothing guaranteed to create ill-feeling and bad publicity quite as much as a badly organized event.

Did You Know ?

The organizers of Sheffield's bid to host the Commonwealth Games in 2002 were forced to pull out at the last minute, because of uncertainties surrounding finances.

A 'blueprint' for success

Having identified the positive opportunities that an event can exploit, as well as some of the problems which can hinder progress, it should be possible to make a 'blueprint' of what needs to be done to make sure that any event is a success. Such a checklist would include:

- Securing funding at an early stage.
- Allowing sufficient time for planning.
- Setting clear objectives.
- Establishing a promotional strategy.
- Liaising with all interested parties.
- Having a contingency plan.
- Recruiting and training staff.
- Establishing a health, safety and security policy.
- Carrying out the event according to the plan.
- Reviewing the event and preparing a report for future use.

Even if all of these points are carried out, however, there is still no guarantee that the event will be a success. There are many unknown factors which can tip the balance between success and failure: the weather, the location, the promotion, the pricing, the theme, the choice of staff and the audience itself, are all difficult to control. Planning well in advance and anticipating problems, however, can minimize the risks associated with any event in leisure and tourism.

Resource implications of events

Making the decision to stage an event is not something which should be entered into lightly. Whatever their size or significance, organizing events demands a great deal of effort, hard work, determination and confidence on the part of all those concerned with planning and management. Organizing an event can also be a very risky business, fraught with pitfalls for the unsuspecting. An organizer of an event needs to be somebody who can combine flair and imagination with a methodical approach – a rare combination, particularly when the job demands nerves of steel as well! Because these talents are seldom found in one individual, event organizers usually adopt a *team approach* to getting the job done, trying to match the natural skills of team members to particular tasks.

Whether an event is organized by one individual or a team approach is adopted, the event itself will have resource implications for the organizers, including:

- Finance
- Premises
- Staffing
- Disruption to other activities
- Environmental constraints
- Health and safety considerations

Finance

The **finance** needed to stage an event will vary depending on the scale and significance of the event itself. A small village summer fete, for example, may need very little funding to get it off the ground. In contrast, the city of Birmingham is estimated to have spent £2 million on its attempt to win the 1992 Olympic Games. Whatever their size, nearly all events will need a degree of financial support at some stage in their development. Organizers can look to local or central government funding, voluntary contributions or the private sector for help. Sponsorship and help 'in kind' often smooth the path of event planning. Once up and running, the finances of the event will need careful monitoring using accepted accountancy practices. A leisure and tourism organization which is planning an event over and above its normal activities must be aware of the extra burden that the event will have on its finances and budget accordingly.

Premises

Depending on the size of an event, **premises** may have to be hired, built, adapted or even demolished. The staging of a major event such as the World Cup or the Olympic Games will involve all of these to a greater or lesser degree. The necessary permissions from local or national authorities will need to be obtained if major alterations or changes of use of premises are envisaged. Time and cost factors will need to be built into the overall event plan if premises which have been altered in some way to accommodate the event have to be reinstated to their original condition once the event is over.

Staffing

Element 3 looks in detail at issues concerning the staffing of an event. In general terms, events call for a rare mix of qualities in those who take on the job of organizers. All **staff**, whether paid or volunteers, will need careful selection and training in their particular role in the event. Teamwork and communication skills are particularly important if the event is to prove successful. Not all staff working in an organization which decides to stage an event for the first time will necessarily feel happy at the prospect of getting involved with something which is outside their normal duties and responsibilities. Management should respect this feeling and, whenever possible, only invite those staff who feel comfortable with the particular qualities and skills that events demand to join the organizing team.

Disruption to other activities

The fact that an event is usually a 'one-off', or at least occurs infrequently, can sometimes present the organizers with something of a headache, since it will **disrupt** the normal operations of a leisure and tourism organization. Unless the organization is solely concerned with organizing an event or series of events, management must accept that some disruption to other activities is inevitable and seek to minimize the impact of the event on the everyday functioning of the establishment. There must also be a recognition that the event not only may disrupt those within the organization but may have an adverse impact on third parties, such as neighbours and the public in general. The organizers of the Great North Run on Tyneside, for example, have to be very sensitive to the needs of the local people on the route of the run, since roads have to be closed and traffic diverted. Prior warning, advance information and a sensitive approach will ensure that local people feel involved in the staging of the event and react positively to the organizers and runners.

Environmental constraints

We have acknowledged that events can cause disturbance to neighbours and others who may be involved with them; noise, congestion, traffic problems, road closures and disruption of normal activities are common causes of complaint. The **environment** too may be harmed during an event or in its build-up or dismantling phases. Events can attract large numbers of people, often concentrated in a small space for a short period of time. Organizers need to be aware of the environmental problems which their event could cause and put in place measures to minimize the impact. Typical environmental concerns which may need addressing include:

- Damage to wildlife, trees and flowers.
- Pollution of rivers, streams, lakes or other water courses.
- Disposal of toxic substances.
- Build-up of litter.
- Physical erosion of a site by feet and vehicles.
- Excessive noise.
- Air pollution from vehicles often stationary with their engines running.

Organizers of a well-planned event should anticipate potential environmental problems and not be left to find solutions on the day of the event.

Did You Know ?

The organizers of major national and international events are increasingly being asked to carry out an environmental impact assessment (EIA), to identify likely problems and put forward solutions.

Health and safety considerations

Every event, no matter how small, must give serious consideration to matters such as **health, safety and security**. As well as any particular statutory requirements which may affect the event, the organizers must remember that they have a common law duty of care to those attending and those assisting on the day. Unit 2 looked in detail at health, safety and security measures in leisure and tourism, but the specific laws and regulations which event organizers are likely to need to consider include:

- Public Order Act.
- Food Safety Act and the Food Hygiene Regulations.
- Health and Safety at Work, etc. Act.
- Trades Description Act.
- The new regulations (from January 1993) needed to implement EU Directives.
- Occupiers' Liability Act.
- Licensing Act.

This list is by no means exhaustive and each event will have its own peculiarities which may require the organizers to take account of other specific legislation. Medical advice and back-up at the event will be particularly crucial; organizers may choose to employ staff with relevant first-aid qualifications and engage the help of voluntary organizations such as the Red Cross or St John Ambulance, as well as alerting the emergency services. In practice a combination of all three approaches will give the best result.

Sources of advice and information

Every event will have its own unique set of circumstances which cannot always be predicted in advance. Organizers should not be afraid to make use of the extensive network of individuals and agencies who have *experience* of event management. The organizers of successful events, whether in Britain or elsewhere in the world, are only too happy to pass on advice and tips on what, and what not, to do. Although every event is unique, there are certain basic principles which apply to all events to a greater or lesser degree. An event organizer, who may 'volunteer' for the position, needs to be aware both of these basic points and those which are specific to his or her event.

As well as the help which can be given by fellow organizers, advice, support and information relating to the management of events is available from a number of different sources.

Professional advice

There are a number of areas where the help of *professionals* is vital if success is to be achieved. No matter how large or small the event, the following specialists are likely to be needed:

- Accountant
- Emergency services staff
- Solicitor
- Environmental health officer
- Insurance agent
- Maintenance staff
- Marketing and PR expert

A local event may be able to use the services of many of these specialists free of charge as their contribution to the event. Some organizers have found, however, that it is sometimes better to pay for the services of the professionals, who then feel more inclined to provide their usual level of professionalism.

Did You Know ?

Major events will set aside significant proportions of their budget to pay fees to professionals and consultants.

Event management companies

There are in Britain today a number of companies which *specialize* in planning and staging events. Increased recognition of the role of events as part of a total promotional package has led to a demand from both the private and public sector for the services of such companies. They are often very small concerns, sometimes just one person, and tend to be people who have been involved in events management for larger organizations and have taken the decision to 'go it alone'. Their impartial advice and expertise can be invaluable, particularly for large and prestigious events.

Other information sources

Public libraries, as well as libraries of colleges and universities, are good sources of information on events management in general. Some may be able to provide organizers with case studies of how successful events have been planned and managed. Collecting promotional literature on events can be a useful way of learning from others. Local authorities sometimes have *events officers*, who may be housed in the recreation, leisure or tourism departments. General books and periodicals on leisure and tourism management may include articles on the management of events and give ideas for further reading.

1. Choose an event that takes place in your local area and list the reasons why it is staged.
_____
_____
_____

2. Why do you think the British government pledged £55 million to the city of Manchester if its bid to host the Olympic Games in the year 2000 was successful?
_____
_____
_____

3. Which leisure and tourism events are most likely to give rise to problems under the Public Order Act?
_____
_____
_____

4. How do rural events such as the Mid Wales Festival of the Countryside help local communities?
_____
_____
_____

Factfile 1: Mid Wales Festival of the Countryside
The Mid Wales Festival of the Countryside is a series of events (some new, some which have been in existence for some time) which take place in the countryside, towns and villages of Mid Wales from June to December each year. Launched in 1985 as a contribution to the World Conservation Strategy, the Festival has grown into a pioneering model of responsible rural tourism. Its aim is to show that informed concern and respect for the environment can go hand-in-hand with economic development, in an area of Britain which is working hard to attract inward investment, create new jobs and improve the social fabric for the local people. Spearheading this work is the Development Board for Rural Wales (DBRW), a government-funded quango (see Unit 1), which considers that high quality tourism can play a significant role in the economic development of the region.

The DBRW is one of the major sponsors of the Festival of the Countryside, along with the Countryside Council for Wales and all eight local authorities in the area. It is staffed by a part-time director, two full-time assistant directors, and associates brought in for specific functions including research and compiling the Festival's annual magazine. An avid supporter of the Festival of the Countryside is the leading environmentalist David Bellamy, who visits Mid Wales every year to take part in events. He said of the Festival recently,

It's the only place I know where the people who have gold chains round their necks and who sit in committees are actively working with conservation to make their landscape wonderful forever and ever.

The Festival, with its base in Newtown in the heart of Mid Wales, acts as an 'umbrella' organization for marketing purposes and as a catalyst for the development of events, linking with individuals, voluntary groups and the private sector.

The aims of the Festival of the Countryside are:

• **Environmental education** – to convey, in an interesting and coherent way, the messages of the countryside and conservation.

• **Enjoyment of the countryside** – to help satisfy the varied recreational demands of residents and tourists.

• **Socio-economic development** – to stimulate the rural economy, support providers of rural attractions and involve the local community in culturally-acceptable ways.

In seeking to achieve these aims, the Festival has had notable success and is now spreading its message through links with rural areas in Europe and beyond. Training for event organizers has been provided through periodic information seminars and local group work, as well as a residential business development course held in 1992. A handbook of good practice in responsible rural tourism has been prepared for use throughout Europe.

(Information courtesy of Mid Wales Festival of the Countryside)

5.2 Presenting a plan for an event

Key stages in event planning

Staging a successful event involves a great deal of effort, time, money, enthusiasm and commitment on the part of many individuals and organizations, sometimes over a long period of time. Above all, what distinguishes a good event from a bad event is excellent planning and organization. Without an organized and methodical approach to all aspects of the staging of an event, it will not reach its full potential or, even worse, will fail miserably, with all the negative publicity and bad feeling which accompany failure.

There are five **key stages** (see Fig. 5.1) which need careful attention to ensure that an event has the best possible chance of success:

• The pre-feasibility stage
• The feasibility study
• The planning phase
• The event itself
• The evaluation stage

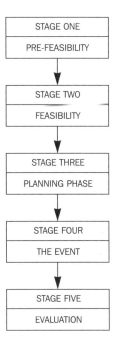

Figure 5.1 Key stages in event planning

Stage one: The pre-feasibility stage

The **pre-feasibility stage** is the stage at which an individual or an organization has an *idea* for an event which may or may not prove viable. Many of the people who work in leisure and tourism are very good at formulating ideas for new events which they believe cannot fail to attract visitors in huge numbers. The aim of the pre-feasibility phase is to look *objectively* at any proposal to see if the event really has the potential to be a winner. In many respects, the pre-feasibility phase is the most important of all; the decision to commit staff, time and money to a full feasibility study will be taken at this stage. The sorts of questions which will need careful consideration are:

- What are the aims of the event?
- Is it in line with the organization's mission or objectives?
- When will it take place?
- Is there a suitable location?
- Can staff be made available or extra people employed?
- Does it have the backing of senior management?
- Will funding be made available?
- Does the organization have the confidence to stage the event?

It is important at this stage to consult widely with people in the organization and to seek advice from respected individuals and organizations outside, remembering always that a degree of confidentiality will be necessary. Their views and concerns will help to answer the question: 'Is the idea a good one?'. Depending on the scale and nature of the proposed event, it may be felt necessary to seek the views of national governing bodies, professional organizations and local or regional groups.

If reactions to the idea are positive and those canvassed consider it worthy of further investigation, it will be necessary to take the idea one stage further by carrying out a feasibility study.

Stage two: The feasibility study

Commissioning a **feasibility study** will help management to evaluate the idea as objectively as possible and to determine whether it is practical, in an operational and financial sense, to stage the event. The study can be undertaken by staff in the organization or carried out by an external consultant; the scale and nature of the event will determine the best method. The written study should include information on:

- The aims and objectives of the event.
- The benefits to the organizers.
- Details of the nature of the event.
- The timescale for planning the event.
- How the event fits into the overall mission of the organization.
- The 'track record' of those proposing the event.
- The resource implications – finance, staff, time, premises, equipment, administration etc.
- Possible problems and their solutions.

The feasibility study should be circulated to key decision-makers for their comments. If they are convinced by the study that the proposed event is viable and will bring benefits to the organization, then the real work can begin. The commitment from senior management is crucial and should preferably be in the form of a written response to the feasibility study. An endorsement in writing will signal the go-ahead for the event and the detailed planning can begin.

If senior personnel are not convinced that the event has potential, it is better that it is stated at this point rather than half way through the planning phase. On the evidence put forward in the feasibility study, they may either reject the proposal altogether or may consider that with a little fine-tuning it could be made to work. Far better that any doubts are raised at this point in order to save valuable time and money later.

> **Did You Know ?**
>
> A feasibility study for an event should include detailed forecasts of anticipated levels of expenditure and income.

Stage three: The planning phase

Having received the approval to proceed, the detailed **planning** to ensure that the event is a success can begin in earnest. The important stages in the planning process are to:

- Publicize the decision to go ahead.
- Select a co-ordinator.
- Elect a committee or steering group.
- Establish an organizational structure.
- Clarify objectives.
- Set timescale targets and deadlines.
- Agree budgets.
- Develop contingency plans.

Publicize the decision to go ahead

It is important to **publicize** the fact that the event is to go ahead for a number of reasons. First, making it generally known when and where your event will take place *should* ensure that other organizers do not choose the same date and venue; in reality, it is practically impossible not to clash with other events taking place on the same day, but it should be possible to avoid events of the same kind on the same day, thus ensuring a good attendance. A second reason for publicizing the event at this stage is to create interest from the general public and, if it is a sports event for example, to give them the opportunity to start training. A third reason is to signal to those who may be interested in helping the event in some way to get in touch.

If there are a number of options as to *when* the event could take place, it is important to give some thought as to the most appropriate date, bearing in mind who it is you are trying to attract. Knowing the dates of school holidays is important if the event is aimed at families; it is also a good idea to avoid meal times for the same reason.

> **Did You Know ?**
>
> It may be important to bear in mind the dates when British Summer Time begins and ends, if an event is to be staged close to either of these two dates.

We have already mentioned that one of the reasons for publicizing the fact that the event is going ahead is to avoid other events occurring on the same day. Equally important is the need to be aware of any other international, national or local events which are already planned to take place. It would be disastrous if the sponsored walk for the local soccer team was inadvertently organized on the same day as the FA Cup Final! Thankfully, the dates of major events are set well in advance.

It is interesting to note the power that television is having over the staging of major events, particularly sporting events. The timing of events often has to be planned to fit in with television schedules. One of the disadvantages that Sydney faced in its bid to host the Olympic Games in the year 2000 was the fact that many of the events would be taking place in the middle of the night European time, because of the time difference between Europe and Australia. As things turned out, Sydney was successful in its bid and will be liaising closely with television companies to ensure maximum coverage of events to satisfy sponsors and those paying to advertise on television.

Select a co-ordinator

Deciding who to appoint to the job of **co-ordinator** is perhaps the most important and difficult decision of all. Time taken at this stage in drawing up a list of qualities which the ideal candidate should have and finding somebody who matches most closely these qualities will pay dividends in the long run. An ineffective co-ordinator can be a liability in the quest for success in the planning of the event. Although every event is unique, any good co-ordinator should have some basic skills and qualities:

- A motivator
- An excellent communicator
- Excellent leadership qualities
- A good organizer
- A persuasive negotiator
- The ability to delegate
- Not afraid of hard work
- Creativity and flair

The event co-ordinator should be appointed with the full confidence of the senior management of the organization, and should be given the necessary resources, authority and support to do the job properly. All those involved in the planning of the event need to be clear where the power and responsibility lie. There should be delegation downwards whenever possible so that paid staff and volunteers feel involved in making the decisions which will ensure that the event is a success.

A good event co-ordinator will realize that he or she cannot operate in isolation, but will want to be involved in the selection of individuals who will collectively take the detailed decisions on planning and managing the event. This most commonly involves the election of a committee.

Elect a committee or steering group

While it may be feasible for a single person to organize an event, particularly if it is small and local, most events will be organized through a **committee**, sometimes referred to as a steering group. For some events, it may be useful to agree a **constitution**, the rules by which the committee will operate; this is often carried out for events which happen every year or have national or international significance.

The committee will have a number of *functions*:

- To take executive decisions on matters relating to the event.
- To oversee the smooth planning of the event (together

with the co-ordinator).
- To ensure that finances are managed appropriately.
- To divide the necessary work amongst individuals and subgroups.
- To free the co-ordinator from routine tasks.
- To develop a promotional plan for the event.
- To agree an organizational structure for the event.
- To ensure that the necessary permissions to stage the event are obtained.

The event co-ordinator should ideally be the chairperson of the committee and be involved in deciding who is invited to sit on the committee, which will be made up of key people who are willing to give the time and effort to the job in hand. If the event is part of the activities of an existing leisure and tourism organization, whether in the public, private or voluntary sector, the committee will include staff from within the organization and, depending on the event's size and importance, people from outside as well. It is often prudent to invite onto the committee individuals from professional bodies, emergency services, sponsors, local authorities and the like, whose support for the event is seen as vital to its success. Depending on the size and type of event, it may be necessary to form **subcommittees** to deal with particular aspects of the planning of the event, such as publicity, traffic management and health and safety.

Every event committee will need a chairperson, secretary and treasurer plus others with special responsibilities peculiar to the particular event being organized. These could include individuals with responsibility for:

- Catering
- Equipment
- Fund-raising and sponsorship
- Staffing and staff training
- Entertainment
- Promotion and marketing

> **Did You Know ?**
> It is sometimes helpful to set up an executive committee, made up of a small group of key individuals, to take decisions in the absence of all committee members.

The event co-ordinator will need to use all his or her skills of persuasion and negotiation to ensure that the organizing committee doesn't become just 'a talking shop' but takes on the role of a working group. Committees are all about fairness and democracy in decision making, but the process can be painfully slow at times. The committee will need to meet regularly to review progress, but members should not be afraid to cancel a planned meeting if there is little to discuss at that particular time; holding a meeting just because a date has been set is time-wasting and can lead to frustration in committee members. Specialists can be **co-opted** onto the committee from time to time to help with particular aspects of the planning of the event.

> **Did You Know ?**
> It is a good idea to invite a well-known person to become president of the committee. This patronage can help promote the event and lend a welcome degree of credibility to proceedings.

Establish an organizational structure

Once the organizing committee is in place, led by the event co-ordinator, it must begin the task of developing a **structure** which will ensure that all aspects of the planning and management of the event are carried out meticulously. One of the first jobs will be to identify **focus** areas, which are broad areas of work, each of which will have a set of *tasks* associated with it. For example, an event such as a county show will have the focus areas and tasks shown in Fig. 5.2.

Focus Area 1: Site preparation and management

Tasks: (1) Public and vehicle access
      (2) Car parking
      (3) Signposting
      (4) Equipment
      (5) Admission

Focus Area 2: Finance and legal

Tasks: (1) Budgetary control
      (2) Fund-raising and sponsorship
      (3) Banking
      (4) Production of accounts
      (5) Legal permissions
      (6) Health, safety and security

Focus Area 3: Staffing

Tasks: (1) Recruitment
      (2) Training
      (3) Payment
      (4) Facilities for staff

Focus Area 4: Event promotion

Tasks : (1) Production of promotional literature
      (2) Advertising
      (3) Media liaison
      (4) VIP guests
      (5) Ticket sales

Focus Area 5: Support services

Tasks : (1) Catering
      (2) First aid
      (3) Toilets
      (4) Lighting and public address (PA) system
      (5) Staff communication system
      (6) Cloakroom
      (7) Facilities for disabled visitors
      (8) Entertainment

Figure 5.2 Focus areas and tasks for a county show

Once the focus areas have been identified, the next job of the co-ordinating committee is to assign an individual or team to develop the *detailed tasks* associated with the focus and accept the responsibility for making sure that the work in this area is correctly planned. The size, nature and significance of the event will determine whether an individual or team approach is needed. Those assigned to this work will report to the event organizer and organizing committee.

It is often useful to draw up an **organization chart** at this stage showing the linkages between the different focus groups and how they relate to the event organizer and the organizing committee. The chart will indicate lines of communication and responsibility. It will help to resolve any problems or areas of overlap between individual focus areas. For major national and international events, it is often necessary to produce an organizational handbook, incorporating an organization chart, to explain in detail the process by which the event is being organized.

Clarify objectives

As soon as the event co-ordinator, co-ordinating committee and focus leaders are all appointed, it is as well to *clarify* exactly what it is the whole team is trying to achieve. This will be a two-stage affair, concentrating first on the overall aims of the event, as detailed in the feasibility study, and then the specific objectives for each focus leader and his or her team. This is best achieved by the event co-ordinator calling a meeting of all event personnel and setting the scene before the work in earnest begins. The work of the focus teams will concentrate on:

- Establishing the tasks within their particular focus area.
- Setting the dates and deadlines by which each of their tasks must be completed.
- Setting spending limits (and income targets, if applicable) for each task in their focus.
- Establishing what level and type of staffing they will need.
- Deciding what other equipment and facilities they will need.

Set timescale targets and deadlines

The focus leaders will need to ensure that they set their **timetables** and **deadlines** within an overall event timescale plan, which will need constant monitoring and refining in response to unforeseen circumstances. It is very helpful to have a **flowchart** or **critical path analysis** detailing the focus areas with key time targets and deadlines incorporated for each one. It is usual practice to work back from the day of the event when deciding on time deadlines. All those involved in staging the event should remember that things often take longer than expected to happen, so it is a good idea to allow extra time for 'contingencies'. It is also sound advice to allow plenty of time at the initial planning stage, so that the systems and procedures adopted can be implemented with as few changes as possible.

Most event organizers work from **checklists**, either ones which they have developed themselves or ones adapted from a reference source (there are a number of good books on event management which give example checklists). The detailed planning process for the event co-ordinator will involve matching the items on his or her checklist with the deadlines being developed by the focus groups, to produce an overall **event planner** giving the full picture of focus areas, tasks and deadlines for completion.

Agree budgets

The co-ordinating committee should be as precise as possible when estimating the likely income and expenditure relating to the event and the **budgets** (if any) needed by the different focus group leaders. Accounting for income and expenditure is particularly important when funds from external sources are being used, e.g. in the form of sponsorship or a grant from a local authority or voluntary trust. They will want assurances and evidence that their investment is being prudently managed. Focus leaders will need to account for their particular expenditure, while the responsibility for overall budgeting and finance lies with the event co-ordinator and the treasurer on the co-ordinating committee.

The financial objectives of events will vary greatly. A local authority, for example, is unlikely to have profit as its main motive when staging an event, but perhaps to make its leisure and tourism facilities and services better known to the local population. An event staged by a private sector leisure and tourism organization, however, may well be expected to generate a healthy profit. While public sector events may well be *subsidized* by the local authority, it will nonetheless be made clear to the organizers that they should aim to minimize expenditure, maximize income and, hopefully, at least *break even* financially on the event. It is important that the event organizer, the organizing committee and the focus leaders are clear about the financial objectives for the event. They will need answers to questions such as:

- Is the event expected to make a profit or a loss?
- What is the level of council subsidy (if any)?
- What is the break-even point?

Without knowing the answers to these questions, the task of planning and managing the finances for the event will be that much harder.

Whether or not the event being staged is a money-making venture or has a non-profit objective, the importance of carefully setting expenditure limits for each focus area and methodically recording what is actually spent is just the same. Even small events in the local community will have costs associated with them and the idea that local authority events are 'free' is far from the truth. Although an event sponsored by a local authority may well be free to enter, local people will have contributed to the cost of organizing the events through their local and national taxes.

There are a number of different **sources of income** which event organizers may explore:

- Sponsorship
- Donations
- Ticket sales
- Grants
- Low interest loans
- Car parking fees
- Sale of advertising space
- Raffles and other competitions
- Income from concessions (businesses given the authority to trade at the event)
- Sale of food and drink
- Income from television or radio companies
- Sale of merchandise

Any income targets for specific focus areas should be realistic and agreed by the focus leader and his or her team from the outset. Estimating income is extremely difficult, particularly when an outdoor event is at the mercy of the weather, and any event is competing with other leisure and tourism activities for customers.

> **Did You Know** ❓
>
> The NutraSweet London Marathon could not operate without the income from its many sponsors.

Develop contingency plans

Events are just as likely as any other aspect of leisure and tourism to fall foul of Murphy's Law, so 'if anything can go wrong it will!' Some things that happen to test the resolve of even the best-prepared event organizer can truly be said to be unforeseen. Many, however, can be predicted and **contingencies** or alternative courses of action can be implemented. In Britain, the weather must be one of the least predictable factors surrounding any event, be it in summer or winter. Organizers can take steps to reassure the public that an outdoor event will go ahead 'whatever the weather' by publi-

cizing this fact from the outset and giving an alternative venue should the worst happen. A cold spell or sudden downpour can also affect attendances at indoor events, with people choosing to stay in the comfort of their own homes rather than venturing out.

Other occurrences will also need contingency plans:

- **Traffic congestion** – is there an alternative point of entry for key personnel?
- **Parts of the site waterlogged** – is there an alternative area available to move into?
- **Failure of power supplies** – is a back-up alternative source of supply needed?
- **A major accident** – have the emergency services been told of the event and means of entry and exit worked out?
- **Non-arrival of key staff or personalities** – are there 'extras' on hand?

There are occasions when an event will have to be called off altogether, often for reasons outside the control of the organizers. Although very disappointing for both organizing staff and the visitors, the same degree of professionalism which was in evidence for the planning of the event must be maintained to deal with this situation. The organizer will need to make the decision either to cancel the event altogether or to postpone it until a future date. Whatever is decided must be communicated as quickly as possible to the general public; an excellent way of doing this is by contacting the local radio station who will gladly broadcast regular information so as to let as many people as possible know. There must be a method by which any advance payments can be returned in the event of cancellation, or tickets can be re-used if the event is only postponed. Those responsible for press and public relations will need to handle the situation sensitively and have their own contingency plan for dealing with any adverse publicity.

Stage four: The event itself

If the event has been planned well in advance and all concerned are familiar with their roles, the day of the **event itself** should be as enjoyable for those who have organized it as for the visitors who support it. It is a good idea to hold an eve of event briefing session to go over the final details, iron out any last minute hitches and confirm any alterations to schedules. It may be that some parts of the event, perhaps the opening and closing ceremonies, will need a final rehearsal. The co-ordinator should not be given specific tasks to carry out on the day itself, except perhaps welcoming and entertaining VIPs, but should be allowed to circulate around the event helping with any difficult situations which may arise and generally maintaining a positive and professional approach.

> **Did You Know** ❓
>
> All staff involved with an event, paid and unpaid, should remember the importance of customer care.

Whether the event is free or customers have paid to enter, it is important that all staff involved in any way with it are mindful of the need to give customers the attention they need so that they can enjoy the event to the full. Visitors with special needs will warrant particular attention. Keeping to any published times is important in order to retain a professional approach to the management of the event. There is nothing more frustrating for visitors than to turn up at a particular time to find that nothing is happening. If changes to the schedule have to be made, make sure that the message is conveyed to those attending the event.

If these points are remembered and all the prior planning has achieved its objectives, then the event should be a memorable celebration for all concerned.

Stage five: The evaluation stage

The process of looking back and **evaluating** is just as important in event management as in any other sector of the leisure and tourism industry.

We all learn from our mistakes and there is invariably something that we would have done in a different way if we had the chance again. Any evaluation of an event should try to answer the following questions:

- Was the organizational structure workable?
- Did the event achieve its financial objectives?
- Were all eventualities covered?
- Did the event achieve its operational objectives?
- What changes would be made if the event was to be staged again?
- Were the sponsors (if any) happy with the outcome?
- Were the customers satisfied with the event?

The event organizer should organize a de-briefing session with staff as soon as possible after the event. At this meeting, the above questions should be considered while still fresh in the minds of all concerned, before a final report on the event is prepared for distribution to interested individuals and organizations, with one copy being retained for future reference. If the event takes place over a number of days, is very large, or is split into discrete activities, more than one de-briefing session may be needed.

Perhaps the most relevant question to ask at the evaluation stage is: 'Was the event worth all the hard work, money, time and effort that went into its planning and staging?' If all those involved in organizing the event can answer yes to this, then it can truly be said to have been a success.

Information which may be helpful during the evaluation phase of an event can come from a number of different sources, including:

- **Feedback from staff** – all staff, whether paid or working in a voluntary capacity, are likely to have useful ideas as to how their particular role could have been improved, as well as general comments about the organization of the event. The event co-ordinator should take the time and trouble to interview key staff and feed their comments into the evaluation process.

- **Records** – any information or data about the event which has been recorded will help in its evaluation. Items such as receipts, financial accounts, attendance figures, video footage, ticket sales, photographs and media coverage, can be used to reflect on the event and draw conclusions.

- **Customer comments** – this can be both formal and informal. Formal feedback can be from surveys carried out during and sometimes immediately after the event. As well as information on the profile of customers attending the event, the organizers can use visitor surveys to discover attitudes and opinions. All staff should be trained to register informal feedback, in the form of comments, complaints and suggestions from customers, since this is often as valuable as the formal data. Events involving large numbers of staff sometimes find it useful to set aside time for an exchange of informal comments.

- **Views from observers** – the organizers of larger events often appoint observers whose role is to look at how the event has been organized and, more importantly, observe how the event comes across 'on the day'. It is useful to have the views of respected individuals who lie outside the organizational framework of the event and whose comments can help the evaluation process.

Factfile 2: The NutraSweet London Marathon

Introduction

First held in 1981, the London Marathon was the brainchild of former British athlete Chris Braisher, now the Chairman of the London Marathon Company which organizes the annual event. The idea came out of seeing other city marathons operating around the world, most notably the New York Marathon. London has hosted a marathon every year since 1981, with the fourteenth event planned for 17 April 1994. Between 65,000 and 80,000 entries are received each year, but the number of starters is restricted to 35,000, made up of club runners, individuals and a field of 'elite' competitors.

What is the event trying to achieve?

One of the main objectives of the event is to generate a surplus of funds which can be used within the London Boroughs to create or improve recreational and leisure facilities for the local people. Approximately £250,000 was distributed after the 1993 event for this purpose. Projects which help those with special needs are particularly supported; for example, one of the recent projects involved installing a hoist for disabled people in a swimming baths. The London Marathon also aims to help British marathon running and to give competitors the opportunity to enjoy themselves. Because the London Marathon is organized by a limited company, it has short-term aims which are similar to those of any commercial sector leisure and tourism organization, namely to ensure that the company continues to exist and continues to generate a working surplus.

How is it financed?

The London Marathon Company has an annual turnover of approximately £2 million. *Sponsorship* is vital to the existence of the Company, and therefore the event; without sponsorship, there would be no London Marathon. Total funds from sponsors amount to around £1 million. The event has attracted a number of major sponsors since it began back in 1981; the first was Gillette, followed by Mars, then ADT and finally NutraSweet, which originally signed a contract for two years but is now negotiating an option to extend beyond this time period. In addition to the main sponsor, there are many 'suppliers' who contribute to the funding of the event in return for publicity. For 1994 these include the sports clothing and footwear company ASICS, Citizen Timing and a host of other companies supplying everything from drinks to cars. The Company aims to maximize revenue from sponsors and suppliers in order to make the surplus available for distribution to charities and worthy causes as large as possible.

Who organizes the event?

Ultimate responsibility for the organization of the London Marathon lies with the General Manager of the London Marathon Company, who is supported by a number of full- and part-time staff, including:

- A Marketing Consultant
- A Press Officer
- An Administrator
- An Entry Co-ordinator
- A Course Director
- An Accountant
- The Start Co-ordinator
- The Finish Director

On the day of the Marathon itself, nearly 5,000 voluntary helpers recruited from clubs and societies assist with all the tasks needed to ensure the success of the event. Team leaders are identified and are asked to attend a two-day briefing session where their roles are clarified. Because of the scale of the event and the logistics involved in making it happen, the organizers use volunteers who have worked with the Marathon before, in order to give continuity and help develop the essential teamwork skills as quickly as possible. There is no dress rehearsal of the event; it has to be right first time!

What is the timescale for planning the event?

The first stage in the planning cycle is fixing the date for the Marathon, which is finalized some 18–20 months in advance. In deciding on a date, the organizers have to consult widely so as not to clash with other events of equal significance. This involves consultation with:

- The Royal Diary (from 1994 the start and finish of the London Marathon will be in the Mall, close to Buckingham Palace)
- Television companies
- The athletics calendar
- The British sporting calendar
- The police and security forces

Once the date has been fixed, detailed planning for the event can begin in earnest.

Is there any community liaison?

The organizers of the Marathon keep local communities up to date with the planning and staging of the event. A representative of the London Marathon sits on committees of all seven London Boroughs through which the route passes. Every house and car on the route is given a leaflet twice before the day of the event to let people know that it is taking place. Local newspapers and radio are kept informed of road closures and other relevant information about the Marathon. Local people are encouraged to join in with the spirit of the event perhaps by organizing a street party or other celebration.

How is the event marketed and promoted?

Much of the marketing effort surrounding the Marathon is concerned with attracting potential sponsors and suppliers. In order to attract sponsorship, organizations are offered advertising space in official programmes and magazines, on vehicles and along the route. There are also VIP hospitality facilities on race day which the sponsors can use. Television coverage is a major incentive when it comes to attracting sponsors; the event is shown live in the UK and Japan, and is distributed to another 50 countries worldwide. In addition to the work on sponsorship, the organizers have to spend time and money to attract the 'ordinary' members of the public who do not read running magazines or who are not members of a running or athletics club. As this group accounts for 50% of all applications to run, the task is by no means an easy one. Local and regional newspapers and local radio stations are used to alert the general public when applications for the Marathon are being accepted.

(Information courtesy of the General Manager of the NutraSweet London Marathon)

5. Why is the pre-feasibility phase of event planning often considered to be the most important of all the stages?
   _____
   _____
   _____

6. Why are television companies so powerful when it comes to the timing of major sporting events?
   _____
   _____
   _____

7. Are there any disadvantages to setting up a committee to oversee the organization of an event?
   _____
   _____
   _____

8. Why is it important to have clear objectives for an event?
   _____
   _____
   _____

9. What are some of the main reasons why local councils sponsor events in their communities?
   _____
   _____
   _____

5.3 Allocating roles and personnel in an event

It is vital that the organizers of an event use their resources wisely to employ the best people available and train them effectively. Success or failure in planning and staging an event often hinges on the quality of the staff given the responsibility of completing the task.

The number of people involved in organizing an event will vary enormously, depending on its size and significance. All events will need a body which sets the framework and policy within which the event will be developed. In the case of a global event such at the the Olympic Games, this function is carried out by the IOC (International Olympic Committee) with representatives of all the competing nations. An event of national or regional significance, such as the Great North Run, will normally have an organizing committee working with an individual event co-ordinator to oversee the planning work. The management of small, local events is sometimes left to a single individual who will make all the necessary decisions. A more usual practice, however, is to form a committee or steering group to ensure fairness and democracy in decision-making; sometimes this is made up of only three people, a chairperson, secretary and treasurer.

Working to the guidelines set by the policy makers will be a number of 'middle managers' who will take on responsibility for specific functions of the staging of the event, e.g. traffic management, staff training or health and safety matters. Element 2 of this unit showed that most events will be divided into focus areas, with **focus leaders** appointed to co-ordinate staff and carry out the necessary tasks associated with the focus.

Once the fact that an event is going to take place is publicized, there will be many people and organizations willing to become involved and help in whatever way they can. Existing employees may be 'seconded' from their normal duties to help to plan or stage the event. Extra staff may need to be employed, particularly if the event is very large, while volunteers may be needed regardless of the size of the event. As well as the staff under the direct control of the event organizers, other support and ancillary staff may be associated with the event, for example security personnel, concessionaires, volunteer medical back-up, creche workers and maintenance staff.

Did You Know ?

The organizers of the NutraSweet London Marathon use 5,000 volunteers to help on the day of the event.

Selection of staff

The process of **staff selection and recruitment** will vary depending on the type of event being organized. An organizer of a local event, for example, is not likely to have the resources available to pay staff and will have to plan the whole thing from start to finish with the help of volunteers. Where an event is of national, regional or even international significance, key staff will need to be appointed and offered an attractive remuneration package; the more significant the event, the more attractive the package will need to be. As we saw in Element 2, finding the right person to take on the role of the *event co-ordinator* is vital. To be considered for the job of an organizer for a major event, the individual is likely to have a good 'track record' in events management and considerable experience of the leisure and tourism industry. Because of success in similar events, a co-ordinator may well be approached by an organization to see if he or she is interested in the position, a process known as 'head hunting'.

Depending on the scale of the event, a standard recruitment and selection procedure similar to that shown in Fig. 5.3 may need to be operated, involving members of the organizing committee.

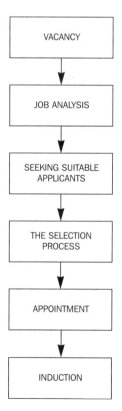

Figure 5.3   The recruitment and selection process for event staff

Staff for events can be found in a number of ways:

- By 'word of mouth'; local councils, youth groups, colleges and voluntary groups may well know of people willing to become involved.
- By sending press releases to newspapers and magazines.
- By advertising in the appropriate newspapers and magazines.
- By contacting voluntary organisations.

Particular attention should be paid to the employment of staff who will be working with children. There are published guidelines on this matter and the advice of the local Social Services Department should be sought at an early stage. They may also be able to help with the recruitment of staff with experience of dealing with disabled visitors and those with other special needs.

Staff training

Staff who are paid to take on a specific role in the organization of an event often have the necessary **training** incorporated into their job specification. When using volunteers, however, it may not be feasible to expect them to give up time, over and above their involvement in the event itself, to attend training sessions. In practice, therefore, tasks which involve a large amount of training will normally be given to paid employees, e.g. health and safety procedures. Volunteers can be issued with written notes relating to their particular tasks or may be asked to attend short briefing sessions.

The event co-ordinator and organizing committee will need to convey to all staff involved in the planning and staging of the event the importance of working as part of a team to achieve the objectives of the event. Larger events may be able to consider separate training sessions in team-building and team interaction (see Unit 7).

Did You Know ?

Funding for staff training for an event may be available through a local college or Training and Enterprise Council (TEC) if the event is seen to be contributing to the economic or social well-being of the area.

Staff welfare

Every member of staff must be made to feel a valued part of the team which has taken on the job of organizing the event. This is when the event co-ordinator and focus leaders have a vital role to play in managing the staff under their control. The particular circumstances of volunteers will need careful and supportive action; pushed too far they may well lose interest in the event. Important ways in which organizers can help staff feel more involved include:

- Thanking them for their help and support throughout the event.
- Paying them a fair rate for the job.
- Giving volunteers a 'reward' for their efforts, e.g. a small gift or contribution towards their travelling expenses.
- Listening to their ideas and suggestions.
- Having clear communication channels.
- Having clear health, safety and security procedures in place.
- Holding a social event for all staff.

- Giving adequate training and briefing.
- Providing refreshments and a rest area.

Above all, management must make it clear that without the help of *all* staff, the event would not have taken place; they are the most valuable resource.

Self Check ✔ **Element 3**

10. Who should be involved in the evaluation of an event?
   _____
   _____
   _____

11. What skills and qualities should an organization look for when selecting an event co-ordinator?
   _____
   _____
   _____

12. Why is it important for event organizers to treat all staff, whether paid or working in a voluntary capacity, equally well?
   _____
   _____
   _____

Self-check Answers

1. There are many reasons for staging an event. It may be to generate income, promote a cause, publicize a facility or improve knowledge and skills.

2. The British government would have seen the £55 million given to Manchester to help with the staging of the Games as an investment. Manchester and the whole of Britain would have benefited enormously if the city had been successful in its bid. It would have stimulated extra investment and jobs in Manchester and would have led to the building of new facilities, which would have been available to local people once the Games had finished.

3. Events causing excessive disturbance to local communities are the most likely to fall within the scope of the Public Order Act. Examples would include rock concerts, motor sport events, car boot sales and late night entertainments.

4. Rural events such as the Festival of the Countryside help local communities in a number of ways. They provide the focus for an influx of visitors to the area, thereby supporting local businesses and sustaining jobs. They also provide local people with an educational and entertaining experience. Events that are well planned and managed can also contribute to the protection of the environment in rural areas and help to sustain public transport provision.

5. The pre-feasibility stage of event planning is when an individual or group of people have a possible idea for an event. The pre-feasibility stage is considered to be important because it is the stage at which the idea's potential can be investigated before the decision to commit time and money to the next stage of development is considered.

6. There is a close liaison between the organizers of major events and the different television companies. The event organizers will want televised coverage of their event, live if possible, so that they can attract sponsors who will pay to have their name appearing on screen. This gives the television companies a great deal of power and influence over the timing of the event, so that it can fit in with normal television schedules.

7. The main disadvantage in electing a committee to oversee the planning of an event is that decision-making is likely to be a slower process. All those represented on the committee will want to have their views heard. An individual event organizer will be able to make faster decisions, but most would agree that the democratic nature of a committee is a preferred way of organizing an event.

8. It is important to have clear event objectives so that all those involved with its planning and management are clear as to what their particular role is. Clear objectives will also make the task of event evaluation much easier.

9. Local authorities will use a proportion of their leisure and tourism budget to finance events for a number of different reasons. They may wish to encourage activities that are considered of benefit to their local areas, in that they will attract extra tourists or provide an outlet for local talent. Larger events will have the potential for creating jobs and helping the local economy.

10. The evaluation of an event should look at as much relevant data and information as possible and should take the views of staff, visitors, councillors, observers and other specialists into consideration.

11. The event co-ordinator should be a positive leader, good communicator, excellent negotiator, supportive manager and excellent organizer.

12. All staff working on an event, whether paid or unpaid, must be treated with the same respect, in order that they maintain their enthusiasm and commitment to their tasks and help ensure the success of the event. Unhappy staff can have a negative impact on all members of the team.

UNIT 6

Providing management information services

Getting Started

Systems for gathering information in one form or another have existed since the beginning of human enterprise. A glance at any history textbook will produce countless examples of military campaigns and power struggles which relied heavily on the establishment of systems to ensure a flow of information to the decision-makers.

When it comes to leisure and tourism, most professionals in the industry would agree that information is the key to effective management. Without reliable information, managers in leisure and tourism are not able to carry out their many functions with any degree of certainty and are liable to make incorrect assumptions and poor decisions. In the past, the provision and use of management information services in many leisure and tourism organizations has not always been seen as a high priority, partly because of insufficient resources and partly because of a lack of awareness of the capabilities of the resources which do exist. The fact that the industry is still in its early stages of development is another reason why information systems have still not fully evolved.

The rapid rise in technology and communications equipment has expanded both the amount and variety of information available to the leisure and tourism manager and the speed with which it can be accessed, processed and communicated. Since the introduction of the *computer*, information systems have been revolutionized, with many mundane tasks previously carried out manually being transferred to automated systems. Sophisticated computer systems can now give managers a whole host of information, from occupancy rates in hotels to break-even points for new leisure and tourism projects.

This unit explores the scope and development of management information services in the leisure and tourism industry. Information needs and their relationship to management information services are the focus of Element 1 of this unit, while Element 2 looks in detail at the different industry contexts and how they manage their information systems. The third section of the unit, Element 3, considers the recording and processing of information, with particular reference to computerized systems.

Back office functions Functions that take place behind the scenes, e.g. accounting and personnel.

Cost centres Identifiable areas within an organization against which expenditure can be allocated.

CRS Refers to computerized reservations system or central reservations system. Examples include Sabre and Galileo.

Data Protection Act Government legislation which aims to protect individuals who have information about themselves held on computer.

Database A stock of information held on computer, e.g. names and addresses of customers.

EPOS Refers to electronic point-of-sale, when cash and stock are managed electronically.

Front office functions Functions that normally take place in reception areas, e.g. welcoming visitors, handling enquiries and taking bookings.

Gateway A system that allows a computer operator to gain access to other computer systems, e.g. a travel agent accessing the computer of a major airline to check flight availability.

Management information system (MIS) A computerized or manual system for the collection, collation and analysis of information and its presentation and use for decision-making purposes.

Revenue centres Specific activities within an organization that generate income.

Essential Principles

What is a management information service?

A **management information service** is the process by which those who make decisions in an organization are presented with information, which will have been collected either manually or with the help of an automated system. A computer-based system will often be referred to as an MIS (management information system), but it would be wrong to assume that all management information services are computerized: a small hotel, museum, café, restaurant or tourist information centre, for example, can function quite well with a manual system based on card indexes, charts or files. Whether a system is manual or automated should not be a prime concern when setting up a management information service. Far more important is deciding exactly what information is required, in what form and at what speed. If the answers to these questions point to a manual system, then a manual system should be used. Too many organizations make the decision to computerize their information system for the wrong reasons, quite often persuaded by sales staff with an eye on their commission rather than the needs of the client. Many organizations find that, rather than cutting down on paperwork, computers actually create more paper, and sometimes fail to provide the information needed for effective decision making.

Information needs

Different contexts within the leisure and tourism industry will have very different **information needs**. The owner of a small seaside hotel, for example, will need access to quite different information from, say, the manager of a local authority leisure centre; the information needed by the administrator of an art gallery will not be the same as that required by the manager of a high street travel agency, and so on.

Deciding what *information* is needed from a management information service is vital to its success; if it is wrong at this stage, all that follows will be rendered useless. Some managers overestimate the quantity of data they think they will need and are often confronted with reams of computer print-out which they have no time to read, let alone use for management purposes. Decisions as to what is needed should start with basic data and finish with more elaborate statistics. The fundamental question to ask at all stages is: 'Will these data really help in decision-making?' Information needs should be primarily determined by the *decisions* that need to be made, which in turn are a reflection of the *objectives* of the organization. Figure 6.1 illustrates this relationship between information, decisions and objectives.

A good way of explaining the relationship shown in Fig. 6.1 is to consider the management of a major commercial theme park such as Chessington World of Adventures. The prime *objective* of the park will be to maximize profits. To be successful in achieving this objective, Chessington employs managers to make *decisions* which will ensure it meets its objectives. To be sure that its decisions are sound, the managers at Chessington will need the sort of *information* on finance, operations and the 'market' which we discuss below.

All leisure and tourism organizations have different information needs, meaning that every management information service will have different characteristics. There are common features, however, which should apply to the *information* produced by all. The information should be:

- Accurate
- Consistent
- Appropriate
- Reliable
- Regular
- Timely
- Precise
- Clearly understood

The information needed by managers in leisure and tourism organizations is likely to fall into one of three broad categories:

- Operational data
- Financial information
- Market information

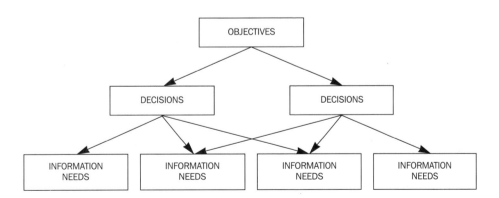

Figure 6.1 The relationship between information, decisions and objectives

Operational data

All leisure and tourism organizations need **data** concerned with the **use and operation** of their facilities, products and services:

- **Occupancy and usage rates** – a leisure centre will need information on the use of the facility as a whole and the take-up on individual activities; a hotel will want to know what percentage of its available bedspaces are occupied and a holiday centre will need to know how many of its self-catering units are let. Tourist attractions, tour operators, airlines and travel agencies will also need data on the use of their facilities and services.

- **Personnel records** – any organization will need to keep information on its staff, their conditions of employment and record of performance. Subject to confidentiality, this information can be held on an MIS, which can also handle the payroll function, providing an automated system for the calculation and payment of wages and salaries. The MIS can also give information on staff turnover and the uptake of staff training.

- **Stock control** – leisure and tourism organizations which operate retail outlets will use their MIS to check availability of stock, e.g. equipment in a sports centre shop, food in a cafeteria and drink in a bar. Many computer-based POS (point of sale) systems will automatically update stock availability figures as goods are sold or used.

Did You Know ?

Under the Data Protection Act, organizations must ensure the security of personnel information held on their computerized management information systems.

Financial information

The need to have accurate **financial data** is often the main reason why many leisure and tourism organizations introduce a computerized MIS. Such a system will provide reliable financial data to enable managers to monitor performance and plan for the future. Details of income and expenditure for the organization as a whole or for specific sections can be made available from the MIS and *trends* can be plotted over time and against 'industry averages' or competitors' performance. Income figures can be produced in a number of different ways, and in the case of a leisure centre could include income related to the:

- **facility** used, e.g. swimming pool, sports hall, bar, catering, sports shop, all-weather pitch, fitness suite, equipment hire etc.
- **type of customer**, e.g. adult, child, senior citizen, groups, off-peak, concessions etc.
- **time of use**, e.g. weekdays, weekends, different times of day, different months of the year etc.
- **type of activity**, e.g. squash, badminton, basketball, indoor football, aerobics etc.

Financial information can be categorized into **revenue centres,** which are the elements of an organization which generate income, and **cost centres**, against which expenditure can be allocated. In a typical hotel, for example, *revenue centres,* could include:

- Rooms
- Food and beverage
- Conference and banqueting facilities

- Retail operations and vending
- Special events
- Telephone and business services
- Valet services

Cost centres, which make it easier to analyse performance, are likely to include:

- Food and beverage purchases
- Marketing and publicity
- Administration costs
- Laundry
- Energy costs
- Maintenance and equipment purchase
- Staffing
- Telephone and postal costs

The arrival of CCT (see page 14) in local authority leisure services has introduced more managers in the public sector to the notion of **financial ratios** and **performance indicators**, which have been widespread in private sector leisure and tourism for some time.

The range of *financial ratios* that can be calculated by an MIS is very broad and could include:

- total revenue : staff costs
- total revenue : number of admissions/visitors
- total revenue : operating expenditure
- revenue per facility : staff costs per facility
- revenue per facility : costs per facility

As well as these ratios which are of use to those managers involved in day-to-day management of facilities, other financial ratios for senior management can be produced by the MIS, including:

- fixed assets : sales
- net profit : sales
- overheads : sales
- gross profit : sales

These ratios will give the decision-makers the necessary information to be able to plan effectively for the future, as well as making any modifications that the figures suggest.

Market information

Units 3 and 4 have already shown us that an effective leisure and tourism organization must have detailed **information about its customers,** in order to be able to provide them with the facilities and services they want and to do so with attention to their desire for a good standard of customer service. An MIS is invaluable for providing such information on the 'market' and can help highlight under-exploited opportunities or areas of an organization which need more promotion. A theatre's *database*, for example, may indicate that residents of particular areas of a city do not visit the theatre in anything like the same proportions as those who live in other areas. The management may investigate why this is so and may feel it worthwhile to mount a publicity campaign in the under-represented areas in order to increase attendance.

In addition to this type of internal information, a leisure and tourism organization may use its MIS to store data on the wider market outside its own organization, sometimes referred to as the external business environment. For example, government statistics, details of competitors' performance and specialist reports may all be part of the MIS. Such data will give the management an idea of its position in the marketplace relative to other organizations and will be an invaluable aid in planning and decision making.

The structure of a management information service

The design of any MIS for a leisure and tourism facility will need to take into account the fact that most organizations divide their functions into 'front office' and 'back office'. In simple terms, the front office (sometimes referred to as 'front of house') refers to the reception area of any leisure and tourism facility, the point at which the customer first makes contact with the organization. The back office (also known as 'back of house') refers to the organization's functions which take place behind the scenes, e.g. accounting and personnel, which the customer is unlikely to be aware of. There must always be a strong link between front and back offices for an MIS to be truly effective; for example, when a guest books into a hotel at reception (the front office), information must be conveyed, possibly manually but more probably via a computer system, to the other departments who need to know, such as housekeeping, accounts, food and beverage, laundry, marketing, etc.

Did You Know ?

Most hotels, leisure/sports centres, travel agencies, visitor attractions, educational establishments, transport companies, catering outlets, entertainment venues and tourist information centres divide their information systems into front office and back office.

The division into front and back office allows management to focus resources on particular functions and train staff in these areas. The selection and training of staff to work in the front office is particularly important since it provides the visitor with his or her first impressions of the organization. Staff with an understanding of customer needs and expectations and who are committed to providing excellence in customer service should be chosen to work in this high-profile area. The environment in which the front office is positioned also needs to be carefully planned and should provide a clean, warm, efficient, welcoming and friendly atmosphere.

The different functions carried out by front and back office staff in leisure and tourism organizations are shown in Fig. 6.2.

Front office functions	Back office functions
Selling services	Membership systems
Welcoming visitors	Cash and credit control
Providing information	Stock control
Handling cash, cheques, cards	Maintenance
Controlling entry	Marketing and publicity
Taking bookings	Accounting
Promoting services	Analysis of management data
Passing information to back office	Food preparation
Issuing equipment	Personnel
Maintaining records	Health and safety
Answering enquiries	Staff training

Figure 6.2 Front and back office functions in leisure and tourism facilities

Security and confidentiality of management information

With so much confidential, personal and commercially sensitive information being held by leisure and tourism organizations, the question of **security** of the management information must be taken very seriously. Loss of any part of the system may affect the viability of the whole MIS. The system must be secured against:

- Accidental interference
- Inquisitiveness
- Theft
- Fraud

Loss of part of the information contained in the MIS will be particularly acute if its loss results in an advantage to a competitor organization. Industrial espionage, involving the deliberate and unlawful entry into a system by unauthorized personnel, is not unheard of in the highly competitive leisure and tourism industry.

Simple security measures can give good protection against theft and wilful damage to components of the MIS. In the case of computer-based systems, these include strict control of access to processing facilities and data storage, as well as careful screening of the staff who are given access to these facilities. Steps can be taken to prevent or at least minimize damage resulting from fire, flood, power failure and civil disorder, including the provision of secure premises and storage facilities designed to combat these threats. Special measures are necessary to protect data in the MIS and to enable the management to reconstruct files from archive material stored in a different location, should the need arise. Issues concerning security of data are particularly important when employing consultants and staff from computer bureaux; rigorous screening of such companies and their personnel is vital.

The Data Protection Act 1984

The increasing use of computer systems to store data on individuals, led to the introduction of the **Data Protection Act** (DPA) in May 1986. Under the Act, individuals who have data held on them have a range of rights in civil law, including:

- Rights of access to the data.
- Rights to apply to have any inaccuracies in the data rectified and, in certain circumstances, rights to have the information erased.
- Rights to compensation for inaccuracy of data.
- Rights to compensation for loss, destruction or unauthorized disclosure of data.

The DPA requires that all organizations which hold personal data about individuals on *automated systems* must register with the Data Protection Registrar and comply with the Data Protection Act. The exact definition of an 'automated system' is open to debate, but in general terms, information held on computer falls within the scope of the Act and that which is processed manually does not. The Act seeks to regulate the way in which data are gathered, stored and disclosed to third parties.

Did You Know ?

Some organizations choose to store certain information on manual systems so that it is not covered by the requirements of the DPA.

The Act establishes eight data protection principles with which data users must comply. Data users are defined as individuals, corporations or other agencies which control the automatic processing of data. The eight principles, which in reality are a set of points of good practice to which data users should aspire, are as follows:

1 That the information held on computer shall be obtained and processed *fairly* and *lawfully*. Data would be said to have been obtained unfairly if the provider was deceived or misled about the purpose for which the information was being obtained.

2 That personal data shall be held only for one or more *specified* and *lawful* purposes. A contravention of this particular principle would be, for example, when an organization holds personal information for staff training purposes but chooses to use it for the selection of staff for redundancy.

3 That data shall not be *disclosed* to persons other than those named in the registration document, nor for any other purpose than that registered under the Act. A tour operator, for example, which collects information on its customers to offer them discounted holidays, cannot then sell the data to another company without contravening this principle.

4 That personal data held for any purpose or purposes shall be *adequate*, *relevant* and *not excessive* in relation to the registered purpose. An organization which holds data which are unrelated to the purpose for which it is registered or is clearly holding far more than are needed to satisfy the purpose, will be in breach of this principle.

5 That personal data shall be *accurate* and *updated* as and when necessary. If an organization, for example, holds a list of customers who have exceeded their annual credit limit but the organization makes no attempt to update the list when further payments are made, it is likely to be considered as having contravened this principle.

6 That personal information held for any purpose or purposes shall not be kept for *longer* than is necessary. A leisure centre which holds a prize draw, and which uses a computer to store the names and addresses of those entering, should destroy these data at the end of the promotion.

7 That an individual shall be entitled, at reasonable intervals and without undue delay or expense, to know whether information is held on him or her and to have *access* to any data which do exist; also to have any data *corrected* or erased as appropriate.

8 That the data user shall take reasonable *security* measures to guard against unauthorized access to, alteration, disclosure, accidental loss or destruction of the personal data.

The extent to which computers are used throughout leisure and tourism means that the Act has important implications for the industry. Databases for marketing and promotional work, membership lists, guests' accounts in hotels, travel agencies and tour operators, to name but a few, all involve the collection and storage of personal data on individuals. Managers therefore need to be aware of the principles of the Data Protection Act and the extent to which it affects their own particular organization.

Evaluation of management information systems

A great deal of the early development work with computerized MIS in leisure and tourism proved disappointing when it came to examining their cost-effectiveness. This was a result of inadequate and inefficient hardware and software, coupled with a lack of clarity in terms of defining management information needs. In the last 10–15 years, however, we have witnessed a transformation in the reliability and capabilities of the technology and an almost universal acceptance of the computer as a useful management tool. This has led to improvements in the efficiency and effectiveness of the various systems in use in leisure and tourism organizations; in other words, an evaluation of the benefits of the MIS compared with its costs has given favourable results.

Although it is sometimes difficult to evaluate all the benefits of a system fully since some may be intangible and therefore hard to quantify, it is important that evaluation of the system once it is operational is seen as an important element of the introduction of any MIS.

Did You Know ?

Management should not forget that informal feedback from staff, customers and managers themselves will prove invaluable in making the MIS as effective as possible.

An objective evaluation of the MIS may highlight actual or potential problem areas, which could include:

- Insufficient storage capability of the system.
- Lack of operational support, including training and maintenance.
- Lack of adequate terminals or work stations.
- Inadequate expansion capability.
- Bottlenecks in interfacing.
- Lack of awareness of capabilities of the system.
- Inadequate security of the system.

If the process of choosing the MIS has been objective, planned and thorough, it is likely that many of these problems will have been anticipated and that the system will function according to the specification drawn up by the purchasing organization.

Self Check ✔ Element 1

1. What benefits does a computerized MIS have over a manual system?
    _____
    _____
    _____

2. What revenue centres would you expect to find in a typical local authority leisure centre?
    _____
    _____
    _____

3. What specific measures should a large leisure and tourism organization take to ensure security of its management information system?
    _____
    _____
    _____

4. Choose a local leisure and tourism facility with which you are familiar and consider how the Data Protection Act has affected its operation.
    _____
    _____

6.2 Selecting and providing management information

Selecting a management information service

The design of any MIS, whether manual or computer-based, must start with an analysis of an organization's immediate and longer-term information **needs**. The information which is accessible via the system must be relevant to its purpose and presented in an appropriate format, which may be text, numerical or graphics. In addition, the information must meet certain quality requirements, in that it must have:

- Validity
- Accuracy
- Currency

Information that is valid is fit for its intended purpose and provides a sound base for management decision making. Accuracy of information, particularly concerning financial data, is essential for short-term and long-term planning. Information must be current, i.e. not out of date, if management are to make effective decisions.

Choosing a computerized management information system

Choosing a computerized MIS can be a very daunting task. Many people working in the leisure and tourism industry have heard stories about computer systems costing many thousands of pounds which have failed to live up to the claims of those who provided them in the first place: systems which are too slow in many of the routine operations they are asked to perform, systems which can provide complex management information but which cannot handle the basics and systems which 'crash' with alarming regularity. Add to these tales of woe the fact that many good systems can be out of date by the time they are 'on line', then it is no wonder that leisure and tourism organizations exercise a great deal of care and attention when it comes to installing or updating a computerized MIS.

There are four basic steps in deciding on a system and its supplier:

- Decide exactly what information is required from the system.
- Draw up a written specification based on the stated information needs.
- Invite tenders from prospective MIS providers.
- Choose the supplier that best matches your requirements.

Decide what information is required from the system

This is no easy task, since it involves a methodical appraisal of everything that happens in the organization at the moment, as well as an attempt to predict what additional information may be needed in the future. All the organization's facilities and services will need to be itemized and all procedures, both formal and informal, will need to be documented.

Draw up a specification based on the stated information needs

The **written specification** will be used by the companies who submit tenders and will give them a detailed picture of what

the organization is looking for in the MIS. The specification is likely to include *detailed information* on the following items:

- The general principles on which the system must be based.
- Details of the products, facilities, activities and services that the system will have to cope with.
- Front office operations – what goes on in the reception area.
- Back office functions – e.g. cash control, accounting etc.
- Membership systems (if applicable).
- Point of sale (POS) systems, including stock control.
- Format of the management information required.
- Security of the system.
- Support, maintenance and training needs.
- Hardware requirements – capability of expansion, portability, flexibility etc.

> **Did You Know ?**
>
> The secret in writing the specification is to express clearly what the management of the organization expects from the MIS while at the same time not making it so specific that any of the tendering companies would have to devise a completely new system in order to comply with it, with all the added expense this would involve.

Invite tenders from prospective MIS providers

Once the specification for the system has been agreed, the process of inviting **tenders** can begin. Advertisements can be placed in relevant leisure magazines such as *Leisure Management* and *Travel Trade Gazette*, asking interested parties to request a specification and tender application form. Details may also be distributed direct to other organizations who may have worked for the organization before or who are known to have carried out similar work for other leisure and tourism facilities. The need for impartiality, however, must be paramount, particularly in the case of local authority facilities where public money is involved. The information sent out must indicate the latest date by which the completed forms should be returned.

Choose the supplier that best matches your requirements

The **evaluation** of the tenders needs to be a very thorough and methodical process carried out in as objective a manner as possible. A company's 'track record' will be an important consideration; it will be necessary to establish whether any companies which are new to leisure and tourism systems, although they may have worked in another business sector for some time, are looking for a 'guinea pig' on which to try out their ideas. On the positive side, however, such a company may be willing to offer a very good deal if they are new to the industry and, if they are open in their negotiations, they may secure the contract on a lower tender price than a more established company.

It will be necessary to establish what proportion of the specification each company can meet without having to make major changes to their 'base' system. It is unlikely that any company will be able to meet all the details on the specification without some adjustments, but it is important to find out how long each modification will take and if it will incur extra costs.

Cost is likely to be a significant factor in the selection process, although it should not be assumed that the company which submits the lowest tender will necessarily win the contract. Cost must be considered along with all the other variables such as experience, expertise and training. Staff training will be a vital consideration, as will updating to software and hardware and on-site maintenance and repair. The suppliers should be asked to itemize the various costs involved in providing the total system and an on-going support and maintenance service.

Once the tenders have been evaluated, a short-list of possible suppliers should be drawn up and the companies invited to make presentations to managers, staff and, in the case of local authority facilities, council representatives. The companies should formally present their system and state how they will meet the requirements listed on the specification. Visits to look at systems in action at other sites may also be part of the 'sifting' process.

Although the process of choosing a supplier for the MIS is planned to be as objective as possible, it is sometimes the case that there are two or three companies who could equally well carry out the job. In these circumstances, the company which eventually is successful in winning the contract may be the one which the management and staff of the facility felt most comfortable with or the one with the most confidence in being able to meet the specification, in the agreed timescale and within budget.

Information needs in different leisure and tourism organizations

The very broad nature of the leisure and tourism industry means that the information needs of managers in its various sectors and contexts are very different. The remainder of this element looks in detail at MISs in the following selection of public and private sector leisure and tourism organizations:

- Travel agencies
- Tour operators
- Airlines
- Leisure centres
- Pubs, bars and catering outlets
- Visitor attractions
- Theatres and other entertainment venues
- Leisure complexes
- Hotels and other accommodation providers

Travel agencies

The need to be able to communicate quickly on a global scale means that the **travel industry** is ideally suited to the use of MISs based on new technology equipment and systems. Computers and sophisticated communications media enable companies to check up-to-date information, make reservations, confirm complex fares, issue tickets and provide information for management purposes. This is not to say that manual management information systems, often using wall charts and card indexes, do not exist in the travel and tourism sector, but they are becoming very rare.

Independent travel agents, as well as those which are owned by one of the well-known multiple chains such as Lunn Poly, Going Places and Thomas Cook, make extensive use of new technology to sell holidays and other travel products to the public. Working as the agents of the large tour operators (the 'principals'), they earn their money from commission on sales, so that access to up-to-date information on product availability is an important part of their operation. A computer system in a typical UK travel agency will be designed to handle:

ITEM	1st Quarter		2nd Quarter		3rd Quarter		4th Quarter	
	Budget	Actual	Budget	Actual	Budget	Actual	Budget	Actual
Rent								
Rates – General								
– Water								
Salaries + NI								
Casual labour								
Lighting								
Heating								
Telephone/Fax								
Telex								
Prestel/Istel								
Postage								
Stationery								
Cleaning								
Insurance								
Travel–Motoring								
–Subsistence								
Maintenance								
Promotions								
Advertising								
Reference books								
Accounts charges								
Legal fees								
Bad debts								
Training								
Petty cash								
Miscellaneous								
Total								

Figure 6.3 Annual expenditure budget

- Front office functions
- Back office functions
- Management functions

Front office functions

The computer terminal or VDU on the counter is now an accepted part of the furniture in any travel agency. In the hands of trained personnel, this **front office system** is a powerful selling tool. It can give access, via a telephone line and the correct computer software known as a 'gateway' system, to the computer reservation systems (CRSs) of major tour operators and airlines, in order to check availability of holidays and flights, check prices and ultimately make bookings on behalf of the clients. One of the first companies to offer this facility was Thomson with its Thomson On-line Program (TOP) introduced in 1986.

Did You Know ?

All Thomson package holidays are now booked through their TOP system in travel agencies.

Back office functions

Back office systems handle the ticketing, accounting, personnel, budgeting and administrative functions of the travel agency. Figure 6.3 shows a typical annual expenditure budget used in an independent travel agency, the completion of which is a relatively simple matter when integrated with a computerised MIS.

An integrated back office system can allow the staff to create client profiles and itineraries, undertake invoicing, issue tickets and generate wordprocessed items. The system can also build a database which can be used for marketing and promotional purposes.

Management functions

One of the main advantages that a computerized MIS has over one which is operated manually is that it can provide accurate information on the performance of the agency at the touch of a button. In times of recession when profit margins are being squeezed, it is even more important to have this regular and up-to-date **management information**. Reports can be requested under a number of different categories, e.g.

- Level of sales by departure airport
- Level of sales by client
- Level of sales by tour operator
- Sales targets of members of staff
- Departures by date

This detailed information will give the manager or owner an accurate picture of the financial state of the business as a whole and accurate data on the different components of the agency's work, which will prove invaluable for decision making purposes.

Tour operators

Unlike travel agents who *sell* the holidays and other travel products, tour operators actually '*construct*' the holidays, putting together packages tailored to the needs of individual travellers. They play the part of wholesalers who buy hotel bedspaces, airline seats and other services in bulk and then re-package them into the holidays that we see offered for sale through travel agents. The information needs of tour operators are therefore quite different from those of travel agents,

who are the retailers in the chain of distribution of holidays. Tour operators will need an MIS which can provide:

- Financial data on agents and their sales performance.
- Level of sales of particular holidays and destinations.
- Data on the availability of accommodation and flights (or other mode of transport).
- Information on competitors and the market in general for package holidays.
- Feedback from clients on their holiday experiences.
- Personnel information (UK and overseas).
- Management accounts showing profit and loss, balance sheet etc.

The largest UK tour operators, including Thomsons, Airtours and First Choice Holidays, all have integrated computerized MISs operating from a central database. This can be accessed by their own reservations staff in response to enquiries or, if a 'gateway' system is in operation, agents can gain access themselves to check availability and make bookings. Small and medium-sized tour operators, which make up the bulk of companies, will often use a mixture of manual and automated systems and can sometimes use standard business software packages for accounts, data processing and database management.

Airlines

The information needs of an airline are broadly similar, whether their principal business is in the scheduled or charter market. Scheduled services operate to a published timetable on defined routes, either domestic or international, and seats are freely available to leisure and business travellers. Charter services have developed in response to the rise in package holidays and are the services which are restricted to passengers who have bought the full package. The distinction between scheduled and charter services is becoming less clear since some charter airlines now offer scheduled services while some scheduled airlines offer charters as well. Much of this is due to the increased demand for 'seat only' sales linked to the growth in independent holidays.

All airlines need an MIS which will provide operational information, such as 'load factors' (seats sold as a percentage of seats available on the aircraft), timetable information, route planning and fare structures. Information relating to capital and operating costs must also be provided by the MIS, as must data concerning marketing and customer satisfaction.

Computer reservations systems have become a major force in the airline industry over the last 20 years or so. These fully integrated systems not only store accurate data on airline fares and services, but also have information on other travel services including car hire, exchange rates, excursions, sporting events, resort and country information, etc., making them attractive to travel agents. Probably the best-known system is American Airlines' Sabre CRS, but European systems including Galileo and Amadeus have been introduced to counter the powerful US threat in this highly competitive sector of the industry.

Leisure centres

Whether a leisure centre is in private or public sector control, it will need to be effectively managed, with the assistance of an efficient MIS. In the UK today, this will invariably mean the use of a computer-based MIS. Leisure centres need reliable information to be able to control costs and provide value-for-money services and facilities for their current and future customers. A good computer system can handle a great deal of tedious administrative work, can provide a database of users, membership lists for promotional work and will enable the centre to handle its finances far more effectively. The management of the centre will be able to track its performance over time, identify trends and compare performance against targets.

The introduction of CCT in local authority leisure services has hastened the need for very detailed information on income, expenditure and usage, both for the operators (known as the 'contractors') of the centres and the 'clients', the local councils themselves. Figure 6.4 shows the type of detailed information which the contractor of a hypothetical local authority leisure centre would be required to provide under the terms of the CCT contract.

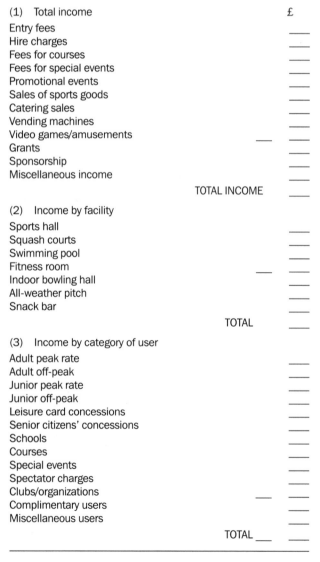

Facility: Fantasia Leisure Centre

Contractor: Hemsterworth Leisure DSO

Client: Hemsterworth District Council Leisure Services Department

Subject: Income Analysis of the Leisure Centre

(1) Total income	£
Entry fees	___
Hire charges	___
Fees for courses	___
Fees for special events	___
Promotional events	___
Sales of sports goods	___
Catering sales	___
Vending machines	___
Video games/amusements	___ ___
Grants	___
Sponsorship	___
Miscellaneous income	___
TOTAL INCOME	___

(2) Income by facility	
Sports hall	___
Squash courts	___
Swimming pool	___
Fitness room	___ ___
Indoor bowling hall	___
All-weather pitch	___
Snack bar	___
TOTAL	___

(3) Income by category of user	
Adult peak rate	___
Adult off-peak	___
Junior peak rate	___
Junior off-peak	___
Leisure card concessions	___
Senior citizens' concessions	___
Schools	___
Courses	___
Special events	___
Spectator charges	___
Clubs/organizations	___ ___
Complimentary users	___
Miscellaneous users	___
TOTAL	___ ___

Figure 6.4 The type of information required under the terms of a CCT contract

The example in Fig. 6.4 is just one small element of what will be needed to satisfy the demands of most CCT contracts concerning the management of leisure centres. As well as detailed data on income, the contractor will have to provide information on a regular basis covering:

- Expenditure levels
- Levels of usage of the facility as a whole and by categories of users
- Total attendance figures and demand for individual facilities

In addition, the management of the leisure centre will be required to furnish information concerning:

- Cleaning
- Operational issues
- Publicity
- Staffing
- Health and safety
- Plant and equipment
- Maintenance

The collection of this information and its subsequent checking by the 'client' (the local authority officers) is all part of the process of monitoring the CCT contract to see if the operator of the leisure centre is meeting the performance standards set out in the specification and is providing the level and quality of service demanded.

The need to collect this detailed management information, which has been common practice with private sector providers for many years, has resulted in an increased demand from leisure centre managers for computer systems which can provide the information both in the detail and format required by the local authority and at the intervals laid down in the CCT contract.

Pubs, bars and catering outlets

Driven by the constant need to reduce costs, increase revenue and provide the high level of customer service that today's consumers are increasingly demanding, **pubs, bars, restaurants, fast-food outlets** and **cafés** all over the UK are introducing new technology systems at a frantic rate, in what has always been a highly competitive sector of the leisure market. Many operators have replaced their old fashioned tills with sophisticated electronic cash registers, pre-programmed with prices for food and drinks. Most large organizations are now giving serious consideration to full-scale *EPOS* (electronic point-of-sale) systems, the sort which have long been used in retail outlets to help control stock and cash. EPOS systems are being introduced in ever-increasing numbers to many leisure sector premises. The only way the customer is likely to know that a facility has an EPOS system is when the staff use their 'touchpads' or 'scatterpads', the small touch-sensitive panels located behind the bar or counter, or sometimes on the cash register itself. The benefits of EPOS are that it:

- improves stock control.
- gives the management control over cash transactions.
- frees staff to concentrate on improving customer care rather than having to calculate prices and issue bills.

As well as performing all the normal functions of an electronic cash register, an EPOS system will log all transactions with time, date, items served, cost, method of payment and the member of staff who dealt with the customer. This not only reduces the possibility of fraud by staff but also allows management to introduce incentives for staff who are meeting and exceeding their sales targets. The system will also mean that the busiest times can be better anticipated and allow better management of staff generally. The detailed management information given by EPOS will mean that stock levels can be monitored more closely, enabling the outlet to hold much smaller levels than would otherwise be the case, thereby improving its cash flow situation.

Factfile 1: Bass Brewers

A very good example of state-of-the-art MISs in the leisure industry is the introduction of a fully integrated system by Bass Taverns into its public houses throughout Britain; Bass is the UK's largest brewer and the fourth largest in the world. By using a front office system combining 'scatterpads' and touch-screen tills, flowmeters which automatically monitor how much beer is drawn from the kegs and a back office system which can review stocks and cash flow, Bass can monitor the operation of all pubs on the system from a central control.

The system begins with staff entering transactions using a scatterpad and touch-screen tills. As a security measure, each till only operates with the electronic identity card of a member of the bar staff. Flowmeters located on the kegs measure the amount of beer used and input data into the network. Each pint pulled is recorded by the flowmeters, which measure to the nearest quarter pint how much beer has been dispensed, while the till is automatically alerted by the flowmeter to expect a payment. If no payment is received, the system sends a warning to the pub manager who operates the back office system. Here, he or she monitors transactions and prepares data for the network. The data are downloaded to the network control which is located in Birmingham and supervises the operation of more than 2,000 pubs.

All 3,000 of Bass's pubs were scheduled to be on this integrated MIS network by the end of 1993, less than two years since the start of the project in January 1992. Every pub manager will have a networked personal computer in his or her office, linked to the network control so that stock details, work rates and cash takings can be downloaded during the night. Using this sophisticated technology, managers at network control have an exact up-to-the-minute picture of what business it is doing in which areas. Regional managers are able to supervise more than 100 pubs in an area by simply connecting a PC or notebook computer to the central network and calling up the data. The system has enabled Bass to manage its public house operation more effectively and has given individual pub managers the chance to use their resources, particularly staff, more efficiently.

The integration of an automatic delivery system into the network is scheduled for 1994. By analysing the stock control data downloaded every night, the system will automatically activate deliveries of beer to the individual pubs. The system will be linked to the brewing arm of Bass in order that demand for beer can be estimated more effectively and wastage can be kept to a minimum.

Looking to the future, Bass sees this as only the start of a revolution in pubs and the way they are managed. There is likely to be even greater use of new technology equipment to monitor energy use, for example, and to offer other services such as cash machines and ordering of theatre tickets.

Visitor attractions

Like any other sector of the leisure and tourism industry, visitor attractions need to compete for customers. They need reliable information on which to base their management decisions. Small attractions catering for a purely local market may not need a computerized MIS but may be able to cope with a manual system. Attractions catering for larger numbers, however,

will need to give serious consideration to computerizing all or part of their operation if they are to remain competitive. Management will need information on:

- The attendance levels
- Visitor characteristics
- Total revenue and costs
- Revenue and costs per facility
- Income from concessions
- Personnel data
- Financial performance

Large visitor attractions are investing in MISs to help them retain their market share in an increasingly competitive marketplace (see Factfile on Alton Towers in Element 3, page 129).

Did You Know ?

Alton Towers has more than 100 terminals and personal computers to store and process its management information.

Theatres and other entertainment venues

There have been great strides in the development of MISs for **theatres**, large and small, and the **indoor and outdoor entertainment venues** which exist throughout the UK, e.g. Wembley Stadium and Wembley Arena, GMEX in Manchester, Sheffield Arena and the Royal Albert Hall. Most venues serving a regional catchment, and quite often many catering only for their local population, will have a computerized MIS controlling front and back office functions. The national venues employ sophisticated systems which can handle the large volume of enquiries and sales which they attract.

The functions carried out by staff in the front office of such venues are in many respects similar to the work carried out by reception staff in leisure centres. The one big difference, however, is that theatres and other entertainment venues sell most of their tickets in advance, rather than taking casual bookings on the day. The main front office functions are:

- Controlling entry and exit.
- Selling tickets – in person, by telephone, by post or by fax.
- Providing information.
- Handling cash and cards.

The front office or reception of an entertainment venue will almost certainly have a VDU (visual display unit) showing a seating plan, seat availability and the prices in the various parts of the venue. This system will include a ticket printer to issue tickets automatically and speedily. The front office system will be connected to a back office computer, responsible for:

- Accounting
- Sales analysis
- Promotion and marketing
- Personnel
- Budgeting

Many venues make extensive use of their database of customer details to market their services. Customers can be targeted according to their tastes and preferences; e.g. a person who books a seat at the snooker championships in the Wembley Arena will automatically be sent details of the same event the following year via the database.

Leisure complexes

Country clubs, health resorts, golf courses and other leisure complexes are a growing part of the leisure and tourism industry in the UK today. Offering facilities for individual and business (corporate) clients, many have invested in fully *integrated* MISs which link all the elements of their operation. Effective systems must provide a fast and efficient service for customers and allow staff to concentrate on developing the highest levels of customer service.

One of the foremost companies providing integrated MISs is Baron Systems, who have worked with companies such as Gleneagles Hotel, the Belfry and Champneys Health Club in London. Figure 6.5 shows the structure of the integrated leisure management system developed by Baron Systems.

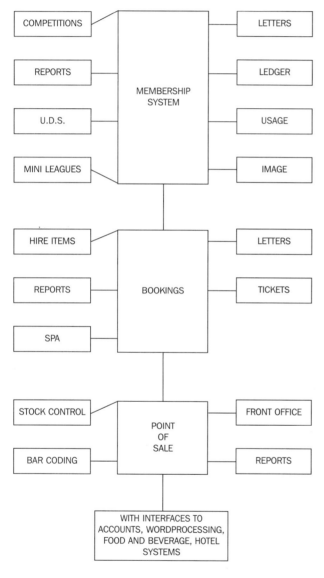

Figure 6.5 The Baron Integrated Leisure MIS (courtesy of Baron Systems Ltd)

Like many systems available for leisure complexes, the Baron MIS offers three integrated 'modules', covering membership, bookings and point-of-sale systems (see Fig. 6.5), all of which can be tailored to the requirements of an individual facility. This modular approach offers the management, staff and customers a system through which all operations can be channelled for enhanced administrative and financial control.

The membership system is often at the heart of any leisure complex and needs flexibility, speed and accuracy of operation. The Baron MIS can record subscription information to speed up renewals, while members' account spends can be controlled by levies or credit controls. The ledger module ensures an efficient storage of transactions and allows the collection of finance at regular intervals. The membership system can be used for marketing purposes with the capability of producing personalized letters for mailing direct to clients.

The bookings system can control all the bookable functions at the complex, including tennis, squash, sauna, spa treatments, golf courses, etc. Good booking systems should offer the facility for bookings to be taken at more than one point in the complex and enquiries for bookings to be made at multiple locations. Various options within the bookings module of the Baron MIS allow the recording of information on hired equipment and the control of members' use of facilities, via magnetic strip cards.

The point-of-sale (POS) system is specifically designed for shops within complexes and clubs. It ensures control of all aspects of the shop's operation, including stock movements, stock taking and stock control. The POS system gives the option to barcode all items giving a faster method of recording sales and stock control information. Analysis of sales can be made under a number of categories, including by supplier, by location, by category of goods, by colour, by size, etc.

One of the most important points about each of the three elements of this MIS, bookings, membership and POS, is that *reports* can be generated from all three modules for use by management. Information on usage and financial performance can be generated by the system. Figure 6.6 shows a sample report from the Baron leisure management system.

Did You Know ?

Integrated MISs offer leisure complexes the opportunity to make maximum use of their resources in order to provide a professional service backed up by sound management practices.

Hotels and other accommodation providers

Hotels have long been at the forefront of developments in MISs for the leisure and tourism industry. The **hospitality sector** in general has evolved with the manual handling of guests' transactions and the production of volumes of paper documenting these activities. The development of computerized MISs has been undertaken as an attempt to simplify the handling of an organization's stock of information, to reduce costs, to increase speed and to offer a higher degree of accuracy than was the case with manual systems. There has also been the assumption that automating many mundane tasks would give staff a greater degree of job satisfaction which would result in improved customer service levels.

A MIS for a hotel or similar accommodation provider is likely to have the following objectives:

* To reduce the amount of unnecessary paperwork.
* To present management with timely, accurate and comprehensive reports.
* To enable the hotel to provide an expanded range of guest services.
* To provide increased operational control.
* To free staff to concentrate on customer service functions.
* To enable management to monitor and control the guest experience better.

SALES GROSS PROFIT REPORT DETAILED EXAMPLE

Date: 07.01.92

Page: 1

Baron Manor Country Club
SALES BY CATEGORY/GROSS PROFIT REPORT

Product Category	Description	P.L.U. Number	Opening Value	Deliveries	Closing Value	Stock Consumption	Actual Sales	Gross Profit	% G.P.
1	Equipment	0000037651480	4005.00	120.00	3460.00	665.00	1234.00	569.00	46.11
		0000045854945	1950.00	130.00	1570.00	510.00	640.00	130.00	20.31
		0000057484844	495.00	0.00	230.00	265.00	386.00	121.00	31.35
1	Equipment		6450.00	250.00	5260.00	1440.00	2260.00	820.00	36.28
2	Clothes	0000005647474	3167.00	179.50	2867.00	479.50	879.50	399.50	45.44
		0000037364644	2483.00	456.00	2461.00	478.00	667.70	189.70	28.41
2	Clothes		5650.00	635.50	5328.00	957.50	1546.70	589.20	38.11
4	Concessions	0004743723737	2020.00	250.00	1960.00	310.00	330.00	20.00	6.06
		0005868668684	2337.60	203.00	2160.00	380.60	450.00	69.40	15.42
4	Concessions		4357.60	453.00	4120.00	690.60	780.00	89.40	11.46
	Total		16457.60	1338.50	14708.00	3088.10	2586.70	1498.60	57.93

Figure 6.6 Sample report from the Baron leisure management system (courtesy of Baron System Ltd)

Hotel information systems follow the classic differentiation into front and back office functions, but must also link with other departments, such as food and beverages, laundry, maintenance, marketing etc.

Self Check ✔ Element 2

5. What short-term and long-term problems is a mass market tour operator likely to face if managers are working with inaccurate financial and operational information?

6. Where can leisure and tourism organizations find details of suppliers of computerized management information systems?

7. What is the 'gateway' system that travel agents use?

8. What is the break-even load factor of a typical charter airline?

9. Choose a leisure or sports centre with which you are familiar and investigate what computer systems it uses.

10. What categories could a theatre use to classify its customers for direct mail campaigns?

6.3 Recording and processing management information

The development of computerized management information systems (MISs)

The dynamic and responsive nature of the leisure and tourism industry has meant that it has always been at the forefront of developments in new technology. The travel industry, including retail travel agencies, tour operators, airlines and other transport providers, has been particularly noteworthy in its willingness to take on-board new developments in computers and telecommunications equipment. The leisure sector has also adapted quickly to the rapid growth in the demand for leisure, sport and recreation services, by installing computer systems to handle many financial and operational aspects of the business.

Why have a computer system?
The principal reason for installing a computerized MIS will be that it will increase the *efficiency* and improve the *effectiveness* of the organization in which it operates. More specific reasons for choosing a computer system will vary enormously between different organizations in the leisure and tourism industry, but could include:

• As a means of expanding the organization – a small company may wish to expand its number of customers but realizes that its manual system will not be able to cope with the extra information.

• In order to provide a better standard of service to its customers – a computer system is likely to speed up the processing of such items as bookings, membership details, cash handling, credit transfers, invoicing, letters and mailing of publicity materials.

• As a way of accessing a remote database – a leisure and tourism organization may introduce a computer system so that it can gain access to data from other organizations. A travel agent, for example, will be able to access information and make bookings with tour operators and airlines directly via a computer link. In the same way, a public sector leisure centre may set up a direct link with its local authority mainframe computer in order to transfer and process data.

- To make better use of staff resources – it is unlikely that a computer system will actually reduce the number of employees once it is introduced, but it will enable the same number of people to do much more, thus improving staff efficiency.
- To provide information for management purposes, which is regular, accurate and in a form which is easily understood.

Microcomputers in leisure and tourism

As well as large-scale, integrated computer MISs, which can handle complex data management functions, the popularity of **microcomputers** has grown rapidly in the leisure and tourism industry over the last 10 years or so. It is becoming increasingly common to find these personal computers (PCs) used not only by administrative staff but also on the desks of the managers themselves. Modern business computers, most of which conform to the standards established by the IBM personal computer, will run wordprocessing, spreadsheets, database and desktop publishing (DTP) programs, depending on the type of software used. Smaller leisure and tourism organizations are able to provide acceptable levels of management information with a MIS based solely on the use of microcomputers.

The components of a computerized management information system

With the first generation of computer-based MISs, organizations followed a **task-by-task** approach to solving their information needs, often starting with specific financial data concerning income and expenditure analysis. Having satisfied one particular need for information, the organization would move on to another data problem to solve. It is only in the last 15 years or so that UK leisure and tourism organizations have begun to commission **integrated** MISs which can perform many tasks and provide a multitude of management information from a single source.

K. J. Radford, in his book on information systems in management, identifies five separate sub-systems which together form the MIS. These are:

- **Common database** – this is the 'hub' of the MIS to which all the other sub-systems are connected. It acts as a storage compartment for information accessed by more than one department or individual in the organization. The accessible nature of the information in the common database means that security of data is an important concern for management. The database is continually updated and altered, as the organization goes about its normal operations. Choice of hardware for the MIS will play an important role in the operation of the common database, since, with inappropriate equipment, the expansion of the database will result in a slowing down of the speed of

response of the MIS. This can be to some extent overcome by the establishment of an 'archive', a separate system into which are transferred data which are not current but may be required at some time in the future.

- **Administrative and operational systems** – these are the components created to support the routine functions within the organization which revolve around the processing of data. Typical functions served by these systems are:

  - Pensions details
  - Payroll
  - Personnel records
  - Accounting ledgers
  - Internal audit
  - Maintenance of inventories of equipment
  - Production of documents
  - Purchasing
  - Sales planning and promotion
  - Maintenance schedules
  - Market research databases

- **Management reporting system** – the function of this system is to provide managers at all levels of an organization with the necessary information on which to base their decisions. These 'reports' will be concerned with either the control of the use of resources, the efficiency of operations or the effectiveness in achieving goals and objectives; depending on which level of management has requested the reports, it may be a mixture of all three.

Did You Know ?

A 'report' from a computerized MIS is often just a printout of current financial and other operational data.

- **Information retrieval system** – this has a similar function to that of the management reporting system (MRS) described above, the main difference being that while the MRS provides structured reports for use by managers in their day-to-day tasks, the information retrieval system gives them the opportunity to receive information from the system on demand, and in a form that is not structured in advance. The manager of a leisure complex, for example, may be asked by a senior executive to provide up-to-date figures on the usage of one of the facilities immediately; an effective information retrieval system should be able to handle such information requests speedily.

- **Data management system** – this is the part of the MIS which arranges and controls the flow of information between the other components of the system. Its major functions are supervising the capture and updating of data on the common database, the accessing of the common database by the other subsystems, generating reports in the formats required by management and providing security for the data in the database against accidental damage, intentional malice or inquisitiveness.

Factfile 2: Alton Towers

Alton Towers is the UK's number one theme park, with around 2 million visitors a year. With such a large number of visitors, it is important that the managers of the theme park have access to detailed information on matters such as:

- Income and expenditure
- Visitor numbers
- Staffing
- Marketing
- Health and safety

In order to remain at the forefront of the attractions market, it was decided to initiate a department-by-department review of the theme park's MIS in 1991. The review has resulted in the introduction of 100 terminals and PCs throughout the business, handling data concerning finance, admissions, marketing, merchandising and catering. The reorganization of the MIS has grouped departments which were hitherto separate, e.g. the retail department has brought together catering, merchandising and amusements. The park's catering function has benefited from the most recent system installation. Catering accounts for 400 of the 700 peak season workforce within retail, with 76 outlets generating in excess of £6.5 million during the 32-week season.

From the outset, the rationalization of the MIS was put into the hands of a team including a departmental head, stores manager and office co-ordinator, as well as a group information technology consultant. This approach encouraged a high degree of commitment to the system and its operation. The park's managers have sought to improve the flow of management data while at the same time recognizing the need for Alton Towers to remain competitive in the marketplace and improve on its already admirable record of customer service.

(Adapted from an article in *Leisureweek*)

Self Check ✔ **Element 3**

11. What advantages would an expanding specialist tour operator gain by changing from a manual to a computerized MIS?
_____
_____
_____

Unit Test This test is one hour long. Answer all the questions.

Focus 1: INFORMATION NEEDS

Question 1
The manager of a heritage centre operated by a city council has been asked to prepare a marketing plan for the facility for the next three years.

Decide whether each of these statements is true (T) or false (F).

(i) An analysis of the characteristics of current visitors to the centre, including age and socio-economic groupings, would not be relevant when collecting information for the plan.
(ii) An analysis of visitors' responses to current promotional activities would be relevant when collecting information for the plan.

Which option best describes these two statements?

A (i) T   (ii) T
B (i) T   (ii) F
C (i) F   (ii) T
D (i) F   (ii) F

Questions 2–4 share the answer options A–D.
Leisure and tourism organizations use a wide range of new technology in order to improve their management information services.

New technology equipment and systems currently in use include:

A 'Gateway' systems
B Electronic tills
C Electronic turnstiles
D Computerized membership lists

Which of these provides:

Question 2
Information which will assist with stock control?

Question 3
Access to the computer reservation systems of airlines and tour operators?

Question 4
The possibility of generating personalized letters for promotional purposes?

Question 5
The financial controller of a specialist tour operator is training two new members of staff in the company's financial procedures.

Decide whether each of these statements is true (T) or false (F).

(i) The company's profit and loss account will indicate the level of overdraft required and at what time in the year it will be needed
(ii) The company's cash flow forecast will show the company's financial position on a particular day in the trading year

Which option best describes these two statements?

A (i) T(ii) T
B (i) T   (ii) F
C (i) F   (ii) T
D (i) F   (ii) F

Question 6
A local authority leisure centre records many items of information on a regular basis as part of normal business practice.

Which of the following is the most important information it needs?

A Names and addresses of local football club secretaries
B The proportion of visitors given discounted admission
C Monthly sales returns
D The level of response to an advertising campaign in the local press

Focus 2: RECORDING AND PROCESSING INFORMATION

Questions 7–9 relate to the following information.
A large hotel has a computerized management information system with the following functions:

A Purchase ledger
B Customer database
C Sales ledger
D Sales performance targets of staff

Which of these would be used in each of the following circumstances?

Question 7
To obtain information on the level of income in the restaurant.

Question 8
To notify all customers of a special weekend break promotion.

Question 9
To find out how much has been spent on food for the grill room.

Questions 10–12 relate to the following information.
Below is a summary of the income and expenditure for a local authority tourist information centre for the last financial year.

Income	£
Commission from accommodation bookings	18,780
Sales of maps, books and guidebooks	7,360
Commission from theatre bookings	3,690
Commission from car hire	3,348
Fees for conference organization	12,450
Total income	45,628
Expenditure	£
Cost of maps, books and guidebooks	4,048
Staff costs	23,500
Office running costs	13,860
Miscellaneous costs	7,468
Total expenditure	48,876
Net profit	–3,248

Question 10
Without the commission from theatre bookings, the net loss would increase to:

A £6958
B £7956
C £6938
D £6638

Question 11

If the local authority had provided the promised subsidy of £12,500 for the year, the tourist information centre would have made a net profit of:

A £9252
B £7522
C £9552
D £5522

Question 12

Decide whether each of these statements is true (T) or false (F).

 (i) Fees for conference organization accounted for more than 25% of total income.
(ii) Staff costs accounted for more than 50% of total expenditure.

Which option best describes these two statements?

A (i) T   (ii) T
B (i) T   (ii) F
C (i) F   (ii) T
D (i) F   (ii) F

Focus 3: LEGAL, SECURITY AND CONTINGENCY ASPECTS AND PROCEDURES

Question 13

The manager of a travel agency has been approached by a local insurance company which is keen to increase its client base. The insurance company wants to buy customer data held on the travel agency's computer system, with a view to contacting clients to sell them travel insurance. Both the travel agency and the insurance company are registered data users.

What information is the travel agency manager allowed to sell?

A Only data that are more than 12 months old
B Any data they have
C Only names and addresses
D No data at all

Questions 14–16 relate to the following information.
A large tour operator, with a networked automated management information system, may use the following security measures:

A Regular back-up copies of data
B Access to certain functions in the system restricted to specified keyholders
C Hard-disk only system
D Allocation of a different password to each system user

Which of these measures would be most appropriate in the following circumstances?

Question 14

Confidential communication between departmental managers of sensitive commercial information.

Question 15

Failure of the electricity supply.

Question 16

Access to the system for all employees to view information, but alterations and amendments only by a limited number of staff.

Question 17

Under the terms of the Data Protection Act, individuals have certain rights concerning the information held about them on computer systems.

Decide whether each of these statements is true (T) or false (F).

 (i) Individuals have a right of access to the data.
(ii) Individuals do not have rights to compensation for inaccuracy of the data.

Which option best describes these two statements?

A (i) T   (ii) T
B (i) T   (ii) F
C (i) F   (ii) T
D (i) F   (ii) F

Question 18

In your role as Assistant Research Officer for a regional tourist board, you have produced a report for the Marketing Manager on the likely future trends in the number of overseas visitors to the region.

Why should the various sources of information be acknowledged in the report?

A It is necessary under copyright law.
B So that the manager can evaluate the validity of the information.
C Disclosing the source of information proves that it is accurate.
D It is a requirement of the Data Protection Act.

Question 19

You are suspicious when one of your employees leaves suddenly to join a rival leisure organization in the same town. You think that the former employee may have copied information on customers from the computer database and passed the data to her new employer. There was no password or user log on your system.

Decide whether each of these statements is true (T) or false (F).

 (i) Keeping back-up copies of information would have prevented the employee from gaining access to the system.
(ii) You will be able to tell if information security has been breached simply by examining your computer data.

Which option best describes these two statements?

A (i) T   (ii) T
B (i) T   (ii) F
C (i) F   (ii) T
D (i) F   (ii) F

Focus 4: RESOURCES AND RECORD-PING

Question 20

An outdoor activity centre is considering buying a microcomputer to help with its management information needs.

Decide whether each of these statements is true (T) or false (F).

(i) It is important to buy a system which can be upgraded in future if necessary.
(ii) The availability of suitable software packages to meet the particular needs of the centre is not important when deciding on which hardware to buy.

Which option best describes these two statements?

A   (i) T   (ii) T
B   (i) T   (ii) F
C   (i) F   (ii) T
D   (i) F   (ii) F

Question 21

The administrator of a small museum is considering which type of printer to buy to accompany her new personal computer. She can't decide whether to buy a dot matrix printer or a laser printer.

Which of the following is NOT a feature of dot matrix printers?

A   They are relatively cheap to buy.
B   They are reliable.
C   They are quiet.
D   Quality of print is not as good as a laser printer.

Question 22

Verity Brown, the owner of a country house hotel in Northumberland, sends out two 'mailshots' each year to her existing customers.

Decide whether each of these statements is true (T) or false (F).

(i) Ms Brown could buy a suitable computer and appropriate software to print personalized letters to her customers.
(ii) 'Mail merge' is a facility offered by the Post Office, allowing bulk users to get discounts on postage costs when carrying out 'mailshots'.

Which option best describes these two statements?

A   (i) T   (ii) T
B   (i) T   (ii) F
C   (i) F   (ii) T
D   (i) F   (ii) F

Question 23

A long-established coach company is resisting the pressure to introduce a computer to replace its existing manual booking and accounts system.

Decide whether each of these statements is true (T) or false (F).

(i) The introduction of a computerized booking system will improve the accuracy of the company's records.
(ii) The introduction of a computerized booking and accounts system will allow the company to give a more personal service to its customers.

Which option best describes these two statements?

A   (i) T   (ii) T
B   (i) T   (ii) F
C   (i) F   (ii) T
D   (i) F   (ii) F

Focus 5: QUALITY AND COST-EFFECTIVENESS

Question 24

A city museum is reviewing its methods of storing information on its exhibits and is considering a microfiche system.

Decide whether each of these statements is true (T) or false (F).

(i) Storing the information on microfiche would be

possible, but would require a large storage area.
(ii) Extra sheets of microfiche information could be photocopied if multiple copies are needed.

Which option best describes these two statements?

A   (i) T   (ii) T
B   (i) T   (ii) F
C   (i) F   (ii) T
D   (i) F   (ii) F

Questions 25–27 share answer options A–D.

External auditors found the following problems contained in a report about the management information system in a large city-centre hotel.

A   The hotel occupancy for the period in question was 56% and not 65% as stated in the report.
B   The report listed maintenance items which needed urgent attention, all of which were carried out before the report was written.
C   The report did not compliment the reception staff on winning the regional 'reception of the year' award.
D   The information on revenue from the hotel's leisure club was in fact related to the revenue from the grill room.

Which problem is mainly a matter of:

Question 25

Currency of the information?

Question 26

Accuracy in calculations?

Question 27

Validity of the information?

Question 28

There are many reasons why leisure and tourism organizations choose to store information on computers rather than in manual systems.

Decide whether each of these statements is true (T) or false (F).

(i) Storing the information on computer systems gives faster access to complicated information.
(ii) Storage of information on computer is cheaper than storage on manual, paper-based systems.

Which option best describes these two statements?

A   (i) T   (ii) T
B   (i) T   (ii) F
C   (i) F   (ii) T
D   (i) F   (ii) F

Questions 29–30 relate to the following information.

The finance department of a large tour operator which employs 15 staff has recently installed a computerized financial management system.

Question 29

This system would be most useful for:

A   Comparing hotel occupancy figures
B   Preparing budgets
C   Generating 'mailshots' for travel agencies
D   Filing personnel records of company staff

Question 30

The financial controller is keen to assess the efficiency and overall security of the new system.

Decide whether each of these statements is true (T) or false (F).

(i) The system should allow finance staff to compare actual with forecast sales.
(ii) The system should be suitable for the needs of all staff in the department if it meets the needs of the financial controller.

Which option best describes these two statements?

A (i) T   (ii) T
B (i) T   (ii) F
C (i) F   (ii) T
D (i) F   (ii) F

Focus 6: RECEIVER'S NEEDS AND WANTS

Question 31
The sales manager of a major international airline is making a presentation to 35 area managers on the subject of sales figures for the last year.

On an overhead projector transparency showing elements of total sales, she is most likely to use:

A A histogram
B A pie chart
C A straight-line graph
D A horizontal bar chart

Question 32
A travel agency clerk is often asked for information on what resorts and hotels are really like.

To enhance long-term goodwill, the travel clerk should:

A Refer the client to the tour operators' brochure descriptions.
B Tell the client to contact the relevant national tourist organization of the particular country.
C Consult reference books and manuals held in the agency and give the client full details.
D Give the client the telephone number of the major tour oper-ators and ask him to contact them direct for the information.

Questions 33–35 relate to the following information.
Large leisure and tourism organizations look for a range of information provision when choosing a management information system, including:

A Financial information
B Market information
C Personnel information
D Operational information

Into which information category does each of the following fall?

Question 33
Data on the changing patterns of demand for leisure and tourism facilities.

Question 34
Forecasts of revenue and costs of operation.

Question 35
Information on the correct storage of dangerous materials.

Question 36
Leisure and tourism organizations sometimes use the terms 'front office' and 'back office' when describing management information systems.

Decide whether each of these statements is true (T) or false (F).

(i) Accounting is commonly thought of as a 'front office' function.
(ii) Personnel is commonly thought of as a 'back office' function.

Which option best describes these two statements?

A (i) T   (ii) T
B (i) T   (ii) F
C (i) F   (ii) T
D (i) F   (ii) F

Self-check Answers

1. A computerized MIS will be able to retrieve complex data much more quickly than a manual system. A computerized system will allow management to carry out 'sensitivity analyses', involving changes in inputs to an organization to measure the effects on outputs. Computerized systems can store the same amount of data as a manual system in a much smaller space.

2. A typical local authority leisure centre will have revenue centres concerned with individual admissions, group bookings, concessions, catering, courses, events, vending, retail operations, etc.

3. Security of information is a very important matter in large, commercial leisure and tourism organizations. In order to ensure security, they should restrict access to computer systems to named keyholders and issue passwords to named individuals. Back-up copies of computer data should be made at regular intervals and stored in a secure place.

4. Your answer will depend on the facility chosen. Why not compare your answer with a friend's?

5. The short-term consequences of using inaccurate financial and operational information will revolve around problems with the cash flow of the business, as a result of wrong product costings. Operational problems may concern overbooking at hotels and incorrect loadings on flights. The longer-term effects are likely to be more serious, possibly affecting the profitability of the company and its eventual survival in the market.

6. Details of suppliers of computerized management information systems can be found from trade associations, professional bodies, the companies themselves, trade magazines and other leisure and tourism operators.

7. A 'gateway' system allows a travel agent to access the database of major airlines and tour operators, so that they can check availability and make bookings on behalf of their clients.

8. The break-even load factor for an airline is the point above which it begins to make a profit on an individual flight. This will typically be when a charter aircraft is 85%–90% full.

10. A theatre could classify its customers according to their tastes or by geographical location. Categories according to customers' tastes could include drama, opera, comedy, pop music, classical music, light entertainment, etc.

11. A tour operator that is expanding will have an increasing volume of data to handle; a computerized MIS will offer the opportunity of dealing with these data at a faster rate than a conventional manual system. A computer system will enable the company to carry out personalized direct mail campaigns and allow a faster response to requests for information. Where storage space is a problem, computer systems have the advantage of a large data storage capacity in a relatively small space.

Answers to Unit Test

1.	C	7.	C	13.	D	19.	D	25.	B	31.	B
2.	B	8.	B	14.	B	20.	B	26.	A	32.	C
3.	A	9.	A	15.	A	21.	C	27.	D	33.	B
4.	D	10.	C	16.	B	22.	B	28.	B	34.	A
5.	D	11.	A	17.	B	23.	D	29.	B	35.	D
6.	C	12.	B	18.	B	24.	D	30.	B	36.	C

Unit test comments

Q1: Answer is C.
When preparing a marketing plan for a leisure and tourism facility, it is important to analyse the characteristics of current visitors, in order to forecast future demand. Responses to current promotional activities should also be studied, since they will indicate which methods proved the most successful.

Q2: Answer is B – electronic tills.
As well as recording details of individual sales, including date, time and name of the member of staff serving, electronic tills can also assist with stock control and stock taking.

Q3: Answer is A – 'gateway' systems.
A 'gateway' system refers to a mix of computer software and hardware which allows an operator to access the main computers of another organization. They are commonly used by travel agents to book holidays and flights with tour operators and airlines.

Q4: Answer is D – computerized membership lists.
New laser printer technology and computerized databases allow even the smallest of leisure and tourism organizations to generate personalized letters for promotional and other purposes.

Q5: Answer is D.
A profit and loss account shows the financial position of an organization after a specified period of trading, normally 12 months. It is the balance sheet that shows the financial position on a particular day in the trading year. The cash flow forecast indicates the financial flows into and out of the organization and is used to predict when any extra borrowing, often in the form of an overdraft, may be needed.

Q6: Answer is C – monthly sales returns.
Without accurate information on the level of sales in the centre, the managers will not be in a position to use their resources effectively. Although details on local club secretaries, responses to advertising and the number of visitors given discounted admission are all relevant to the management of the centre, nothing is as important as information on its financial performance.

Q7: Answer is C – sales ledger.
The hotel's sales ledger will record the total revenue as well as the income for individual elements of the business, sometimes known as 'revenue centres'. These will include restaurant, bars, special functions and leisure suite income.

Q8: Answer is B – customer database.
Computerized databases can be used for a number of different purposes, including sending existing customers details of special events, offers and incentives.

Q9: Answer is A – purchase ledger.
The hotel's purchase ledger will include details of total purchases made by the hotel, with a subdivision into 'cost centres' such as food, equipment and casual labour.

Q10: Answer is C – £6938.
Without the commission from theatre bookings the total income would fall to £41,938. Total expenditure would stay the same at £48,876, giving a net loss of £6938.

Q11: Answer is A – £9252.
The subsidy of £12,500 would have made the total income rise to £58,128. Total expenditure would have stayed the same at £48,876, giving a net profit of £9252.

Q12: Answer is B.
Fees for conference organization accounted for 27.3% of total income, while staff costs accounted for 48.1% of total expenditure.

Q13: Answer is D – no data at all.
Under the Data Protection Act, registered data users are not allowed to disclose information to persons other than those named in their registration document. In this case, the travel agency is only likely to have named itself on its document; the name of the insurance company will not have been included.

Q14: Answer is B – access to certain functions in the system restricted to specified keyholders.
Neither allocating a different password to each system user, nor making regular back-up copies of data, nor using a hard-disk-only system would give the organization the degree of confidentiality it needs in this situation.

Q15: Answer is A – regular back-up copies of data.
Saving information onto floppy disks at regular intervals will guard against losing large amounts of data should there be a power failure.

Q16: Answer is B – access to certain functions in the system restricted to specified keyholders.
Option B will allow all employees to gain access to the system to view information, but will restrict alterations and amendments to be made only by a certain number of specified members of staff.

Q17: Answer is B.
The Data Protection Act gives members of the public the right to know whether information on them is held on an organization's computer and to have access to any data which do exist, at reasonable intervals and without undue delay or expense. Individuals also have rights to compensation for inaccuracy of data and loss, destruction or unauthorized disclosure of the information.

Q18: Answer is B – so that the manager can evaluate the validity of the information.

Quoting a source of information in a report does not necessarily prove that it is accurate, but it does allow the reader to assess whether the information has come from a valid source.

Q19: Answer is D.

The usual ways of controlling access to a computer system are to issue passwords to users or to allow access by specified key-holders only. Keeping back-up copies of information, however, will ensure that information is not lost should there be a failure of the computer system or its power supply. It is not possible to tell if the security of a computer system has been breached simply by examining the computer data.

Q20: Answer is B.

Constant developments in technology mean that it is sensible to buy a computer system that can be upgraded in the future if necessary. When purchasing a system, it is necessary to investigate both hardware and software at the same time, in order to buy a system that will meet the centre's particular requirements.

Q21: Answer is C – they are quiet.

When comparing a dot matrix to a laser printer, it is true that the dot matrix will be cheaper, will be reliable, but will not give as good a print quality as the laser printer. The dot matrix, however, is noisier than the laser printer.

Q22: Answer is B.

'Mail merge' is a facility on some computer software that allows one set of data to be merged with another, in order to produce a composite document. A good example is a mailing list being merged with a standard letter to produce personalized correspondence.

Q23: Answer is D.

Although the introduction of a computerized booking system can have benefits, such as the ability to deal with large volumes of data at great speed, it will not by itself improve the accuracy of the company's records; the information that comes out is only as good as the information that went in. Neither can a computerized booking system guarantee a more personal service to customers.

Q24: Answer is D.

One of the great benefits of a microfiche or microfilm system for storing data is that it takes up a very small amount of space; statement (i) is therefore false. It cannot, however, be photocopied, since the copy would be illegible. Extra copies need to be made professionally.

Q25: Answer is B – the report listed maintenance items which needed urgent attention, all of which were carried out before the report was written.

Information which is out of date is of little use when included in management reports; indeed, it may lead to incorrect management decisions.

Q26: Answer is A – the hotel occupancy for the period in question was 56% and not 65% as stated in the report.

All calculations to be included in management reports, particularly those concerning financial transactions, must be thoroughly checked before publication, so as to avoid embarrassing and sometimes costly mistakes.

Q27: Answer is D – the information on revenue from the hotel's leisure club was in fact related to the revenue from the grill room.

Information must be valid, i.e. fit for its intended purpose, in order to be of value for management purposes. Clearly, in this case the data on revenue from different parts of the hotel's operation had become mixed up.

Q28: Answer is B.

While one of the benefits of storing information on computer is that it gives faster access to complicated information, manual systems may well be cheaper to operate. Organizations often find that the introduction of a computer system results in greater volumes of paper rather than less.

Q29: Answer is B – preparing budgets.

The computer system for a finance department would not normally be used for promotional purposes such as sending out 'mailshots', nor for filing the personnel records of the company. Although occupancy figures will have a bearing on financial performance, the system will be most useful for preparing budgets.

Q30: Answer is B.

One of the most important aspects of monitoring the financial performance of an organization is to be able to compare actual sales with forecast sales, by studying the budgets. Any deviations from the predicted figures are known as variances. Different staff in a finance department will have different needs when it comes to the operation of the computerized system. The controller will tend to focus on management information, while other staff may be concerned with sales and purchase ledgers, taxation and payroll.

Q31: Answer is B – a pie chart.

Any diagram which tries to show the constituent parts of a total figure is best shown as a pie chart, with each element clearly indicated. Typical uses for a histogram and a horizontal bar chart would be monthly sales figures and monthly temperatures in a resort. Straight-line graphs are used to show the trend and fluctuations in a set of figures, e.g. annual sales figures.

Q32: Answer is C – consult reference books and manuals held in the agency and give the clients full details.

The descriptions of hotels and resorts given by tour operators in their brochures are sometimes a little over-flattering! A good travel agent will have a range of reference manuals which will give more objective details.

Q33: Answer is B – market information.

Information on the market for a particular leisure and tourism product or facility, including the origin of visitors, numbers of visitors and their characteristics, will be invaluable for planning future developments.

Q34: Answer is A – financial information.

Data on finance is often the most important information held on a management information system. Without accurate, timely and current information, management may not be able to deploy its resources to best effect.

Q35: Answer is D – operational information.

Operational information covers not only the storage of materials but also stock levels, usage levels and maintenance schedules.

Q36: Answer is C.

The distinction between 'front office' and 'back office' functions is not always totally clear, but in general such tasks as accounting, personnel and security management are considered to be 'back office', while reception, welcoming visitors, handling enquiries and taking bookings are 'front office'.

UNIT 7

Working in teams

Getting Started

It is difficult to think of many instances in the leisure and tourism industry where *teamwork* is not vital to the success of an organization. All sectors and contexts of leisure and tourism rely heavily on teams, large and small, to get things done. Building and motivating an effective and efficient team is one of the most difficult tasks faced by any leisure and tourism manager.

Contrary to popular belief, leisure and tourism products, services and facilities don't just happen, but are the result of concerted effort by groups of people seeking to achieve a common goal. By the same token, the skills of teamwork are not always built into an individual's character but frequently have to be learned through training and experience. It is important to remember that teamwork is both a *philosophy* and a *skill*; it is one of the roles of the leisure and tourism manager to create the organizational culture within which teamwork is encouraged and supported and to allow staff to develop the skills needed to operate as an effective team member.

This unit investigates how effective teams are built and managed in the leisure and tourism industry. Element 1 starts by looking at the characteristics of teams and discusses the importance of good communication. It continues by considering the role of the team leader, along with the qualities that go to make an effective team. Element 2 focuses on the interaction of team members and the stages in building an effective team. The final element of the unit, Element 3, examines the importance of evaluating team performance as a whole and the performance of individuals within a team.

Ad hoc teams Formed to tackle a specific problem or opportunity, over a short period of time.

Formal teams Often found in the workplace and characterized by having an elected leader with clear lines of authority and responsibility.

Informal teams Develop organically rather than in a planned fashion. May form for social or work-related reasons.

Innovator A member of a team who is good at thinking of new ideas and different ways to tackle problems. Sometimes called an "ideas person".

Inter-personal skills Skills and techniques which allow people to interact with each other more effectively, e.g. communication skills, negotiation skills and team building skills.

Non-verbal communication A powerful means of communication, used either instead of the spoken word (bodily contact, facial expressions etc.) or at the same time as we are speaking to reinforce a message (a speaker at a conference who bangs the table to make a point).

Peer Appraisal This is the review and evaluation of the performance of a team member by the other members of the group.

Team objectives A statement outlining what a team hopes to achieve in the short and long-term. Sometimes referred to as team goals.

Team rationale The reasons for a team's very existence.

Two-way communication When two or more people both send and receive messages and are, therefore, able to enter into an effective dialogue.

Essential Principles

What is a team?

A **team** is a group of individuals working together towards a clearly defined goal or objective. The ideal team will be made up of individuals who are all committed to the task in hand and have been given the necessary resources to do the job properly. It will operate in an 'open' and democratic fashion where all ideas and concerns are shared by the members of the team. As well as having the necessary resources to operate effectively, the team must be given the authority to make its own decisions and commit resources. Finally, for a team to be wholly effective in its tasks, it must have the full support of the senior management within the organization.

We are all familiar with the many examples of teams operating in the leisure and tourism industry, including:

- The crew of an Airtours jet flying from Manchester to Palma in Majorca with 190 holidaymakers on board.
- An English couple who own and run a wine bar in Alicante.
- A specialist tour operator with a team of four sales and reservations staff.
- A team of four students carrying out a visitor survey for a local tourist attraction.
- A conference organizer and his team of two who organize business conferences and meetings at a country house hotel.
- A school's basketball team.
- A team responsible for organizing a charity event such as a fun-run.
- The cast of a major West End musical such as Grease.

Types of teams

A team may develop formally or informally. An example of a **formal team** is given in Fig. 7.1, showing the structure of a regional tourist board. A formal team often operates within the work environment and is characterized by having a leader appointed by the organization, in this case the chief executive.

As well as having an appointed leader, formal teams also:

- Are established to carry out specific tasks and to help achieve organizational objectives.
- Have clearly identified channels of communication.
- Assign specific roles to each team member.
- Have clear lines of authority and responsibility.

Informal teams also exist in leisure and tourism organizations. They tend to develop organically rather than through an organizational structure and may form for social or work-related reasons. In the work situation, colleagues often find it easier to make decisions through talking informally rather than in a formal setting, such as at a meeting or group presentation. The importance of informal teams should not be underestimated, but there should be mechanisms in place to channel the outcome of informal gatherings into the more formal team setting.

> **Did You Know ?**
>
> The term *ad hoc* is sometimes given to a team which is set up at short notice to work on a particular problem or opportunity.

The benefits of team operation

Effective teamwork brings benefits both to the organization which sets up the team and to the individual team members. Benefits to the organization will vary depending on its size, structure and culture, but are likely to include:

- **Increased sales** – a teamwork approach to selling holiday insurance by telephone is likely to yield increased sales compared with the same activity carried out individually.

- **A happier workforce** – teamwork allows individuals to work to their full potential and feel good about themselves and their work.

- **Increased efficiency** – an example of this could be that an effective team working in the information department of a national tourist office will be able to handle more enquiries from customers.

- **Less staff conflict** – a team which is trained to take responsibility for its own work and decision making is likely to be better at resolving its own internal problems, thus saving valuable management time.

- **Increased loyalty** – teamwork instils a sense of loyalty and commitment into members of staff.

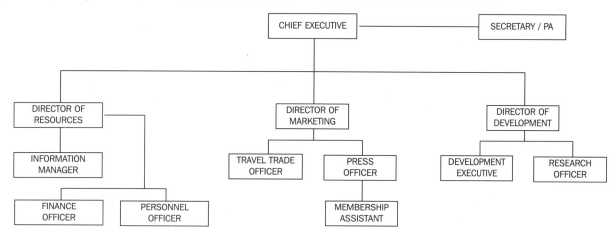

Figure 7.1 A formal team structure in a regional tourist board

- **Reduced absenteeism** – staff who see themselves as valued members of a team are likely to be more content and take less time off work.

- **A more creative workforce** – team members are more likely to come forward with ideas for improving work practices, reducing costs or increasing efficiency.

A vital part of establishing a team to carry out a task is that it will operate more *efficiently*. For example, three people who previously prepared meals in a fast-food restaurant individually and were able to prepare 10 meals each per hour would be expected to deliver more than 3×10 meals per hour when working as a team.

Many of the tasks carried out in leisure and tourism organizations can *only* be accomplished through the efforts of a team of people. Tasks such as staging a banquet for 150 guests or hosting a major tennis championship are too large and complex to be left to a single individual or workers who neither communicate with each other nor work as part of a team; in many cases, a team approach is the only solution.

Benefits to *individual* team members from working as part of a team include:

- The chance to be innovative and creative.
- An enhanced sense of their worth within the organization.
- Greater job satisfaction.
- Increased status within the organization.
- The ability to use their talents to the full.
- The support of other team members.
- Increased rewards for their work made possible as a result of greater efficiency, e.g. a productivity bonus or extra 'perks'.

The characteristics of an effective team

Leisure and tourism teams will vary in their composition, structure and methods of operation. However, common features are displayed by the most **effective teams**, such as:

- A commitment from all team members to the task in hand.
- An informal atmosphere within which ideas are developed.
- A leader whose role is that of 'facilitator', i.e. creating the culture which allows others to work to their full potential.
- Good communication among team members.
- A system which ensures accurate recording of decisions made by the group.
- Clear identification of who is responsible for taking action and by when.
- Members who have a clear idea of what the team is trying to achieve.
- Team members selected on the basis of their skill at working with others.
- Regular team meetings in an appropriate environment.
- A known 'lifespan' if the team has been formed for a specific project.
- Access to the necessary resources to achieve the task.
- The support of senior management in the organization.

All leisure and tourism organizations, in an ideal world, would like to be able to develop teams which exhibit all of the above characteristics. However, as we are all aware, the reality of working in leisure and tourism, particularly in times of economic recession, is often far from 'ideal'; budgets may not be increased or, even worse, may be cut, staff may be made redundant and other cost-cutting measures may be implemented. While these pressures will have an undoubted effect on team operation, many of the characteristics of effective teams listed above are *internal* to the team itself and its members. The team will be responsible, for example, for its own internal communication and for setting an atmosphere which is informal yet conducive to getting the task done. To some extent, therefore, a team can still operate effectively even in a difficult economic climate; indeed it could be argued that it is *more* important to develop effective staff teams when the economy is in recession, in order that an organization remains competitive in the leisure and tourism industry.

Leadership in teams

The members of a team must have effective **leadership** if they are to work to their full potential and the team achieve its ultimate goal. Many people would argue that having a strong leader is the single most important factor in determining whether a team will achieve success.

The team leader

We have acknowledged that organizations in the leisure and tourism industry often have to operate in an imperfect world. The jobs of staff working for a local authority, for example, may be at risk because the council is forced to make cuts in the provision of leisure services for local people. A country house hotel may be having a bad season and cannot afford the cost of the extra staff that it desperately needs to maintain its high levels of customer service. A travel agency may still be using out-dated computer equipment which should have been replaced 12 months ago. A shortage of capital may mean that an airline has to postpone the introduction of a new fleet of aircraft until business picks up. Against these difficult situations, finding **team leaders** who are able to lead and motivate staff, as well as being able to give them all the 'tools' to carry out an effective job, is not an easy task. When looking for a team leader, however, it is important to appoint the 'best' person for the job, whether it is somebody already working for the organization or a candidate from outside. When looking for the 'perfect' team leader, an organization needs to find an individual who will:

- Plan and co-ordinate, with all team members, the strategy that the team will adopt, while keeping the objectives of the team constantly in mind.
- Accept the challenge and responsibility of leading the team from day one.
- Acknowledge the achievements of team members and publicize successes both internally and externally.
- Be enthusiastic about the task and spread this enthusiasm to all members of the team.
- Communicate effectively with other team members and those outside the team who need to be kept abreast of developments.
- Develop skills and qualities in other team members so that they may achieve their full potential.
- Promote an 'open' style of management by discussing all matters of concern to the group and by listening to the views and concerns of all team members.
- Adopt an action-orientated approach to making things happen, by first identifying what needs to be done in a

certain situation and then stating the action which needs to be carried out, who is responsible for carrying it out and a date or time by which it must be completed.

- Constantly promote a positive approach to solving problems and pushing the work of the team forward in a positive manner.
- Involve all team members in the decision-making process.
- Manage the evaluation process to identify any ways in which the team could have worked more effectively or how particular problems could have been resolved.
- Not be afraid of admitting mistakes, but will build on them and actively work towards quality in all aspects of team operation.

Did You Know ?

It is essential that a team leader is more than just a figurehead, but an effective manager as well.

Once the decision has been taken to form a team to carry out a specific task or tasks, the choice of leader must be the first consideration. He or she must be involved in all stages of **team development** (see Fig. 7.2).

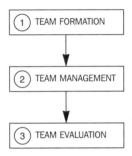

Figure 7.2   The stages in team development

In many cases, a team leader will not have the luxury of selecting a complete team from scratch. He or she will often be in the position of taking over an existing team of people who may have been together for a long period of time. Whenever feasible, the leader must be involved at the **team formation stage** in selecting team members for a new team or one which is being reorganized. An organization which arbitrarily selects team members over the head of the team leader is immediately undermining the leader's position.

The leader will act as a facilitator during the **team management stage** when the real work of the team is under way. The leader should not try to dominate proceedings but rather should create the right atmosphere to give team members the best chance of success.

The leader will need constantly to monitor how the team is functioning and will need to reflect on how well it performed at the **team evaluation stage**. Evaluation is all about measuring team effectiveness, in other words discovering how well the team performed. If clear objectives have been set for the team, it will be easier to answer this question (see Element 3 of this unit for more on evaluation of team performance).

The importance of communication in teamwork

A team which is unable to develop an 'open' culture, with effective **communication** channels both within the team and with outside agencies will not achieve its full potential. The team leader will have a crucial role to play in ensuring that effective communication takes place and, just as importantly, takes place in a way that encourages team members to perform to their maximum; handled badly, communication can be a distinct disincentive to good performance.

Did You Know ?

Poor communication is one of the most common reasons why a team fails to reach its goal.

Communication within a team means more than just the occasions when the team members are talking to each other in a meeting. This **verbal communication**, to which can be added talking on the telephone, is obviously very important, but is only a small part of the total communication process. Communication by team members can also be in *written form*, perhaps a report on a particular subject, minutes of meetings or fax/telex/telephone messages. Often as important as written and verbal communication is the way in which information is sent, received and understood by others; this is the subject known as **non-verbal communication** (NVC). The most talked-about type of NVC is body language, the process by which we send and receive messages without using words. A team leader who is making an important point during a meeting may well bang the table or wave his or her arms about to stress the importance of what is being said. Body language is sometimes classified as follows:

- **Posture** – whether standing, sitting, lying down, walking or running, there is often something about our body posture which relays a message to those around us, either consciously or unconsciously.
- **Physical proximity** – the distance we feel we need to keep between ourselves and other people, e.g. as a spectator at a football match.
- **Orientation** – where we place ourselves in relation to others. By tradition, a leader running a team meeting will sit at the head of the table.
- **Bodily contact** – shaking hands, for example.
- **Gestures** – we all make gestures from time to time to signal approval or disapproval, e.g. a 'thumbs up' to show you agree with what is being suggested.
- **Eye contact** – whether we are aware of it or not, we pay a great deal of attention to a person's eyes when they are communicating with us.
- **Facial expression** – the face can transmit an enormous range of messages and emotions, either consciously or subconsciously. Like much non-verbal communication, facial expressions can sometimes be misinterpreted.

Promoting two-way communication

Effective teams must develop good two-way communication channels. An example of two-way communication in a leisure and tourism team situation is as follows:

Paul, the product manager of a large tour operator, has called a meeting of the two product executives under his control to explain the introduction of a new pricing structure for the company's Florida programme. Dawn, a product executive who has only just joined the team from a rival operator, asks Paul a question on discounted child prices for the programme. Paul is able to respond to the question and give Dawn the necessary information. However, she is still not clear about part of the answer and so asks a further question. Paul finally answers all Dawn's points and thanks her for raising the matter.

Paul and Dawn were able to ask questions of each other and clarify any points about which they were unclear. An alternative way of explaining the new pricing structure would have been to circulate a memo; this is an example of **one-way communication** since it gives the person receiving it no immediate answers to any points which are unclear or could be misinterpreted. **Two-way communication** has many advantages, although it is initially more time consuming, and should be used whenever practical.

Self Check ✔ **Element 1**

1. Think of a selection of teams which operate in the leisure and tourism industry in your own area.

2. Why is it important for a team to have the full support of senior management?

3. Why is it important to encourage two-way communication in a team situation?

7.2 Working with others in teams

Effective team building

The recognition of the importance of teamwork in leisure and tourism is a recent phenomenon. While it is true that some organizations have used a team approach to providing leisure and tourism services since Victorian times, it is only in the last 20 years at best that **team building** and team development have been given a high priority in the management of facilities. Today's most effective and efficient leisure and tourism organizations, in the private, public and voluntary sectors, have recognized that time, money and effort spent on team building pays dividends. Using techniques and practices developed in the USA, Europe and the Far East, many UK leisure and tourism organizations have changed their structures, increased their staff training and developed a culture which is based on decision making by teams of people rather than individuals. These organizations have become more successful in achieving their objectives and individual employees have benefited from a more 'open' management style and a more cohesive approach to work.

The six main stages in building an effective team are shown in Fig. 7.3.

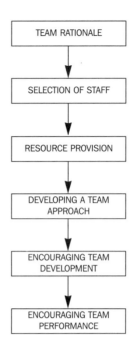

Figure 7.3   The stages in building an effective team

Stage one – team rationale

The **rationale stage** of team building is concerned with whether it is necessary to set up a team to achieve a particular objective. It tries to answer such questions as 'Do we really need a team?' and 'Is there a better (and cheaper) way of achieving the same end?' If an organization is convinced that a team approach *is* the best way forward, it must then consider the *objectives* of the team and the *parameters* within which it will work.

The **parameters** (or **constraints**) could include:

- The timescale within which the team must operate. The team members should know how long they will be working together, and if there are any interim time targets which they will have to meet for specific elements of their work.
- The budget which the team will be allocated. The team should be given at the outset the limits of any expenditure they can incur and any income targets which they have to meet.
- The maximum number of staff who can be invited to join the team. In a small organization, it may be felt that only two or three people can be spared to join the team, or otherwise normal operations may be adversely affected.
- Specific individuals who cannot join the team. If the team is being established in an existing organization, these will usually be members of staff who have a full workload at present and cannot be released. If the team is being put together for a specific event, there may be many reasons why particular individuals are not invited to join the team, ranging from confidentiality to personality clashes.

In relation to the aims of the team, the leader may be given a broad goal by the organization and asked to develop with the team the specific objectives which will need to be achieved in order to reach the goal. For example, a tour operator which at present only organizes holidays to Spain may set up a team with a goal 'to expand operations into long-haul holidays to the West Indies'. The team will then identify specific **objectives** which could include:

- To sell 1,000 holidays to the West Indies in the first year.
- To set up contracts with 20 hotels in the West Indies for the first season.
- To have a turnover of £5 million on holidays to the West Indies within three years.
- To establish a network of agents to sell the holidays.
- To be known for offering a high quality product within the industry.
- To train all staff in the importance of customer service.

The team will organize themselves to work to these objectives within the budget and timescale given by the organization. In some cases, specific objectives will already have been developed and the team will be asked to comment on them and suggest any modifications which they may feel are appropriate.

It is important to remember that building a team is not always the most effective way of achieving a task. Managers must be skilled at deciding when a team approach to solving a particular problem or tackling a job is the *best* course of action. Many day-to-day management decisions are taken by individuals without recourse to a team. There are occasions when a manager will set up a team to tackle a particular issue to hide the fact that he or she is unable, or unwilling, to take on the responsibility for making the necessary decision. Senior management must be aware of this practice which is wasteful of scarce resources.

Stage two – selection of staff

The **team leader** is often the most important appointment to the team. We discussed in Element 1 of this unit the characteristics of the 'ideal' team leader and the qualities he or she will need to mould a successful team (see page 138). The team leader may be somebody already working for the organization or may be appointed to head up a team working on a specific project or event. Unless they have very strong characters, leaders who already work for an organization sometimes find it difficult to adapt to their new roles and responsibilities. The **staff selected** to join the team may also find it hard to accept that the leader has a new function in the organization and may themselves have to change the way they deal with the leader. For these reasons, leisure and tourism organizations sometimes prefer to appoint a new person from outside the organization to be the team leader. The disadvantage of this situation is that the leader will then have the difficult task of selecting team members from a pool of staff about which he or she knows very little. The leader will also need to be sensitive to the fact that some of the team members will feel insecure and perhaps uncomfortable in their new positions. A leader with great tact and diplomacy will be needed to 'win over' some members of the team.

How big should the team be?

There is no 'best' size of team which will apply in all circumstances. The number of people who are chosen to form the team will depend on many factors, including:

- **The size of the organization** – the bigger the organization, the less likely it is to suffer when team members are released from their normal work duties.
- **The size and significance of the task** – a team which is formed to plan and stage an international sporting event, for example, is going to need to be large in order to cover the multitude of complex tasks involved.
- **The type of task to be undertaken** – a team which is brought together to deal with a very technical task, e.g. involving language translation, is likely to need more 'specialists'.
- **The length of time it is likely to take to complete** – a project which will run for months or even years, may be managed by a small team who may, from time to time, change roles and responsibilities.
- **The abilities and skills of the team members** – a small team of highly experienced individuals may be able to achieve the same outcomes as a larger team made up of staff with less experience and training.
- **The time of year** – many leisure and tourism organizations operate on a seasonal basis, thus making it possible for a larger team to be formed outside the peak season than would be the case if it was formed at the busiest time of year.

Research suggests that teams can become unwieldy and difficult to control once the number of members reaches double figures. The team leader can begin to experience difficulties with communication and co-ordination when numbers go beyond 10 people. There may be occasions when the task that the team has been set is so large that no *single* team could be expected to cope with all that is expected. In such circumstances, the leader may well decide to split the team into subgroups and identify a group leader who would report back on progress. This is the situation which often exists in the management of hotels, for example, when a general manager delegates authority to section managers who control the working of a team of staff.

> **Did You Know** ❓
>
> A team size of six to nine members is likely to function effectively and be of a size which is capable of being managed by the team leader.

Team training

Depending on the task that the team has been set, resources will need to be made available for **staff training** in a number of different areas, including:

- **Training in inter-personal skills** – all team members will benefit from training in such matters as communication, decision-making, listening skills, problem-solving, working collaboratively and a host of others. The team leader may need specialist training in, for example:

  - Managing team meetings
  - Developing team skills
  - Negotiation skills
  - Evaluating team performance
  - Resolving conflict
  - Communication skills

  This sort of training can be carried out 'in house' or

with the help of an outside trainer. An increasingly popular way of learning team building and other inter-personal skills is for team members to spend time at an activity centre, where they are given physical and mental challenges to help develop management skills. Two of the leading companies offering this type of training are The John Ridgeway School of Adventure, based in the Highlands of Scotland, and Outward Bound, with its headquarters in Aberdovey, Mid Wales.

- **Training in technical skills** – it is likely that some members of the team will need specific technical training in order to be able to fulfil their roles effectively. Taking the example of the food and beverages section of a large hotel, some members of the team working in the kitchens will need technical training in, for example, food hygiene and food storage. A team which has been developed to change the admissions procedure at a visitor attraction may need specialist training in computer spreadsheets and databases. Members of a team working on a new fitness suite for a leisure centre will need instruction and training in the technical aspects of the equipment being installed.

- **Training in administrative skills** – whether or not a team is lucky enough to have good administrative support, it is helpful if at least some team members have a grasp of basic administrative skills, such as note-taking, wordprocessing and report writing. All teams will need to process day-to-day paperwork. It is useful to have a team member who can interpret financial data and train others in the group to be able to do the same, perhaps with the help of computer software.

Team interaction

The mix of personal characteristics in members of a team is a major determinant of its success or failure. Simply bringing together the individuals with the greatest technical expertise, best qualifications or most experience does not guarantee success in a team. These qualities are obviously important, but just as important is the way in which the team members **interact**. The most important characteristics which can affect the team's performance are background, personality, age and experience of work:

- **Background** – team members who have a similar background are more likely to gel into an effective team quickly and understand the task in hand. Differences in culture, language, education and social status can sometimes lead to problems of team cohesion. Team members with similar hobbies or interests will have a common talking point from the outset, which will help team development.

- **Personality** – all human beings are unique and will react in different ways when in a team situation. Some will be quiet and reflective while others will be loud and try to dominate the group. It is the team leader's role to give all team members the opportunity to state their views, while building on the positive characteristics of individuals. The leader must anticipate potential conflict and have measures ready to resolve any problems caused by differing personalities.

- **Age and experience of work** – team members who are roughly the same age and with similar lengths of time in

their jobs are likely to form into an effective team on the basis of their shared experiences.

Stage three – resource provision

In addition to any budgets that the team may need, it should also be given the physical **resources** in order to complete its task effectively. We shall look at some of the more important resources that the team will need, starting with the equipment that may be necessary.

Equipment

Access to the necessary **equipment** will be vital to the team if it is to stand any chance of meeting its objective. Depending on the nature and size of the team's task, and the leisure and tourism context in which it operates, the team members may need access to:

- Technical equipment, e.g. specialist ovens for kitchen staff.
- The use of vehicles for transporting people and equipment.
- Specialist computer software, e.g. for a central reservations system (CRS).
- Communications equipment, e.g. fax machine, telex, telephones, audio-visual aids etc.

Given the right level of equipment, the team will feel comfort-able about having sufficient resources to do the job it has been set.

The work environment

Team members who share the same office are more likely to form into a cohesive group than colleagues who are in distant locations. Where it is not possible for all the members of a team to be housed together, perhaps because the group is simply too large, there must be effective means of communi-cation so that ideas and decisions can be swiftly conveyed to all staff. The nature of many leisure and tourism organiza-tions will mean that the **work environment** for the team will be the facility itself, e.g. a leisure centre, hotel, museum, aircraft or outdoor activity centre. Working in close proxim-ity to colleagues in these situations with few physical barriers can mean that teams perform particularly well and that a tremendous team spirit is built up. Team leaders need to be aware, however, of the potential pressures and conflicts which can arise in such circumstances and be prepared to take what-ever action is necessary to manage the situation.

Did You Know ❓

Teams invariably function best when their members all work in the same location or at least in close proximity to each other.

Support staff

There will be times when the team will need the **support** of other people in order to function effectively. These people may be from inside the organization, so it is important that the whole workforce is aware of the team's existence and has a feel for what it is trying to achieve. A team leader may some-times feel that it would be helpful to employ somebody from outside the organization to join the team, perhaps for a short period of time or for a particular task which cannot be carried out by the current team members. Consultants can be employed to take on the role of 'facilitator' or 'observer', and so give an objective view of how the team is performing and pinpoint any ways in which it could improve its effectiveness.

Stage four – developing a team approach

Once the team members have been selected and sufficient resources have been made available, consideration must be given to the many factors which influence the way in which a **team approach** can be developed, including:

- Group motivation
- Style of leadership
- External threats
- Personnel policies and practices

Group motivation

Success breeds **motivation**, so the more successful the team, the more motivated its members are likely to be, and vice versa. The leader should aim to maintain this cycle of motivation and success, which will lead to effective team performance, by praising individuals and the team as a whole when successes have been achieved. There may be times when the team deserves more than just praise from the team leader or senior management, but has earned a reward for its efforts. Rewards and incentives can act as positive motivators if handled carefully and in such a way that they do not build resentment between those in the organization, but outside the team, who do not receive the reward. Typical incentives for teams could include bonus payments, social events, free holidays or short breaks.

Style of leadership

We have already emphasized the crucial role that the team leader plays in managing the work of the team. He or she should not try to dominate proceedings within the group but rather act as a 'catalyst' who creates the right environment and conditions in which the team can operate effectively. While the leader of the team may have a very 'open' management **style**, he or she may be constrained by the decisions of senior management, who may appear distant and bureaucratic. For a team to be completely effective, the senior management of the organization must also adopt the same supportive style of management and give the leader and team members the freedom to take risks in seeking to achieve their objectives. Compare, for example, the management style of Virgin Atlantic Airways, with their charismatic Chairman Richard Branson, with that of British Rail, a state-controlled monopoly. Virgin is characterized as an organization which is willing to take risks to achieve its objectives and, in so doing, is committed to an 'open' style of management with team decision making in evidence throughout the organization. British Rail, on the other hand, has a very hierarchical structure which some say leaves little room for team innovation and swift decision making.

External threats

Threats from outside the team can often have a very positive effect in helping to develop cohesion among the team members. Human nature dictates that individuals will co-

operate more effectively in the face of external threats. In the world of leisure and tourism, threats could come from a number of different sources. It could be the appointment of a new manager or new team leader from outside the organization or a threat from a competitor who is about to open a similar facility nearby. Perhaps an airline is trying to gain permission to fly its planes on one of your most profitable routes. Even if the threat is subsequently removed, team development will have been helped and a more cohesive team will result. It has been known for some organizations to create mythical threats, perhaps by circulating a rumour, in order to develop team cohesion.

Personnel policies and practices

Organizational policies concerned with **personnel** matters should reflect the importance that is given to teamwork within the organization. It is pointless for a major commercial leisure company, for example, to say that it puts a high priority on teamwork in the management of its facilities and then to have no budget for training in teamwork skills. Similarly, systems for appraisal, promotion and personal development should reflect a commitment to team operation and development. Personnel practices should also treat all members of teams in an equitable fashion and should not create antagonism between those members of staff who work in teams and those who do not, by virtue of the fact that members of teams are perceived as being favoured by management.

Stage five – encouraging team development

During the initial stages of the formation of the group, when the objectives and team roles are being clarified, team members are likely to feel anxious and will be trying to establish their credentials and develop a rapport with both the team leader and the other members of the team. The leader too may feel unclear about the capabilities of team members and be unsure about his or her own performance. Once individual team members get to know each other, they will be more willing to enter into debate and challenge colleagues on issues that they are concerned about. This should be encouraged by the team leader since, if handled constructively, it will often lead to the team as a whole clarifying its rationale and the way in which it operates. Having a clarified purpose will also help to mould the team into an effective force.

> **Did You Know** ?
>
> Some leaders use 'ice breaker' games to help team members get to know each other.

At an early stage in its development, the team will need to set the guidelines, standards and levels of acceptable behaviour under which it will function; in other words, establish the **ground rules** for all team members. At this stage, the team leader may feel the need to intervene when decisions made by the team could be seen as controversial or contrary to organizational policy. Having set the ground rules, the team will then be in a position to perform the role or roles for which it was established, with a cohesive team framework allowing all team members to contribute to the attainment of their objectives.

Stage six – evaluating team performance

The team leader should encourage all team members constantly to **monitor** their individual activities and the performance of the team as a whole. **Evaluation** of team performance involves looking back at how effective the team was, either at the end of the project or event for which it was formed, or at clearly identified stages in its development. Evaluation is an important tool for both management and the team itself, so that lessons are learnt, performance is rewarded and mistakes are analysed. Element 3 of this unit looks in detail at evaluating team performance.

Poor performance in teams

It is not always easy to identify exactly why a team does not perform well or fails to meet its objectives. Poor performance can sometimes be a result of one or more of the following factors:

1 Unclear goals
2 Poor communication
3 Ineffective leadership
4 Group dynamics
5 Vested interests
6 Inability to maintain momentum

1 **Unclear goals:** One reason why teams fail to achieve their full potential is that they are not given, or do not develop, clear *goals* from the outset. If members of a team are unclear as to what it is they are supposed to be achieving, then their performance will suffer and their work will lack direction and purpose.

2 **Poor communication:** This is another reason why teams sometimes fail. Team leaders need to establish the mechanism by which decisions are conveyed both inside and outside the team, and develop an 'open' culture which encourages feedback, questioning and debate among team members.

3 **Ineffective leadership:** This can mean that a team fails to achieve its full potential. A leader who does not recognize potential in individual members, who cannot prioritize or lead by example, will lack credibility and may even become a liability to the team.

4 **Group dynamics:** Selecting individuals to be part of a team is not an easy task. Leisure and tourism managers who think that building a team involves nothing more than selecting the brightest staff and locking them away in a room are in for a nasty shock. It is essential to be aware of *group dynamics*, i.e. how individuals relate to and interact with each other, when choosing staff for a team. A lack of awareness of group interaction is one of the most common reasons for teams failing to achieve their objectives.

5 **Vested interests:** These can sometimes lead to the downfall of a team. For example, a group of local council sports development officers which has come together to mount a major county-wide sports promotion event may be hampered in its efforts by one of their number who insists that his district must always have the last word when any decisions are made. Individuals who put their own vested interests before the 'corporate good' are of little use to a team which is trying to be as effective as possible.

6 **Loss of momentum:** A failure to maintain *momentum* can lead to a team not being able fully to meet its aims. The team leader should anticipate that after an initial period of excitement and commitment from team members, their enthusiasm may falter, and he or she will need to have ideas and mechanisms to hand to be able to generate a new tide of effort from all team members. It is a good idea to plan social events and gatherings where team members can 'let their hair down' and forget about the challenges they face at work. Changing the venue of team meetings can be another good way of maintaining momentum.

Conflict in teams

There are two main types of **conflict** situations that may develop in leisure and tourism organizations: those which occur within the team (*intra-team*) and those which may exist between teams (*inter-team*).

Intra-team conflict usually arises from a clash of personalities between one or more members of the team. For example, there may be a member of the team who is:

- **Cynical** – sees no point in going on.

- **Aggressive** – often contributes unnecessarily hostile comments.

- **Critical** – cannot think positively about the team and its work.

- **A time waster** – continually interrupts with insignificant remarks.

- **A perfectionist** – who is constantly revising decisions and ideas.

- **A liar** – is out to dismantle the team at all costs.

- **A gossip** – constantly spreads rumours.

Conflict may develop between the team leader and a member or members of the team. In this situation, senior management may well need to intervene to sort things out.

In the case of **inter-team** conflict, i.e. conflict which exists *between* one or more groups in the same organization, there is often more to the problem than personality clashes alone. Inter-team conflict can result in one group becoming hostile to another, can lead to a breakdown in communication or a mistrust of one group by another. If we take as an example a large tourist attraction such as Beaulieu in Hampshire, with many different teams controlling the activities, events, attractions, car parking, catering, maintenance, litter and a host of other duties, a little rivalry between teams is to be encouraged in order to increase job satisfaction and team performance. Conflict could arise, however, when one team is regarded by some of the others as being of a lower status; the staff responsible for car parking, for example, may be considered of less value than those organizing events. This could be overcome by rotating jobs on a regular basis, so that the events organizer in week one takes on the role of the car park attendant in week two, and so on. Management must also continually stress that every member of staff is crucial to the success of the organization.

Inter-team conflict can also arise when one team considers that it is not being treated the same as another team. Management must strive to treat all teams on an equal basis and, if there are reasons why one team is rewarded better than another, then an explanation is given.

Why is it important to deal with conflict?

Most organizations in leisure and tourism will have to deal with conflict in their staff from time to time. Teams, which by their very nature are made up of people working closely together, are perhaps more prone to conflict situations, particularly if the same team members are together over an extended period of time or are sharing the same workspace. A degree of healthy debate and criticism within a team is not of itself necessarily a bad thing; it is only through open discussion of issues that good decision making and problem solving can take place. Conflict, however, is a stage removed from healthy debate and discussion and, if not managed well, can have serious implications for the organization in which the team is working. Conflict in teams can lead to:

- A high turnover of staff
- Reduced staff morale and commitment
- Poor levels of customer service
- Increased staff absenteeism
- Increased disciplinary problems
- More management time being devoted to dealing with the problem
- Reduced profitability

It is when conflict becomes so serious as to damage the operation and viability of an organization that the problem must be managed. Some organizations are of the opinion that conflict can be anticipated, and there may well be occasions when potential conflict situations can be diffused before any real harm is done. Much conflict, however, is hard to predict because of its very spontaneous nature.

Did You Know **?**

If not handled sensitively, team conflict can have serious effects on staff morale and performance.

Managing conflict in teams

In the example of Beaulieu above, we saw one solution to a particular conflict situation, namely the *rotation* of jobs between team members. As well as this, and other, specific measures, there are some general principles that can be employed to deal with conflict in team situations, such as adopting a positive management style and stressing the importance of all team members working towards the same goal.

Management style

We have compared the different **styles of management** employed at Virgin Atlantic and British Rail from the point of view of leadership and the development of a team approach to decision making. Management style is also very important when considering how to deal with conflict in a team. The style of management of the team leader and the organization itself will determine how well conflict situations are handled.

In leisure and tourism organizations, management styles differ greatly between one organization and another. Figure 7.4 gives some common examples of styles of management found in leisure and tourism.

STYLE ONE	PASSIVE MANAGEMENT
STYLE TWO	COMMITTEE MANAGEMENT
STYLE THREE	ADMINISTRATIVE MANAGEMENT
STYLE FOUR	AGGRESSIVE MANAGEMENT
STYLE FIVE	MOTIVATIONAL MANAGEMENT

Figure 7.4 Common management styles in leisure and tourism

Style one, passive management, is characterized by a manager who does the bare minimum in any given situation, will generally resist change and will operate with an unhealthy degree of 'slackness'.

In **style two, committee managers** will tend to steer a middle course on most matters and will try to remain popular with the members of the team. They will avoid open conflict and praise achievement, almost to the point of flattery.

Style three, administrative management, will be carried out by the person who likes to do everything 'by the book'. The administrative manager will tend to be conscientious rather than innovative and will develop systems within the team for most operations.

In **style four,** the **aggressive manager** is generally not a good listener but will request that everything is done his or her way, often without recourse to team discussion. He or she will give the impression of not worrying unduly about creating conflict within the team.

Style five, motivational management, involves a manager agreeing goals with team members and inspiring the team to perform well and achieve its aims. He or she will be supportive if staff are experiencing difficulties in their work. The motivational manager will consult widely with team members and make clear where each person's responsibilities lie.

When it comes to selecting which is the most effective management style when we are looking at how best to deal with conflict, most organizations would agree (except perhaps those which exhibit styles one to four!) that style five, motivational management, is likely to achieve the most positive outcome. The motivational management style is:

- 'Open' rather than defensive
- Supportive rather than destructive
- Critical in a positive rather than negative fashion
- Assertive rather than aggressive
- Praises rather than undermines staff achievement
- Advocates good communication

Managers who practise this type of management are far more likely to resolve conflict by confronting it in a calm and logical manner.

Working towards the same goal

Whenever conflict does develop within a team or between teams, it is important to stress to the conflicting parties that they are all striving for the same goal and are part of the same organization. If the staff can focus on their own and their team's part in achieving the goal, then they can all feel valued members of the organization and so be part of the 'winning team'. This message is often best conveyed by bringing the conflicting groups or individuals together and raising the level of debate above their own areas of conflict to the level of the common goal of the organization. Management may decide to hold a series of regular informal meetings where members from all teams are given the opportunity of raising issues of concern and putting forward new ideas for team operation.

Self Check ✔ **Element 2**

4. Why is it important for a team to have clear aims and objectives?

   _____
   _____
   _____

5. How can the personalities of individual team members influence team interaction?

   _____
   _____
   _____

6. Can you think of any internal threats which may have a positive effect on a leisure and tourism team?

   _____
   _____
   _____

7. Why is it that vested interests can sometimes result in a team failing to achieve its aims?

   _____
   _____
   _____

8. Why is a team leader with an aggressive management style unlikely to build an effective team?

   _____
   _____
   _____

7.3 Evaluating team performance

As we saw in Fig. 7.2 on page 139, **team evaluation** is the final stage in the process of team development, following team formation and team management. Evaluation is an area which is not always given the attention it deserves. Indeed, many teams fail, not because their initial planning and development lacks direction, but because they commit little, if any, time to review their effectiveness and to ensure that the gains, agreements and decisions made by the team are being implemented. Without time being set aside for evaluating performance, the team members will not fully learn from their experiences and management will not have an objective view on how well the team has performed.

What is the purpose of team evaluation?

Teamwork in leisure and tourism is a means to an end, rather than an end in itself. It is a process and, as such, evaluation should look at all stages of team development and team operation. Any evaluation of team performance will be trying to answer some or all of the following questions:

* Were the channels of communication effective?
* Did individual team members perform to the best of their ability?
* Did the team as a whole achieve its objectives?
* Was the team leader effective?
* Were any weaknesses identified?
* Were measures put in place to rectify weaknesses?
* What were the strengths of the team and its members?
* Was good performance commended or rewarded?
* Did the team identify any new directions for future work?
* Were there examples of outstanding performance?

The methods used to evaluate team performance and the personnel involved in the process will differ from one organization to another. It is generally agreed, however, that the people who should *not* be left out of any evaluation are the team members themselves. They will have the most knowledge about how the team operated and will be aware of its successes and failures. Their perception of how the team performed will, of course, be subjective, i.e. their conclusions will be from their own viewpoint as members of the team. Nonetheless, their views are critical to obtaining a valid evaluation of performance.

To arrive at a more objective view of the team's performance, the team leader may carry out an appraisal of the relative performance of each member. A member of the senior management of the organization may be allocated the job of appraising the team leader, individual team members or the team as a whole. This same senior manager may be given the task of reviewing the team's performance against its objectives to see if, for example, it has achieved any financial targets it was set or reached any quotas on use by particular members of the local community, e.g. disabled people.

Observers are sometimes used to increase further the objectivity of the evaluation exercise. Usually from outside the organization, an observer will view the team's progress from the outset and be able to comment on performance and development issues. Consultants, staff from leisure and tourism departments at colleges and universities, local authority personnel and staff from professional bodies can be called upon to take on the role of observer to a leisure and tourism team.

How is the evaluation carried out?

There are a number of tried and tested ways of carrying out team evaluation, including:

* Team review
* Staff performance review
* Peer appraisal
* Self-appraisal

Team review

As soon as it is practical after the team has finished its work, or at pre-planned stages of its development, the team should carry out a **review** and evaluation exercise. This is likely to take the form of a meeting of all team members and will include both formal and informal feedback. Useful feedback from the team members will include their personal views and comments on their own performance and the effectiveness of the whole team, including the team leader. While informal feedback is a very useful tool for identifying broad areas of success and failure, a more formal reporting mechanism will be needed to measure team effectiveness. It is likely that the team will have identified its objectives at the start of its work. The more precise the objectives, and any associated performance criteria, the easier it will be for the team to measure its effectiveness in meeting its targets. For example, a member of a team which has been set up to introduce a new customer care programme into a leisure centre may have been set performance criteria which could include:

* Answer the telephone within five 'rings'.
* Record every complaint on an official complaint form.
* Write a letter to each person who complained apologizing on behalf of the organization and keep a copy for reference.
* Carry out visitor perception surveys at monthly intervals.

It will be a relatively straightforward matter to check whether these tasks have been carried out and so reach a conclusion on this element of the person's work performance.

Staff performance review

Individual team members may be interviewed by either their line manager or the team leader, who may in fact be the same person, to formally assess their **individual performance** in the team. This may be part of a wider staff appraisal exercise which links pay to performance. The interview will seek to identify good performance by the team member and areas where performance needs to be enhanced, perhaps by a particular type of staff development activity, e.g. going on a course which improves decision making or telephone technique. The outcome of the performance review should be a written development plan, agreed by both the reviewer and member of the team, which should list personal development objectives and the activities needed to meet the objectives.

Peer appraisal

This is the evaluation of a member of the team by his or her peers, i.e. the other members of the team. Formal rather than informal **peer appraisal** is more useful, since it can prevent the

exercise becoming too personal. If managed effectively by the team leader, however, it can be very enlightening and can help to identify strengths and weaknesses in individual team members, who can use the outcomes to identify any remedial measures which may be necessary.

Self-appraisal

Team members may be asked to formally evaluate their own performance against objectives and performance criteria by carrying out a **self-appraisal** which, if undertaken in as objective a way as possible, can produce useful feedback both for the individual and his or her line manager. Such an appraisal can be fed into any wider staff appraisal exercise which the organization may undertake.

Self Check ✔ **Element 3**

9. Who should be involved in carrying out a team evaluation?

10. What part can performance criteria play in evaluating team performance?

Unit Test This test is one hour long. Answer all the questions.

Focus 1: THE PURPOSE AND STRUCTURE OF TEAMS

Question 1
Following expansion of a major tour operator's long-haul programme, the three marketing assistants in the product development department have been told to report to the newly appointed assistant product manager, instead of reporting directly to the product manager as before.

This is because:

A   The product manager thinks the team will work harder
B   The manager is no longer involved in staff appraisal
C   The manager does not want to be part of a team any more
D   The manager thinks this will help the newly expanded team to work more effectively

Question 2
The manager of an out-of-town indoor arena has discovered an unexpected and unusual problem which must be resolved quickly and will require a team with an unusual mix of expertise and skills.

How should the manager handle the problem?

A By employing agency staff to form a permananent team
B By taking on new members of staff to form a new team
C By setting up an *ad hoc* team of existing members of staff
D By asking senior managers to 'shelve' their current responsibilities and form a new team to tackle the problem

Questions 3–4 relate to the following information.
Look at the following staffing structure of a typical high street branch of a major travel agency chain.

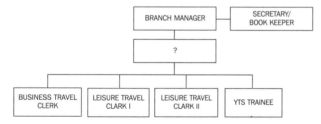

Question 3
Which of the following job titles is missing from the chart?

A   Regional manager
B   Sales manager
C   Travel supervisor
D   Foreign exchange clerk

Question 4
The branch is reviewing its staff training policy.

Decide whether each of these statements is true (T) or false (F).

(i) The leisure travel clerk II is likely to take responsibility for training the YTS trainee.
(ii) The branch manager is unlikely to need further training.

Which option best describes these two statements?

A   (i) T   (ii) T
B   (i) T   (ii) F
C   (i) F   (ii) T
D   (i) F   (ii) F

Question 5
The members of a sales team for a major international airline are discussing their individual roles and responsibilities.

Decide whether each of these statements is true (T) or false (F).

(i) It is more important for the telephone sales staff than the sales representatives to be trained in customer care techniques.
(ii) It is usual for the sales director to report to the area sales managers.

Which option best describes these two statements?

A   (i) T   (ii) T
B   (i) T   (ii) F
C   (i) F   (ii) T
D   (i) F   (ii) F

Question 6
A theme park asks a member of staff from the safety department to attend a meeting of a small management team which has been set up to investigate health and safety matters within the park.

Will the role of the member of safety staff be to:

A   Take minutes
B   Lead the team
C   Give technical advice
D   Represent office staff

Focus 2: TEAMWORK

Questions 7–9 relate to the following information.
Although staff working in a hotel will share the company's overall aims and objectives, teams of staff will have different long-term and short-term objectives, such as :

A   To achieve an increase in the number of guests
B   To identify potential hazards
C   To achieve reductions in wastage
D   To provide an efficient and courteous service

Which is the specific objective of the following teams?

Question 7
A team set up to run a special promotion.

Question 8
The health and safety working party.

Question 9
The team on reception.

Question 10
A member of a coach company's health and safety committee has been unable to attend the last two meetings.

Which is the best way of letting the committee member know what has happened?

A   Ask another member of the committee to brief her
B   Ask the chair of the committee to telephone her with the details

C   Send her copies of the minutes of the meetings
D   Send her the agenda for the next meeting

Questions 11–13 share answer options A–D.
Leisure and tourism organizations which consist of one or
more work teams normally set up effective methods of
internal communication so that management decisions can
be conveyed to all team members.

Four possible reporting methods currently used include:

A   Individual letters to members of staff
B   Formal written report to all staff
C   Notices placed on staff notice boards
D   Formal meetings with minutes taken

Which method would be most appropriate in the following
situations?

Question 11
All staff are informed of the new five-year company
strategy.

Question 12
All staff are informed of new salary scales.

Question 13
All staff are informed of additions to the social events
planned by the company's social committee.

Focus 3: CONSTRAINTS AND CONFLICTING ROLES

Question 14
Achieving goals for a team of sales representatives will be
easier if:

A   Vested interests are encouraged
B   The team has many different aims
C   Clear communication channels are established
D   The team is made up of 20 or more members

Questions 15–17 share answer options A–D.
The organizer of a regional swimming championships is worried about the increasing number of clashes between members
of the publicity team and members of the security team for the
event. He is worried that the constant conflicts will affect the
success of the event.

He has decided to:

A   Reduce the numbers in each team
B   Clarify the objectives of each team
C   Introduce a bonus payment if all goes well before and
    during the event
D   Hold a joint meeting between the two teams

Which of the above actions will achieve the following benefits?

Question 15
Provide an incentive for both teams to co-operate.

Question 16
Give the teams an opportunity to resolve their problems.

Question 17
Ensure that each team knows what is expected of it.

Question 18
The administrator in a stately home is finding it difficult to
organize her team effectively.

Decide whether each of these statements is true (T) or false
(F).

(i) It will not reduce the effectiveness of the team if one
    member is disruptive.
(ii) The members of the team will be looking to the
    administrator for leadership and encouragement.

Which option best describes these two statements?

A   (i) T   (ii) T
B   (i) T   (ii) F
C   (i) F   (ii) T
D   (i) F   (ii) F

Questions 19–21 relate to the following information.
Your outdoor activity centre has been vandalized by a
group of youths from a nearby town. You have enlisted the
help of a local venture scout group to spend a weekend
cleaning and refurbishing the centre. When the venture
scouts turn up on the Saturday morning, you note the
following problems:

A   Only one of the scouts has done any decorating before
B   There are only enough overalls for half of the team
C   The job must be completed by Sunday lunch-time
D   One of the scouts suffers from asthma

Select the category under which the above problems may
be identified:

Question 19
Materials.

Question 20
Time.

Question 21
Skills.

Focus 4: TEAM EFFECTIVENESS

Question 22
A newly appointed manager at a local authority tourist
attraction is keen to promote a more 'open' management
style among the workforce. He has decided to introduce
monthly meetings where staff and management can meet to
discuss team performance.

Decide whether each of these statements is true (T) or false
(F).

(i) New and useful ideas are unlikely to emerge from such
    meetings.
(ii) Only management can evaluate the performance of a
    staff team effectively.

Which option best describes these two statements?

A   (i) T   (ii) T
B   (i) T   (ii) F
C   (i) F   (ii) T
D   (i) F   (ii) F

Questions 23–25 share answer options A –D.
The most effective teams usually have a balance of team
members who adopt different roles, including:

A   Innovator
B   Reviewer
C   Leader
D   Administrator

Decide which role will be taken by the team member who:

Question 23
Co-ordinates and directs the team's progress.

Question 24
Contributes creative ideas.

Question 25
Monitors the team's progress.

Question 26
The sales manager of a timeshare company is concerned that the level of positive enquiries achieved by the telesales team has dropped significantly in the last quarter.

Which of the following actions is most likely to result in improved performance by the team members?

A   Make sales calls up to 9.00 pm rather than finishing at 8.00 pm as at present.
B   Inform the team members that two staff will be sacked if performance does not improve.
C   Offer financial incentives to the team as a whole in return for increased sales.
D   Offer the sales manager a productivity bonus.

Question 27
Effective teams are crucial to the success of many leisure and tourism facilities.

Decide whether each of these statements is true (T) or false (F).

(i) There is no link between the availability of resources and the effectiveness of a team.
(ii) Teams cannot operate effectively without the support of senior management.

Which option best describes these two statements?

A   (i) T   (ii) T
B   (i) T   (ii) F
C   (i) F   (ii) T
D   (i) F   (ii) F

Focus 5: EVALUATING TEAM PERFORMANCE

Question 28
It is sometimes difficult to evaluate the effectiveness of teams working in leisure and tourism.

Decide whether each of these statements is true (T) or false (F).

(i) Individual team members evaluating their own performance is not a valid method of evaluation.
(ii) It is easier to evaluate the effectiveness of a team if outcomes can be easily measured.

Which option best describes these two statements?

A   (i) T   (ii) T
B   (i) T   (ii) F
C   (i) F   (ii) T
D   (i) F   (ii) F

Question 29
In the absence of a team leader who is yet to be appointed, a small team working for a conference planning company has been allocated specific tasks by a senior manager who is unaware of their individual skills and interests.

The team has decided that its effectiveness could be improved by changing:

A   The membership of the team
B   The senior manager
C   The objectives of the team
D   The roles of team members

Questions 30–32 relate to the following information.
A travel agency clerk will receive feedback on his performance from a number of sources, including:
A   Customers
B   Self-evaluation
C   Peer evauation
D   His line manager

Which of the above sources is most closely associated with the following?

Question 30
A client satisfaction survey.

Question 31
Completion of a daily training log.

Question 32
A staff development review.

Question 33
Which of the following is the most effective way for an individual to receive feedback from other team members?

A   Over the telephone
B   Via questionnaires
C   Via open discussion
D   Via written reports

Question 34
Performance targets are sometimes used by leisure and tourism organizations as a way of evaluating team effectiveness.

Decide whether each of these statements is true (T) or false (F).

(i) Performance targets are not favoured by some organizations since their use does not indicate to team members what is expected of them.
(ii) Performance targets are not favoured by some organizations since they cannot be linked to financial incentives for team members.

Which option best describes these two statements?

A   (i) T   (ii) T
B   (i) T   (ii) F
C   (i) F   (ii) T
D   (i) F   (ii) F

Question 35
The leader of a team which has been formed to plan and implement a new marketing strategy for a car hire company has repeatedly made decisions alone and, most recently, has decided to join forces with a major hotel chain without consulting the other members of the team.

The effectiveness of the team is most likely to be improved by changing:

A   The frequency of team meetings
B   The objectives of the team
C   The members of the team
D   The leader of the team

Self-check Answers

2. Without the full support of senior management, a team may not gain access to the resources it needs to achieve its tasks. Team members also like to feel that senior management knows what they are doing and appreciate it when managers take the time to seek their views on matters concerning the organization of the event.

3. Two-way communication is by far the most effective form of communication between team members. Whenever possible, it should be encouraged since it minimizes the risk of misunderstandings between individuals, is likely to give a faster response to a situation and will promote openness between team members.

4. Without clear aims and objectives, a team will be unsure as to what it is trying to achieve. Individual members of the team may be unsure of the boundaries of their work, leading to unnecessary duplication of effort. Team evaluation will also be a much easier task if clear objectives have been set from the outset.

5. All human beings have unique personalities, making the task of managing the members of a team a not inconsiderable one! A team member with an aggressive style, if not handled positively, can lead to instability within a group situation. Domineering characters will need careful handling by the team leader so that they do not dominate proceedings. Quieter members of the team will need encouragement to put forward their own points of view.

6. A threat from within the team, such as a member who says that he is considering leaving, may well have a positive effect on the working of the team as a whole, by 'cementing' relationships and encouraging the team to strive for even better results.

7. Team members with vested interests, in other words those who are more interested in their own outcomes rather than the success of the team as a whole, can have a disruptive influence on team performance by frustrating the normal operation of the team and preventing it achieving its aims.

8. A team leader with an aggressive management style may not convince other team members that he or she has the correct mix of qualities needed. He or she may not be effective when it comes to communicating and negotiating with outside agencies and may not gain the confidence of some members of the group. An assertive rather than aggressive style is more beneficial to a team leader.

9. All members of the team should certainly be involved in the team evaluation, whether they are paid members of staff or volunteers. People outside of the team, such as senior managers, observers, councillors, board members or consultants, should also be encouraged to become involved with the task.

10. A team that has set itself clear performance criteria, such as a target attendance figure or income per visitor, will find it easier to evaluate its performance. It will have an objective yardstick against which to measure its success.

Answers to Unit Test

Answers

1.	D	8.	B	15.	C	22.	D	29.	D
2.	C	9.	D	16.	D	23.	C	30.	A
3.	C	10.	C	17.	B	24.	A	31.	B
4.	D	11.	A	18.	C	25.	B	32.	D
5.	D	12.	A	19.	B	26.	C	33.	C
6.	C	13.	C	20.	C	27.	C	34.	D
7.	A	14.	C	21.	A	28.	C	35.	D

Unit test comments

Q1: Answer is D – the manager thinks this will help the newly expanded team to work more effectively.
This is an example of delegation, where the product manager has delegated authority and responsibility to the assistant product manager. This change will not of itself make the team work harder, nor will it mean that the manager will no longer be involved in staff appraisal, but it will help the organization and the team to work more effectively. The product manager will continue to be a member of a team of senior managers.

Q2: Answer is C – by setting up an *ad hoc* team of existing members of staff.
In a situation such as this, when a new team needs to be set up quickly, it is better to look inside the organization for team members, since they will be more familiar with work practices and will produce results more quickly than employing outside staff. Asking senior managers to switch from their normal duties is likely to be problematic, in that important management tasks will not be completed.

Q3: Answer is C – travel supervisor.
An experienced travel supervisor will oversee the work of the travel clerks and the YTS trainee, providing support and advice when necessary. A regional manager will be responsible for a number of branches in an area, while the sales manager is likely to be a head office position, with responsibility for overall sales performance of the travel agency chain. If the branch has a foreign exchange clerk, he or she would not normally supervise the work of the travel clerks.

Q4: Answer is D.
Although the YTS trainee will often be given help and advice by other travel clerks, the responsibility for his of her training will rest with the travel supervisor. The branch manager will continue to need training in such matters as financial management, marketing management and human resource management.

Q5: Answer is D.
It is equally important for both the telephone sales staff and the sales representatives to be trained in customer care techniques; they both have vital roles to play in helping to achieve success for the airline. The sales director will be a senior management position, often reporting directly to the chief executive of an airline. Area sales managers will report to a sales manager who in turn will report to the sales director.

Q6: Answer is C – give technical advice.
Minutes of a meeting will normally be taken by a secretary or administrator. Since the member of staff is not from the administration department, he or she would not be expected to represent the office staff. A member of staff is unlikely to be asked to lead a management team.

Q7: Answer is A – to achieve an increase in the number of guests.
Teams are often set up in leisure and tourism organizations to plan and implement special promotions, such as exhibitions, discount schemes and public events, with the aim of increasing business.

Q8: Answer is B – to identify potential hazards.
The health and safety working party will have a formal team structure and clear terms of reference, covering the identification of potential safety hazards and measures to reduce risks in the hotel.

Q9: Answer is D – to provide an efficient and courteous service.
The team on reception will need very good communication and customer service skills. They will also need well developed teamwork skills in order to provide an efficient and courteous service to guests. Shift work will be part of the normal work pattern of reception staff.

Q10: Answer is C – send her copies of the minutes of the meetings.
To ensure that the member of the committee receives an accurate account of proceedings at the meeting, it is best if she is sent copies of the minutes. Verbal accounts are unlikely to cover all the relevant points, while the agenda for the next meeting will not include details of the previous meetings.

Q11: Answer is A – individual letters to members of staff.
It is good internal public relations if all employees are informed in writing of any new company policies.

Q12: Answer is A – individual letters to members of staff.
Personal information on employees, their pay and conditions of service, should be conveyed in letters to the individuals concerned.

Q13: Answer is C – notices placed on staff notice boards.
Information that is not personal and is concerned with matters such as social events and staff associations is best displayed on notice boards, where all employees will have the opportunity of reading it.

Q14: Answer is C – clear communication channels are established.
Having clear channels of communication is essential if a team is to achieve its stated aims. Team members with vested interests can sometimes hinder effective team development, while a team with many different aims may find it difficult to focus on its primary goal. The number of team members is not a crucial issue when it comes to the team achieving its objectives.

Q15: Answer is C – introduce a bonus payment if all goes well before and during the event.
In a situation such as this, offering a bonus may well encourage the two parties to co-operate with management and with each other.

Q16: Answer is D – hold a joint meeting between the two teams.
A meeting involving the two teams may well 'clear the air', by giving all present an opportunity to state their views, hear the other side's views and agree a positive way forward.

Q17: Answer is B – clarify the objectives of each team.
Having objectives which are not only clear, but also realistic and achievable, will ensure that each team and team member knows what is expected of them.

Q18: Answer is C.
Just one disruptive member of a team can have a serious impact on its effectiveness. The leader will have to be a strong character who can deal with potentially disruptive individuals. The leader will also be the person that the rest of the team members look to for leadership and encouragement. The administrator will be concerned with secretarial and administrative support for the team.

Q19: Answer is B – there are only enough overalls for half of the team.

Q20: Answer is C – the job must be completed by Sunday lunch-time.

Q21: Answer is A – only one of the scouts has done any decorating before.

Q22: Answer is D.
Regular meetings between management and staff are not only a very good way of showing that an organization values its staff, but they may also generate new and useful ideas. Evaluating the performance of a team can be carried out by many people, not just the management. For example, team members and observers can usefully add to the evaluation process.

Q23: Answer is C – leader.
Team leaders play an essential role in team operation, by co-ordinating and directing progress. They will also be an important part of the team evaluation process.

Q24: Answer is A – innovator.
Innovators, sometimes referred to as 'ideas people', are very good at suggesting new ideas and new approaches to problems. They cannot always combine a creative mind with the ability to see a task through, however. Team leaders have an important part to play in matching the different skills of their team members.

Q25: Answer is B – reviewer.
The job of the reviewer, who may be a member of the team or an outside observer, is to monitor the progress of the team to ensure that it is working towards meeting its objectives.

Q26: Answer is C – offer financial incentives to the team as a whole in return for increased sales.
Asking staff to work an extra hour may well make the situation worse and create more resentment, as will threatening team members with the sack. Offering the manager a productivity bonus may not result in increased sales for the team as a whole; some team members may also feel that the manager has been singled out for special attention.

Q27: Answer is C.
Teams which are not given the resources to do their job properly are unlikely to achieve their full potential; statement (i) is therefore false. In order to function effectively, teams also need the full support of senior management, who must be prepared to devote the necessary time and resources to the successful operation of the team.

Q28: Answer is C.

Self-evaluation can be a very effective way of measuring an individual's performance in a team, especially when coupled with such techniques as peer appraisal and team review and evaluation. If the outcomes of a team's performance can be measured, by the use of performance criteria for example, then it will be easier to evaluate team effectiveness.

Q29: Answer is D – the roles of the team members.

It is important for team leaders to assess the strengths and weaknesses of their individual team members and allocate roles on this basis whenever possible. In this case, team members have been given roles which do not match with their skills and experience.

Q30: Answer is A – customers.

Feedback from customers is clearly crucial to the success or otherwise of a travel agency. A client satisfaction survey is a good way of collecting their views on a formal basis; informal feedback, such as favourable comments and complaints, can also be very valuable.

Q31: Answer is B – self-evaluation.

The completion of a daily training log, particularly by new members of staff, will identify the skills they are developing and should highlight areas that need further training and development.

Q32: Answer is D – his line manager.

A staff development review, sometimes called a staff appraisal, normally takes the form of an interview between a member of staff and his or her immediate superior. Both parties look back at the individual's performance and agree targets and objectives for the future. Some organizations link staff appraisal and performance to pay and other benefits.

Q33: Answer is C – via open discussion.

Feedback from peers (those with whom you work) on an individual's performance as part of a team is best carried out on an informal, face-to-face basis. Questionnaires and written reports are more appropriate for formal appraisal situations.

Q34: Answer is D.

Statement (i) is false, since one of the major benefits of setting performance targets for staff is that they know exactly what is expected of them. Targets can also be linked to financial incentives in order to increase staff performance.

Q35: Answer is D – the leader of the team.

A team leader who repeatedly ignores the views of other team members or makes unilateral decisions cannot hope to gain the confidence of team members, which results in a team that becomes demoralized and loses its commitment. In such circumstances, it is better to replace the leader.

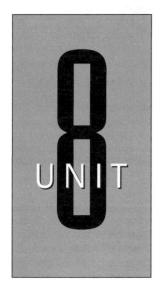

Evaluating the performance of facilities

Getting Started

All leisure and tourism organizations need to know how well they are performing, in order to rectify any shortcomings in performance or build on aspects of good performance. Managers and owners will be keen to compare the performance of their own organization with those offering similar products and services elsewhere. They will also want to know how well their staff are performing and how well the organization is making use of its other resources.

There is a strong link between the management of facilities and their performance. In simple terms, an organization which has an ineffective management team will not perform to its full potential. Management is all about planning, organizing, controlling and evaluating a range of resources, including:

* **Human resources** – full-time staff, part-time staff and seasonal staff.

* **Physical resources** – including buildings, land and equipment.

* **Financial resources** – revenue and capital which flows into and out of the organization.

A leisure and tourism organization which manages its human, physical and financial resources well is likely to benefit from a steady improvement in performance.

To discover how well it is performing, a leisure and tourism organization must be able to **evaluate** its performance. This unit examines the process of performance evaluation in the industry by starting, in Element 1, with an analysis of organizational objectives and their importance in leisure and tourism. Element 2 goes on to look at the key aspects of performance which are used when planning the evaluation of an organization. Element 3 is concerned with performance evaluation in an individual facility and looks at such matters as the environmental and community impacts of leisure and tourism.

Balance Sheet A statement of an organisation's financial position at a given point in time; a 'snapshot' of the financial health of the business.

Cash flow statement Shows the flow of funds into and out of a business over a given period of time.

Effectiveness A measure of how well an organization has met its objectives.

Efficiency The optimum use of resources by an organization.

Financial accounting The preparation of the financial information that an organization is required by law to produce, including the profit and loss account, balance sheet and cash flow statement.

Management accounting The provision of financial information to help with business decision-making and for control purposes.

Management by objectives (MBO) An approach to management that concentrates on setting objectives, devising strategies for the achievement of the objectives, implementing the strategies and evaluating their effectiveness.

Performance indicators Objective indicators by which management can evaluate the performance of a range of resources.

Profit and loss account Shows an organization's income and expenditure over a given period of time, usually 12 months, as a result of normal trading activities.

ROCE Refers to return on capital employed. This is the most widely used indicator of the profitability of an organization.

Stakeholders All those individuals and groups who have an interest in the management and development of an organization, e.g. shareholders, councillors and customers.

Essential Principles

Organizational objectives

All leisure and tourism organizations set themselves **objectives** or goals in order to provide a framework within which all their resources can be used to best effect and their performance can be measured. Objectives for individual organizations will be very diverse and will be affected by a number of factors, including:

- The **philosophy** of the owners or managers – some organizations will want to maximize their profits while others will be happy with a lower profit margin in return for a less stressful lifestyle.
- The **size** of the organization – the objectives of large companies may be influenced by the fact that they have shareholders to satisfy.
- Its **stage** of development – an organization that is just starting out will have quite different objectives from one which has been in operation for some time.
- The **sector** in which it operates – organizations in the private, public and voluntary sectors of leisure and tourism have very different objectives, as we shall see in the next section of this element.

Private sector organizations

The leisure and tourism industry in the UK is dominated by **private sector or commercial organizations**. Some of the best-known names in the industry are private companies, such as British Airways, Nike, Mecca, Forte, Thomson Holidays and Thomas Cook. The private sector is made up of large and small organizations owned by individuals or groups of people whose primary aim is to make a profit. Many individuals rely on the profits generated by commercial organizations for a substantial part of their income.

Profit maximization is an important objective for a number of reasons, since it:

- Rewards risk taking.
- Encourages efficiency and innovation.
- Provides resources for further expansion of a business.
- Enables a business to respond to the needs of its customers.

Although profit maximization is the primary objective of most private sector companies, it is by no means the *only* objective of all commercial leisure and tourism organizations. A lot of small businesses in the leisure and tourism industry are run by people who used to work for larger companies but became frustrated with the high level of bureaucracy they encountered. Operating your own business in leisure and tourism can give a great deal of job satisfaction and the feeling that you have control over the decisions that are made. We saw in Unit 1, however, that there are also disadvantages to being a sole trader or partner (see page 15). Some owners will not seek to maximize profits to the full, but may be content with a level of profit which gives them the type of lifestyle they are happy with; after all, why work in an industry concerned with leisure, holidays and travel and have no time to enjoy yourself and have fun!

> **Did You Know** ?
>
> Profit maximization is not always the only objective of private sector leisure and tourism organizations.

It is currently very fashionable for organizations in the private sector to develop **mission statements**, which are intended to convey to all those with an interest in the organization, be they staff, shareholders or the public in general, what objectives it is trying to achieve and where it sees itself going. Some mission statements introduce an element of the organization's philosophy and values as well. Mission statements vary enormously in their complexity; some are very short and to the point, e.g. British Airways:

> To be the best and most successful company in the airline industry.
> (BA Annual Report and Accounts 1992–3)

Although its mission statement is very succinct, the Annual Report 1992–3 lists the seven detailed objectives (which they call goals) that the company hopes to fulfil in order to achieve its mission. These are:

- **Safe and secure** – to be a safe and secure airline.
- **Financially strong** – to deliver a strong and consistent financial performance.
- **Global leader** – to secure a leading share of the air travel business worldwide with a significant presence in all major geographical markets.
- **Service and value** – to provide overall superior service and good value for money in every market segment in which we compete.
- **Customer driven** – to excel in anticipating and quickly responding to customer needs and competitor activity.
- **Good employer** – to sustain a working environment that attracts, retains and develops committed employees who share in the success of the company.
- **Good neighbour** – to be a good neighbour, concerned for the community and the environment.

Some people are very sceptical about the value of mission statements and see them as nothing more than a public relations exercise. What the mission statement can do is set out in very broad terms the direction in which an organization is hoping to progress in the future and provide a framework for the development of its more specific objectives.

Non-commercial organizations

Non-commercial leisure and tourism organizations, falling within the public or voluntary sectors of the economy, do not have 'profit maximization' as their primary objective. They have been developed with wider social objectives in mind: a council-run leisure centre, for example, will have as a primary aim 'the provision of a wide range of leisure and recreational services and facilities for the benefit of all sectors of the local community'. Although profit maximization is not the primary objective of non-commercial organizations in leisure and tourism, those which are part of local government or are agencies of central government (e.g. the quangos) are expected to offer value for money and meet targets and agreed performance criteria. Many local authorities have recruited staff from the private sector and have implemented private sector management practices in order to achieve their objectives.

There are many examples of **non-commercial organizations** in leisure and tourism, including:

- Charitable trusts
- Local authorities
- Clubs and societies
- Public corporations
- Quangos

Charitable trusts

Many **charitable trusts** are established to conserve or preserve our national and local heritage. The most well-known and respected is the National Trust which today protects more than 600,000 acres of land in England, Wales and Northern Ireland as well as over 200 houses and parks (see Factfile 5 in Unit 1, page 16). The Civic Trust, established in 1957, is a registered charity which aims to uphold high standards of environmental quality and management throughout the UK.

Local authorities

Local councils play a major role in the provision of leisure and tourism facilities in Britain. Without their involvement, facilities such as recreation grounds, parks, libraries, museums, leisure centres, tourist information centres and visitor attractions would not exist. The general move towards privatization, market testing and compulsory competitive tendering has meant that local authorities are now functioning much more like private sector operators and the distinction between commercial and non-commercial is becoming blurred.

Many local authority leisure and tourism departments summarize their objectives in the form of a policy statement, which is similar to the mission statement that we discussed under the private sector. The policy statement for a typical, progressive borough council would be as follows:

> Daltingworth Borough Council takes pride in the standards of service it delivers to the residents of the Borough. Our primary responsibilities are to promote services of the highest possible quality within the resources we have, at a cost acceptable to Council Tax payers, tenants and users of our leisure services. We therefore place great emphasis on caring for the needs of our customers and on being cost-conscious and efficient.
>
> We aim to deliver services through an effective partnership of councillors and employees. We endeavour to ensure that our staff are well trained and are aware of the aims and objectives of the Council.
>
> The Council's belief is that the residents of the Borough expect a high level of efficiency in the services they use, and are looking for a dynamic and forward-looking approach towards building on its services for a growing population, thus enhancing the quality of life for all.

Clubs and societies

Set up by local people with a specific purpose in mind, these organizations will aim to break even on their finances and may apply for some financial help from their local authority. A good example is a local photographic society.

Public corporations

The main **public corporation** linked to the leisure and tourism industry is British Rail, offering a service to both business and leisure travellers. Privatization has meant that the former state-owned enterprises of British Airways and the British Airports Authority (BAA) are now in private hands. BR is itself scheduled for privatizaton in the very near future.

Quangos

Quangos (quasi-autonomous non-governmental organizations) are primarily financed from the public purse but have a high degree of autonomy. Examples in leisure and tourism are the Sports Council, Countryside Commission and the British Tourist Authority.

The **Arts Council**, a quango funded largely by the Department of National Heritage, has the following objectives:

- To open the arts to all
- To promote excellence among artists of all kinds
- To encourage innovation in the arts
- To keep alive our heritage in the arts
- To serve as a national forum of thinking and planning in the arts

It seeks to achieve these aims by:

> (1) Encouraging people to recognise the contribution made by artists and those who work in the arts to the quality of life
>
> (2) Pressing the case for the arts and their public funding
>
> (3) Encouraging and supporting all other sources of arts funding
>
> (4) Using its financial resources to achieve its aims in Scotland, Wales and England
>
> (5) Collaborating with individuals and organizations who share its aims
>
> (6) Making its own organization open and accessible.
>
> (Arts Council of Great Britain Annual Report and Accounts 1991–2).

Did You Know ?

The Arts Council spent nearly £200 million in 1992 in pursuit of its objectives.

Stakeholders and objectives

Objectives of leisure and tourism organizations will be developed and refined by all those who have an interest in the organization, sometimes referred to as '**stakeholders**'. They include:

- **The owners or managers** – who will be concerned that the objectives are realistic and achievable and provide a reward for their effort, skill and management expertise.

- **The staff** – will want to be sure of their conditions of employment and future prospects in terms of promotion and the growth, or otherwise, of the organization.

- **Shareholders** – will be looking to the owners and/or managers to provide them with a growing return on capital invested in the organization (the dividend).

- **Visitors or users** – will be concerned with the experience they receive and whether they think the organization gives value for money.

- **Local councillors** – representing the local community, will be keen to see that public facilities are being used to the maximum, objectives are being achieved and that local authority funds are being wisely deployed.

- **Members** (of a club or association) – will be actively involved in setting objectives and helping to achieve them.

- **Society in general** – has a stake, to a greater or lesser extent, in the aims and objectives of leisure and tourism organizations. The benefits of faster travel, instant entertainment and access to a wealth of activities and facilities needs to be balanced against the wider issues and concerns of social and environmental exploitation, problems of congestion and changes in the nature of work and leisure in society.

Conflicting objectives

Establishing objectives in leisure and tourism organizations cannot be seen as a once-and-for-all operation, but as an evolving process concerning all those who have a stake in the organization. Leisure and tourism is a dynamic industry, which is constantly adapting in response to changing customer expectations, new technological developments and wider changes in the nature of society in general. Leisure and tourism organizations must reflect this dynamism by constantly reviewing their objectives and methods of operation.

The process of modifying objectives can sometimes lead to **conflict** within organizations. A local tourist attraction, for example, funded by the town council, which has for many years offered an excellent service to local school children may be required to adopt a more commercial approach to its activities in order to provide an income to offset against its council subsidy. This change from an educational to a financial objective may be resented by the staff at the attraction who see their job as providing an educational resource and not running a business. At a national level, questions have been raised about institutions such as the Victoria and Albert Museum and the National History Museum charging for admission. Both museums used to admit visitors for free, but decided to introduce an admission charge to offset rising operating costs. Some people fear that commercial activities at the museums will detract from the educational and conservation objectives for which they were established.

Some tourist companies are criticized for taking little heed of the negative environmental and social effects that their activities can have on destinations, particularly those fragile areas which are new to tourism. All too often, there is a conflict between the purely commercial objective of maximizing profits by selling as many holidays as possible and the wider social and environmental objectives of disturbing places and people as little as possible.

There may be conflict when a leisure organization says that it has one objective which states that it will endeavour to provide a range of facilities and services for all sectors of the community and a second which says that it will be 'a good neighbour, respectful of community feelings and concerns'. If it happens to organize events which cause disturbance and disruption to local people, there may be bad feeling in the local community which may lead to the organization reviewing its operation and objectives.

Management by objectives

All managers in leisure and tourism organizations set themselves and their staff objectives in order to achieve results. Some organizations have gone one step further by implementing the formal technique known as MBO (**management by objectives**), which is widespread in many sectors of the UK economy. To call MBO a technique undervalues its true purpose: it is better thought of as a **total management approach** or management style which encourages participation by all employees and rewards openness. The basis of MBO is the involvement of managers and employees in setting a mutually acceptable set of objectives. It examines the current status of an organization, highlights areas that need improvement or amendment, specifies means of achieving the changes and gives time limits within which they will be made. When the time limit is reached, the results are reviewed, new objectives may be set and the process is repeated. Figure 8.1 sets out the cyclical nature of MBO.

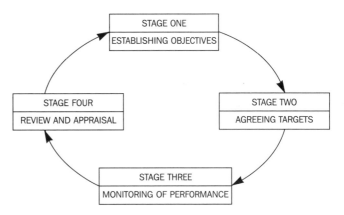

Figure 8.1   The cyclical nature of MBO (management by objectives)

The process of MBO can be illustrated by the following example of staff appraisal.

Stage one – establishing objectives

A manager or supervisor meets with an employee to discuss how that employee can best contribute to the overall effectiveness of the organization by jointly agreeing objectives for the individual. The sort of **objectives** which may be agreed by an employee and manager working in leisure and tourism could include:

- Increased turnover in the shop at a golf course or fitness suite.
- Increased sales in a high street travel agency.
- Improving the level of customer service in a restaurant or fast-food outlet.

- Increase in occupancy, attendance or usage rates for a facility such as a hotel, tourist attraction or sports centre.
- Reduction in staff turnover in the reservations department of a tour operator or airline.
- Control of stock levels and wastage in the catering function of a major visitor attraction.
- Improved security in a major out-of-town entertainment venue.
- Increased levels of guest spending on ancillary services in a self-catering villa complex.

Stage two – agreeing targets

This stage is concerned with the manager and employee **agreeing targets** against which to measure whether or not the objectives have been met. These targets, sometimes known as **performance indicators** (PIs), should be:

- **Realistic** – a target is only an incentive to the employee if he or she considers that it is realistic and achievable. A target of reducing customer complaints to zero, for example, is totally unrealistic and therefore not appropriate.
- **Set within a time frame** – e.g. increase the use of a local authority leisure centre by disabled people from 1% to 4% within 12 months.
- **Easily measurable** – e.g. reduce the number of customer complaints by 20% or increase turnover by 10%.
- **Specific** – targets must be specific and unambiguous; general statements are unlikely to be measurable.

Did You Know ?

A central feature of MBO is that objectives and targets should not be imposed by management but rather should be agreed between management and employees. Staff feel more comfortable with the process if they are asked to accept responsibility for achieving targets rather than being told exactly what to do without consultation.

Stage three – monitoring of performance

Stage three of the MBO process involves the periodic **monitoring of the performance** of the individual member of staff against the agreed targets. This is likely to be an informal process and will take the form of a manager overseeing the work of a particular employee or group of employees and giving support and advice on work methods and systems, highlighting any areas which may need adjustment or further action.

Stage four – review and appraisal

Manager and employee will hold a more formal **review and appraisal** meeting at which the performance of the member of staff will be judged against the original targets, which may have been modified as part of the monitoring process. The outcome of the appraisal may be linked to the employee's pay via a performance related pay scheme or other incentives. Stage four of the MBO process should end with a statement of objectives and targets for the next period of time, in order to continue the cycle.

Advantages and disadvantages of MBO

The MBO system has many potential *benefits* to the leisure and tourism industry. If it is part of a wider participative style of management which encourages openness, it can:

- Allow management to deploy resources profitably.
- Let staff know exactly what is expected of them.
- Allow management to measure the efficiency and effectiveness of their organization accurately.
- Highlight areas of the organization which need further development.
- Help management to plan for the future.
- Encourage motivation on the part of employees.
- Encourage the review of the organization's structure.
- Encourage innovation from employees and managers.
- Identify staff and management training needs.

Although MBO, if properly installed, has a number of potential advantages to a leisure and tourism organization, the system does have its critics. Some people point to the rigidity and inflexibility of MBO which does not fit well into an industry which is by its very nature very dynamic and responsive to the changing habits, fashions and tastes of its consumers. Those who favour the MBO approach would argue that all organizations *must* set themselves objectives and targets, since, without them, success or failure cannot be accurately measured. A well-developed MBO system should be able to take into account the dynamic nature of the leisure and tourism industry by, for example, shortening the length of time between monitoring and appraisal meetings.

The MBO system offers one way for the management of a leisure and tourism organization to set objectives and targets and review its performance. Whether MBO or some other management philosophy or system is followed, one thing is quite clear: the setting of objectives is only the first part of evaluating performance of individual members of staff and the efficiency and effectiveness of the leisure and tourism organization generally. In order that the objectives can be realized, the organization must translate them into workable practices and achievable targets. It is this process of linking objectives and performance that we will look at in the next two elements of this unit.

Self Check ✔   Element 1

1. Why is it important for a leisure and tourism organization to have clearly defined objectives?

2. What is a 'mission statement'?

3. Investigate the objectives of the leisure services department in your own local authority.

4. Which organizations and individuals are likely to have an interest in developing the objectives of a local authority leisure centre?

5. What do you understand by the term 'MBO'?

8.2 Planning the evaluation of a facility's performance

The role of performance evaluation

Most leisure and tourism managers concentrate on their organization's internal operations when **evaluating performance**. Whether in the public, private or voluntary sector, they establish systems and processes to measure their performance for a number of reasons:

- To find out if financial and staff resources are being used to best effect.
- To discover how well they are performing in relation to competitor organizations.
- To identify weaknesses in management systems, including communication and decision-making, and to highlight training needs.
- To find out if the objectives they have been set are being met.
- To establish whether customers and users are happy with the service and facilities.

In addition to evaluating these internal factors, organizations are increasingly being encouraged to measure the impact that they have outside of their immediate environment. Depending on the size and nature of the organization, it will need to evaluate its performance in relation to economic, environmental and social/cultural factors. A large tourist attraction, for example, will certainly have an impact on the economy of the local area by creating jobs and attracting visitors who will spend money on local goods and services. At the same time, it may have an adverse effect on the local environment and its operations will need to be constantly monitored and evaluated. If not planned carefully, the attraction may, for example, generate traffic congestion in its vicinity, thereby causing problems for local people.

Did You Know ?

Performance evaluation is not just about internal factors but should include consideration of factors outside the organization as well.

Using performance indicators

Performance indicators (PIs) are an essential feature of the evaluation of efficiency and effectiveness of any leisure and tourism organization. By *efficiency*, we mean the optimum use of resources, i.e. the maximum output from the resources used. *Effectiveness* is a measure of how well an organization has met its objectives. At senior management level, the most important performance indicators are those which help with the evaluation of financial and operational performance, for example the income per visitor to an attraction or the number of staff employed per 1,000 seats sold in a theatre. PIs are often expressed as **ratios**, for example:

- retail spend per visitor : total spend per visitor
- number of visitors : total income
- staff costs : total income
- number of staff : total income
- operating costs : total income

Ratios give a manager an easy and quick way of comparing performance over a particular time period or between different departments or teams of staff. They are commonly used in the commercial sector of the leisure and tourism industry and are now being adopted in the public sector in response to compulsory competitive tendering (CCT) and other efficiency initiatives. The hospitality sector of leisure and tourism has long used PIs and ratios to evaluate performance and thus there is a wealth of information available which can facilitate performance evaluation within a particular hotel and even between hotels with similar characteristics; the use of this 'industry standard' data can help the management of new ventures to gauge their levels of performance. In public sector leisure and recreation, the Chartered Institute of Public Finance and Accountancy (CIPFA) publish comprehensive data and statistics on the finances and operation of leisure centres which are useful for purposes of comparison.

There are literally thousands of different performance indicators, expressed as ratios, which can be developed for any leisure and tourism organization. It is important, therefore, to specify only those ratios which will give meaningful information and will aid management decision making. A glance at some CCT specifications and contracts for leisure or sports centres will clearly show that there is a tendency to include ratios which yield little useful data. It is also important to remember that ratios and PIs are only one measure of performance of a facility or organization and should not be treated in isolation. Performance indicators concerning queuing times at a theme park, for example, should be supplemented by direct observation of the situation in order to give a true picture of what is happening. PIs are based on information gathered over a period of time and must be used in conjunction with other management techniques to highlight where performance is average, or better or worse than expected. If the latter is the case, the PIs should trigger an investigative process to identify the cause of the poor performance and suggest ways of improving the situation.

Key aspects of performance

Having considered the part that performance indicators play in the overall evaluation of performance, we now need to look in detail at the **key areas** of performance which a manager in leisure and tourism will need to evaluate. These will vary from one organization to another and may be implemented in a slightly different way depending on which sector of the industry is being measured. There are a number of aspects, however, which will be of concern to all organizations, including:

- Operational performance
- Financial performance
- Customer satisfaction

Operational performance

The level of occupancy or usage of a facility is an important **operational performance** indicator for a whole range of leisure and tourism facilities. Theatres, leisure centres, swimming pools, self-catering units, coaches, hotels, aircraft and conference facilities, to name but a few, can all be appraised on the basis of the extent of their use. Occupancy ratios, usually expressed as percentages, can be calculated and compared over time and between different organizations in order to gauge performance.

The **occupancy ratio** can be calculated as follows:

$$\frac{\text{actual number of bookings, seats, spaces etc. taken up}}{\text{total number of bookings, seats, spaces etc. available}} \times 100\%$$

As an example of this ratio, if we assume that a coach has 42 of its 56 seats sold on an excursion, the occupancy ratio is calculated as follows:

$$\frac{42}{56} \times 100 = 75\% \text{ occupancy}$$

In local authorities, under CCT, targets for occupancy and usage levels of leisure centres and other facilities are usually set by the client. For example, a leisure centre operator may be required, as part of the CCT contract, to achieve the following usage levels and targets over a 12-month period:

- 55% use of the indoor bowls hall.
- Offer a children's activity programme during the school holidays.
- 80% use of the main sports hall.
- 45% use of the fitness suite.
- Attract one national and a minimum of 10 regional sporting events.
- 65% use of the squash courts.

Other useful performance indicators related to the operation of leisure and tourism organizations are:

- Total number of clients booking with a travel agent.
- Length of stay of visitors.
- Total throughput of visitors.
- Ratio of cost of cleaning to area cleaned.
- Load factor (number of seats occupied in relation to the number available).
- Number of destinations offered by a tour operator.
- Ratio of maintenance costs to total costs.

Did You Know ?

The range of operational performance indicators and ratios is virtually endless and management must be very clear to specify only those which will help in the difficult task of performance evaluation.

Social performance

Many leisure and tourism organizations, particularly those in the public and voluntary sectors, will have objectives which are not easily quantifiable and which are therefore harder to measure. These **social** or **community aims** are varied, but could include:

- A special event may be staged for an ethnic minority group which will achieve a community objective.
- An art gallery which welcomes school parties will be fulfilling an educational role.
- A visitor attraction may offer special rates and services for disadvantaged young people.
- A leisure centre may admit disabled visitors free of charge.

Although these, and other, **qualitative** objectives are sometimes difficult to evaluate, the introduction of CCT and other efficiency initiatives has forced local authorities to begin to **quantify** them so that they can be measured along with more conventional objectives relating to financial and operational performance. An example of this would be a local authority museum which has as one of its objectives:

To provide the best possible educational service for all pupils in the borough.

Although this is an aim which would be applauded by all concerned, how does the management of the museum know if it has been successful in meeting the objective? What is 'the best possible' service? In order to quantify this objective, the museum would need to draw up a list of all the services and facilities which it considers are contributing to providing the educational service, e.g. the building itself, any worksheets and factsheets produced for the school children, the catering service, promotional literature, etc. The next step would be to devise performance indicators or targets for each of these components. For the catering service, these could include:

- To provide a food and drink service whenever the museum is open.
- To offer four different types of cold drink.
- To have no more then 10 people waiting in the payment queue at any one time.

Once these targets have been set, all staff and management must be involved in making sure that they are committed to meeting or even exceeding them. Quantifying aims and measuring performance in this way will go a long way towards informing management and the local borough council if the educational objective is being met.

Financial performance

Ask any manager in leisure and tourism to comment on the success or otherwise of his or her facility, operation, department or organization and it is very likely that the first set of statistics consulted will be those relating to **financial performance**. Whether we like it or not, the main criteria used to evaluate the success of a venture will be those concerned with its finances. Managers may be able to produce a whole list of positive features and statistics about their organization, such as a range of glossy promotional materials, total numbers of visitors, amount of coverage in the local and national media or a state-of-the-art computer management information system. At the end of the day, however, if the organization has unhealthy finances when 'the bottom line' is investigated, no amount of clever public relations activity will conceal this weakness.

Very few **public sector** leisure and tourism facilities actually make a profit. They are subsidized from central and local government funds because they are considered important to the social well-being of the community and society at large. It must be remembered, however, that local authority spending on leisure and tourism, on such things as play areas, tourist information centres, swimming pools, leisure centres and museums, is purely discretionary; there is no statutory duty on a local council to provide leisure and tourism facilities and services in the same way that they are obliged to provide, for example, housing and education. In reality, they all do provide a range of leisure and tourism services related to their budget allocation. Increasing pressure from central government to reduce spending on local services has meant that there have been, and will continue to be, cuts in local services, and a corresponding need for local authority leisure and tourism departments to perform as efficiently as possible in all aspects of their financial and operational management.

The need for sound financial performance has long been

important in the **private sector**, which is why it is commercial leisure and tourism organizations which have been at the forefront in developing a range of performance indicators and financial ratios in order to have accurate data on which to base their decisions. Put very simply, there is a limit to the amount of time that a company which is not making a profit can be financed, either from external sources or from other departments or companies within the same group. There will come a point at which the company will cease trading.

Carrying out an assessment of the financial performance of an organization involves the management in preparing the detailed information on which the appraisal will be based and having sufficient expertise and experience to be able to interpret the data. The next section of this element will concentrate on the role of accounts and accounting conventions in the process of performance evaluation.

Types of accounting in leisure and tourism

Accounting methods used by leisure and tourism organizations mirror closely those used by organizations in many other sectors of the economy. In order for a manager to be able to make the necessary day-to-day and longer-term planning decisions about his or her organization, financial information such as the annual accounts and interim financial statements must be readily available. Accounting in leisure and tourism can be divided into two categories:

• Financial accounting
• Management accounting

Financial accounting
Financial accounting is concerned with the preparation of

that financial information which an organization is required by law to produce. In the private sector, these statutory accounts comprise:

• The profit and loss account
• The balance sheet
• If the company is a plc, it is also required by an accounting standard to produce a cash flow statement.

The **profit and loss account** shows an organization's income and expenditure over a period of time, usually 12 months, as a result of its normal trading activities. Figure 8.2 shows the profit and loss account for the year ended 31 December 1992 of a tourist attraction in Mid Wales, the Centre for Alternative Technology, which is unusual in that it is a relatively small operation which has chosen to become a public limited company (PLC).

Figure 8.2 shows the typical layout of a profit and loss account, starting with the turnover (sales) for the year, from which is deducted a figure for the cost of sales to produce the gross profit. In this example the net profit (or loss) is shown as the operating profit (or loss). All profit and loss accounts will show whether the organization is carrying forward either a surplus or a deficit into the next accounting period and are useful for comparing financial performance over different periods of time.

The **balance sheet** for any leisure and tourism organization is a statement of its financial position at a given point in time: a 'snapshot' of the financial health of the business at a particular point in time. Balance sheets are constructed at least on an annual basis and often more frequently than this, depending on the financial systems of the organization. Figure 8.3 shows a typical balance sheet for a leisure and tourism business.

CENTRE FOR ALTERNATIVE TECHNOLOGY PLC
PROFIT AND LOSS ACCOUNT
FOR THE YEAR ENDED 31 DECEMBER 1992

	Notes	£	1992 £	£	1991 £
TURNOVER	2	£85,74	805,710		678,166
Cost of sales			297,609		264,271
GROSS PROFIT			508,101		413,895
Administration expenses			(495,978)		(445,430)
			12,123		(31,535)
Other operating income	3		17,701		19,502
OPERATING PROFIT/(LOSS)	4/5		29,824		(12,033)
Interest receivable and similar income	6	8,574		40,721	
Interest payable and similar charges	7	(10,300)		(8,758)	
			(1,726)		31,963
PROFIT ON ORDINARY ACTIVITIES BEFORE TAXATION			28,098		19,930
Tax on profit on ordinary activities	8		–		338
RETAINED PROFIT FOR THE YEAR			28,098		20,268
Retained (deficit) brought forward			(70,276)		(90,544)
RETAINED (DEFICIT) CARRIED FORWARD			£(42,178)		£(70,276)

Figure 8.2 Profit and loss account of the Centre for Alternative Technology PLC (courtesy C.A.T.)

```
                   CENTRE FOR ALTERNATIVE TECHNOLOGY PLC
                              BALANCE SHEET
                          AS AT 31 DECEMBER 1992

                                        1992                    1991
                          Notes    £          £          £          £
FIXED ASSETS
Tangible assets             9    950,943               799,337

CURRENT ASSETS
Stocks                     10     54,480                66,185
Debtors                    11     37,755                21,596
Cash at bank and in hand          77,843               229,959
                                 170,078               317,740

CREDITORS–amounts falling
due within one year        12    (41,477)              (95,056)

NET CURRENT ASSETS                          128,601               222,684

TOTAL ASSETS LESS CURRENT LIABILITIES     1,079,544             1,022,021
CREDITORS–amounts falling due
after more than one year   13               (71,720)              (53,045)

NET ASSETS                               £1,007,824              £968,976

Financed by
CAPITAL AND RESERVES
Called up share capital    16             1,050,002             1,039,252
Profit and loss account                     (42,178)              (70,276)

                                         £1,007,824              £968,976

These financial statements were approved by the board of directors on...............................................
```

Figure 8.3   Balance Sheet of the Centre for Alternative Technology PLC (courtesy C.A.T.)

As Fig. 8.3 shows, the balance sheet revolves around an organization's assets and liabilities, the difference between the two being the working capital that it has available to use for day-to-day operations. Fixed assets include buildings, machinery and equipment, while current assets represent debtors, stock and cash which will convert into cash in the normal course of trading. Current liabilities are liabilities which fall due within a relatively short period of time, usually within 12 months, such as taxation and short-term bank loans.

The **cash flow statement** of a leisure and tourism organization shows the flow of funds into and out of the operation for a given period of time. Figure 8.4 gives the cash flow statement of the Centre for Alternative Technology for the year ended 31 December 1992.

A cash flow statement provides a link between an organization's profit and loss account and its balance sheet. It forms part of the audited accounts and shows the funds which have entered the company, how they have been used and how any net surplus or deficiency in short- and long-term funds have been applied.

Management accounting

While financial accounting is concerned with the production of statutory accounts, **management accounting** focuses on the provision of financial information to help with business decision-making and for control purposes. The managers of all leisure and tourism organizations need accurate financial data to manage on a day-to-day basis and to plan for the future. This makes management accounting just as important in the public and voluntary sectors of the industry as it is in the commercial sector. Managers need information to be able to analyse the viability of various courses of action and to test options before making a final decision. Effective control, on the other hand,

requires frequent and accurate data so that actual performance can be measured against original plans and targets, thereby allowing corrective action, if needed, to be implemented as soon as possible.

Management accounts will provide the leisure and tourism manager with information on such items as:

- Costs of the operation
- Total sales or turnover
- Profit for the organization as a whole
- Profits for individual activities, facilities or services
- Cash flows

It is vital that managers have precise information on the **costs** of running their organization. Costs are generally classified as either *fixed*, which remain relatively static regardless of the level of business activity, or *variable* which go up or down in direct proportion to the level of activity. Fixed costs include rent, interest payments or leasing charges which have to be met whether the organization is trading successfully or struggling to survive. In service sector industries such as leisure and tourism, the biggest variable cost is nearly always that related to employing staff, both permanent and temporary. Other significant variable costs in the industry include telephone and postage charges, especially for tour operators, travel agents and airlines, maintenance charges in the visitor attractions sector, and the cost of raw materials such as food in hotels, restaurants and fast-food outlets.

Controlling the flow of funds into and out of the organization, known as **cash flow**, is vital if it is to survive and expand. Maintaining a positive cash flow position is particularly difficult for new businesses or for organizations which have chosen to expand their operation by the addition of new buildings, plant or machinery. In these circumstances, banks and other providers of finance may be able to offer short-term loans or overdrafts until such time as the cash flow is stabilized. It is not

CENTRE FOR ALTERNATIVE TECHNOLOGY PLC
CASH FLOW STATEMENT
FOR THE YEAR 31 DECEMBER 1992

	Notes	£	1992 £	£	1991 £
Net cash inflow/(outflow) from operating activities	18		50,470		31,942
Returns on investments and servicing of finance					
Interest received		8,574		40,721	
Interest paid		(10,300)		(8,758)	
Net cash inflow from returns on investments & servicing of finance			(1,726)		31,963
Taxation					
Corporation tax		–		5,252	
Tax paid					(5,252)
Investing activities					
Payments to acquire tangible fixed assets		182,032		733,913	
Receipts form sale of tangible fixed assets		(623)		–	
Net cash flow from investing activities			(181,409)		(733,913)
Net cash outflow before financing			(132,665)		(675,260)
Financing					
Issue of ordinary share capital			10,750		402,200
(Decrease)/Increase in cash & cash equivalents	18		£(121,915)		£(273,060)

Figure 8.4 Cash flow statement of the Centre for Alternative Technology PLC (courtesy C.A.T.)

always apparent to the world outside that an organization is experiencing difficulties in its cash flow position. It may seem that an organization is trading normally, but the true position may be that it has insufficient funds coming in to be able to meet its payments and other financial obligations. A recent case in point was the collapse of the International Leisure Group (ILG) who were best known for their Intasun tour operating subsidiary.

Management accounts tend to be used purely within an organization and there is no statutory requirement for them to be published. There is a great deal of confidential and commercially sensitive information held in the management accounts, so it is important that the management information system (MIS) which stores the data is designed with security in mind and that access to the MIS is restricted to authorized personnel only.

The interpretation of financial data

The accounts of an organization are an important source of information which enable the management to examine and evaluate its financial performance. All leisure and tourism organizations, regardless of which sector they are in, are striving towards effective management and control which should lead to a healthy profit and loss account and balance sheet. These statements, together with other performance indicators, should be used by managers to assess efficiency and indicate areas which may need adjustment to improve the overall outcome. It is common practice for organizations to develop ratios from the accounts which can be used for performance appraisal.

Financial ratios
Financial ratios tend to be the most common method by which managers interpret information so as to give them an

easy way of comparing performance both within and between organizations. Comparisons between one year and another, between similar organizations in the same sector or comparisons with budgeted targets are much more useful than actual figures. It is important not to consider a single ratio in isolation or make decisions based on a single set of figures. It is much better to study a number of ratios in order to assess the state of health of the organization.

> **Did You Know ?**
>
> Financial ratios can only be as good as the financial information from which they are compiled; inaccuracies in the original data will result in ratios which give a false picture of performance.

Profitability ratios
The most widely used indicator of the profitability of an organization is based on the **return on capital employed** (ROCE), since it is meaningless to look at profitability without also analysing the resources which have been used to generate the profit. In simple terms, the ROCE is calculated as follows:

$$\text{return on capital employed } = \frac{\text{profit}}{\text{capital employed}}$$

This is known as the primary ratio. It has many variations and this leads to a lack of consistency and distortion. In particular, there are a number of interpretations of resources or capital employed in a business. Different organizations will have different methods of determining the figure for capital employed but, whichever is chosen, the same basis should be used from one year to the next to produce consistency.

Other **profitability ratios** used by leisure and tourism organizations include:

- **Net profit : sales ratio** – this is generally expressed as a percentage rather than a ratio. It will give a figure for profit (or loss) made per £ of income. The percentage profit on sales varies between different sectors, so it is essential to compare the ratio with similar businesses and also to make allowance for the prevailing economic conditions.

- **Sales : capital employed** – this ratio measures the efficiency with which an organization uses its capital in relation to its sales. Again this ratio will vary according to the type of business; most tour operators, for example, work on low profit margins with a high turnover, whereas a country house hotel will have a higher profit margin but with a lower turnover.

Public sector financial ratios

Most **public sector** leisure and tourism organizations are subsidized from either central or local government funds and are not normally expected to make a profit. It is still important, however, to measure the **ratio of income to expenditure** in order to calculate to what extent the income from such items as ticket sales and admission charges can be offset against operating costs. The ratio, usually expressed as a percentage, is calculated as follows:

$$\frac{income}{operating\ expenditure} \times 100\%$$

Another useful ratio for public sector organizations is the **level of subsidy per visitor or user**, which is calculated as follows:

$$\frac{net\ operating\ expenditure}{number\ of\ admissions}$$

This ratio can be applied to a whole range of leisure and tourism facilities provided by local councils, including leisure centres, swimming pools, theatres, museums and entertainment venues.

A number of other **primary ratios** can be applied to public sector provision, including:

- bar gross profit : bar revenue
- income : number of admissions (to give spend per head)
- catering income : number of admissions
- staff costs : operating expenditure
- catering gross profit : catering revenue
- bar income : number of admissions

The number and range of **secondary ratios** which can be developed for public sector leisure and tourism organizations is immense. It is important to calculate only those ratios which will contribute to the manager's decision-making process. From the revenue point of view, common ratios which could prove useful include:

- shop income : total income
- bar income : total income
- catering income : total income

Ratios related to expenditure include:

- cleaning costs : operating expenditure
- energy costs : operating expenditure
- marketing expenditure : total operating expenditure

It must be remembered that whether financial ratios are being applied in the private, public or voluntary sector, they are just one of the methods by which financial performance can be measured. Decisions taken on the basis of financial ratios alone will not produce the desired satisfactory outcome.

Customer satisfaction

One of the most important aspects of a service industry such as leisure and tourism is for operators to provide facilities and services that the **customers** are happy with. The level of customer satisfaction can also be a very potent weapon when it comes to evaluating performance of an organization; get it wrong, and you won't have any customers to ask if they are happy with the service! There is a general acceptance in the industry that customers and users have increasing expectations from the leisure and tourism organizations they use, and that they are becoming more assertive in demanding higher levels of customer service (see Unit 3 for more detail on the importance of customer service in leisure and tourism).

The importance of customer feedback

Customer-centred leisure and tourism organizations will gear all their activities and operations to the needs of the customer. Customers and users will form the focus of a total management system which acknowledges that they are the reason for the organization's very existence: without them there would be no organization. These enlightened and 'open' operations will welcome **feedback** from customers, both positive and negative, and will use it as a way of improving organizational performance.

Did You Know ?

Monitoring feedback is vital to effective management and should be built in to evaluation procedures and practices from the outset, rather than being considered as an additional and onerous duty.

Information from customers on their attitudes to a particular leisure and tourism organization can be gathered either informally or formally. **Informal customer feedback** is often spontaneous, making it just as valuable as information which is given in a more formal manner. Indeed, many would say that a customer is more likely to reveal his or her true feelings and attitudes in an unprompted chat with a member of staff than when that same member of staff is carrying out a survey of users with the help of a questionnaire. Informal feedback can take many forms, including:

- A member of staff overhearing customers praising the standard of service received at a golf club.
- A child heard complaining to his father about the length of time they are having to queue for a 'ride' at a theme park.
- A remark to a holiday representative about the poor standard of the food in a resort hotel.

It is important that management establish a mechanism by which this informal feedback is collected and monitored. We are all well aware of the influence that unhappy customers can have on the image of an organization and thereby its success. We all like to talk about our leisure and tourism experiences, which, if unhappy, can spread very quickly by 'word of mouth'. This powerful mechanism can also be beneficial for those organizations which have provided a good standard of service.

Many leisure and tourism operators now have regular staff meetings at which employees are invited to share any informal feedback that they have picked up. They are also encouraged to record comments from customers on specially designed feedback forms, so that management can monitor the situation to see if corrective action is needed in any areas.

Did You Know ?

All staff at EuroDisney are trained in customer service skills and have regular training sessions at which they discuss the importance of informal feedback and share their experiences with other employees.

Formal customer feedback can be collected in a number of ways, including:

- Interview surveys
- Customer comment forms
- Suggestion boxes
- 'Mystery shoppers'
- Focus groups

- **Interview surveys:** These are an invaluable way of gaining useful feedback from customers on their attitude to the facilities provided and of gaining information which can be used to build up customer profiles and form the basis of future product development and promotional activities. It is sometimes helpful to carry out user surveys, aimed at those customers currently using the facility, and non-user surveys which aim to discover why some people do not use the service. Carrying out interview surveys is a very skilled task, encompassing questionnaire design, training interviewers, collating the data and analysing the results.

- **Customer comment forms:** These give visitors an immediate opportunity to tell the management what they think of the service and facilities they have used. Figure 8.5 shows an example of a customer care survey used on cross-channel ferries.

Customer comment forms are in widespread use throughout all sectors of the leisure and tourism industry, including tour operators, travel agencies, leisure centres, hotels, transport operators, destinations and tourist information centres.

- **Suggestion boxes:** These are a novel way of inviting customer feedback. A simple form can be provided, which, when completed, is put into the box to be looked at by staff and management. Suggestion boxes often highlight ways in which leisure and tourism organizations can make simple alterations to facilities which will improve the customer experience. They can help in the process of monitoring customer complaints; management should aim to keep these to a minimum by

Stena Sealink
LINE

SOUTHAMPTON•CHERBOURG

PASSENGER AREA & TOILETS SURVEY

Dear Passenger,

We would be obliged if you could find time during your trip to fill in this simple survey and give us your opinion of the passenger area and toilets. This will allow us to improve our quality of service.

Once you have filled in the survey please hand it to a member of staff or put it into the special box provided at the Information Desk.

Many thanks for your assistance!

PASSENGER AREA AND TOILETS						
Passenger area	- overall impression					
	- decor					
	- seating availability					
	- storage of baggage					
	- signposting					
	- cleanliness					
	- disabled facilities					
Toilets	- overall impression					
	- cleanliness					
	- hygiene facilities					
	- disabled facilities					
		1	2	3	4	5

With the exception of the journey you are making, how often have you travelled with Stena Sealink Line on this particular route over the past 12 months?

Not at all ☐ 0 Once ☐ 1 Twice ☐ 2 3-4 times ☐ 3
5-6 times ☐ 4 7-10 times ☐ 5 More than 10 times ☐ 6

Age:

-14 ☐ 1 15-19 ☐ 2 20-24 ☐ 3 25-34 ☐ 4 35-44 ☐ 5
45-54 ☐ 6 55-59 ☐ 7 60-64 ☐ 8 65+ ☐ 9

Sex: Male ☐ 1 Female ☐ 2

Nationality:

British ☐ 1 French ☐ 2 Spanish ☐ 3 German ☐ 4
Italian ☐ 5 Other ☐ 6 *Please specify* ______

Figure 8.5 A typical customer comment form (courtesy Stena Sealink)

setting targets for the number of complaints received which should be reduced over time.

- **Mystery shoppers:** A 'mystery shopper' is somebody who is employed by an organization to visit a facility or use a product or service anonymously and report back to management on his or her experiences. It can be used to gain information on the performance of staff, for example, in the management's own organization or to look into the service offered by competitors. The technique is widely used in the commercial sector of leisure and tourism, most notably in airlines and travel agencies.

- **Focus groups:** Market research organizations are sometimes asked to assemble *focus groups* to look in detail at what influences people when they are deciding which product or service to buy. A small number of customers who already use a particular product, or those with specific social and economic characteristics, are invited to spend a couple of hours with a trained interviewer, employed by a company or group of companies to help them increase their market share. Although not widespread in the leisure and tourism industry, there are examples of airlines holding focus group sessions with business travellers and some conference and business organizers are known to use the technique.

Self Check ✔ Element 2

6. What are performance indicators?

_____

_____

7. What is the difference between quantitative and qualitative objectives?

_____

_____

8. What is the purpose of a leisure and tourism organization's profit and loss account?

_____

_____

9. Explain the difference between management accounting and financial accounting.

_____

_____

10. How does a leisure and tourism facility calculate its level of subsidy per visitor or user?

_____

_____

11. How can customers be involved in the evaluation of an organization's performance?

_____

_____

8.3 Evaluating the performance of a facility

Whether a leisure and tourism organization decides to use its own staff to carry out the **evaluation** of the performance

---

of its facility or whether it employs an outside consultant or agency to do the job, the following guidelines will apply:

- The evaluation must use information sources which are relevant, valid and current.
- The information gathering and analysis methods must be accurate and suitable for their purpose.
- The evaluation should identify both internal and external influences on facility performance.
- The opportunities for improvement in facility performance must be correctly identified.
- Any obstacles to improvement in facility performance must be highlighted.
- The evaluation should be applied to the facility's objectives as the basis for appraisal.
- The evaluation should use a range of information sources, both internal and external to the organization.
- The findings of the evaluation should be presented in an appropriate fashion to the facility management.
- The security and confidentiality of information should be ensured.

Compliance with health and safety and other legal requirements

The vast amount of **legislation** covering health and safety and other legal aspects of running a leisure and tourism organization means that managers are constantly being monitored, and their performance evaluated, by public agencies outside of their own organization. Although the present government has set itself the aim of reducing to a minimum the amount of 'red tape' surrounding organizations, there is still a great deal of legislation which starts its life in Brussels through the European Union (formerly the European Community). Legislation and codes of practice covering health and safety at work, food hygiene, the control of hazardous substances, workplace conditions and fire precautions, to name but a few, all place a duty on the owners and managers of leisure and tourism organizations to carry out audits or risk assessments to highlight any problems they may have. Once highlighted, procedures must be put in place to deal effectively with the problems.

Environmental impact

The performance of organizations in relation to the impact that they have on the **environment** is becoming a major issue for the 1990s. No leisure and tourism organization can operate without having positive and negative effects on its immediate natural environment and, in some cases, on the environment thousands of miles away. Western societies are becoming increasingly concerned about the threats to the environment posed by many leisure and tourism developments. The 1980s saw the growth of the 'green consumer' who not only looks for environmentally sound products in the supermarkets but also looks for leisure and tourism products which are developed in harmony with the environment. Many tourism developments in particular have been criticized for their lack of concern for environmental issues, while many argue that the whole of the tourism industry is, by its very nature, environmentally destructive.

Evaluating environmental performance

The rise in the awareness of, and concern for, the environment has meant that leisure and tourism organizations are becoming more involved in measuring their environmental effects. This is often as a direct result of a national or local government regulation linked to the planning and development process. It is now very common for large leisure and tourism projects to be asked to carry out an appraisal of the costs and benefits of the development from an environmental point of view. The most common technique for carrying out such an evaluation is the **environmental impact assessment** (EIA), which can be applied to a wide range of planned developments in leisure and tourism. The EIA is a structured process which aims to:

- Identify the costs and benefits of a particular development.
- Establish who will lose and who will gain if the development goes ahead.
- Examine alternative courses of action and their likely impacts.
- Consider ways of reducing impacts if the project is given the green light.

For leisure and tourism enterprises which are already in existence, the technique of **environmental auditing** is gaining in popularity. Some pioneering work by the Inter-Continental Hotel Group, which has resulted in a manual of procedures giving consideration to the environmental consequences of all its business activities, has led to many large hotel companies, airlines and tour operators looking at their activities and processes from a different angle. Some organizations have used their concern for the environment as a marketing tool, hoping to tap into the growing market for leisure and tourism products and services which are truly respectful of the world in which we live.

Did You Know ?

'Green' or sustainable issues concerning leisure and tourism will grow in importance in the 1990s.

Economic, social and cultural impacts

We have seen that leisure and tourism organizations are beginning to evaluate the impact that they are having on the environment, both close to home and further afield. An equally important concern is their effect on the **ecomonic, social and cultural** fabric of local communities and society in general. Leisure and tourism can bring enormous benefits to people, by providing leisure facilities locally, by giving them the chance to travel widely, by boosting economies with the provision of jobs and income, and by introducing them to new people with different cultures and traditions. There are, however, disadvantages at the local, national and international levels.

There will be many occasions when an organization is asked to *quantify* the benefits and costs of its activity in relation to, for example, its local community. It may be seeking financial help from central or local government in the form of a grant or a loan, or may be trying to obtain permission to expand its operations by building new premises. Economic points are always much easier to quantify and evaluate than benefits relating to social and cultural factors. Some new projects are now being asked to provide an impact assessment concerning these factors in the same way that they may be asked for an EIA.

Self Check ✔ Element 3

12. What is the difference between environmental auditing and an environmental impact assessment?

13. How could a mass market outbound tour operator measure its performance in terms of its social and cultural impacts?

Unit Test This test is one hour long. Answer all the questions.

Question 1
Providing an educational experience in a local authority leisure facility can sometimes conflict with achieving the financial targets set by the council.

Decide whether each of these statements is true (T) or false (F).

(i) Local authority leisure facilities should always give priority to financial rather than educational objectives.
(ii) A local authority leisure facility which has an educational objective will always run at a loss.

Which option best describes these two statements?

A   (i) T   (ii) T
B   (i) T   (ii) F
C   (i) F   (ii) T
D   (i) F   (ii) F

Question 2
The management of a cinema complex has outlined specific ways of enhancing the quality of the leisure experience it provides for its customers.

Decide whether each of these statements is true (T) or false (F).

(i) One way would be to install a new computer system for financial planning and monitoring.
(ii) One way would be to carry out hourly checks on the toilet facilities.

Which option best describes these two statements?

A   (i) T   (ii) T
B   (i) T   (ii) F
C   (i) F   (ii) T
D   (i) F   (ii) F

Questions 3–5 relate to the following information.
Leisure and tourism organizations will have very different aims and objectives, including:

A   Profit maximization
B   Creation of jobs
C   Provision of access to facilities for all sectors of the community
D   Conservation of the environment

Which of the above objectives is most closely associated with each of the following?

Question 3
A local authority economic development department.

Question 4
A commercial leisure organization.

Question 5
A local authority leisure services department.

Question 6
A major drinks company has decided to sponsor the next national schools' athletics championships which is to be covered live on television.

Decide whether each of these statements is true (T) or false (F).

(i) The main aim of the sponsorship is to make a profit on the sale of drinks at the event.

(ii) The image of the drinks company could be harmed if the event was badly organized.

Which option best describes these two statements?

A   (i) T   (ii) T
B   (i) T   (ii) F
C   (i) F   (ii) T
D   (i) F   (ii) F

Question 7
The following diagram shows the cycle of objectives of a local authority leisure centre, but is incomplete:

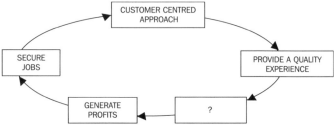

Choose one statement from the list below which completes the diagram.

A   Satisfied management
B   Satisfied customers
C   Satisfied councillors
D   Satisfied organization

Question 8
The National Trust is one of the largest voluntary sector leisure and tourism organizations in the UK.

Its principal aim is to:

A   Create jobs in the countryside
B   Generate funds for the government
C   Preserve land and buildings
D   Create Areas of Outstanding Natural Beauty (AONBs)

Question 9
In order to measure whether it is meeting its objective of providing a high standard of customer care, a large tourist attraction in Wales regularly conducts surveys of its visitors.

Decide whether each of these statements is true (T) or false (F).

(i) To obtain the same number of responses, a face-to-face interview survey will cost more to carry out than a survey which use self-completed questionnaires.
(ii) Qualitative information from the surveys is easier to analyse than quantitative data.

Which option best describes these two statements?

A   (i) T   (ii) T
B   (i) T   (ii) F
C   (i) F   (ii) T
D   (i) F   (ii) F

Questions 10–12 share the answer options A–D.
The following are examples of indicators that a self-catering complex may use to examine its performance:

A   Monthly income per unit

B   Analysis of reasons for repeat bookings
C   Average overnight spend in the region
D   Analysis of reasons for staff absence

Which performance indicator would be best researched by:

Question 10
Customer survey?

Question 11
Internal financial records?

Question 12
Reference to secondary data?

Question 13
In order to establish whether financial objectives are being met for a Tourist Information Centre's accommodation booking service, data would be gathered from an analysis of:

A   Its budget for the next nine months
B   Customer satisfaction surveys
C   Occupancy levels in local accommodation
D   Invoices for commission

Focus 3: ASPECTS OF PERFORMANCE

Question 14
A specialist tour operator is concerned about the negative environmental and socio-cultural impacts its operation may be having on one of the countries offered in its programme. It decides to establish an objective of improving its performance in relation to the local community and environment in the country concerned.

Decide whether each of these statements is true (T) or false (F).

(i) This objective could be achieved by setting targets, increasing annually, for the percentage of people from its headquarters in London working in the country concerned.
(ii) This objective could be achieved by carrying out an impact study and establishing a plan for reducing negative impacts in the country concerned.

Which option best describes these two statements?

A   (i) T   (ii) T
B   (i) T   (ii) F
C   (i) F   (ii) T
D   (i) F   (ii) F

Question 15
Although the total number of visitors using a tourist attraction is important, a private sector organization will often consider that making a profit is its main objective.

Which of the following performance indicators could a stately home use to determine success in making a profit?

A   Grade of tourist board classification
B   Margin on sales
C   Staff absenteeism
D   Share of the market

Question 16
Many leisure and tourism organizations are actively working towards certification of the quality of their operation, via systems such as BS5750/ISO9000.

Decide whether each of these statements is true (T) or false (F).

(i) This award is given to organizations when they achieve an agreed number of visitors per year.
(ii) This award is given to organizations when senior management attend a quality training seminar.

Which option best describes these two statements?

A   (i) T   (ii) T
B   (i) T   (ii) F
C   (i) F   (ii) T
D   (i) F   (ii) F

Questions 17–19 share answer options A–D.
Different leisure and tourism facilities will have different interest groups assessing their performance, including:

A   Councillors
B   Trustees
C   Visitors
D   Shareholders

Which group is most likely to use the following assessment criteria for evaluating the performance of a facility?

Question 17
Benefits to the local community.

Question 18
Level of profits.

Question 19
Value for money.

Question 20
The owner of a private hotel is concerned when she hears that a major hotel group is planning to open a new hotel within 800 yards of her own.

Identify which aspect of the performance of the private hotel would be affected by the competition from the new hotel.

A   Complying with health and safety requirements
B   Speed of service in the restaurant
C   Level of profitability
D   Quality of the customer service

Question 21
The management of an international airline is reviewing its performance in relation to its commitment to customer loyalty.

Decide whether each of these statements is true (T) or false (F).

(i) Customer loyalty cannot be measured quantitatively.
(ii) The recent decrease in the volume of repeat business indicates that its commitment to customer loyalty is achieving its objective.

Which option best describes these two statements?

A   (i) T   (ii) T
B   (i) T   (ii) F
C   (i) F   (ii) T
D   (i) F   (ii) F

Focus 4: PLANS AND REPORTS

Question 22
You have been asked to carry out some research to forecast

attendance figures at an indoor arena over the next three years.

Decide whether each of these statements is true (T) or false (F).

(i) The forecasts are likely to influence the future programme of events held at the arena.
(ii) The use of 'sensitivity analysis' will indicate the results of changes to certain variables in your forecast.

Which option best describes these two statements?

A   (i) T   (ii) T
B   (i) T   (ii) F
C   (i) F   (ii) T
D   (i) F   (ii) F

Questions 23–24 relate to the following information.
You have been employed by a major visitor attraction to carry out research about the quality of the customer service at the attraction.

Question 23
The best method to research this is:

A   By carrying out a face-to-face interview survey with a sample of visitors
B   By carrying out a telephone survey with a sample of visitors
C   By consulting secondary research data
D   By carrying out a postal survey of a sample of visitors

Question 24
Having carried out the research, you have produced a report for the management of the visitor attraction.

Decide whether each of these statements is true (T) or false (F).

(i) Incorrect figures in the report are unlikely to lead to incorrect management decisions.
(ii) Such reports should include an executive summary for those who do not wish to read the full report.

Which option best describes these two statements?

A   (i) T   (ii) T
B   (i) T   (ii) F
C   (i) F   (ii) T
D   (i) F   (ii) F

Question 25
You have been given the task of producing and circulating the monthly management report for a casino, but notice a small error in the computer's analysis of the results.

What is it most important for you to do?

A   Correct the error in the report before circulation
B   Put a note in the report explaining the error
C   Find out how the error occurred
D   Contact the computer maintenance company

Question 26
In your capacity as Tourism Officer for a local authority, you have been invited to give a talk to a group of children in a local primary school.

Decide whether each of these statements is true (T) or false (F).

(i) Using pictograms would be good for presenting numerical information, since they are eye-catching.
(ii) As long as any charts and tables you use during the talk are accurately drawn, you will not need to explain them to the audience.

Which option best describes these two statements?

A   (i) T   (ii) T
B   (i) T   (ii) F
C   (i) F   (ii) T
D   (i) F   (ii) F

Focus 5: OPPORTUNITIES AND OBSTACLES

Question 27
Commercial coach operators measure their performance by their profitability or by the size of their turnover.

Decide whether each of these statements is true (T) or false (F).

(i) An increase in the number of bookings means an increase in turnover.
(ii) A decrease in the number of bookings means a drop in profits.

Which option best describes these two statements?

A   (i) T   (ii) T
B   (i) T   (ii) F
C   (i) F   (ii) T
D   (i) F   (ii) F

Questions 28–30 relate to the following information.
As part of its future marketing plan, a large city-centre hotel has employed a marketing consultant to carry out a SWOT (strengths, weaknesses, opportunities and threats) analysis.

The consultant has noted the following factors which may affect the hotel's performance in the near future:

A   A multinational corporation is relocating its European headquarters to the city in six months' time
B   Forte is about to open a Travelodge on the outskirts of the city
C   The hotel has only one member of staff who speaks a foreign language
D   The hotel is part of a national marketing consortium

Which of these factors is:

Question 28
A threat.

Question 29
A weakness.

Question 30
An opportunity.

Question 31
Which is the least reliable guide to the long-term performance of a local museum?

A   The number of visitors
B   The value of goods sold in the shop
C   The number of complimentary letters received
D   The revenue from the museum café

Questions 32–34 relate to the following information.
The owner of a stately home which is open to the public wants to expand its activities and improve facilities for visitors.

There are a number of obstacles, however, to expanding and improving the stately home, including:

A   Environmental impacts
B   Seasonal variations

C   Competitor activities
D   Economic conditions

Under which heading should each of the following obstacles be listed?

Question 32
A theme park is under construction five miles away.

Question 33
A local pressure group is objecting to the felling of more trees.

Question 34
The volume of business is often low in the 'shoulder months'.

Focus 6: CONFIDENTIALITY AND SECURITY

Questions 35–37 relate to the following information.
The owners of a small tour operator specializing in trekking holidays to the Himalayas are reviewing the security and confidentiality of their information, some held in paper systems and some held on computer.

Question 35
Decide whether each of these statements is true (T) or false (F).

(i) The company's newly installed modem will only allow authorized users to access the computer data.
(ii) Using passwords to protect files and then storing data on floppy disks will help to keep the data confidential.

Which option best describes these two statements?

A   (i) T   (ii) T
B   (i) T   (ii) F
C   (i) F   (ii) T
D   (i) F   (ii) F

Question 36
The owners have decided to renew all staff contracts, after inserting a clause concerning confidentiality.

The main reason for this is to:

A   Improve the company's image
B   Improve staff productivity
C   Ban staff from disclosing company information to third parties
D   Ban staff from leaving without giving six months' notice

Question 37
The company keeps details of clients on file but is concerned about the security of the system.

Decide whether each of these statements is true (T) or false (F).

(i) Only senior management should be given access to clients' details.
(ii) Clients' details need to be kept secure under the requirements of the Data Protection Act.

Which option best describes these two statements?

A   (i) T   (ii) T
B   (i) T   (ii) F
C   (i) F   (ii) T
D   (i) F   (ii) F

Self-check Answers

1. All leisure and tourism organizations, whether in the private, public or voluntary sectors, must devise objectives that are clear, realistic and measurable. Without clear objectives, an organization and its staff will be unclear about its purpose and the reasons for its very existence. Clearly defined objectives will also allow those with an interest in the organization to measure whether it has achieved its aims.

2. A mission statement seeks to alert people inside and outside an organization as to its policy and aims. Many mission statements include an element of an organization's philosophy and values, as well as its vision for the future. They are currently very fashionable in the private and public sector.

4. Those with an interest in the objectives of a local authority leisure centre will include its customers and users, local Council Tax payers, elected councillors, council officers and the staff in the centre.

5. MBO stands for management by objectives, a management philosophy that begins with a clear statement of objectives, identifies strategies by which the objectives will be achieved, implements the strategies and evaluates the outcome of the process.

6. Performance indicators (PIs) are objective yardsticks against which performance, which may be financial or operational, can be measured. Financial performance is often evaluated with the help of financial ratios. PIs are used to measure the efficiency and effectiveness of leisure and tourism organizations, in both the private and public sectors.

7. Quantitative objectives are expressed in clearly defined terms, e.g. as percentages or other statistics. Qualitative objectives are rather less precise and may include social and environmental objectives which are harder to measure.

8. The purpose of a profit and loss account is to show an organization's income and expenditure over a given period of time, generally one year.

9. Management accounting is concerned with the provision of financial information for an organization's decision-making purposes. Financial accounting is concerned with the preparation of the financial information that an organization is required by law to produce.

10. The level of subsidy per visitor (the amount that the local authority pays towards the cost of an individual visitor) is calculated by dividing the net operating expenditure of the centre by the number of admissions.

11. It is important that customers are given the opportunity to be involved in the evaluation of an organization's performance; after all, the organization is in business to meet the needs of the customer. Customers may be asked to complete attitude surveys, fill in comment forms or take part in focus groups, so that their views can be heard and taken into consideration.

12. An EIA (environmental impact assessment) aims to identify the costs and benefits of a particular development and indicate the likely impacts on the environment if it goes ahead. Environmental auditing involves studying organizations that are already operating to see if their environmental impacts can be reduced by adaptations to existing work practices and systems.

13. The tour operator could carry out an impact study in the countries where it operates, identifying particular social and cultural impacts that need to be addressed. The impact study should indicate ways in which any negative impacts could be minimized.

Answers to Unit Test

1.	D	9.	B	17.	A	25.	A	33.	A
2.	C	10.	B	18.	D	26.	B	34.	B
3.	B	11.	A	19.	C	27.	B	35.	C
4.	A	12.	C	20.	C	28.	B	36.	C
5.	C	13.	D	21.	D	29.	C	37.	C
6.	C	14.	C	22.	A	30.	A		
7.	B	15.	B	23.	A	31.	C		
8.	C	16.	D	24.	C	32.	C		

Unit test comments

Q1: Answer is D.
Local authorities have a very difficult job to do in trying to meet financial, social and educational objectives in their leisure facilities. It is not true to say that they should always give priority to financial objectives. They must, however, always strive to give value for money and make maximum use of their available resources. Statement (ii) is also false, since there is no direct link between a facility having an educational objective and it always making a loss.

Q2: Answer is C.
Although the installation of a new computer system should help the financial operation of the cinema, it is unlikely to have a direct bearing on the quality of the customers' experience. Regular inspections, however, will result in facilities that are clean, thus adding to the quality of the customers' experience.

Q3: Answer is B – creation of jobs.
Economic development departments have been created to stimulate investment and the creation of businesses in their local areas, leading ultimately to more job opportunities.

Q4: Answer is A – profit maximization.
Most leisure organizations in the private sector will have profit maximization as their main, but not always their only, objective.

Q5: Answer is C – provision of access to facilities for all sectors of the community.
The primary aim of a local authority leisure department is to provide a range of services and facilities for as wide a cross-section of their local community as possible, within the resources at their disposal.

Q6: Answer is C.
The main reason for sponsoring this particular event will be to gain exposure on television, rather than making a profit on the sale of drinks. A badly organized event may well reflect badly on the sponsoring companies; people may associate bad organization with a bad product.

Q7: Answer is B – satisfied customers.
A leisure centre with a customer-centred approach, i.e. putting the customer at the hub of the organization's activity, is likely to provide them with a quality experience, which will result in satisfied customers.

Q8: Answer is C – preserve land and buildings.
The National Trust is a voluntary sector organization which has no direct links with government organizations. Its activities do create jobs in the countryside, but its primary aim is the preservation of land and buildings. AONBs are the responsibility of the Countryside Commission in England.

Q9: Answer is B.
To obtain the same number of responses, a face-to-face interview survey will cost more than a self-completed questionnaire survey, since there will be payment for training and employing interviewers. Quantitative data tend to be easier to analyse because they are more objective and questionnaires can be designed with a greater number of 'closed' questions than is the case with qualitative information.

Q10: Answer is B – analysis of reasons for repeat bookings.
A survey of customers will allow the managers of the complex to discover the reasons why customers are making repeat bookings, as well as providing data on the proportion of customers who are booking for the first time.

Q11: Answer is A – monthly income per unit.
The company's financial records will provide data on the total revenue for all units and the monthly income per unit. This will allow an analysis of booking patterns, in terms of both individual units and seasonality factors.

Q12: Answer is C – average overnight spend in the region.
This information will not be available from internal sources since it relates to the wider regional picture. Reference to secondary data, often produced by the Regional Tourist Boards in the form of factsheets, will give this general information.

Q13: Answer is D – invoices for commission.
Although analysis of operational objectives relating to customer satisfaction and occupancy levels is important, it will not indicate whether financial objectives are being met. The budget will be looking forward to the next nine months, leaving the commission invoices the only reliable method of establishing whether the financial objectives have been met. Tourist Information Centres earn a commission (or sometimes charge a fee) on any bookings for accommodation made through them.

Q14: Answer is C.
Increasing the proportion of staff from its headquarters in London who work in the countries will mean that fewer local people are employed by the tour operator. This will not help the socio-cultural problems of the countries, which would be better served by employing more local people. An impact study would certainly help to reduce negative impacts by planning for the future.

Q15: Answer is B – margin on sales.
While they are important performance indicators, tourist board classification and staff absenteeism will not relate directly to the objective of making a profit. Share of the market is not relevant, since it bears no direct relationship to profitability.

Q16: Answer is D.
Quality systems such as BS5750/ISO9000, stipulate that organizations must devise and implement systems and procedures related to the quality of all their functions and tasks. Having a target number of visitors per year would not normally be a condition of accreditation. Management may well be required to attend a training seminar, but this will be only one of a whole range of measures.

Q17: Answer is A – councillors.
Councillors, being the elected representatives of the local people, will be keen to see that the local community gains maximum benefit from its leisure and tourism facilities.

Q18: Answer is D – shareholders.
Shareholders will want to see that their investment is giving them a healthy return (dividend).

Q19: Answer is C – visitors.
While councillors and trustees will be concerned with value for money in relation to leisure and tourism facilities, it will be of greatest concern to the visitors to the facilities, who may take their custom elsewhere if they feel that they are not being given good value for money.

Q20: Answer is C – level of profitability.
Factors such as the quality of customer service, compliance with health and safety requirements and speed of service should not be influenced unduly by the new hotel. What may well suffer, however, is the private hotel's level of profitability, given that the new hotel may take business away from the established hotel. The owner of the private hotel may need to consider its product range and marketing strategy in response to the threat.

Q21: Answer is D.
Customer loyalty can in fact be measured quantitatively; a 'frequent flyer' programme, for example, will give objective information on those customers who continue to use the services of an airline and those who take their business elsewhere. A decrease in repeat business will show that the steps the airline is taking to enhance customer loyalty are not working.

Q22: Answer is A.
The forecasts are likely to have a direct bearing on the programme of events at the arena; if it is predicted, for example, that attendance figures will drop, large scale events such as rock concerts may not be sustainable. 'Sensitivity analysis' will indicate the likely differences in outcomes when a range of factors, such as inflation, entrance costs and group sizes, are taken into account.

Q23: Answer is A – by carrying out a face-to-face interview survey with a sample of visitors.
A face-to-face interview survey will be the best way of getting the qualitative data needed to assess the customers' thoughts on the quality of the service they receive. It will give a better response rate than either a postal or a telephone survey, assuming that the visitors' details were available. Secondary research data would not give the required information.

Q24: Answer is C.
The data and information must be as accurate as possible, so as to minimize the likelihood of incorrect management decisions; statement (i) is therefore false. It is good practice to include an executive summary covering the main points of the report for those who do not wish to read the report in full.

Q25: Answer is A – correct the error in the report before circulation.
From a presentational point of view, this is a better option than putting a note in the report. Finding out how the error occurred, perhaps by contacting the maintenance company, would take place after the report had been corrected.

Q26: Answer is B.
Pictograms are a highly visual form of graphical representation which would appeal to young children. Even though any charts and tables may be accurately drawn, they will still need explanation, especially to this age group.

Q27: Answer is B.
Statement (i) is true, since an increase in bookings means an increase in income (turnover), although not necessarily an increase in profits. A decrease in the number of bookings does not necessarily mean a drop in profits; a tour operator, for example, may decide to go 'up market' by offering a higher priced product to a smaller number of people.

Q28: Answer is B – Forte is about to open a Travelodge on the outskirts of the city.
This would be regarded as a threat since the Travelodge may well take custom away from the city-centre hotel.

Q29: Answer is C – the hotel has only one member of staff who speaks a foreign language.
This is a weakness that the management may wish to address, since it may well be limiting the amount of business from overseas visitors and companies.

Q30: Answer is A – a multinational corporation is relocating its European headquarters to the city in six months time.
This will be a good opportunity to increase corporate (business) and leisure clients, given that friends and relatives of employees will be visiting.

Q31: Answer is C – the number of complimentary letters received.
Items such as the number of visitors, value of goods sold and revenue from the museum cafe are reliable and objective indicators of performance. Complimentary letters, while very welcome, are rather subjective, but may be used for promotional purposes.

Q32: Answer is C – competitor activities.
A competing nearby theme park will have an undoubted influence on visitor levels and hence profitability at the stately home.

Q33: Answer is A – environmental impacts.
An increase in environmental awareness and respect mean that new leisure and tourism developments are subject to greater environmental scrutiny, including direct action by pressure groups and the need to carry out environmental audits and impact studies.

Q34: Answer is B – seasonal variations.
'Shoulder months' is the term used to denote the months either side of a facility's peak season; in the case of a stately home, these are likely to be the months either side of July and August.

Q35: Answer is C.
A modem will allow access to remote databases via a telephone line, but will not protect the security of the system. Confidentiality and security, however, will be protected by the use of passwords and storing data on floppy disks.

Q36: Answer is C – ban staff from disclosing company information to third parties.
The travel industry is highly competitive, meaning that security of information is crucial to success. Many private sector companies have confidentiality clauses in staff contracts to prevent their employees disclosing commercially sensitive information to third parties, including competitors.

Q37: Answer is C.
It is impractical to allow only senior management to have access to clients' details. All members of staff will need this access to carry out their normal day-to-day activities. Under the requirements of the Data Protection Act, organizations that are registered data users must take steps to ensure the security and confidentiality of any client information held on their computer systems.

The Portfolio

This final chapter of the book is devoted to the **portfolio of evidence** that you will compile in order to achieve your GNVQ. Most of the chapter examines closely the various skills that might be involved in putting together a portfolio.

Nature of the portfolio

Once the evidence you have collected for a unit has been assessed as satisfactory and you have passed the external test (if any), you will be credited with a pass in that particular unit. Passing all eight mandatory, four optional and the three core skill units will give you your Advanced GNVQ in Leisure and Tourism. Individual units on the GNVQ are not graded, i.e. you either have or have not reached the required standard for the unit, but a grade is awarded for the overall qualification, at pass, merit or distinction level; this is determined by your **portfolio of evidence**.

Throughout your GNVQ course, you will be collecting many different types of evidence to show that you have successfully completed elements and units. This all needs to be stored in your portfolio in such a way as to allow your tutors or teachers (and staff from the awarding bodies) to decide whether the grade you receive for the Advanced GNVQ should be at pass, merit or distinction level. In coming to a decision on what overall grade to award, they will judge your work against three important **themes**:

- **Planning** – how you have set out the way in which you will approach particular tasks and activities.

- **Information seeking and handling** – how well you have identified and used information sources.

- **Evaluation** – how you have reflected on the tasks that you have undertaken and suggested alternative courses of action and their implications.

We shall look at these three important areas in more detail later in the chapter (see page 194).

Your portfolio will contain evidence relating to:

- Mandatory units
- Optional units
- Core skill units
- Grading activity
- Performance in external tests
- Comments from your tutors or teachers

In order to give yourself the chance of getting the best possible grade, make sure that your portfolio is well structured, with a clear index. Your tutors or teachers will provide you with the necessary forms and charts to complete and insert into your portfolio.

What will a portfolio contain?

The portfolio is likely to contain a *variety* of evidence. Listed below are some of the most common forms of evidence:

- Questionnaire surveys
- Reports of observations
- Photographs, audio and videotapes
- Computer-generated material
- Role playing
- Organizing an event or service
- Demonstrations and discussions
- Presentations and displays
- Tests set by your tutors
- Notes from lectures or classes
- Activities carried out on work experience
- Records of visits to leisure and tourism organizations
- References and certificates from previous work or study
- Log books and records of achievement

Whatever type of evidence you choose to put forward to claim credit for an element or a unit, you will need to remember a number of important points:

1   The evidence must be **valid**, i.e. fit for its purpose. In other words, does the evidence you are submitting really satisfy the performance criteria laid down in the element? If not, you will need to change some of the evidence or add to it and re-submit it for assessment. Use the performance criteria as a checklist against which you compile your evidence.
2   The evidence must be **authentic**. Your tutors will check to see that the evidence you submit is genuine and that it is all your own work. This will be especially important when it comes to group work. Working as part of a team is an essential skill that you will need to develop, but you must be able to provide evidence to show that you have played a full part in the working of the group.
3   There must be **sufficient** evidence to be able to claim full credit for the element or unit. Your tutor will give you guidance on whether or not you have collected enough evidence to satisfy the requirements.
4   You must have obtained **permission** to use evidence from other people. There shouldn't be a problem recording and using information that is collected in your school or college, but when you are using data and information from outside sources, perhaps from a part-time job or work placement, you must make sure that you have

permission before the evidence is used. Leisure and tourism is a very competitive industry, making security of information an important consideration.

The stages in continuous assessment

Although the exact nature of a piece of assessed work will vary between one school or college and another, there are a number of clearly defined **stages** that you will go through when carrying out continuous assessment, namely:

Stage 1: Receiving written and/or verbal instructions from your tutor about an assessment that will provide evidence to meet the requirements of a particular element or group of elements.

Stage 2: Discussing the practicalities of carrying out the work with your teacher or tutor and perhaps with other members of your group.

Stage 3: Devising an 'action plan' (see page 196) for the assessment, indicating time deadlines, tasks and sources of information.

Stage 4: Discussing the action plan with your teacher or tutor, who may suggest alterations or improvements to make your task easier.

Stage 5: Carrying out the assessment in line with your action plan.

Stage 6: Having your written and/or oral work checked by your tutor, who will either confirm that it is of the required standard or indicate that more needs to be done to reach the standard.

Stage 7: When completed, claiming credit from your teacher or tutor for the particular element or elements covered, and filing your evidence in your portfolio.

Who marks the assessments?

You will find that studying for a GNVQ is quite different from any other courses of study you may have done. Just as you won't be spending a great deal of time sitting in classrooms taking notes from your teacher or tutor, you will notice differences when it comes to having your work marked as well. You will be expected to take responsibility for setting your own realistic timescales for achieving tasks and handing in evidence to your tutors. Under the GNVQ system, the person who checks to see that your evidence is of the right quality and quantity is called an **assessor**. This will usually be the teacher or tutor who set the assignment or task. In order to make sure that all the assessors in your school or college are assessing at the same level, one of the team of staff teaching you will take on the role of an **internal verifier**. The internal verifier is often the course tutor or course co-ordinator for the Advanced GNVQ in Leisure and Tourism at your school or college, who oversees the smooth operation of your course and maintains fairness in the assessment process. If you feel that your work has not been fairly assessed, you can appeal to the internal verifier to look at your work again. He or she will also look at a sample of assessment work from different students at regular intervals to see that standards are consistent across all units and between all assessors. All assessors and internal verifiers have to be trained in the operation of GNVQ assessments so as to ensure consistency of standards throughout the country.

In addition to staff from your own school or college who check your evidence and assess your work, there is another independent check by a person known as an **external verifier**. External verifiers are employed by the awarding bodies (BTEC, RSA or City & Guilds) to see that the methods of assessing GNVQ students at your school or college are working prop-

erly. They will visit your school or college from time to time to check that the assessment system is fair and in line with other centres running GNVQs throughout the country. They will want to talk to students about how the GNVQ is running and whether there are any concerns that can be investigated. Do not be afraid of telling the external verifier what you think of the course; they welcome feedback just as much as you do.

We now look at how the **core skills** mentioned in the introduction to this book can be demonstrated within the portfolio.

Core Skills

GNVQs have been developed to provide a broad education which may be used as a basis for employment or entry into higher education. This is done by ensuring that students develop:

- A knowledge and understanding of leisure and tourism subject matter.
- A wide range of skills which underpin many different jobs.

Apart from the evidence of achievement you will be required to produce in order to pass the eight mandatory units and the four optional units, you will also need to produce *evidence of achievement* in the three **core skill** unit areas of:

- Communication
- Application of number
- Information technology

Unlike the mandatory and optional units, you will not find the core skill units taught as separate subjects. As far as is possible the teaching, development and assessment of the core skill units will be integrated into the teaching and assessment of these other units.

In order to claim that you have developed certain skills, you will have to provide **evidence** of achievement. Many schools and Colleges provide students with a **log book** (detailing the skills performance criteria) for this purpose. This will be incorporated into your portfolio of evidence at the end of the course. While assessments will often be the method by which you will demonstrate that you have acquired certain skills, there are other possibilities. These would include:

- Work experience
- Audio-visual presentations
- Your domestic situation
- Social or leisure activities
- Previous study

During your Advanced GNVQ course you will find that many of the skills listed in the following pages are covered by your assessments or other evidence of achievement several times. This is no bad thing, since it allows you to improve on these skills and thus claim a merit or distinction rather than a pass. From time to time it is also useful to review your progress in the core skills and, in conjunction with your tutor, develop an action plan to remedy deficiencies or improve on the minimum pass grade.

In the following pages we state the **performance criteria** for each of the skills and how you could provide evidence of their achievement. To help you build up your portfolio of evidence we also provide space for you to record *how* you have achieved, or intend to achieve these skill criteria. These statements may eventually be included in your portfolio of evidence.

It is very important to ensure that your portfolio of evidence shows your full abilities in these core skill areas. Some aspects of the presentation and handling of data relevant to all three core skills will be considered in the next section of this chapter.

Communication

Element 3.1

Take part in discussions with a range of people on a range of matters.

This means you should:

Make contributions in discussions which are relevant and expressed effectively.

Make contributions in a tone and manner which is suited to the audience.

Encourage others to contribute, and listen carefully to what they say.

Clarify any points which others make if you do not understand.

Possible evidence:

Discussions may take place, face-to-face or over the telephone with:

tutors	colleagues
peer group	family
customers/clients	etc.

When dealing with routine tasks, solving problems or dealing with sensitive issues.

Date	Evidence	Page reference in Portfolio

Element 3.2

Prepare written material on a range of matters.

This means you should ensure that:

Any information you provide is accurate and meets the requirements of the audience.

All documents are easily read. You should use highlighting and indentation to enhance meaning.

Sentence construction, paragraphs, spelling grammar and punctuation are correct.

A suitable format for presentation is used.

Possible evidence:

Responding to tutors, colleagues, family or customers by producing:

Assessments	Leaflets
Reports	Booklets
Memoranda	Log book entries
Letters	Publicity material.

Date	Evidence	Page reference in Portfolio

Element 3.3

Use images to illustrate points made in writing and in discussions with a range of people on a range of matters.

You should ensure that:

A range of illustrative material is used to improve other people's understanding of the points you make.

Illustrative material clarifies the points you wish to make.

Illustrative material is used at appropriate points in your work.

Possible evidence:

Organization charts   Pictographs
Diagnostic and flow charts   Tables
Pie and bar charts   Histograms
Photographs   Graphs.
Sketches

Date	Evidence	Page reference in Portfolio

Element 3.4

Read and respond to written material and images on a range of matters.

You should:

Identify accurately the main points in the text.

Discover the meaning of unfamiliar words, phrases or illustrative material.

Refer to appropriate sources for help.

Possible evidence:

Sources to use include:

manuals, dictionaries
tutors, supervisors, colleagues

when dealing with reports, memos, letters, assessments.

Date	Evidence	Page reference in Portfolio

Information technology

Element 3.1

Set system options, set up storage systems and input information.

You should:

Enter information using the correct procedures.

Enter information so that editing may be carried out efficiently.

Keep copies of source information and drafts.

Save and store information so that it is easily retrieved.

Use security routines to avoid loss of work or unauthorized access.

Select changes in systems operations which result in more efficient working.

Ensure changes in system operations do not adversely affect other users.

Possible evidence:

Copies of information produced showing IT applications such as documents created or saved.

Report on evaluation of IT used, including systems options such as:

Mouse speed
Changing cursor
Changing screen colours.

Date	Evidence	Page reference in Portfolio

Element 3.2

Edit, organize and integrate complex information from different sources.

You should be able to:

Retrieve information using retrieval routines effectively.

Protect information from accidental deletion.

Use edit, search or calculation routines to minimize the number of steps taken.

Use editing, moving and copying routines so as to minimize the likelihood of deleting or disrupting information.

Save or arrange information in such a way that it is easy to transfer.

Correct any discrepancies which arise between source material and new files/ records.

Possible evidence:

Using IT applications such as databases, wordprocessing and spreadsheets produce:

Reports with chapters and subsections

Tables of figures

Complex graphical information

Databases (e.g. of employee details)

Documents incorporating different IT applications (e.g. graphs and wordprocessing).

Date	Evidence	Page reference in Portfolio

Element 3.3

Select and use formats for presenting complex information.

You should be able to:

Provide printouts of information which are legible, accurate and complete.

Provide printouts of information that meet user requirements.

Ensure waste is minimized.

Ensure that information is presented effectively using format options.

Provide a final version of information drawn from different sources that is clear and easy to understand.

Possible evidence:

Using IT applications such as databases, spreadsheets, wordprocessing and desktop publishing produce:

Documents with page numbers, indexes, justified paragraphs, different character styles etc.

Documents with imported tables, graphs etc

Tables of figures.

Date	Evidence	Page reference in Portfolio

Element 3.4

Evaluate features and facilities of applications already available in the setting.

You should be able to:

Explain the importance of accuracy and precision when using IT.

Explain the importance of using procedures designed to protect information from deletion or unauthorized use.

Describe and evaluate the use of IT applications in the workplace.

Describe and evaluate some IT applications used to improve day-to-day working.

Compare and evaluate the above applications with other non-IT means of information handling.

Possible evidence:

Using IT applications such as databases, wordprocessing or spreadsheets produce:

Reports on the use of IT in an organization

Reports into the feasibility of introducing IT into an organization.

Date	Evidence	Page reference in Portfolio

Element 3.5

Deal with errors and faults at level 3 (Advanced).

You should be able to:

Use IT equipment in accordance with health and safety requirements.

Identify simple errors and faults and take action to rectify them.

Identify more complex errors and faults and report them to an appropriate member of staff.

Avoid harm to persons or equipment when errors or faults occur.

Warn others of IT problems so as to prevent disruption of their activities.

Possible evidence:

Arising out of the use of IT equipment in school/college workshop or work experience, produce:

  A report on health and safety procedures to note when using IT

  A statement of a problem experienced with IT equipment and procedures followed

  A copy of a fault report made in a log book.

Date	Evidence	Page reference in Portfolio

Application of number

Element 3.1

Gather and process data at core skill level 3 (Advanced).

You will ensure that:

Correct techniques are selected.

The techniques are used properly.

Mathematical terms are interpreted correctly.

Data are recorded in the correct units and format.

Records are accurate and complete.

Possible evidence:

Making and checking estimates using measures such as lengths, weights, speeds, etc.

Converting between different measurement systems (e.g. £ and $ or yards and metres) using tables, graphs, scales.

Design and use a form to collect and record data.

Design and use a questionnaire to survey opinion.

Classify data into different groups.

Date	Evidence	Page reference in Portfolio

Element 3.2

Represent and tackle problems at core skill level 3 (Advanced).

You will ensure that:

Appropriate methods are used to solve problems.

The problem solving technique adopted is used properly and to an appropriate level of precision so as to obtain the correct answer.

Mathematical terms are explained in layman's language.

Rough estimates are used to check calculations.

Mathematical aids (e.g. rulers, calculators, compasses) are used correctly.

Conclusions drawn from results are well founded.

Explanations for your conclusions can be given.

Possible evidence:

Solving problems using simple arithmetic.

The correct use of fractions, decimals, ratios and percentages to describe facts such as profitability, absenteeism, etc.

The correct use of simple formulae or equations (e.g. to calculate return on capital investment projects or economic order quantities).

The use of diagrams to solve problems (e.g. breakeven charts, flow diagrams, decision trees).

Solving geometrical problems such as finding areas, volumes or perimeters for various shapes and solids (e.g. product packaging, product transportation).

Use shorthand symbols to express series of numbers that are arranged in a particular way.

Solve more complicated equations.

Date	Evidence	Page reference in Portfolio

Element 3.3

Interpret and explain mathematical data at core skill level 3 (Advanced).

You should be able to:

Identify trends or significant features in data.

Draw the correct conclusions or make the correct predictions from data.

Explain the mathematical terms used.

Justify the conclusions or predictions you have made.

Follow conventions or standard rules for presenting data.

Represent data accurately using symbols and diagrams.

Possible evidence:

Using mathematical terms to describe common shapes (e.g. cylinders for cans, cubes for blocks).

Construct and explain statistical diagrams (e.g. pie or bar charts).

Calculate and explain the arithmetic mean of a set of figures.

Explain the implications of combing two separate events (e.g. age structure : activity ratios).

Calculate the probability of an event given the probability of other events.

Date	Evidence	Page reference in Portfolio

Presenting and analysing data

In many assignments you can demonstrate *evidence* of the 'core skills' and of the other skills required for a merit/distinction grade by the ways in which you present and analyse data.

Presenting information and data

We shall first look at some of the ways in which information can be **presented** in your assignments. The visual presentation of research results in the form of tables, charts or diagrams can make patterns in the research stand out more forcefully. It therefore helps you to see what your research has discovered, as well as enabling anyone who reads the assignment to grasp more clearly the results of your research. The ability to construct and interpret statistical diagrams is also a requirement of the Core Skills Unit 'Application of number'. It is important, however, to choose the right form of presentation. You should consider carefully the advantages and disadvantages of the alternatives available to you and decide which method of presentation is the most appropriate for the findings you have to present.

Grouping data

Data needs to be **grouped** and classified before it can be analysed. This means sorting the bits of information you have obtained into logical groupings. If a small range of figures or responses is involved this is usually straightforward. If for instance you asked visitors to a resort to grade the quality of information they had received *before* reaching their destination on a scale of 1 (inadequate) to 4 (excellent), you would only need to sort the responses into these four categories. Here the groupings suggest themselves, but if a large range of figures is involved you need to reduce them to a smaller number of groupings.

Imagine for instance that in a survey, 1,000 adults were asked to fill in a questionnaire. Their responses would be easier to analyse if you put them into groups according to age. Usually you need around 5–10 groupings. Fewer than this may mean you are generalizing too much and obscuring the details of your findings; more than this and the purpose of grouping the data (which is to make it more manageable by summarizing it) begins to be lost. You also need to ensure that each grouping covers a similar range. In this case you might use the following groupings:

> 18 and under 30 years
> 30 and under 40 years
> 40 and under 50 years
> 50 and under 60 years
> 60 and under 70 years
> 70 and under 80 years
> 80 years and above.

Tables

A **table** is defined as an arrangement of data in labelled rows and columns. The main purposes of presenting data using a table format are:
- To present crude data in an orderly manner
- To make it easier to identify trends
- To summarize different types of information

Each table should include all that is relevant but exclude anything which is unnecessary. All tables must be clearly labelled, units marked and the source of data given, as in the table below looking at the age distribution of different ethnic groups in Great Britain.

Great Britain

| | Age group (percentages) | | | | |
	0–15	16–29	30–44	45–59	60 and over
Ethnic group					
West Indian or Guyanese	24	30	19	19	9
Indian	29	25	25	14	6
Pakistani	44	23	20	11	3
Bangladeshi	46	26	15	11	3
Chinese	25	28	29	13	5
African	31	28	28	10	2
Arab	23	30	33	9	5
Mixed	54	24	13	6	3
Other	27	27	31	10	4
All ethnic minority groups	34	26	22	13	5
White	19	21	21	17	21
Not stated	36	22	16	11	15
All ethnic groups[a]	20	22	21	17	20

[a]Including White and Not stated.   (*Social Trends* 1993)

Table 9.1   The Age Distribution of Different Ethnic Groups in Great Britain.

Line graphs

Line graphs are one way of showing changes and trends more clearly. They can be used to indicate the relationship between two variables. In the case of a teenage drinking survey, for example, you want to establish if there is any significant relationship between the ages of teenagers and the amount that they drink. A line graph will help you to see if your findings suggest there is such a relationship.

The first stage in constructing a line graph is to sort your data into two groups of figures. One of these groups will be plotted on the horizontal axis (known as the x axis) and the other on the vertical axis (known as the y axis). It is usual to place the *dependent variable* on the y axis and the *independent variable* on the x axis. Essentially, the dependent variable is something that is determined by, or depends upon, another variable. In the case of the teenage drinking survey, the dependent variable is the amount of alcohol consumed because its value depends upon the age of the teenagers concerned. The opposite is clearly not true – the age of the teenagers does not in any way depend upon the amount that they drink. The age of the teenagers is therefore the independent variable and is plotted along the horizontal axis.

Next you must choose a *scale* for each of your axes. The point at which your axes cross is referred to as the *origin* and it is usual for all variables to have a value of zero at the origin. Bearing this in mind your scale should be large enough to make clear the way in which the variable you are plotting has behaved over time. Sometimes the choice of a scale is easy, but what if the first observation you wish to plot has a value of several thousand million pounds? This would be the case if you were plotting UK expenditure on consumer goods and services over time. Some information on the way this has changed over time is given in Fig. 9.1. Note the use of a zig-zag to break the y axis enabling us to show the range £62m–£75m. Without the zig-zag, our line graph would occupy such a small proportion of the diagram it would be less clear and considerably more difficult to interpret.

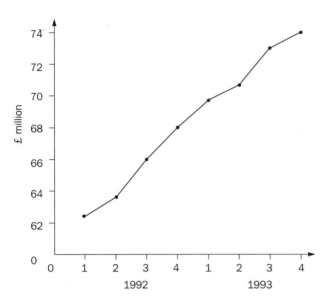

Figure 9.1 Line graph of quarterly expenditure of UK consumers.
Source: Economic Trends, February, 1994, HMSO.

Line graphs are popular because they highlight *trends* and *relationships* in data that are not so easy to spot if data are simply presented in the form of a table. When constructing your own line graphs remember the following points of good practice:

- Label your axes showing clearly the units of measurement. For example, the variable on your *x* axis might be time and this might be measured in quarters of a year as in Fig. 9.1.
- Give the original source of the information plotted.
- Give the graph a title indicating what it shows.
- Plot the *independent variable* on the *x* axis. This variable should be the one that is changed to assess the impact on a different (*dependent*) variable.
- Plot the *dependent variable* on the *y* axis.
- Choose a scale that enables you to identify changes in the dependent variable.
- When the same axes are used to plot more than one graph, draw each graph in a *different colour* so that they are easily distinguished. Remember to include a *key* showing which variable is shown by which graph.

Bar charts

These are one of the most widely used techniques for presenting economic data related to leisure and tourism. It is possible that you will want to use a **bar chart** in your assignment. It is therefore important for you to understand how to construct one. However, it is also important for you to understand how to interpret a bar chart, since you are almost certain to come across them when you examine economic data.

Bar charts can either be drawn vertically or horizontally. Which is preferable is a matter of personal choice, though vertical bar charts are more commonly used. Whichever way you present information, it is important that you give your diagram a *title* and a *scale*. You should also ensure that the original *source* of your information is given.

A bar chart can be used to show the importance of the *different components of a given aggregate*. For example, we could use a bar chart to show the *proportion* of an individual's expenditure on a given day on different goods and services purchased. Thus, an individual's total purchases can be itemized as:

Bus fares	£1.20	Stationery	£1.25
Lunch	£0.80	Refreshments	£0.75

This can be represented in the form of a bar chart, as in Fig. 9.2. More usually, there are three main types of bar chart you can use:

1 Simple bar chart
2 Component bar chart
3 Multiple bar chart

A **simple bar chart** is a set of non-joining bars of equal width whose height is proportional to the frequency it is represent-

Figure 9.2 Bar chart

ing. They can be drawn in a vertical or horizontal format and can show negative as well as positive values (Fig. 9.3).

A **component** or **segmented bar chart** is useful to illustrate a breakdown in the figures, e.g. the total sales of XYZ Co. could be broken down into sales by product (see Fig. 9.4). The constituent parts of each bar are always stacked in the same order with the height of each part representing the values of sales of that product.

A **multiple bar chart** uses a separate bar to represent each constituent part of the total. The data in Fig. 9.4 can be represented in multiple bar chart form (see Fig. 9.5).

Pie charts

A **pie chart** is a circle divided into segments. The circle represents a whole number, and each segment represents a share or proportion of that number. We can use the information in Fig. 9.2 above and show it this time as a pie chart so that at a glance you can see the proportion of the individual's expenditure spent on each item.

To construct a pie chart you will need a compass and a protractor. Let us use the information about personal expenditure

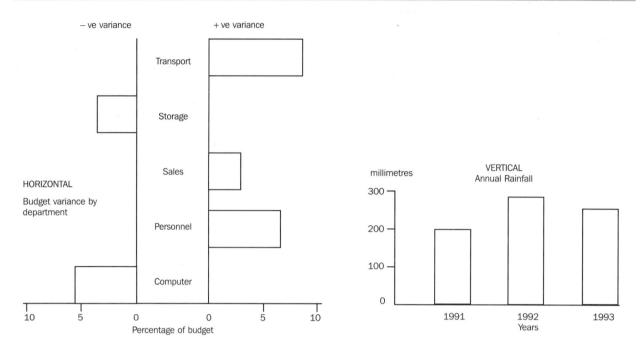

Figure 9.3 Simple bar charts

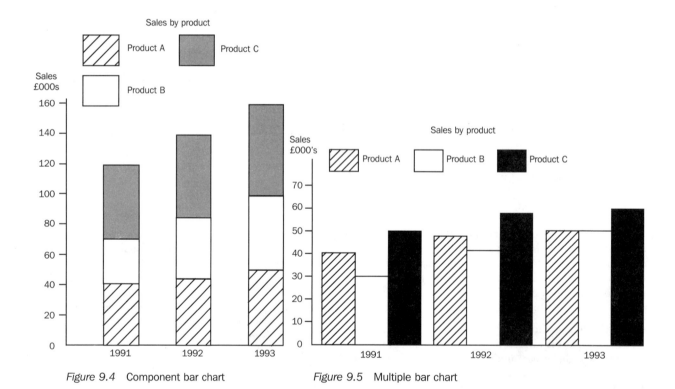

Figure 9.4 Component bar chart

Figure 9.5 Multiple bar chart

given on page 189 as an example. First you must draw a circle of any radius – it must, of course, be big enough to enable you to illustrate the information you intend to illustrate! The circle represents the total. In our case it represents total spending by an individual on a given day. The problem now is to divide the circle into its component parts, i.e. expenditure on bus fares, lunch and so on. This is where you will need your protractor. There are 360° in a circle, and therefore each component of the circle has to be represented as a *proportion* of 360°. Refer to the information given on page 189 and you will see that total spending on

this day was £4 of which £1.20 was spent on bus fares. We can calculate what percentage of total spending this represents:

$$\frac{£1.20}{£4.00} \times 100 = 30\%$$

This means that the segment of our pie chart which represents expenditure on *bus fares* is equal to 30% of the area of the circle. To be able to draw this segment we must first multiply 360° by 30%.

$$\frac{30}{100} \times 360° = 108°$$

Now find the mid-point of the circle and draw a radius. Next, use your protractor to mark of an angle of 108° and draw another radius to that point, so that the angle between the two radii you have drawn is 108°.

To obtain the next segment of the pie chart simply repeat the procedure. For example, as a percentage of total expenditure, *lunch* is equal to £0.80/£4.00 × 100 = 20%. This means we require an angle of 20/100 × 360° = 72°. Taking your protractor and using one of the radii you have already drawn, mark off an angle 72°. Draw another radius such that the angle between the radius you have constructed and the one you have previously drawn, is 72°.

Figure 9.6 represents the expenditure of our individual as a pie chart. To help you we show the *angles* as well as the *percentage contribution* of each component.

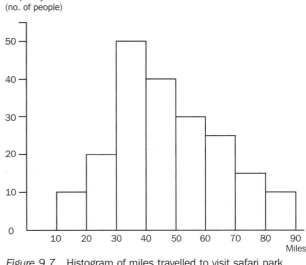

Figure 9.7 Histogram of miles travelled to visit safari park

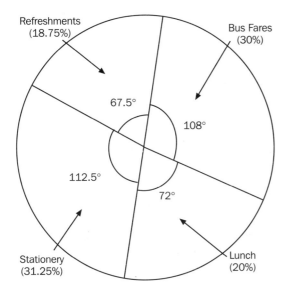

Figure 9.6 Pie chart

Histogram

Visually, **histograms** are similar to bar charts except the bars connect together rather than having spaces between them. They are used to present **continuous data** rather than data that has been divided into *categories*, such as products A, B and C. The histogram is a set of *rectangles*, with the *area* of each rectangle representing the frequency of a particular class interval. From the histogram we can gain a quick visual impression as to where the bulk of the distribution lies. For example, in Fig. 9.7 we can see that most people (50) in the survey have travelled between 30 and 40 miles to visit the Safari Park.

Because the *areas* of each rectangle are proportional to the class frequencies, you must remember to adjust the *height* of any rectangle where the *base* (class interval) is different from that of the other rectangles. For example, if one rectangle had 20 miles instead of 10 miles for its base, then you would need to *halve* the height (frequency) of the rectangle since the base was *double* that of other rectangles.

Scattergrams and correlation

A **scattergram** is a useful diagram for indicating the type of relationship (if any) between two variables. Each point on the scattergram is a *co-ordinate*, i.e. the value of *x* and *y* represented as a point on the diagram. If variables *are* related, we often use the term **correlation** between the variables.

In Fig. 9.8(a) there is a *positive correlation* between the two variables: both tend to rise (or fall) together. In Fig. 9.8(b) there is a *negative correlation* between the two variables: as one variable rises, the other falls. In Fig. 9.8(c) there is *no correlation* between the two variables.

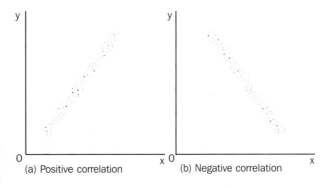

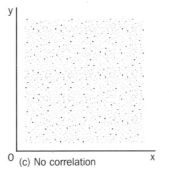

Figure 9.8 Types of scattergram

Scattergrams are useful because they can give a quick visual impression of the relationship between two variables. However, you should remember that a strong correlation between two variables does not necessarily mean that the relationship between them is one of cause and effect – an increase in one variable is not necessarily the reason for the increase or decrease in the other. The correlation may be the result of other factors or of coincidence.

Analysing information and data

Once you have undertaken research and collected together relevant data for an assignment, you need to **analyse** the results of your research and present your findings in a logical and coherent manner. While you will hope in your completed assignment to display your writing skills, some of your assignments will also need to incorporate diagrams and statistical analysis. Here we concentrate on some of the numerical and statistical ways in which you can make sense of your information and data.

Fractions, decimals and percentages

Fractions, decimals and percentages are all ways of expressing parts or divisions of a whole.

Fractions are calculated by dividing the number that refers to the part by the number that refers to the whole. Thus if a survey found that one out of four guests in a hotel was dissatisfied with the meals served, we can express this as a fraction: $\frac{1}{4}$. If the number referring to the part and the number referring to the whole have a common denominator, i.e. a number by which both can be divided, we divide the two numbers by the common denominator. Thus if instead of one out of four guests our findings involved three out of twelve guests, we would first express this in fraction form as $\frac{3}{12}$. As 3 is the common denominator and of 3 and 12 we divide both numbers by 3 and arrive again at $\frac{1}{4}$. The fraction is the same in both cases because the proportion of guests expressing dissatisfaction (i.e. the part or division of the whole) is the same in both instances.

Fractions can be a useful way of simplifying your findings or of making a trend or pattern in the findings more obvious. If you conducted a survey in a holiday resort, for example, and found that 37 out of 72 people questioned considered the leisure information they had received to be inadequate, you might observe in your discussion of the findings that 'around half of the people interviewed felt that the leisure information they had received had been inadequate'.

A **decimal** is a fraction with a denominator of 10, or of some power of 10 such as 100, 1000 and so on. A decimal is calculated by dividing the upper part of a fraction by the lower part, adding noughts to the upper number as required. Before the first nought is added a decimal point is inserted in your answer and for each additional nought the point is moved one place further to the left. Thus $\frac{1}{4}$ can be converted to a decimal as follows:

$$\frac{1}{4} = \frac{1.0}{4} = \frac{1.00}{4} = 0.25$$

We find a **percentage** by multiplying the decimal (or fraction) by 100.

$$0.25 \times 100 = 25\%$$

Again these calculations can easily be performed on a calculator. In the first of the above examples the stages in the calculation are:

$$1 \div 4 \times 100 = 25\%$$

Percentages are useful in analysing the responses to questions in a questionnaire. If for example a survey found that seven out of thirty-two mothers questioned at a playgroup found the facilities unsatisfactory, this could be expressed as a percentage. The part (7) is divided by the whole (32) and the resulting fraction is multiplied by 100:

$$\frac{7}{32} \times 100 = 21.875\%$$

It is the usual practice to express such percentages to the nearest whole number, or to one decimal place. This is done by rounding figures of 5 or more up, and figures that are less than 5 down. The above percentage therefore becomes:

22% to the nearest whole number
21.9% to one decimal place

Percentages can also be used to express the response rate to a questionnaire. If you distribute 100 questionnaires and 83 are returned, the response rate would be 83%. A further use of percentages is to make your findings easier to comprehend. Imagine, for example, that you have found out from your local authority that the most recent estimate of the population of the borough in which you live is 115,073. These are distributed among the following types of property:

52,203	owner-occupied properties
37,411	council-owned properties
21,879	private rented accommodation
3,580	other accommodation / unaccounted for

These figures might be easier to grasp if they were expressed as percentages:

45%	owner-occupied properties
33%	council-owned properties
19%	private rented accommodation
3%	other accommodation / unaccounted for

Averages

When you have a group of figures or scores it is often useful to have one figure which indicates the overall tendency. In everyday language this is known as an **average**, but in statistics there are different kinds of average, including *mean*, *median* and *mode*.

- **Mean:** The most commonly used in the mean, which is the simple arithmetic average. It is calculated by adding all the scores and dividing the total by the number of scores. Imagine for example that you asked 10 teenage smokers to record how many cigarettes they smoked on a particular day and the reported totals were as follows:

5, 15, 12, 40, 10, 10, 4, 9, 5, 10

The mean is calculated by adding these scores and dividing by the number of scores:

$$120 \div 10 = 12$$

An advantage of the mean is that it takes into account all the individual scores. A disadvantage is that extreme scores can influence the mean so that the mean actually gives a misleading impression. In the above example, there is one extreme score – 40 – and this makes the mean greater than it would otherwise be. If the score of 40 were omitted, the mean of the other scores would be 9 (to the nearest whole number). If a report on these findings stated 'On average the teenagers in the survey smoked 12 cigarettes a day' this would be quite misleading as in fact only three of the teenagers smoked 12 or more cigarettes.

- **Median:** The median is the middle score of a group of scores. It is found by placing the scores in numerical order and identifying the number that is in the middle. Thus if eleven scores were arranged in numerical order the median would be the sixth score because this would have five scores to the left of it and five scores to the right. If there are an even number of scores the median is the arithmetic average (the mean) of the two middle numbers. To return to the above example, if we place the scores in numerical order we have the following:

  4, 5, 5, 9, 10, 10, 10, 12, 15, 40

  As there are an even number of scores there is not a single middle number but two (10 and 10). The mean of these two numbers is 10, which is therefore the median. (If the middle numbers were 10 and 12, the median would be 11; if they were 10 and 11, the median would be 10.5.)

  An advantage of the median is that it is less influenced than the mean by extreme scores and is therefore more representative than the mean when there are extreme scores. In the example of the smoking survey, 10 cigarettes per day is a more representative average score than 12 cigarettes per day. A disadvantage however is that it is mathematically less precise than the mean and does not give a true arithmetic average.

- **Mode:** The mode is simply the number that occurs most frequently in any given set of scores. Thus if we take the original set of scores in the smoking survey

  5, 15, 12, 40, 10, 10, 4, 9, 5, 10

  the mode is 10, because this score occurs three times, which is more frequently than any of the other scores. An advantage of the mode is that it is usually easy to find. However, difficulties arise if the same rate of frequency is shared by more than one number. It is also a crude measure of the average score, especially if there is not a great difference in the frequencies of the scores (in the above example, 5 occurs almost as frequently as 10).

If you mention an average in an assignment, always explain whether it is a mean, median or mode. If the average seems in any way unrepresentative or misleading (if it has been distorted by an extreme score, for example) point this out also.

Range and standard deviation

As well as the *average* we are often interested in how the data are distributed (or *dispersed*) around the average. The *range* and *standard deviation* are ways of indicating how scores are distributed within a set of figures. They are useful because they can show if the scores are close together or far apart.

- **Range:** The range is the difference between the highest and lowest scores. In the smoking survey the highest score was 40 and the lowest 5, so the range was 35:

  40 − 5 = 35

  A disadvantage of the range is that it only uses the extreme scores and so can give a misleading impression if one number is markedly higher or lower than the

rest. In the smoking survey, the range becomes very different if we omit 40 from the list of scores. The lowest number is still 5 but the highest now is 15, so the range drops to 10. This original range (35) was misleading because it implied that the scores were more highly scattered than they in fact are.

- **Standard deviation:** A more satisfactory measure of distribution is the *standard deviation*. This is a measure of the spread of scores around the mean value. If the scores are grouped closely around the mean value, the standard deviation is small. If the scores are widely distributed, the standard deviation is large. The distribution curves in Fig. 9.9 represent large and small standard deviations. The small standard deviation curve indicates that most of the scores are close together; the large standard deviation curve indicates that they are spread quite widely.

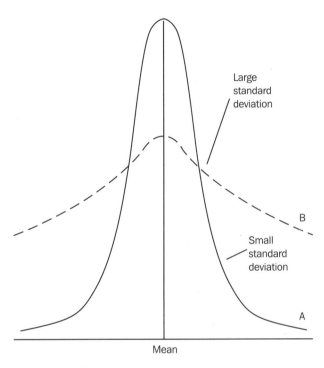

Figure 9.9 Dispersion around the average (mean)

Although a knowledge of range is a GNVQ requirement, a knowledge of standard deviation is not. However, you may wish to make use of the concept of standard deviation in your assignments. You should be able to find a more detailed explanation of standard deviation in any book on statistics, or your teacher may be able to help.

Spreadsheets

Many of the calculations we have been discussing in this 'Analysing information and data' section can be performed on a computer using a spreadsheet program. A **spreadsheet** is a program for handling numerical information. On screen it appears as a grid of boxes or 'cells', each of which can contain a number or a formula to act upon the contents of other cells. For example, a very simple calculation would be to add the numbers in two cells together; another would be to express one number as a percentage of another, or as a percentage of the total of all the numbers on the spreadsheet. Not only can a spreadsheet perform a large range of calculations, it can also present numerical information that has been entered, and the results of calculations that have been carried out, as charts and graphs.

This section on presenting and analysis data is by no means exhaustive of all the possibilities. Nevertheless it has covered many of the ways in which you can provide *evidence* of the *core skills* of communication, application of number and information technology. Using such techniques can also help in providing evidence of the *themes* required if you are to be awarded a merit or distinction. It is to these that we now turn.

Assessment criteria for pass, merit and distinction

To achieve a pass, merit or distinction, your portfolio must contain consistent evidence which covers the following three **themes**:

- Planning
- Information seeking and handling
- Evaluation

NB A fourth theme 'quality' is being introduced at Advanced GNVQ level. Check with your tutor.

You will be given the chance to develop these skills throughout your programme of study and should be given the opportunity to add further evidence to your portfolio.

Some of the assessments you are given to complete may not be appropriate for obtaining a merit or distinction. For example, if all of the activities that you need to complete are listed clearly for you and do not require you to obtain any further information, then this may not fall into the category of a graded assessment. Although some of your assessments may be categorised as pass only, your tutor will give you sufficient opportunities to allow you to obtain a *merit* or *distinction* grade overall.

For an assessment to be of a **merit standard**, the tasks you undertake must be *discrete* and for a **distinction** the tasks must be *complex*.

Discrete' means that:

- The tasks are self-contained
- The overall method of working is well defined
- The number of different things you have to do within the task is limited

'**Complex**', on the other hand, means that:

- You often are asked to deal with a number of inter-related tasks
- You will be expected to define the problem, method of working, targets, timescale, etc., rather than having this information presented to you
- The problem you are asked to work on will contain a number of complicated activities

Your tutor will tell you whether the assessment you are given will qualify for a merit or distinction. The criteria (standards) needed for you to obtain a merit or distinction in your assessments are shown in the table below.

You will notice from the table that one of the main differences between merit and distinction grading is the ability of a student to work on his or her *own initiative*. Grading at merit level implies a greater input to your work from your tutors than is the case with grading at distinction level, where more independent action is rewarded.

Merit (discrete tasks)	Distinction (complex tasks)
Planning	
1 Draw up plans and prioritize your work on your own	Draw up plans and prioritize your work on your own
2 Be able to monitor and perhaps revise your plan of action with the guidance of your tutor	Be able to monitor and perhaps revise your plan of action on your own
Information seeking and handling	
3 On your own be able to identify, access and collect information from main sources and use additional sources provided by your tutor	On your own be able to identify, access and collect information from a range of sources and justify your selection
4 On your own check the validity of the information using methods given to you	On your own check the validity of the information applying your own methods
Evaluation	
5 You must be able to judge outcomes and identify and apply alternative criteria	You must be able to judge outcomes and identify and apply a range of alternative criteria
6 You must be able to justify how you have approached the assessment	You must be able to justify your approaches pointing out the advantages and disadvantages

Table 9.2 Criteria for obtaining a merit or distinction.

Planning

In **planning** your work you must write down how you intend to approach and monitor the tasks given, before you start on the tasks. To begin with, we suggest that you:

1 Read carefully through the activity/tasks that you have to complete.
2 Read through the material again and start to think about what it entails.
3 Have a short break and, at the same time, continue to think about what is required.
4 Get a piece of paper and write down the following:

  (i) The type of information you need to find out.
  (ii) What you need to do to get that information.
  (iii) In what order – some tasks will take longer than others. For instance you may have to write to an organization to ask for information. If so, you need to allow plenty of time for the information to be sent. Writing a letter of this type will need to be one of your earlier activities.

5 Having compiled your initial list, think about what you have written. Have you missed anything out? Are you sure that you have done them in the right order?
6 When you feel happy that everything is in order, rewrite your list in date order. To do this we suggest that you:

  (i) Work out the number of weeks you have been given to complete the tasks/activities.
  (ii) Make the last date your assignment 'hand in' date.
  (iii) Place the first task in and realistically estimate the time it will take to complete.
  (iv) Place the other tasks in order of priority

(v) Ensure you allow sufficient time to check your assignment before the 'hand in date'..

(vi) Check your plan and ask yourself the following questions:

- Have I allowed sufficient time for the tasks?
- Have I listed the tasks in the correct order?
- Have I allowed time to check my work?

It is imperative that you allow yourself sufficient time to check through your work, to correct any minor errors which could count against you. Many students receive lower grades because they do not plan their work. They think that they have 'lots of time' to complete the tasks and leave them to the 'last minute'. This results in them rushing the work, leaving things out or making silly mistakes.

Remember, you will be assessed on skills as well as performance criteria. Allow sufficient time to check your grammar, punctuation and spelling.

If you are asked to use information technology in the production of the activities/tasks, make sure that you build in 'hands on' time. Many students who have not planned their work effectively will make a 'last minute dash' to the IT workshops to wordprocess their work. This causes a great deal of anxiety and frustration as they often find that they cannot get access to a computer. Tutors and teachers often hear phrases such as:

I could not get onto a computer.

There was no printer paper left.

There was a 'bug' on the machine and I lost my work.

The printer ribbon/cartridge ran out and a replacement is not available until tomorrow.

I thought I could work on the computer today, but all the second year students were there.

Colleges and schools have a limited number of computers to cater for their students' needs. The number they have is calculated on an even throughput of student usage. If, for instance, 40 first year GNVQ advanced students all demand access to them at the same time, there is sure to be insufficient computer space, especially considering the other courses that need to use them and that are perhaps timetabled in to use them on that day. We cannot stress enough:

- ALLOW SUFFICIENT TIME TO COMPLETE ALL TASKS
- BUILD IN AN ACCURATE AMOUNT OF TIME FOR USING I.T. FACILITIES
- BUILD IN TIME TO CHECK YOUR WORK BEFORE THE HAND-IN DATE

7 Once you are sure of the above, build into your plan a column that will allow you to monitor your courses of action. You will need to state, against each activity or task whether you have achieved your completion date. If not, you need to identify the reason why and decide what you must now do to overcome this problem.

Figure 9.10 shows a complete **action plan** for a group assignment which involved developing a business plan to set up a leisure and tourism business. The students had to identify what information was needed to carry out the task, what they had to do to obtain the information, who was going to undertake which task and by when they expected to complete the tasks. Each member of the group had £20,000 to put into the venture; if they needed more, they could obtain a bank loan for up to half of the capital invested.

Action plans are an ideal way of keeping track of the progress of an assessment and checking that tasks are being completed on time.

Information seeking and information handling

A good way of identifying possible **sources of information** is to write down any that immediately spring to mind. This is called 'brainstorming' and is often used in leisure and tourism organizations. The idea is to list anything that comes to mind; don't think about it too much or this may limit the exercise. Having completed your brainstorming session, you can start to identify (or dismiss) the relevant or irrelevant sources. It is then time for a short break to clear your mind. Come back to the task and carefully check your list until you are happy that the relevant sources have been included. Below we have identified some of the sources that we think may help you in the skill of information seeking:

- Books
- Magazines
- Catalogues
- Leaflets
- Brochures
- Newspapers
- Trade catalogues
- Libraries
- Dictionaries
- Databases
- Businesses/work placement providers/part time employers
- Parents and relatives
- Observation
- Questionnaires
- Yellow pages
- Radio and television
- Exhibitions

The important points to remember about any information you collect are that it must be relevant, it must be valid and it must be current. You will need to consult your information sources regularly to ensure that you have collected sufficient to enable you to complete the tasks. Quite often, students leave this part of their assessments too late; you must make sure that you sustain the momentum of information collection and do not just rely on an initial burst of enthusiasm. It is no good realizing that you are missing vital information the day the assessment has to be completed. Tutors often hear these sorts of comments from their students:

I thought I had all the information I needed.

I didn't realise that I needed to collect information on that task.

I collected lots of information, but when it came to completing the tasks I was missing some.

How to list research and information sources

You must *list* all the sources of information you use, whether from a book, an interview or a television programme, for example. Remember, this will form part of your evidence for your grading themes and will be used by your tutor and the external verifier in the assessment of your work. It is a good

ACTION PLAN Group members: Kay Smith, John Ford, Indira Singh				
What we need to find out	What we need to do	Date to be completed	Date completed	Completed by
Business activity we could run	Brain storm – business ideas, taking into account our skills and expertise	Jan 26	Jan 26	All
Types of business formations	Decide on the formation of the organization	Jan 27	Jan 27	All
How to produce CV	Produce C.V's – book IT time	Feb 3	Feb 2	All
Whether business is feasible	Talk to organizations	Feb 4	Feb 14	All
Businesss formation for our group	Write up the introduction	Feb 5	Feb 15	Kay
Memorandum of association	Visit library, use class notes,write up memorandum	Feb 5	Feb 15	John
Articles of association	As above	Feb 5	Feb 15	Indira
Market research	Research, class notes, look at types of methods	Feb 19	Feb 21	Indira
Questionnaires	Produce draft questionnaire	Feb 21	Feb 28	Kay and John
As above	Analyse questionnaires	Mar 4	Mar 4	All
Research for suitable premises	Look in newspapers, commercial estate agents	Mar 9	Mar 10	Indira
Advertising techniques	Class notes, results of questionnaires, books, look at types of advertising used by other companies	Mar 12	Mar 13	John
Find out costs of advertising	Find prices of: radio, newspaper, leaflet drops, hoardings, bus advertising	Mar 14	Mar 14	All
Contents of a projected cash flow	Draw on formal input, class notes, obtain bank. Start your own business pack	Mar 14	Mar14	Kay
How to create a corporate image	Produce business cards, decide on logo, decide on letter heads	Mar 14	Mar 16	All
Best way of producing posters etc.	Produce posters etc. for advertising	Mar 14	Mar 16	All
Costs associated with above	Use information already obtained for premises, find costs of heat and light, wages. Trade catalogues for cost of office equipment. Use other sources for cost of producing service	Mar 19	Mar 19	John and Kay
Cash flow production	Produce projected cash flow	Mar 25	Mar 26	John
Profit and loss and balance sheet production	Draw on formal input, class notes	Mar 28	Mar 29	Indira
Potential of business	Produce an evaluation – identify whether business is profitable and liquid. Decide on potential and write conclusion	Mar 30	Mar 30	All

Figure 9.10   A typical action plan for an assessment

idea to make use of a *diary* for this part of your work, listing information sources on a day-by-day basis. You should record your information sources for inclusion in your portfolio in the following manner:

- **Book** – state the name of the author, title of the book, date of publication and the name of the publisher.

- **Newspapers and magazines** – state the name of the author, title of the article, name of the newspaper/magazine, date of publication.

- **Quotes** – in addition to the above information, quotes must include the page number of the publications from which they are taken.

- **Interviews** – state the name of the person with whom the interview took place, the reason for the interview, the date it took place and where the interview was carried out. Remember that interviews and discussions can take place with many different people, e.g. owners of businesses, public sector officials, parents, tutors, etc.

- **Radio and television** – state the programme name, the channel or radio station, the date and time, as well as the nature of the programme and details of any relevant individuals who took part.

Quite often you will need to write to various organizations to collect information to help you with your assessments. Make sure you include copies of any letters you send and any replies you receive. Even if you don't receive any information back, the fact that you have tried will count in your favour.

Evaluation

Evaluation is the third of the grading themes that your evidence will be assessed against. While planning and information seeking/handling are relatively easy to understand, evaluating the work that you have done can sometimes be a little daunting. You may find yourself thinking:

> How can I evaluate my work when I don't know where I may have gone wrong and haven't yet had any feedback from tutors?

This is a natural reaction and one which you should not become worried about. It is important to remember that you are expected to develop the skill areas of planning, information seeking/handling and evaluating throughout your course of study; nobody expects you to get everything right first time! To begin with, you will be guided by your tutors and teachers who will help you with evaluation and the other grading themes. As time progresses, you will gradually take on this responsibility yourself, so that you can work towards completing all tasks proficiently on your own.

What is evaluation?
In terms of your Advanced GNVQ in Leisure and Tourism, *evaluation* is the way you look back at:

- The tasks you have completed.
- The activities you have undertaken.
- The decisions you have taken in the course of your work.
- Any alternative courses of action open to you.
- The implications of the particular actions you carried out.

When evaluating your work, you must be able to justify how you have approached the tasks. You should get into the habit of writing down why you thought it was necessary to complete tasks in a particular way and how you expected to achieve those tasks. You should ask yourself questions, such as:

- What were the advantages in tackling the assessment in this way?
- What were the disadvantages?
- If I was given the chance to do the work again, what would I change?
- What areas need improvement?
- How could the improvements be implemented?
- Which areas am I satisfied with and why?
- Which areas am I dissatisfied with and why?
- Would I complete the tasks in the same order?
- Did I allow myself enough time for information collection?
- Did I allow myself sufficient time for IT inputs to the work?
- Did I check my sources of information?
- Would I try to obtain further or different information next time?

Being able to evaluate your own work critically requires time and training; many senior managers working in the leisure and tourism industry find it a very difficult task! If you adopt a structured approach to the problem, using the type of questions listed above, you will be a long way towards developing your skills of evaluation.

Sample assessments

This section will give you an understanding of how assessments are structured and how you can ensure the best possible grade for your own pieces of work. Completing assessments shows that you have met the requirements of mandatory, optional and additional units on your GNVQ. Although the external tests for the mandatory units are important and must be passed, most of the work that you will do on your Advanced GNVQ in Leisure and Tourism will revolve around the type of assessments we will be looking at in this section. In particular, we will look at:

---

1 The structure of typical assessments.
2 How the assessments meet the requirements of the units.
3 Pointers to make sure that you achieve the best possible grade.

We will look in detail at two sample assessments covering the following units:

- Mandatory Unit 1
- Mandatory Unit 4

Using the information and advice given for these two units, you will be able to develop action plans for tackling all the assessments you will be expected to complete for your Advanced GNVQ in Leisure and Tourism.

Mandatory Unit 1 – investigating the leisure and tourism industry

You will notice from the specification for this unit that it covers a very broad range of topics and aims to give you a general appreciation of the scope and nature of the leisure and tourism industry. Much of what you learn from completing tasks and assessments for this unit will prove invaluable in helping you to tackle work in the other mandatory, optional and additional units that you study. The precise way in which tutors plan the assessments for mandatory Unit 1 will vary between one school or college and another, but it is likely that the structure of any assessment will be similar to the following example.

Sample assessment

Advanced GNVQ in Leisure and Tourism

Mandatory Unit Assessment

UNIT: 1 Investigating the Leisure and Tourism Industry

ASSESSMENT TITLE: Leisureview UK

RATIONALE AND AIMS

This unit assessment provides you with the opportunity to demonstrate the skills and knowledge outlined in Unit 1, Investigating the Leisure and Tourism Industry. During your work on this assessment, you will be able to demonstrate successful achievement in the three core skill areas of communication, application of number and information technology. In particular, you will be able to:

- Demonstrate an ability to analyse relevant sources of information.
- Reflect on the past development of the UK leisure and tourism industry.
- Analyse present and likely future trends in the different industry contexts.

You will be expected to:

- Undertake desk research into past, present and future developments in the leisure and tourism industry.
- Investigate local, national and international leisure and tourism provision.
- Gather and present up-to-date information on the funding of the leisure and tourism industry.

BACKGROUND

Context

Leisureview UK is a small company specializing in leisure and tourism consultancy services for private and public sector organizations. The Managing Director is Jim Bell, who previously worked for 18 years in local authority leisure services. The company employs a team of six full-time staff, with other specialists being employed on a contract basis depending on the nature of the work in hand.

Circumstances

Leisureview has just been awarded a substantial contract to provide technical information and advice to a number of private and public sector leisure and tourism organizations located throughout England and Wales. The organizations have been successful in gaining funds from the European Union to carry out a number of feasibility studies in their areas, to investigate the economic potential of increasing their involvement in leisure and tourism developments. Leisureview will carry out some of the feasibility studies and provide general information and advice.

Role

You have been employed as a research assistant reporting directly to the head of research at Leisureview.

Your Tasks

Task One

Before the leisure and tourism organizations can make any firm decisions about how best to invest in facilities and products, they need detailed and up-to-date information on the leisure and tourism industry.

Working on your own, you are to prepare an initial report for the head of research, focusing on the scale and context of the leisure and tourism industry. The report should be wordprocessed and use appropriate displays of statistical information. The report is to be supported by an oral presentation.

(a) Use a range of publications and information sources to identify and comment on the following:
- Recent historical developments in leisure and tourism.
- The current patterns of leisure and tourism activity of the UK population and leisure and tourism provision in selected European countries.
- The importance of the different contexts of the leisure and tourism industry.
- The factors that influence an individual's participation in leisure and tourism.
- Future trends in the industry.

(b) The organizations are particularly interested to know about employment in the leisure and tourism industry, both nationally and locally. Using a range of data sources, you are to identify and comment on the following:
- The trends in employment in all contexts of the UK leisure and tourism industry.
- The career opportunities that the industry can offer.
- The skills needed to be an effective employee in leisure and tourism.

(c) Being aware of the competition from other leisure and tourism organizations will be important in terms of planning products and facilities that are likely to be successful. Part of your initial report, therefore, should focus on existing UK leisure and tourism products. In particular, you should:
- Investigate the main products in all contexts of the industry and analyse their relative importance.
- Identify on a map the principal tourist receiving areas in the UK.
- Investigate the UK travel infrastructure.
- Analyse the effects of climate, topography and other physical factors on the development of leisure and tourism products.

Task Two

A sound information base is essential if the leisure and tourism organizations are to be able to plan effectively for the future. Their knowledge of what is going on in their local areas in terms of leisure and tourism is very patchy and much of the data is out of date.

Working as a member of a group, you are to investigate the range of leisure and tourism facilities, products and services that exist in your local area and analyse the impact that they have on the local environment and local people. Your findings are to be presented in the form of a set of factsheets, to be used by the members and officers of the local council and local businesses interested in getting involved in leisure and tourism. In researching and compiling your factsheets, you should pay particular attention to:

- How the needs of different types of customers are satisfied.
- Whether the facility, product or service is provided by a public, private or voluntary sector organization.
- The variety of facilities, products and services in the various contexts of the leisure and tourism industry.
- The various types of impacts, both positive and negative, that are evident locally in terms of the leisure and tourism industry.

Task Three

All of the leisure and tourism organizations will be keen to have as much advice as possible on the financial aspects of operating leisure and tourism facilities, products and services.

Working on your own, you are to prepare an initial report for the head of research on the various sources of income available to leisure and tourism organizations. The report should be word processed and use appropriate displays of statistical information. Using a range of publications and information sources, your report should identify and comment on the following:

- Sources of income for different sectors of the leisure and tourism industry.
- Sources of income for different contexts of the leisure and tourism industry.
- The relative importance of different income sources to leisure and tourism organizations.

How does this assessment meet the requirements of the unit?

In order to be able to answer this question fully, you will need to look at the printed *specification* for the unit and match the tasks in the assessment to the elements, performance criteria and range statements given in the specification. You will also need to refer to the specifications for the Core Skill Units. If you do not already have copies of these, ask your tutor or teacher. They are also available direct from the three awarding bodies. Figure 9.11 shows how the tasks you are asked to undertake and the resulting evidence you provide meet the particular requirements of the unit. This sort of information is often contained in a frontsheet which will be attached to the assessment when it is handed out by your tutor.

Some assessments you are given will cover all the elements and performance criteria for a particular unit. This is the case with the example on Unit 1 included in this section. Assessments such as these will involve you in a lot of research and collection of information. Others will focus on a particular element or performance criteria, involving less information gathering and presentation, but still contributing to the overall achievement of a particular unit. Make sure you are clear what the assessments or activities that you are given are planned to achieve; you will get no credit for gathering evidence which is not relevant to the assessment!

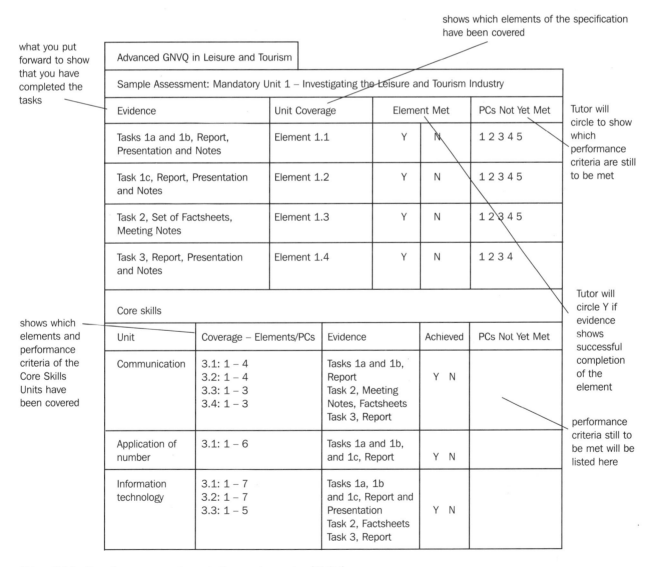

Figure 9.11   How the assessment meets the requirements of Unit 1

Pointers to achieving a good grade

Earlier we looked at the general principles concerning grading in GNVQs. Put very simply, satisfying the requirements of the eight mandatory units, four optional units and three core skill units, will mean that you will be awarded a pass grade in your Advanced GNVQ in Leisure and Tourism. You can gain a merit or distinction grade **for the whole award**, however, by:

- For a **merit award** – producing at least one-third of your portfolio of evidence at merit standard.
- For a **distinction award** – producing at least one-third of your portfolio of evidence at distinction standard.

In deciding whether your portfolio of evidence falls into either of the above categories, your tutors and the external verifier will judge it against the following three factors:

- **Planning** – how well you planned your work.
- **Information seeking and handling** – the relevance and reliability of the information you collected and presented.
- **Evaluation** – how well you have justified your actions and whether alternative courses of action were investigated.

These three areas of planning, information seeking and handling, and evaluation are investigated more fully earlier in this chapter (see pages 194–197).

Carrying out the sample assessment for Unit 1

It is important that you make good use of your time when completing your GNVQ assessments. For each piece of work, you must decide what needs to be done and the date by which it must be completed and, if your assessment involves group work, you should also indicate who is responsible for each task. This is best achieved by developing an **action plan** for each assessment (see page 196).

The boxes below indicate what you need to do when working on the sample assessment for Unit 1, to ensure that your finished work has the best chance of being considered of merit or distinction standard within your overall portfolio of evidence.

Element 1.2   Investigate UK leisure and tourism products

Performance criteria	Pointers to achieving a good grade
1.2.1 The principal UK leisure and tourism products and services in each context are described clearly and concisely using relevant and up-to-date sources of information.	Make sure you cover the full range of UK leisure and tourism products. Remember that 'products' can include purpose-built facilities as well as 'packaged' elements.
1.2.2 The principal UK receiving areas are correctly located and accurately described.	Include not only the 'traditional' seaside resorts, but also inland resorts located in urban and rural areas.
1.2.3 The travel infrastructure serving principal tourist receiving areas is accurately described.	Remember that infrastructure includes road, rail, air and port services and facilities.
1.2.4 Regional variations in participation levels in leisure activities are explained.	As well as including data on regional differences, give realistic analyses of why the variations exist.
1.2.5 The features and benefits of tourist receiving areas and leisure activities are described in relation to the needs and requirements of their principal customers.	Be sure to include a full range of both man-made and natural features and benefits as well as categorizing different customer types.

Element 1.1   Describe the scale and contexts of the leisure and tourism industry

Performance criteria	Pointers to achieving a good grade
1.1.1 Selected authoritative sources are used to describe the scale and contexts of the industry.	Make sure that the data you use are reliable, up to date and cover all contexts of the industry.
1.1.2 Past changes in scale are identified and explained.	Be careful that you not only refer to past developments in the industry, but also that you give reasons for why it has evolved in the manner that we now see.
1.1.3. Current trends in scale are identified and likely developments described.	Make sure that any future developments that you highlight are backed up with authoritative evidence and are not just your own 'hunches'.
1.1.4 Relationships between trends in different parts of the industry are accurately described.	Be sure to compare and contrast the relative importance of all contexts of the leisure and tourism industry.
1.1.5 The main areas of employment growth and decline and of career opportunities are identified.	State clearly which sectors and contexts have shown growth and decline in the recent past.

Element 1.3   Investigate the variety of local services and products

Performance criteria	Pointers to achieving a good grade
1.3.1 The main services and products represented locally in each context are correctly identified and described clearly and concisely.	Make sure that you include all contexts of the leisure and tourism industry found locally.
1.3.2 Local patterns of provision of services and availability of products in contexts and sectors are described.	Identify clearly whether the products and services are provided by public, private or voluntary sector organizations.
1.3.3 Key differences between the national and local components of each context are explained.	Include valid national data on the scale of the industry contexts to highlight local variations.
1.3.4 The responses of leisure and tourism facilities to the expectations and needs of different customer types are described and explained.	Be sure to consider individuals, groups, those with special needs, different cultural groups, members of clubs and societies.
1.3.5 The local impact of services and products is described clearly.	Make sure you include both positive and negative environmental, economic and socio-cultural impacts.

Element 1.4   Identify sources of income for leisure and tourism facilities

Performance criteria	Pointers to achieving a good grade
1.4.1 Information used to identify sources of income is current and reliable.	Be sure to use up-to-date sources of information, such as company reports, trade journals, local authority budget information etc.
1.4.2 Sources of income for different products and services are accurately and clearly described.	Remember to include a full range of both public and private sector sources of income.
1.4.3 Key common sources of income for similar types of facility are identified and explained.	Collect information across all sectors and contexts before looking for similarities in income sources.
1.4.4 The importance of different sources of income to facilities are described and explained.	Be sure to include information on how the size of leisure and tourism facilities can influence the importance of different

Taking note of the points listed above, and bearing in mind the three grading factors of planning, information seeking and handling, and evaluation, will ensure that the *evidence* you put forward for this sample assessment will give you every opportunity of producing work of a high standard, capable of contributing towards a merit or distinction grade for the overall award.

Mandatory Unit 4 – marketing in leisure and tourism

Being able to identify customers' needs and produce products and services to satisfy their requirements is a crucial part of success in the leisure and tourism industry. Marketing is considered by many people in the industry to be the most important part of their work; an organization may have the best leisure facilities or most exciting holiday products, but without effective marketing to develop and promote the right products and services it will not be completely successful. Mandatory Unit 4 will give you a broad understanding of the basic principles of marketing and how they are applied in the leisure and tourism industry.

Sample assessment

Advanced GNVQ in Leisure and Tourism

Mandatory Unit Assessment

UNIT: 4 Marketing in Leisure and Tourism

ASSESSMENT TITLE : Ski-scope

RATIONALE AND AIMS

This unit assessment provides you with the opportunity to demonstrate the skills and knowledge outlined in Unit 4, Marketing in Leisure and Tourism. The skills and knowledge developed while undertaking the assessment will enable you to operate competently at a junior level in a leisure and tourism organization with a marketing function. Completion of the

assessment will also offer the opportunity for further study, skills development and career progression. You will be able to:

- Analyse a range of information sources.
- Demonstrate an ability to analyse market research.
- Plan and evaluate promotional activities.

You will be expected to:

- Undertake desk research into past, current and future demand for holidays.
- Design and conduct a small scale survey into holiday habits and preferences.
- Relate your research to the development of a new holiday product.
- Investigate promotional objectives in leisure and tourism.
- Propose appropriate promotional techniques and methods.
- Evaluate promotional activities.

BACKGROUND

Context

Ski-scope is a well-established, medium-sized specialist UK tour operator, offering skiing holidays to the French Alps and selling through ABTA agents throughout Britain. Its head office is in London.

Circumstances

The company has been in business for 15 years, but has recently seen its market share decrease as a result of intense competition from large and small operators. In order to retain its profitability, the company is planning to offer a new product, by diversifying into offering activity holidays in France, concentrating on walking and cycling. The directors believe that UK holidaymakers are increasingly looking for active holidays and short breaks. This factor, coupled with the popularity of France as a holiday destination with the British, should generate a healthy demand for the new product.

Role

You have recently joined Ski-scope as the assistant product executive, reporting directly to the product manager, who has overall control over the tour programmes on offer, pricing, contracting with hoteliers and promotion of the holidays. Your post has been established to work specifically on the new activity holidays.

Your Tasks

Task One

Working on your own, write an initial report for the product manager. The report should be wordprocessed and contain relevant statistical data presented in an appropriate manner. The report should focus on the future market patterns and trends for overseas package holidays taken by UK holidaymakers. The report is to be supported by an oral presentation.

(a) Use a range of information sources and publications to identify and comment on the following:

- The current demand for package holidays.
- Demand for package holidays over the past 25 years.
- Changing patterns of demand for overseas holidays.

(b) Offer possible explanations as to the ways in which the patterns and trends identified might affect demand for different types of package holidays in the future. Explanations should include the following factors:

- Economic
- Demographic
- Environmental
- Socio-cultural
- Technological

Task two

You will have formed a good idea of the general demand for overseas package holidays from the desk research carried out in task one.

(a) Working as a member of a group, you are to design and carry out a small scale survey into the holiday habits of a sample of the UK population and their reactions to the proposed activity holidays in France. Choose and justify an appropriate survey method, which could include a postal questionnaire, face-to-face interview survey, self-completed questionnaire, focus group or telephone survey. The survey should identify the following primary data:

- The main destinations of the holidaymakers
- Preferred types of holiday
- Patterns of holiday taking
- Ratio of UK to overseas holidays
- Profile characteristics of those sampled (e.g. age, gender, etc.)
- Patterns of awareness and demand for active holidays generally
- Opinions and likely demand for the proposed activity holidays in France.

(b) The results of the survey should be analysed and the findings discussed by your group. You will need to consider:

- Customer preferences for different types of holidays.
- Preferences for particular holiday destinations.
- The holiday habits and preferences of different types of customers.
- The attitudes of those interviewed towards France as a holiday destination and the proposed activity holidays.
- The appropriateness of the methodology – accuracy, sampling, costs, speed, time, ease of use etc.
- The relationship between the findings of the secondary data (task one) and the primary research (task two).

You are to give an oral presentation of your findings.

(c) Working on your own, present the group's findings in a written report, using appropriate statistical displays to support the findings. Evaluate the methodology employed in the primary research and make recommendations for further full-scale research.

Task three

Ski-scope have acted on your recommendations and have just concluded a market research study into the viability of the proposed activity holidays in France. The study has indicated that, if developed and promoted effectively, the holidays are likely to be a success and contribute to the overall profitability of the company.

Task three involves you in developing a promotional plan for the new activity holidays to France.

(a) Working as a member of a group, you are to investigate a range of possible methods and techniques that could be used to promote sales of the activity holidays. You must justify your final choice of methods, which could include advertising, public relations, personal selling, sales promotions and direct marketing. Your choice of promotional techniques should reflect the findings of your secondary and primary research. The total promotional budget for the first year is £40,000, excluding brochure production costs.

Your promotional plan should be presented as a group report, which must be word processed and include relevant statistical and financial data. Your group will also be asked to make a formal presentation of your proposals. In particular, you should focus on:

- The promotional objectives

- Potential customers
  - Timescale for implementation
  - The theme(s) of the promotional campaign
  - Budget information

(b) Part of your group report must concentrate on the evaluation of the promotional activities that you have recommended. In particular, you should:

- Suggest reliable evaluation criteria
- Relate the objectives of the promotional work to its expected achievements
- Recommend any changes to future promotional activities

You will be expected to comment on your evaluation methods as part of the formal presentation.

How does this assessment meet the requirements of the unit?

Reference to the unit specification and Core Skill Units will show how this sample assessment meets the requirements of the mandatory Unit 4, Marketing in Leisure and Tourism. Figure 9.12 shows how the tasks you are asked to complete and the resulting evidence you provide, match with the elements and performance criteria for the unit

Carrying out the sample assessment for Unit 4

We have stressed the importance of drawing up an action plan for each assessment you are given. A suitable **action plan** for this particular sample assessment would be as follows.

Sample Assessment 4: Marketing in Leisure and Tourism

ACTION PLAN

Task	To be completed by
Research for task one	End of week one
Completion of task one, initial report	End of week two
Preparation for oral presentation	End of week three
Group formation and allocation of tasks between group members (task two)	End of week four
Completion of survey and allotted tasks	End of week six
Analysis of data	End of week seven
Preparation for oral presentation (task two)	End of week seven
Completion of written report (task two)	End of week eight
Group formation and allocation of tasks (task three)	End of week nine
Research for task three	End of week ten
Completion of group report (task three)	End of week eleven
Preparation for formal presentation	End of week twelve

It may be necessary to revise the action plan in the light of unforeseen events or circumstances. Don't worry if this happens, but simply agree a revised action plan with the other members of the group. Make sure that all members of the group are clear about their particular roles and responsibilities. Elect a group leader to make sure that everybody is contributing to the tasks equally.

The boxes below indicate what you need to do when working on the sample assessment for Unit 4, to ensure that your finished work has the best chance of being considered of merit or distinction standard within your overall portfolio of evidence.

Advanced GNVQ in Leisure and Tourism				
Sample Assessment: Mandatory Unit 4 – Marketing in Leisure and Tourism				
Evidence	Unit Coverage	Element Met		PCs Not Yet Met
Tasks 2, Survey, Presentation Task 1, Report	Element 4.1	Y	N	1 2 3 4 5 6 7
Task 1, Report and Presentation	Element 4.2	Y	N	1 2 3 4 5 6
Task 3a, Promotional plan in the Group Report, Formal Presentation	Element 4.3	Y	N	1 2 3 4 5 6 7 8
Task 3a and 3b, Promotional plan in the Group Report, Formal Presentation	Element 4.4	Y	N	1 2 3 4 5 6

Core skills				
Unit	Coverage – Elements/PCs	Evidence	Achieved	PCs Not Yet Met
Communication	3.1: 1 – 4 3.2: 1 – 4 3.3: 1 – 3 3.4: 1 – 3	Tasks 1 and 3, Reports Task 2, Meeting Notes, Presentations	Y N	
Application of number	3.1: 1 – 6 3.3: 1 – 6	Tasks 1 and 3, Reports Task 2, Survey	Y N	
Information technology	3.1: 1 – 7 3.2: 1 – 7 3.3: 1 – 5	Task 1, Report Task 2, Survey Task 3, Report and Presentation	Y N	

Figure 9.12 How the assessment meets the requirements of Unit 4

Element 4.1 Identify market needs for products and services

Performance criteria

Pointers to achieving a good grade

4.1.1 Research and analysis plan is developed to identify market needs.

Make sure that your research and analysis is focused clearly on establishing market needs.

4.1.2 Research and analysis methods used are efficient and cost effective.

Be sure to justify exactly why you have used a particular research or analysis method.

4.1.3 Market needs are correctly identified.

Make sure your identification of needs is based on sound research.

4.1.4. Customers are accurately described.

Be sure to describe customers in terms of their characteristics, needs and expectations.

4.1.5 Report is presented using appropriate formats.

Make sure that the structure and content of your report is suited to its intended reader(s).

4.1.6 Any difficulties encountered and solutions found are described.

Constant monitoring and evaluation of your work is important.

4.1.7 Any justifiable variations from the research and analysis plan are described.

Be sure to produce written evidence of any alterations to action plans.

Element 4.2 Identify market opportunities

Performance criteria

Pointers to achieving a good grade

4.2.1 Market needs are compared with current provision to determine market opportunities.

You must show that there is a clear gap in the market, as shown by your own research.

4.2.2. Identified market opportunities accommodate customer needs, anticipated provision and the facility's capacity to deliver.

The products and services that you recommend must be realistic and stem from researched customer needs and requirements.

4.2.3 The key features of the market opportunities are described.

Make sure that you include sufficient detail of the scale of the opportunity and the expected return.

4.2.4 Recommendations are viable and take into account effects on the local community and the environment.

Remember that there is a growing awareness among customers of environmental and socio-cultural factors.

4.2.5 Likely advantages and disadvantages of suggested further action relating to different opportunities are explained.

Make sure that any suggestions are commercially sound and will add to overall profitability.

4.2.6 Necessary measures to maintain the confidentiality of commercially sensitive information are taken.

Your recommendations must take account of the very competitive nature of the leisure and tourism industry, especially in the private sector.

Element 4.3 Plan promotional activities

Performance criteria

Pointers to achieving a good grade

4.3.1 Promotional objectives are identified and the plan describes how they will be met.

It is essential to give a lot of thought to what you are hoping to achieve with your recommendations for promotional activities.

4.3.2 Potential customers are identified and described.

Be sure to consider both existing and potential customers.

4.3.3 Promotional activities are planned to make optimum use of resources.

Give consideration to management and staff time, money, skills, premises and equipment.

4.3.4 Viable budgets are set in relation to anticipated benefits.

Be careful to set realistic budgets and financial targets.

4.3.5 Sources of expert advice and assistance are identified.

Consider whether the expert advice of advertising and PR agencies is relevant.

4.3.6 Draft promotional materials have clear explanations of their purpose and use.

Be careful when drafting promotional materials that they are designed with the target markets in mind and are in sufficient detail.

4.3.7 All necessary stages in the promotional campaign are identified and accurately described.

Be sure to include an action plan of the total campaign and its constituent parts, including time deadlines.

4.3.8 Relevant evaluation criteria for the campaign are identified and described.

Evaluation must be built into the campaign from the outset, not merely 'bolted on' at the end.

Element 4.4   Evaluate promotional activities

Performance criteria	Pointers to achieving a good grade
4.4.1 The evaluation criteria and techniques used are reliable, cost effective and yield useful information.	Whatever techniques you recommend must be set within the resources of the company and be of use to management.
4.4.2 Valid and accurate comparisons are made between the objectives of the promotional activities and their achievements.	Remember that the clearer the initial objectives, the easier it will be to measure the effectiveness of the promotional work.
4.4.3 Recommendations are made to enhance subsequent promotional activities.	Make sure you consider pricing, product mix, timing of promotion and presentation techniques.
4.4.4 Implications for other products/services of the facility arising from the evaluation are explained.	Be sure to give full consideration to the effects on the current products offered by the company when the new holidays are introduced.
4.4.5 Any needs for further evaluation of the promotional activities are identified.	Try to look to the future and suggest what type and extent of evaluation may be needed in the future in order for the new product to remain successful.
4.4.6 Means of ensuring the security of information are described.	Be sure to highlight the commercially sensitive nature of private sector leisure and tourism.

Organizing your assessments

The assessments that you are given as part of your GNVQ course will encourage you to investigate and produce evidence in a variety of ways and from many different sources. You will quickly realize that to learn effectively, and to get the most out of the opportunity you have been given to study for an Advanced GNVQ in Leisure and Tourism, you will generate a great deal of paperwork which forms the basis of your evidence. GNVQs encourage the production of reports, the planning and staging of events, oral presentations, questionnaire surveys and the analysis of case studies, to name but a few. Planning and design tasks include work on posters, plans, maps, charts and photographs. Assessments are used to generate, among other things, reports, letters, memoranda, speeches, notes and codes of practice.

To be able to deal effectively with such a large volume and wide range of items, calls for a very *organized* and *methodical* approach to compiling your portfolio of evidence. You may decide to use a ring binder or series of binders, envelope folders or box files. What is important is that there is an explanation of how the evidence contained in the portfolio meets the requirements for the award of the Advanced GNVQ in Leisure and Tourism, plus the standards for a merit or distinction award, if either is being claimed. Your tutor will be able to provide you with the necessary forms that record your progress through the GNVQ in the mandatory, optional, core skill and (if applicable) additional units. Your portfolio must be divided into sections with a detailed index, so that your tutors and the external verifier can find the relevant information and documentation quickly and easily.

Although you should agree the final structure of your portfolio of evidence with your tutor or teacher, it is likely to include the following items:

- A title page with your name, centre name and number, and the name of the qualification (Advanced GNVQ in Leisure and Tourism)
- A contents page
- Copies of the unit specifications for mandatory, optional and core skills units
- An index of assessments showing how these relate to the specifications
- A claim sheet explaining how the assessment meets particular elements and performance criteria
- An index of core skills evidence indicating how the requirements of the three core skills of communication, application of number and information technology have been satisfied
- An index of evidence for the three grading criteria of planning, information seeking and handling, and evaluation.

The process of compiling a good portfolio of evidence is in itself an example of many of the core skills that go to make up the GNVQ award. A well organized and indexed portfolio will show your tutors and the external verifier that you have a logical approach to your studies and that you are keen to progress to employment in the industry or to further study.

Student materials with assessor comments

In order to highlight points of good practice and areas that could be improved upon, we will now look in detail at a piece of work that a student has completed as part of the sample assessment for Mandatory Unit 4. The part of the assessment we will investigate is task three, where, as part of a group exercise, the student is asked to produce a promotional plan for the new activity holidays in France.

Name: Mary Smith

Assessment Title: Ski-scope

Task Number: 3 – Preparing a Promotional Plan

Introduction

Promotion is a very important part of marketing. If a company does not promote its products correctly, it will not make a profit. Promotion is one of the four Ps – price, product, place, promotion, sometimes called the marketing mix. Product is the most important part of the 4 Ps but promotion is vital as well. Most promotion is concerned with advertising, as it is more effective than any other type of promotion. Some other types of promotion are special offers and free gifts.

Tutor comment: It is a good idea to have an introduction to each task that you submit, so that you can set the scene surrounding the task and let the reader know what it is you are attempting to do. This particular introduction, however, fails to cover either of these points. It should include a statement on the aim of the task and the way in which it has been tackled; e.g.

This task will show how the group set about preparing a promotional plan for Ski-scope's new range of activity holidays to France. It is divided into the following sections:

1 The promotional objectives
2 Potential customers
3 Timescale
4 Campaign themes
5 Budgets

The final part of the report looks at the evaluation of each of the proposed promotional methods.

Having established the aims of the task, the introduction can then include specific detail about promotion. This example correctly states that promotion is one of the 4 Ps, but gives no further information as to how these four elements relate to each other. The statement that 'product is the most important of the 4 Ps but promotion is vital as well' shows that the student has not grasped that the balance between the 4 Ps will vary between one organization and another and is dependent on many factors. A newly established theme park, for example, will spend a greater proportion of its budget on promotion than an established hotel, simply because it has to work harder to make its name known. The introduction incorrectly states that 'most promotion is concerned with advertising'. In reality, leisure and tourism organizations use a wide range of promotional techniques; the introduction should indicate that advertising is just one form of promotional activity and should list others, including direct mail, public relations, personal selling and sales promotions.

It would also have been useful in the introduction for the student to have shown how promotion (and the development of promotional plans) ties in with the overall concept of marketing. A diagram such as the following would have clearly covered this:

MARKET RESEARCH
↓
DEVELOPING PRODUCTS AND SERVICES
↓
PROMOTION
↓
EVALUATION

A short explanation of the diagram to indicate the interrelationship of the four elements would have shown that the student was well aware of the importance and function of promotion in the total marketing activity.

Part 1 – Promotional objectives

An objective is a goal, something which is aimed at or striven for. A leisure and tourism organization must be clear about its objectives before it can begin to market its products. As well as overall objectives for the organization, e.g. to be the number one tour operator to a particular country, a company must also set specific aims related to its promotional work – its promotional objectives. The promotional objectives of Ski-scope in terms of its new activity holidays in France are as follows:

1 To sell as many holidays as possible
2 To make people aware of the new holidays
3 To identify likely customers
4 To offer a high standard of customer care
5 To make the promotion as cost effective as possible

In order to meet these objectives, I think that the following methods of promotion should be used:

- Newspaper advertising
- Advertising in magazines
- Mailshots
- Exhibitions

The newspaper advertising should be in high-class papers such as *The Times* and *Sunday Telegraph*, because these are the most likely people to buy the activity holidays to France. Magazine advertising will concentrate on women's magazines, as they have the most influence on where a family takes a holiday. Mailshots will be to people who are members of walking and cycling clubs to let them know about the holidays and how much they cost. The company will take an exhibition stand at the World Travel Market in London to publicize its new holidays.

It is important to remember that these objectives may change slightly as the holidays become better known.

Tutor comment: This section on promotional objectives is quite well structured but is lacking in depth in certain areas. The student is right to stress that an organization will have overall objectives for its work, as well as specific promotional objectives, and that it must be clear what its objectives are before it can market itself effectively. She fails to mention, however, that objectives must be measurable, concise, realistic, achievable and set within a particular timescale.

The particular promotional objectives listed are all realistic, but need to be a little more clearly defined. Objective number 1, for example, 'to sell as many holidays as possible', will be very difficult to assess. Exactly how will the company be able to measure that it has achieved this particular objective? Far better would be an objective which is related to a particular number of holidays sold or perhaps capturing a certain percentage of the market for activity holidays in France. Objective number 2, 'to make people aware of the new holidays', could have been developed a little further by stating that a very important part of any promotional work for a new product, facility or service is raising awareness among potential customers.

In putting forward the four particular promotional methods chosen, the student makes a number of statements that need further clarification and support from statistical and other sources, i.e. 'because these (readers of high-class papers) are the most likely people to buy the activity holidays in France' and 'as they (women) have the most influence on where a family takes a holiday'.

One major weakness of this section is that there is little indication as to why these four particular promotional techniques have been chosen. There is no mention of the findings of the student's research in task one or task two, although task three specifically mentions this. It is very likely that the research will have indicated the type of people likely to be interested in the holidays and their lifestyle characteristics – very useful data when a decision is being made on possible promotional techniques and methods. There is also no mention of using public relations as a promotional tool: this is a serious omission, since a company of this size will rely heavily on press and other media coverage through editorials and journalists' familiarization trips, to name but two PR techniques.

As a general point, it is advisable not to write in the first person (I think that... I recommend that...), but use phrases such as 'data showed that', 'it is recommended that' etc. Be careful also when distinguishing between people of different social classes; avoid using phrases such as 'upper class' or 'lower class'.

Part 2 – Potential customers

There has been a growth in recent years in the popularity of activity holidays taken by British people. The population is now more concerned about its health and fitness, meaning that there should be a ready demand for Ski-scope's new activity holidays. There has also been a tremendous growth in the number of British holidaymakers visiting France; the numbers are bound to increase with the opening of the Channel Tunnel. All in all, there should be no problem in selling the new activity holidays to France.

The sort of people who will be attracted to the product are families who like the outdoor life and who are interested in walking and cycling. The holidays should also appeal to young couples and possibly groups. The company will need to make sure that the prices of the holidays are in line with the type of people they are aimed at.

Tutor comment: While this section covers some important points, the student has failed to substantiate the many claims made by providing statistics and evidence. For example, there should be figures or quotes from authoritative sources to back up the claims that:

- Activity holidays are now more popular.
- The population is more concerned about its health and fitness.
- There has been a 'tremendous' growth in the number of British holidaymakers visiting France.
- The opening of the Channel Tunnel will increase the number of British people taking holidays in France.

There should also be mention of the primary and secondary research carried out in tasks one and two, which should have indicated the type of customers likely to be interested in this type of holiday.

Part 3 – Timescale for implementation

Any promotional work needs careful planning to make sure that it has the best possible impact. The promotional activities will need to be planned alongside the development of the activity holidays themselves. Working back from the date of the launch of the holidays, the promotional work will look as follows:

Stage of development of the activity holidays	Promotional activity
Pre-launch	Advertising in newspapers and magazines
	Attending World Travel Market
Launch	Advertising in newspapers and magazines
	Mailshots
Post-launch	Advertising in newspapers and magazines
	Mailshots

It is best if the new holidays are launched in the autumn preceding the first summer of operation, so as to be able to compete with other tour operators' products on the market.

The promotional plan will need to be reviewed regularly, at least every year.

Tutor comment: This is quite a good section, in that it distinguishes clearly between the different promotional activities that are needed at different times of the year. Where it does fall down, however, is that it doesn't mention the purpose of the activity at the different times, i.e. the pre-launch activity is geared towards raising the awareness of the existence of the new holidays; the activity at launch time is to stimulate sales; while the post-launch activity is to reinforce the sales message, maintain the sales momentum and focus on the quality and value for money of the product.

On the point of the range of promotional techniques used, we highlighted earlier that PR was missing from the list. PR can play a very important role in raising the awareness of a new product among its potential market. Also, personal selling and sales promotions (such as incentives, free gifts and competitions) will be an important part of the total promotional campaign.

Part 4 – Theme(s) of the promotional campaign

As the activity holidays are centred around walking and cycling, these are the two areas that will be used as themes for the promotional campaign. All advertising and mailshots will feature the two themes, while the exhibition stand at the World Travel Market will be an open plan 'mock up' of a countryside scene, with staff dressed as walkers and cyclists. A suitable logo will be produced to give a feeling of fresh air, health and activity.

It is important that any promotional activity highlights the fact that the holidays are based in France. The Ski-scene brochure featuring the activity holidays, as well as all advertising and mailshots, will focus on items and scenes that will appeal to the clients, e.g. wine, vineyards, garlic, the French flag, some French phrases, French bread, fields of sunflowers, etc.

Throughout the promotional campaign, the importance of personal service, value for money and attention to detail will be strongly featured.

Tutor comment: This part of the task has been completed well. It sets out clearly the importance of relating the themes to the likely travellers' tastes and preferences. The need to keep the same themes across all types of promotional activities so as to maximize impact is also acknowledged. One area of weakness, however, is that the student has not included any visual material showing, for example, the style and layout of a typical advertisement or the design of the stand at the World Travel Market. It is important to include such material, even if you are not particularly gifted at art, since it is important to show that you have a grasp of the need for consistency of design and themes.

Part 5 – Budget information

We have been told that the total budget for promotional work is £40,000 for the first year. This excludes the costs of producing the brochure. The £40,000 will be used as follows:

	£
• Advertising in *The Times*, *Independent*, *Guardian*, *Observer*, *Sunday Times*	20,000
• Advertising in *Family Circle*, *You Magazine*, *Bella*, *Mail on Sunday Magazine*	8,000
• Mailshots	4,000
• Stand at the World Travel Market	8,000
Total	£40,000

It will be important not to go over budget and to monitor which type of promotion works best so as to know which to concentrate on in the future.

Tutor comment: Although the student has given a breakdown of promotional expenditure, it lacks sufficient detail, including:

- What type of advertisements will be placed? Display, semi-display, classified or a mixture of all three?
- How many times will the advertisements appear?
- When will they appear? This could be shown as a breakdown in the budget for pre-launch, launch and post-launch promotional work.
- Will the advertisements be in colour or black-and-white?
- Who will the mailshots be directed at?
- What will the direct mail package consist of?
- How is the £8,000 for the World Travel Market stand broken down?

Without this sort of detail, the student will not produce a convincing report.

The problem previously mentioned, of not including PR activity, personal selling and sales promotions in the total promotional package, will mean that the budget data presented by the student here will not be totally comprehensive.

Part 6 – Evaluation of the promotional activities

In Part 1 of this task, I listed four promotional techniques – newspaper advertising, magazine advertising, mailshots and exhibitions – as the ones that I would recommend for the promotion of the new activity holidays in France. This is how I will go about evaluating how good each of the four is.

- **Newspaper advertising** – all newspaper advertisements will include a tear-off coupon with a particular code printed on it, e.g. the advertisement in the *Guardian* will carry a 'G' code, plus the date to see if advertising at particular times is better. Staff will be trained to ask all telephone callers where they heard of the company.

- **Magazine advertising** – again the advertisements will carry a tear-off slip with a printed code and staff will be trained to ask all callers where they heard of Ski-scene.

- **Mailshots** – these should be quite easy to monitor. A postcard or competition form will be included with the mailshot letter and brochure. Clients will post this back. It will have a unique code for that client.

- **Exhibitions** – this will not be so easy. The World Travel Market is a trade only event, meaning that the public is not allowed. The aim of the exhibition stand will be to let travel agents know about the new range of activity holidays to France. There will be a prize draw or competition to encourage travel agents to leave their name, address and business card. After the exhibition, a list will be compiled from all the names taken. These agents will be sent stocks of brochures.

Although evaluation is sometimes difficult, it must be attempted so that the company does not waste valuable money on advertising or other promotion that does not work.

Tutor comment: This section deals well with the difficult area of evaluation of promotional activities. Specific ideas are put forward that are realistic and workable. The same criticism that we have mentioned earlier, namely that PR activities, personal selling and sales promotions are not included in the overall promotional plan, is relevant here as well.

Index